ART HISTORY

Portable Edition | Book 4 Fifth Edition

ART HISTORY

Fourteenth to Seventeenth Century Art

MARILYN STOKSTAD

Judith Harris Murphy Distinguished Professor of Art History Emerita
The University of Kansas

MICHAEL W. COTHREN

Scheuer Family Professor of Humanities
Department of Art, Swarthmore College

PEARSON

Boston   Columbus   Indianapolis   New York   San Francisco   Upper Saddle River
Amsterdam   Cape Town   Dubai   London   Madrid   Milan   Munich   Paris   Montréal   Toronto
Delhi   Mexico City   São Paulo   Sydney   Hong Kong   Seoul   Singapore   Taipei   Tokyo

Editorial Director: Craig Campanella
Editor in Chief: Sarah Touborg
Senior Sponsoring Editor: Helen Ronan
Editorial Assistant: Victoria Engros
Vice-President, Director of Marketing: Brandy Dawson
Executive Marketing Manager: Kate Mitchell
Marketing Assistant: Paige Patunas
Managing Editor: Melissa Feimer
Project Managers: Barbara Cappuccio and Marlene Gassler
Senior Operations Supervisor: Mary Fischer
Operations Specialist: Diane Peirano
Media Director: Brian Hyland
Senior Media Editor: David Alick
Media Project Manager: Rich Barnes
Pearson Imaging Center: Corin Skidds
Printer/Binder: Courier / Kendallville
Cover Printer: Lehigh-Phoenix Color / Hagerstown

This book was designed by
Laurence King Publishing Ltd, London
www.laurenceking.com

Editorial Manager: Kara Hattersley-Smith
Senior Editor: Clare Double
Production Manager: Simon Walsh
Page Design: Nick Newton
Cover Design: Jo Fernandes
Picture Researcher: Evi Peroulaki
Copy Editor: Jennifer Speake
Indexer: Vicki Robinson

Cover image: Workshop of the Master of Flémalle, Mérode Altarpiece (Triptych of the Annunciation). c. 1425–1430s. Oil on wood panel, center 25¼″ × 24⅞″ (64.1 × 63.2 cm); each wing approx. 25⅜″ × 10¼″ (64.5 × 27.6 cm). Metropolitan Museum of Art, New York/Art Resource/Scala, Florence.

Credits and acknowledgments borrowed from other sources and reproduced, with permission, in this textbook appear on the appropriate page within text or on the credit pages in the back of this book.

Library of Congress Cataloging-in-Publication Data
Stokstad, Marilyn
  Art history / Marilyn Stokstad, Judith Harris Murphy Distinguished
Professor of Art History Emerita, The University of Kansas, Michael W.
Cothren, Scheuer Family Professor of Humanities, Department of Art,
Swarthmore College. -- Fifth edition.
      pages cm
  Includes bibliographical references and index.
  ISBN-13: 978-0-205-87347-0 (hardcover)
  ISBN-10: 0-205-87347-2 (hardcover)
1. Art--History--Textbooks. I. Cothren, Michael Watt. II. Title.
  N5300.S923 2013
  709--dc23
                              2012027450

10 9 8 7 6 5 4 3 2 1

Prentice Hall
is an imprint of

www.pearsonhighered.com

ISBN 10:   0-205-87379-0
ISBN 13: 978-0-205-87379-1

Contents

CHAPTER 18 Fourteenth-Century Art in Europe 530

CHAPTER 19 Fifteenth-Century Art in Northern Europe 562

CHAPTER 20 Renaissance Art in Fifteenth-Century Italy 594

CHAPTER 21 Sixteenth-Century Art in Italy 632

Letter from the Author

Dear Colleagues

Energized by an enthusiasm that was fueled by conviction, I taught my first introductory art history survey course in the late 1970s, soon after the dawn of a period of crisis and creativity in the discipline of art history that challenged the fundamental assumptions behind the survey and questioned the canon of works that had long served as its foundation. Some professors and programs abandoned the survey altogether; others made it more expansive and inclusive. We all rethought what we were doing, and the soul searching this required made many of us better teachers—more honest and relevant, more passionate and convincing. It was for the subsequent generation of students and teachers, ready to reap the benefits of this refined notion of art history, that Marilyn Stokstad conceived and created her new survey textbook during the 1990s, tailored for students whose lives would unfold in the twenty-first century. It is a humbling honor to have become part of this historic project.

Reconsidering and refining what we do as professors and students of art history, however, did not cease at the turn of the century. The process continues. Like art, our teaching and learning changes as we and our culture change, responding to new expectations and new understandings. Opportunities for growth sometimes emerge in unexpected situations. Recently, while I was inching through sluggish suburban traffic with my daughter Emma—a gifted fifth-grade teacher—I confessed my disappointment in my survey students' dismal performance on the identification portion of their recent exam, lamenting their seeming inability to master basic information about the set of works I expected them to know. "Why," I asked rhetorically, "was it so difficult for them to learn these facts?" Emma's unexpected answer, rooted in her exploration of Grant Wiggins and Jay McTigue's *Understanding by Design* during a graduate course on curriculum development, shifted the question and reframed the discussion. "Dad," she said, "you are focusing on the wrong aspect of your teaching. What are you trying to accomplish by asking your students to learn those facts for identification on the exam? Question and explore your objectives first, then determine whether your assessment is actually the best way to encourage its accomplishment."

Emma's question, posed while I was planning this fifth edition of *Art History*, inspired me to pause and reflect more broadly on what it is that we seek to accomplish in art history survey courses. I initiated a series of conversations with professors across the country to take me beyond my own experience and into a national classroom. Many of you provided illuminating feedback, sharing goals and strategies, searching with me for a way of characterizing a shared set of learning outcomes that underlie the survey courses we teach as a way of introducing our students in the present to the study of art from the past. Talking with you helped me formulate language for the essential ideas we want our students to grasp, and characterize succinctly the kinds of knowledge and skills that are required to master them. From these conversations and your feedback, I developed a set of four fundamental outcomes envisioned for the book as a whole, outcomes that would be reflected within each chapter in four coordinated learning objectives at the beginning, and four assessment questions at the end. These overall learning outcomes aim to encompass the goals we share as we introduce the history of art to beginners. Thinking about them has already helped me refocus on what it is I am trying to accomplish in my own classroom. It certainly has alleviated the frustration I shared with Emma about my students' performance on slide IDs. I am now working on new ways to assess their engagement in relation to two fundamental goals—the "big ideas" that are embodied in these learning outcomes: building a knowledge base to anchor cultural understanding, and encouraging the extended examination of works of art, what I call "slow looking."

I hope these ideas, goals, and outcomes resonate as much with you as they have with me, that they will invite you to continue to think with me about the reasons why we believe the study of art history is meaningful and important for our students. After all, our discipline originated in dialogue, and it is rooted in the desire—maybe even the need—to talk with each other about why works of art matter and why they affect us so deeply. I would love to hear from you—mcothre1@swarthmore.edu.

Warm regards,

Michael Cothren

What's New

WHY USE THIS NEW EDITION?

Art history—what a wonderful, fascinating, and fluid discipline that evolves as the latest research becomes available for debate and consideration. The fifth edition of *Art History* has been revised to reflect these new discoveries, recent research and fresh interpretive perspectives, and also to address the changing needs of the audience—both students and educators. With these goals in mind, and by incorporating feedback from our many users and reviewers, we have sought to make this fifth edition an improvement over its earlier incarnations in sensitivity, readability, and accessibility without losing anything in comprehensiveness, in scholarly precision, or in its ability to engage readers.

To facilitate student learning and understanding of art history, the fifth edition is centered on four key Learning Outcomes. These overarching outcomes helped steer and shape this revision with their emphasis on the fundamental reasons we teach art history to undergraduates:

LEARNING OUTCOMES FOR *ART HISTORY*

Explore and understand the developing traditions and cultural exchanges represented by major monuments of world art by

1. Identifying the hallmarks of regional and period styles in relation to their technical, formal, and expressive character;
2. Understanding the principal themes, subjects, and symbols in the art of a variety of cultures, periods, and locations;
3. Probing the relationship of works of art to human history by exploring their cultural, economic, political, social, spiritual, moral, and intellectual contexts, and
4. Recognizing and applying the critical thinking, creative inquiry, and disciplined reasoning that stand behind art-historical interpretation, as well as the vocabulary and concepts used to describe and characterize works of art with clarity and power.

Each chapter opens with **Learn About It** objectives to help students focus on the upcoming chapter material and ends with corresponding **Think About It** assessment questions. These tools are rooted in the four learning outcomes stated above and help students think through, apply the chapter material, and synthesize their own viewpoints.

OTHER HIGHLIGHTS OF THE NEW EDITION INCLUDE THE FOLLOWING:

- The chapters are coordinated with significantly expanded MyArtsLab resources that enrich and reinforce student learning (see p. xvi).
- Crosscurrent Questions at the end of each chapter encourage students to compare works from different chapters and probe the relationship of recurrent themes across cultures, times, and places.
- Enriched **Recovering the Past** boxes document the discovery, re-evaluation, restoration, or conservation of works of art, such as the bronze She-Wolf that was once considered Etruscan and has recently been interpreted as medieval.
- **Closer Look** features appear in each chapter, guiding students in their exploration of details within a single work of art and helping students to understand issues of usage, iconography, and style. Each Closer Look is expanded and narrated within MyArtsLab to explore technique, style, subject matter, and cultural context.
- **Broader Look** boxes in each chapter offer an in-depth contextual treatment of a single work of art.
- **Global coverage has been deepened** with the addition of new works of art and revised discussions that incorporate new scholarship, especially in the area of South and Southeast Asia, whose chapters have been expanded.
- Throughout, **images have been updated** whenever new and improved images were available or works of art have been cleaned or restored.
- **New works have been added** to the discussion in many chapters to enhance and enrich what is said in the text. For example, the Disk of Enheduanna, Sphinx of Taharqo, garden mural from Livia's villa at Primaporta, and monastery of St. Catherine's on Mount Sinai. In addition, the following artists are now discussed through new, and more representative, works: Bihzad, Giovanni Pisano, Duccio, Verrocchio, Giambologna, Bronzino, Gentileschi, Hals, Steen, Rubens, Sharaku, Turner, Friedrich, Monet, Degas, Gauguin, Cézanne, and Warhol.
- **New artists have been added**, notably, Sultan Muhammad, Joan Mitchell, Diane Arbus, and Ed Ruscha.
- The **language used to characterize works of art**—especially those that attempt to capture the lifelike appearance of the natural world—has been **refined and clarified** to bring greater precision and nuance.
- In response to readers' requests, **discussion of many major monuments** has been revised and expanded.
- **Byzantine art** has been separated from the treatment of Jewish and Early Christian art for expanded treatment in a new chapter (8) of its own.

MyArtsLab lets your students experience and interact with art

This program will provide a better teaching and learning experience for you and your students. Here's how:

The new MyArtsLab delivers proven results in helping individual students succeed. Its automatically graded assessments, personalized study plan, and interactive eText provide engaging experiences that personalize, stimulate, and measure learning for each student.

- ▶ The Pearson eText lets students access their textbook anytime, anywhere, and any way they want—including downloading to an iPad or listening to chapter audio read by Michael Cothren and Brian Seymour. Includes a unique scale feature showing students the size of a work in relation to the human figure.

- • Personalized study plan for each student promotes critical-thinking skills. Assessment tied to videos, applications, and chapters enables both instructors and students to track progress and get immediate feedback.

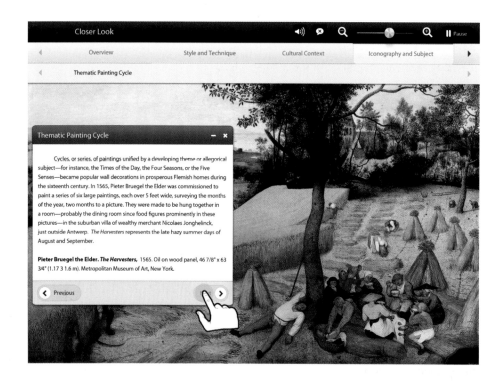

- • **New:** Henry Sayre's *Writing About Art* 6th edition is now available online in its entirety as an eText within MyArtsLab.

- ◀ **New and expanded:** Closer Look tours—interactive walkthroughs featuring expert audio—offer in-depth looks at key works of art. *Now optimized for mobile.*

- • **New and expanded:** Over 75 in total, 360-degree architectural panoramas and simulations of major monuments help students understand buildings—inside and out. *Now optimized for mobile.*

► **New:** Students on Site videos—over 75 in total, produced and edited by students for students, these 2–3 minute videos provide "you are there" impressions of major monuments, reviewed and approved by art historians. To learn more about how your students can participate, please visit **www.pearsonfreeagent.com**

BREAK THROUGH TO A NEW WORLD OF LEARNING

MyArtsLab consistently and positively impacts the quality of learning in the classroom. When educators require and integrate MyArtsLab in their course, students and instructors experience success. Join our ever-growing community of 50,000 users across the country giving their students access to the high quality rich media and assessment on MyArtsLab.

"Students who use MyArtsLab perform better on their exams than students who do not."
—*Cynthia Kristan-Graham, Auburn University*

"MyArtsLab also makes students more active learners. They are more engaged with the material."
—*Maya Jiménez, Kingsborough Community College*

"MyArtsLab keeps students connected in another way to the course material. A student could be immersed for hours!"
—*Cindy B. Damschroder, University of Cincinnati*

"I really enjoy using MyArtsLab. At the end of the quarter, I ask students to write a paragraph about their experience with MyArtsLab and 97% of them are positive."
—*Rebecca Trittel, Savannah College of Art and Design*

Join the conversation!
www.facebook.com/stokstadcothren

Give Your Students Choices

ORDERING OPTIONS

Pearson arts titles are available in the following formats to give you and your students more choices—and more ways to save.

MyArtsLab with eText: the Pearson eText lets students access their textbook anytime, anywhere, and any way they want, including listening online or downloading to an iPad.

MyArtsLab with eText Combined: 0-205-88736-8
MyArtsLab with eText Volume I: 0-205-94839-1
MyArtsLab with eText Volume II: 0-205-94846-4

Build your own Pearson Custom e-course material. Pearson offers the first eBook-building platform that empowers educators with the freedom to search, choose, and seamlessly integrate multimedia. *Contact your Pearson representative to get started.*

The **Books à la Carte edition** offers a convenient, three-hole-punched, loose-leaf version of the traditional text at a discounted price—allowing students to take only what they need to class. Books à la Carte editions are available both with and without access to MyArtsLab.

Books à la Carte edition Volume I: 0-205-93840-X
Books à la Carte edition Volume I plus MyArtsLab: 0-205-93847-7
Books à la Carte edition Volume II: 0-205-93844-2
Books à la Carte edition Volume II plus MyArtsLab: 0-205-93846-9

The **CourseSmart eTextbook** offers the same content as the printed text in a convenient online format—with highlighting, online search, and printing capabilities. **www.coursesmart.com**

Art History **Portable edition** has all of the same content as the comprehensive text in six slim volumes. If your survey course is Western, the Portable Edition is available in value-package combinations to suit Western-focused courses (Books 1, 2, 4, and 6). Portable Edition volumes are also available individually for period or region specific courses.

Book 1 – Ancient Art (Chapters 1–6): 978-0-205-87376-0
Book 2 – Medieval Art (Chapters 7–9, 15–18):
   978-0-205-87377-7
Book 3 – A View of the World, Part One (Chapters 9–14):
   978-0-205-87378-4
Book 4 – Fourteenth to Seventeenth Century Art (Chapters 18–23):
   978-0-205-87379-1
Book 5 – A View of the World, Part Two (Chapters 24–29):
   978-0-205-87380-7
Book 6 – Eighteenth to Twenty-first Century Art (Chapters 30–33):
   978-0-205-87756-0

INSTRUCTOR RESOURCES

All of our instructor resources are found on MyArtsLab and are available to faculty who adopt *Art History*. These resources include:

PowerPoints featuring nearly every image in the book, with captions and without captions.

Teaching with MyArtsLab PowerPoints help instructors make their lectures come alive. These slides allow instructors to display the very best rich media from MyArtsLab in the classroom—quickly and easily.

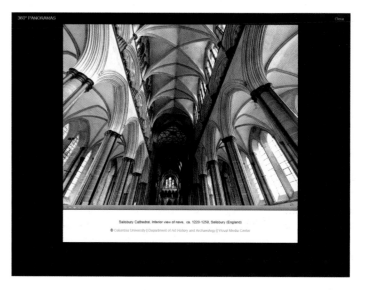

Instructor's Manual and Test Item File
This is an invaluable professional resource and reference for new and experienced faculty.

The Class Preparation Tool collects these and other presentation resources in one convenient online destination.

Acknowledgments and Gratitude

Art History, which was first published in 1995 by Harry N. Abrams, Inc. and Prentice Hall, Inc., continues to rely, each time it is revised, on the work of many colleagues and friends who contributed to the original texts and subsequent editions. Their work is reflected here, and we extend to them our enduring gratitude.

In preparing this fifth edition, we worked closely with two gifted and dedicated editors at Pearson/Prentice Hall, Sarah Touborg and Helen Ronan, whose almost daily support in so many ways was at the center of our work and created the foundation of what we have done. We are continually bolstered by the warm and dedicated support of Yolanda de Rooy, Pearson's President of the Social Sciences and the Arts, and Craig Campanella, Editorial Director. Also at Pearson, Barbara Cappuccio, Marlene Gassler, Melissa Feimer, Cory Skidds, Brian Mackey, David Nitti, and Carla Worner supported us in our work. At Laurence King Publishing, Clare Double, Kara Hattersley-Smith, Julia Ruxton, and Simon Walsh oversaw the production of this new edition. For layout design we thank Nick Newton and for photo research we thank Evi Peroulaki. Much appreciation also goes to Brandy Dawson, Director of Marketing, and Kate Stewart Mitchell, Marketing Manager extraordinaire, as well as the entire Social Sciences and Arts team at Pearson.

FROM MARILYN STOKSTAD: The fifth edition of *Art History* represents the cumulative efforts of a distinguished group of scholars and educators. Over four editions, the work done in the 1990s by Stephen Addiss, Chutsing Li, Marylin M. Rhie, and Christopher D. Roy for the original book has been updated and expanded by David Binkley and Patricia Darish (Africa); Claudia Brown and Robert Mowry (China and Korea); Patricia Graham (Japan); Rick Asher (South and Southeast Asia); D. Fairchild Ruggles (Islamic); Claudia Brittenham (Americas); Sara Orel and Carol Ivory (Pacific Cultures); and Bradford R. Collins, David Cateforis, Patrick Frank, and Joy Sperling (Modern). For this fifth edition, Robert DeCaroli reworked the chapters on South and Southeast Asia.

In addition, I want to thank University of Kansas colleagues Sally Cornelison, Susan Craig, Susan Earle, Charles Eldredge, Kris Ercums, Sherry Fowler, Stephen Goddard, Saralyn Reece Hardy, Marsha Haufler, Marni Kessler, Amy McNair, John Pulz, Linda Stone Ferrier, and John Younger for their help and advice. My thanks also to my friends Katherine Giele and Katherine Stannard, William Crowe, David Bergeron, and Geraldo de Sousa for their sympathy and encouragement. Of course, my very special thanks go to my sister, Karen Leider, and my niece, Anna Leider.

FROM MICHAEL COTHREN: Words are barely adequate to express my gratitude to Marilyn Stokstad for welcoming me with such trust, enthusiasm, and warmth into the collaborative adventure of revising this historic textbook, conceived and written for students in a new century. Working alongside her—and our extraordinary editors Sarah Touborg and Helen Ronan—has been delightful and rewarding, enriching, and challenging. I look forward to continuing the partnership.

My work was greatly facilitated by the research assistance and creative ideas of Moses Hanson-Harding, and I continued to draw on the work of Fletcher Coleman and Andrew Finegold, who helped with research on the previous edition. I also have been supported by a host of colleagues at Swarthmore College. Generations of students challenged me to hone my pedagogical skills and steady my focus on what is at stake in telling the history of art. My colleagues in the Art Department—especially Stacy Bomento, June Cianfrana, Randall Exon, Laura Holzman, Constance Cain Hungerford, Patricia Reilly, and Tomoko Sakomura—have answered all sorts of questions, shared innumerable insights on works in their areas of expertise, and offered unending encouragement and support. I am so lucky to work with them.

Many art historians have provided assistance, often at a moment's notice, and I am especially grateful to Betina Bergman, Claudia Brown, Elizabeth A.R. Brown, Brigitte Buettner, David Cateforis, Madeline Harrison Caviness, Sarah Costello, Cynthia Kristan-Graham, Joyce de Vries, Cheri Falkenstien-Doyle, Sharon Gerstel, Kevin Glowaki, Ed Gyllenhaal, Julie Hochstrasser, Vida J. Hull, Penny Jolly, Barbara Kellum, Alison Kettering, Benton Kidd, Ann Kuttner, Anne Leader, Steven A. LeBlanc, Cary Liu, Elizabeth Marlowe, Thomas Morton, Kathleen Nolan, David Shapiro, Mary Shepard, Larry Silver, David Simon, Donna Sadler, Jeffrey Chipps Smith, and Mark Tucker.

I was fortunate to have the support of many friends. John Brendler, David Eldridge, Stephen Lehmann, Mary Marissen, Denis Ott, and Bruce and Carolyn Stephens, patiently listened and truly relished my enjoyment of this work.

My preparation for this work runs deep. My parents, Mildred and Wat Cothren, believed in me from the day I was born and made significant sacrifices to support my education from pre-school through graduate school. From an early age, Sara Shymanski, my elementary school librarian, gave me courage through her example and loving encouragement to pursue unexpected passions for history, art, and the search to make them meaningful in both past and present. Françoise Celly, my painting professor during a semester abroad in Provence, by sending me to study the Romanesque sculpture of Autun, began my journey toward art history. At Vanderbilt, Ljubica Popovich fostered this new interest by teaching me about Byzantine art. My extraordinary daughters Emma and Nora remain a constant inspiration. I am so grateful for their delight in my passion for art's history, and for their dedication to keeping me from taking myself too seriously. My deepest gratitude is reserved for Susan Lowry, my wife and soul-mate, who brings joy to every facet of my life. She is not only patient and supportive during the long distractions of my work on this book; she has provided help in so very many ways. The greatest accomplishment of my life in art history occurred on the day I met her at Columbia in 1973.

If the arts are ultimately an expression of human faith and integrity as well as human thought and creativity, then writing and producing books that introduce new viewers to the wonders of art's history, and to the courage and visions of the artists and art historians that stand behind it—remains a noble undertaking. We feel honored to be a part of such a worthy project.

Marilyn Stokstad   *Michael W. Cothren*
Lawrence, KS   *Swarthmore, PA*
Spring 2012

IN GRATITUDE: As its predecessors did, this fifth edition of *Art History* benefited from the reflections and assessments of a distinguished team of scholars and educators. The authors and Pearson are grateful to the following academic reviewers for their numerous insights and suggestions for improvement: Kirk Ambrose, University of Colorado, Boulder; Lisa Aronson, Skidmore College; Mary Brantl, St. Edward's University; Denise Budd, Bergen Community College; Anne Chapin, Brevard College; Sheila Dillon, Duke University; William Ganis, Wells College; Sharon Gerstel, University of California, Los Angeles; Kevin Glowacki, Texas A&M University; Amy Golahny, Lycoming College; Steve Goldberg, Hamilton College; Bertha Gutman, Delaware County Community College; Deborah Haynes, University of Colorado, Boulder; Eva Hoffman, Tufts University; Mary Jo Watson, University of Oklahoma; Kimberly Jones, University of Texas, Austin; Barbara Kellum, Smith College; Sarah Kielt Costello, University of Houston; Cynthia Kristan-Graham, Auburn University; Paul Lavy, University of Hawaii at Manoa; Henry Luttikhuizen, Calvin College; Elizabeth Mansfield, New York University; Michelle Moseley Christian, Virginia Tech; Eleanor Moseman, Colorado State University; Sheila Muller, University of Utah; Elizabeth Olton, University of Texas at San Antonio; David Parrish, Purdue University; Tomoko Sakomura, Swarthmore College; Erika Schneider, Framingham State University; David Shapiro; Richard Sundt, University of Oregon; Tilotttama Tharoor, New York University; Sarah Thompson, Rochester Institute of Technology; Rebecca Turner, Savannah College of Art and Design; Linda Woodward, LSC Montgomery.

This edition has continued to benefit from the assistance and advice of scores of other teachers and scholars who generously answered questions, gave recommendations on organization and priorities, and provided specialized critiques during the course of work on previous editions.

We are grateful for the detailed critiques from the following readers across the country who were of invaluable assistance during work on the third and fourth editions: Craig Adcock, University of Iowa; Charles M. Adelman, University of Northern Iowa; Fred C. Albertson, University of Memphis; Kimberly Allen-Kattus, Northern Kentucky University; Frances Altvater, College of William and Mary; Michael Amy, Rochester Institute of Technology; Susan Jane Baker, University of Houston; Jennifer L. Ball, Brooklyn College, CUNY; Samantha Baskind, Cleveland State University; Tracey Boswell, Johnson County Community College; Jane H. Brown, University of Arkansas at Little Rock; Stephen Caffey, Texas A&M University; Charlotte Lowry Collins, Southeastern Louisiana University; Roger J. Crum, University of Dayton; Brian A. Curran, Penn State University; Cindy B. Damschroder, University of Cincinnati; Michael T. Davis, Mount Holyoke College; Juilee Decker, Georgetown College; Laurinda Dixon, Syracuse University; Rachael Z. DeLue, Princeton University; Anne Derbes, Hood College; Caroline Downing, State University of New York at Potsdam; Laura Dufresne, Winthrop University; Suzanne Eberle, Kendall College of Art & Design of Ferris State University; April Eisman, Iowa State University; Dan Ewing, Barry University; Allen Farber, State University of New York at Oneonta; Arne Flaten, Coastal Carolina University; John Garton, Cleveland Institute of Art; Richard Gay, University of North Carolina, Pembroke; Regina Gee, Montana State University; Rosi Gilday, University of Wisconsin, Oshkosh; Mimi Hellman, Skidmore College; Julie Hochstrasser, University of Iowa; Eunice D. Howe, University of Southern California; Phillip Jacks, George Washington University; Evelyn Kain, Ripon College; Nancy Kelker, Middle Tennessee State University; Patricia Kennedy, Ocean County College; Jennie Klein, Ohio University; Katie Kresser, Seattle Pacific University; Cynthia Kristan-Graham, Auburn University; Barbara Platten Lash, Northern Virginia Community College; William R. Levin, Centre College; Susan Libby, Rollins College; Henry Luttikhuizen, Calvin College; Lynn Mackenzie, College of DuPage; Elisa C. Mandell, California State University, Fullerton; Pamela Margerm, Kean University; Elizabeth Marlowe, Colgate University; Marguerite Mayhall, Kean University; Katherine A. McIver, University of Alabama at Birmingham; Dennis McNamara, Triton College; Gustav Medicus, Kent State University; Lynn Metcalf, St. Cloud State University; Janine Mileaf, Swarthmore College; Jo-Ann Morgan, Coastal Carolina University; Johanna D. Movassat, San Jose State University; Beth A. Mulvaney, Meredith College; Dorothy Munger, Delaware Community College; Jacqueline Marie Musacchio, Wellesley College; Bonnie Noble, University of North Carolina at Charlotte; Leisha O'Quinn, Oklahoma State University; Lynn Ostling, Santa Rosa Junior College; Willow Partington, Hudson Valley Community College; Martin Patrick, Illinois State University; Ariel Plotek, Clemson University; Patricia V. Podzorski, University of Memphis; Albert Reischuck, Kent State University; Margaret Richardson, George Mason University; James Rubin, Stony Brook University; Jeffrey Ruda,

University of California, Davis; Donna Sandrock, Santa Ana College; Michael Schwartz, Augusta State University; Diane Scillia, Kent State University; Joshua A. Shannon, University of Maryland; Karen Shelby, Baruch College; Susan Sidlauskas, Rutgers University; Jeffrey Chipps Smith, University of Texas, Austin; Royce W. Smith, Wichita State University; Stephanie Smith, Youngstown State University; Stephen Smithers, Indiana State University; Janet Snyder, West Virginia University; Laurie Sylwester, Columbia College (Sonora); Carolyn Tate, Texas Tech University; Rita Tekippe, University of West Georgia; James Terry, Stephens College; Michael Tinkler, Hobart and William Smith Colleges; Amelia Trevelyan, University of North Carolina at Pembroke; Julie Tysver, Greenville Technical College; Jeryln Woodard, University of Houston; Reid Wood, Lorain County Community College. Our thanks also to additional expert readers including: Susan Cahan, Yale University; David Craven, University of New Mexico; Marian Feldman, University of California, Berkeley; Dorothy Johnson, University of Iowa; Genevra Kornbluth, University of Maryland; Patricia Mainardi, City University of New York; Clemente Marconi, Columbia University; Tod Marder, Rutgers University; Mary Miller, Yale University; Elizabeth Penton, Durham Technical Community College; Catherine B. Scallen, Case Western University; Kim Shelton, University of California, Berkeley.

Many people reviewed the original edition of *Art History* and have continued to assist with its revision. Every chapter was read by one or more specialists. For work on the original book and assistance with subsequent editions thanks goes to: Barbara Abou-el-Haj, SUNY Binghamton; Roger Aiken, Creighton University; Molly Aitken; Anthony Alofsin, University of Texas, Austin; Christiane Andersson, Bucknell University; Kathryn Arnold; Julie Aronson, Cincinnati Art Museum; Michael Auerbach, Vanderbilt University; Larry Beck; Evelyn Bell, San Jose State University; Janetta Rebold Benton, Pace University; Janet Berlo, University of Rochester; Sarah Blick, Kenyon College; Jonathan Bloom, Boston College; Suzaan Boettger; Judith Bookbinder, Boston College; Marta Braun, Ryerson University; Elizabeth Broun, Smithsonian American Art Museum; Glen R. Brown, Kansas State University; Maria Elena Buszek, Kansas City Art Institute; Robert G. Calkins; Annmarie Weyl Carr; April Clagget, Keene State College; William W. Clark, Queens College, CUNY; John Clarke, University of Texas, Austin; Jaqueline Clipsham; Ralph T. Coe; Robert Cohon, The Nelson-Atkins Museum of Art; Alessandra Comini; James D'Emilio, University of South Florida; Walter Denny, University of Massachusetts, Amherst; Jerrilyn Dodds, City College, CUNY; Lois Drewer, Index of Christian Art; Joseph Dye, Virginia Museum of Art; James Farmer, Virginia Commonwealth University; Grace Flam, Salt Lake City Community College; Mary D. Garrard; Paula Gerson, Florida State University; Walter S. Gibson; Dorothy Glass; Oleg Grabar; Randall Griffey, Amherst College; Cynthia Hahn, Florida State University; Sharon Hill, Virginia Commonwealth University; John Hoopes, University of Kansas; Reinhild Janzen, Washburn University; Wendy Kindred, University of Maine at Fort Kent; Alan T. Kohl, Minneapolis College of Art; Ruth Kolarik, Colorado College; Carol H. Krinsky, New York University; Aileen Laing, Sweet Briar College; Janet LeBlanc, Clemson University; Charles Little, The Metropolitan Museum of Art; Laureen Reu Liu, McHenry County College; Loretta Lorance; Brian Madigan, Wayne State University; Janice Mann, Bucknell University; Judith Mann, St. Louis Art Museum; Richard Mann, San Francisco State University; James Martin; Elizabeth Parker McLachlan; Tamara Mikailova, St. Petersburg, Russia, and Macalester College; Anta Montet-White; Anne E. Morganstern, Ohio State University; Winslow Myers, Bancroft School; Lawrence Nees, University of Delaware; Amy Ogata, Cleveland Institute of Art; Judith Oliver, Colgate University; Edward Olszewski, Case Western Reserve University; Sara Jane Pearman; John G. Pedley, University of Michigan; Michael Plante, Tulane University; Eloise Quiñones-Keber, Baruch College and the Graduate Center, CUNY; Virginia Raguin, College of the Holy Cross; Nancy H. Ramage, Ithaca College; Ann M. Roberts, Lake Forest College; Lisa Robertson, The Cleveland Museum of Art; Barry Rubin; Charles Sack, Parsons, Kansas; Jan Schall, The Nelson-Atkins Museum of Art; Tom Shaw, Kean College; Pamela Sheingorn, Baruch College, CUNY; Raechell Smith, Kansas City Art Institute; Lauren Soth; Anne R. Stanton, University of Missouri, Columbia; Michael Stoughton; Thomas Sullivan, OSB, Benedictine College (Conception Abbey); Pamela Trimpe, University of Iowa; Richard Turnbull, Fashion Institute of Technology; Elizabeth Valdez del Alamo, Montclair State College; Lisa Vergara; Monica Visoná, University of Kentucky; Roger Ward, Norton Museum of Art; Mark Weil, St. Louis; David Wilkins; Marcilene Wittmer, University of Miami.

Use Notes

The various features of this book reinforce each other, helping the reader to become comfortable with terminology and concepts that are specific to art history.

Starter Kit and Introduction   The Starter Kit is a highly concise primer of basic concepts and tools. The Introduction explores the way they are used to come to an understanding of the history of art.

Captions   There are two kinds of captions in this book: short and long. Short captions identify information specific to the work of art or architecture illustrated:

> artist (when known)
> title or descriptive name of work
> date
> original location (if moved to a museum or other site)
> material or materials a work is made of
> size (height before width) in feet and inches, with meters and
>   centimeters in parentheses
> present location

The order of these elements varies, depending on the type of work illustrated. Dimensions are not given for architecture, for most wall paintings, or for most architectural sculpture. Some captions have one or more lines of small print below the identification section of the caption that gives museum or collection information. This is rarely required reading; its inclusion is often a requirement for gaining permission to reproduce the work.

Longer, discursive captions contain information that complements the narrative of the main text.

Definitions of Terms   You will encounter the basic terms of art history in three places:

> **In the Text,** where words appearing in boldface type are defined, or glossed, at their first use.

> **In Boxed Features,** on technique and other subjects, where labeled drawings and diagrams visually reinforce the use of terms.

> **In the Glossary,** at the end of the volume (p. 771), which contains all the words in boldface type in the text and boxes.

Maps   At the beginning of each chapter you will find a map with all the places mentioned in the chapter.

Boxes   Special material that complements, enhances, explains, or extends the narrative text is set off in six types of tinted boxes.

Art and Its Contexts and A Broader Look boxes expand on selected works or issues related to the text. A Closer Look boxes use leader-line captions to focus attention on specific aspects of important works. Elements of Architecture boxes clarify specifically architectural features, often explaining engineering principles or building technology. Technique boxes outline the techniques and processes by which certain types of art are created. Recovering the Past boxes highlight the work of archaeologists who uncover and conservators who assure the preservation and clear presentation of art.

Bibliography   The bibliography at the end of this book beginning on page 780 contains books in English, organized by general works and by chapter, that are basic to the study of art history today, as well as works cited in the text.

Learn About It   Placed at the beginning of each chapter, this feature captures in bulleted form the key learning objectives, or outcomes, of the chapter. They point to what will have been accomplished upon its completion.

Think About It   These critical thinking questions appear at the end of each chapter and help students assess their mastery of the learning objectives (Learn About It) by asking them to think through and apply what they have learned.

MyArtsLab prompts   These notations are found throughout the chapter and are keyed to MyArtsLab resources that enrich and reinforce student learning.

Dates, Abbreviations, and Other Conventions   This book uses the designations BCE and CE, abbreviations for "Before the Common Era" and "Common Era," instead of BC ("Before Christ") and AD ("Anno Domini," "the year of our Lord"). The first century BCE is the period from 99 BCE to 1 BCE; the first century CE is from the year 1 CE to 99 CE. Similarly, the second century CE is the period from 199 BCE to 100 BCE; the second century CE extends from 100 CE to 199 CE.

100's	**99–1**	**1–99**	**100's**
second	first	first	second
century BCE	century BCE	century CE	century CE

Circa ("about") is used with approximate dates, spelled out in the text and abbreviated to "c." in the captions. This indicates that an exact date is not yet verified.

An illustration is called a "figure," or "fig." Thus, figure 6–7 is the seventh numbered illustration in Chapter 6, and fig. Intro-3 is the third figure in the Introduction. There are two types of figures: photographs of artworks or of models, and line drawings. Drawings are used when a work cannot be photographed or when a diagram or simple drawing is the clearest way to illustrate an object or a place.

When introducing artists, we use the words *active* and *documented* with dates, in addition to "b." (for "born") and "d." (for "died"). "Active" means that an artist worked during the years given. "Documented" means that documents link the person to that date.

Accents are used for words in French, German, Italian, and Spanish only. With few exceptions, names of cultural institutions in Western European countries are given in the form used in that country.

Titles of Works of Art   It was only over the last 500 years that paintings and works of sculpture created in Europe and North America were given formal titles, either by the artist or by critics and art historians. Such formal titles are printed in italics. In other traditions and cultures, a single title is not important or even recognized.

In this book we use formal descriptive titles of artworks where titles are not established. If a work is best known by its non-English title, such as Manet's *Le Déjeuner sur l'Herbe (The Luncheon on the Grass)*, the original language precedes the translation.

Starter Kit

Art history focuses on the visual arts—painting, drawing, sculpture, prints, photography, ceramics, metalwork, architecture, and more. This Starter Kit contains basic information and addresses concepts that underlie and support the study of art history. It provides a quick reference guide to the vocabulary used to classify and describe art objects. Understanding these terms is indispensable because you will encounter them again and again in reading, talking, and writing about art.

Let us begin with the basic properties of art. A work of art is a material object having both form and content. It is often described and categorized according to its *style* and *medium*.

FORM

Referring to purely visual aspects of art and architecture, the term *form* encompasses qualities of *line, shape, color, light, texture, space, mass, volume,* and *composition*. These qualities are known as *formal elements*. When art historians use the term *formal*, they mean "relating to form."

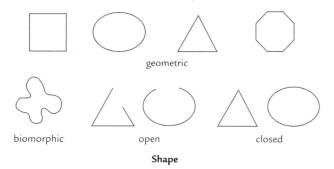

geometric

biomorphic   open   closed

Shape

Line and **shape** are attributes of form. Line is an element—usually drawn or painted—the length of which is so much greater than the width that we perceive it as having only length. Line can be actual, as when the line is visible, or it can be implied, as when the movement of the viewer's eyes over the surface of a work follows a path determined by the artist. Shape, on the other hand, is the two-dimensional, or flat, area defined by the borders of an enclosing *outline* or *contour*. Shape can be *geometric*, *biomorphic* (suggesting living things; sometimes called *organic*), *closed*, or *open*. The *outline* or *contour* of a three-dimensional object can also be perceived as line.

Color has several attributes. These include *hue, value,* and *saturation*.

Hue is what we think of when we hear the word *color*, and the terms are interchangeable. We perceive hues as the result of differing wavelengths of electromagnetic energy. The visible spectrum, which can be seen in a rainbow, runs from red through violet. When the ends of the spectrum are connected through the hue red-violet, the result may be diagrammed as a color wheel. The primary hues (numbered 1) are red, yellow, and blue. They are known as primaries because all other colors are made by combining these hues. Orange, green, and violet result from the mixture of two primaries and are known as secondary hues (numbered 2). Intermediate hues, or tertiaries (numbered 3), result from the mixture of a primary and a secondary. Complementary colors are the two colors directly opposite one

another on the color wheel, such as red and green. Red, orange, and yellow are regarded as warm colors and appear to advance toward us. Blue, green, and violet, which seem to recede, are called cool colors. Black and white are not considered colors but neutrals; in terms of light, black is understood as the absence of color and white as the mixture of all colors.

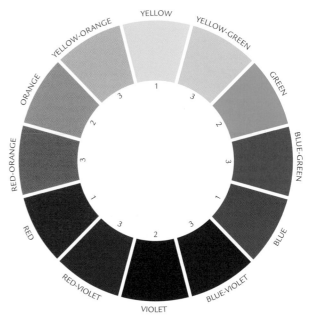

Value is the relative degree of lightness or darkness of a given color and is created by the amount of light reflected from an object's surface. A dark green has a deeper value than a light green, for example. In black-and-white reproductions of colored objects, you see only value, and some artworks—for example, a drawing made with black ink—possess only value, not hue or saturation.

Value scale from white to black.

+ WHITE   PURE HUE   + BLACK

Value variation in red.

Saturation, also sometimes referred to as *intensity*, is a color's quality of brightness or dullness. A color described as highly saturated looks vivid and pure; a hue of low saturation may look a little muddy or grayed.

PURE HUE   DULLED   PURE HUE

Intensity scale from bright to dull.

Texture, another attribute of form, is the tactile (or touch-perceived) quality of a surface. It is described by words such as *smooth*, *polished*, *rough*, *prickly*, *grainy*, or *oily*. Texture takes two forms: the texture of the actual surface of the work of art and the implied (illusionistically described) surface of objects represented in the work of art.

Space is what contains forms. It may be actual and three-dimensional, as it is with sculpture and architecture, or it may be fictional, represented illusionistically in two dimensions, as when artists represent recession into the distance on a flat surface—such as a wall or a canvas—by using various systems of perspective.

Mass and volume are properties of three-dimensional things. Mass is solid matter—whether sculpture or architecture—that takes up space. Volume is enclosed or defined space, and may be either solid or hollow. Like space, mass and volume may be illusionistically represented on a two-dimensional surface, such as in a painting or a photograph.

Composition is the organization, or arrangement, of forms in a work of art. Shapes and colors may be repeated or varied, balanced symmetrically or asymmetrically; they may be stable or dynamic. The possibilities are nearly endless and artistic choice depends both on the time and place where the work was created as well as the objectives of individual artists. Pictorial depth (spatial recession) is a specialized aspect of composition in which the three-dimensional world is represented on a flat surface, or *picture plane*. The area "behind" the picture plane is called the *picture space* and conventionally contains three "zones": *foreground*, *middle ground*, and *background*.

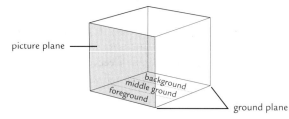

Various techniques for conveying a sense of pictorial depth have been devised by artists in different cultures and at different times. A number of them are diagrammed here. In some European art, the use of various systems of *perspective* has sought to create highly convincing illusions of recession into space. At other times and in other cultures, indications of recession are actually suppressed or avoided to emphasize surface rather than space.

TECHNIQUE | Pictorial Devices for Depicting Recession in Space

overlapping

In overlapping, partially covered elements are meant to be seen as located behind those covering them.

diminution

In diminution of scale, successively smaller elements are perceived as being progressively farther away than the largest ones.

vertical perspective

Vertical perspective stacks elements, with the higher ones intended to be perceived as deeper in space.

atmospheric perspective

Through atmospheric perspective, objects in the far distance (often in bluish-gray hues) have less clarity than nearer objects. The sky becomes paler as it approaches the horizon.

divergent perspective

In divergent or reverse perspective, forms widen slightly and imaginary lines called orthogonals diverge as they recede in space.

intuitive perspective

Intuitive perspective takes the opposite approach from divergent perspective. Forms become narrower and orthogonals converge the farther they are from the viewer, approximating the optical experience of spatial recession.

linear perspective

Linear perspective (also called scientific, mathematical, one-point and Renaissance perspective) is a rationalization or standardization of intuitive perspective that was developed in fifteenth-century Italy. It uses mathematical formulas to construct images in which all elements are shaped by, or arranged along, orthogonals that converge in one or more vanishing points on a horizon line.

CONTENT

Content includes *subject matter*, but not all works of art have subject matter. Many buildings, paintings, sculptures, and other art objects include no recognizable references to things in nature nor to any story or historical situation, focusing instead on lines, colors, masses, volumes, and other formal elements. However, all works of art—even those without recognizable subject matter—have content, or meaning, insofar as they seek to communicate ideas, convey feelings, or affirm the beliefs and values of their makers, their patrons, and usually the people who originally viewed or used them.

Content may derive from the social, political, religious, and economic *contexts* in which a work was created, the *intention* of the artist, and the *reception* of the work by beholders (the audience). Art historians, applying different methods of *interpretation*, often arrive at different conclusions regarding the content of a work of art, and single works of art can contain more than one meaning because they are occasionally directed at more than one audience.

The study of subject matter is called *iconography* (literally, "the writing of images") and includes the identification of *symbols*—images that take on meaning through association, resemblance, or convention.

STYLE

Expressed very broadly, *style* is the combination of form and composition that makes a work distinctive. *Stylistic analysis* is one of art history's most developed practices, because it is how art historians recognize the work of an individual artist or the characteristic manner of groups of artists working in a particular time or place. Some of the most commonly used terms to discuss *artistic styles* include *period style*, *regional style*, *representational style*, *abstract style*, *linear style*, and *painterly style*.

Period style refers to the common traits detectable in works of art and architecture from a particular historical era. It is good practice not to use the words "style" and "period" interchangeably. Style is the sum of many influences and characteristics, including the period of its creation. An example of proper usage is "an American house from the Colonial period built in the Georgian style."

Regional style refers to stylistic traits that persist in a geographic region. An art historian whose specialty is medieval art can recognize Spanish style through many successive medieval periods and can distinguish individual objects created in medieval Spain from other medieval objects that were created in, for example, Italy.

Representational styles are those that describe the appearance of recognizable subject matter in ways that make it seem lifelike.

    Realism and **Naturalism** are terms that some people used interchangeably to characterize artists' attempts to represent the observable world in a manner that appears to describe its visual appearance accurately. When capitalized, Realism refers to a specific period style discussed in Chapter 31.

    Idealization strives to create images of physical perfection according to the prevailing values or tastes of a culture. The artist may work in a representational style and idealize it to capture an underlying value or expressive effect.

    Illusionism refers to a highly detailed style that seeks to create a convincing illusion of physical reality by describing its visual appearance meticulously.

Abstract styles depart from mimicking lifelike appearance to capture the essence of a form. An abstract artist may work from nature or from a memory image of nature's forms and colors, which are simplified, stylized, perfected, distorted, elaborated, or otherwise transformed to achieve a desired expressive effect.

    Nonrepresentational (or Nonobjective) Art is a term often used for works of art that do not aim to produce recognizable natural imagery.

    Expressionism refers to styles in which the artist exaggerates aspects of form to draw out the beholder's subjective response or to project the artist's own subjective feelings.

Linear describes both styles and techniques. In linear styles artists use line as the primary means of definition. But linear paintings can also incorporate *modeling*—creating an illusion of three-dimensional substance through shading, usually executed so that brushstrokes nearly disappear.

Painterly describes a style of representation in which vigorous, evident brushstrokes dominate, and outlines, shadows, and highlights are brushed in freely.

MEDIUM AND TECHNIQUE

Medium (plural, *media*) refers to the material or materials from which a work of art is made. Today, literally anything can be used to make a work of art, including not only traditional materials like paint, ink, and stone, but also rubbish, food, and the earth itself.

Technique is the process that transforms media into a work of art. Various techniques are explained throughout this book in Technique boxes. Two-dimensional media and techniques include painting, drawing, prints, and photography. Three-dimensional media and techniques are sculpture (for example, using stone, wood, clay or cast metal), architecture, and many small-scale arts (such as jewelry, containers, or vessels) in media such as ceramics, metal, or wood.

Painting includes wall painting and fresco, illumination (the decoration of books with paintings), panel painting (painting on wood panels), painting on canvas, and handscroll and hanging scroll painting. The paint in these examples is pigment mixed with a liquid vehicle, or binder. Some art historians also consider pictorial media such as mosaic and stained glass—where the pigment is arranged in solid form—as a type of painting.

Graphic arts are those that involve the application of lines and strokes to a two-dimensional surface or support, most often paper. Drawing is a graphic art, as are the various forms of printmaking. Drawings may be sketches (quick visual notes, often made in preparation for larger drawings or paintings); studies (more carefully drawn analyses of details or entire compositions); cartoons (full-scale drawings made in preparation for work in another medium, such as fresco, stained glass, or tapestry); or complete artworks in themselves. Drawings can be made with ink, charcoal, crayon, or pencil. Prints, unlike drawings, are made in multiple copies. The various forms of printmaking include woodcut, the intaglio processes (engraving, etching, drypoint), and lithography.

Photography (literally, "light writing") is a medium that involves the rendering of optical images on light-sensitive surfaces. Photographic images are typically recorded by a camera.

Sculpture is three-dimensional art that is *carved*, *modeled*, *cast*, or *assembled*. Carved sculpture is subtractive in the sense that the image is created by taking away material. Wood, stone, and ivory are common materials used to create carved sculptures. Modeled sculpture is considered additive, meaning that the object is built up from a material, such as clay, that is soft enough to be molded and shaped. Metal sculpture is usually cast or is assembled by welding or a similar means of permanent joining.

Sculpture is either free-standing (that is, surrounded by space) or in pictorial relief. Relief sculpture projects from the background surface of the same piece of material. High-relief sculpture projects far from its background; low-relief sculpture is only slightly raised; and sunken relief, found mainly in ancient Egyptian art, is carved into the surface, with the highest part of the relief being the flat surface.

Ephemeral arts include processions, ceremonies, or ritual dances (often with décor, costumes, or masks); performance art; earthworks; cinema and video art; and some forms of digital or computer art. All impose a temporal limitation—the artwork is viewable for a finite period of time and then disappears forever, is in a constant state of change, or must be replayed to be experienced again.

Architecture creates enclosures for human activity or habitation. It is three-dimensional, highly spatial, functional, and closely bound with developments in technology and materials. Since it is difficult to capture in a photograph, several types of schematic drawings are commonly used to enable the visualization of a building:

Plans depict a structure's masses and voids, presenting a view from above of the building's footprint or as if it had been sliced horizontally at about waist height.

Plan: Philadelphia, Vanna Venturi House

Sections reveal the interior of a building as if it had been cut vertically from top to bottom.

Section: Rome, Sta. Costanza

Isometric drawings show buildings from oblique angles either seen from above ("bird's-eye view") to reveal their basic three-dimensional forms (often cut away so we can peek inside) or from below ("worm's-eye view") to represent the arrangement of interior spaces and the upward projection of structural elements.

Isometric cutaway from above: Ravenna, San Vitale

Isometric projection from below: Istanbul, Hagia Sophia

Introduction

Intro-1 • Mark Rothko MAGENTA, BLACK, GREEN, ON ORANGE (NO. 3/NO. 13)
1949. Oil on canvas, 7'1⅜" × 5'5" (2.165 × 1.648 m). Museum of Modern Art, New York.

The title of this book seems clear. It defines a field of academic study and scholarly research that has achieved a secure place in college and university curricula across North America. But *Art History* couples two words—even two worlds—that are less well focused when separated. What is art? In what sense does it have a history? Students of art and its history should pause and engage, even if briefly, with these large questions before beginning the journey surveyed in the following chapters.

WHAT IS ART?

Artists, critics, art historians, and the general public all grapple with this thorny question. The *Random House Dictionary* defines "art" as "the quality, production, expression, or realm of what is beautiful, or of more than ordinary significance." Others have characterized "art" as something human-made that combines creative imagination and technical skill, and satisfies an innate desire for order and harmony—perhaps a human hunger for the beautiful. This seems

---

LEARN ABOUT IT

I.1 Explore the methods and objectives of visual analysis.

I.2 Assess the way art historians identify conventional subject matter and symbols in the process called iconography.

I.3 Survey the methods used by art historians to analyze works of art and interpret their meaning within their original cultural contexts.

I.4 Trace the process of art-historical interpretation in a case study.

((•—[Listen to the chapter audio on myartslab.com

relatively straightforward until we start to look at modern and contemporary art, where there has been a heated and extended debate concerning "What is Art?" The focus is often far from questions of transcendent beauty, ordered design, or technical skill, and centers instead on the conceptual meaning of a work for an elite target audience or the attempt to pose challenging questions or unsettle deep-seated cultural ideas.

The works of art discussed in this book represent a privileged subset of artifacts produced by past and present cultures. They were usually meant to be preserved, and they are currently considered worthy of conservation and display. The determination of which artifacts are exceptional—which are works of art—evolves through the actions, opinions, and selections of artists, patrons, governments, collectors, archaeologists, museums, art historians, and others. Labeling objects as art is usually meant to signal that they transcended or now transcend in some profound way their practical function, often embodying cherished cultural ideas or asserting foundational values. Sometimes it can also mean they are considered beautiful, well designed, and made with loving care, but this is not always the case. We will discover that at various times and places, the complex notion of what is art has little to do with standards of skill or beauty. Some critics and historians argue broadly that works of art are tendentious embodiments of power and privilege, hardly sublime expressions of beauty or truth. After all, art can be unsettling as well as soothing, challenging as well as reassuring, whether made in the present or surviving from the past.

Increasingly, we are realizing that our judgments about what constitutes art—as well as what constitutes beauty—are conditioned by our own education and experience. Whether acquired at home, in classrooms, in museums, at the movies, or on the Internet, our responses to art are learned behaviors, influenced by class, gender, race, geography, and economic status as well as education. Even art historians find that their definitions of what constitutes art—and what constitutes artistic quality—evolve with additional research and understanding. Exploring works by twentieth-century painter Mark Rothko and nineteenth-century quilt-makers Martha Knowles and Henrietta Thomas demonstrates how definitions of art and artistic value are subject to change over time.

Rothko's painting, **MAGENTA, BLACK, GREEN, ON ORANGE (NO. 3/NO. 13)** (**FIG. Intro-1**), is a well-known example of the sort of abstract painting that was considered the epitome of artistic sophistication by the mid-twentieth-century New York art establishment. It was created by an artist who meant it to be a work of art. It was acquired by the Museum of Modern Art in New York, and its position on the walls of that museum is a sure sign of its acceptance as art by a powerful cultural institution. However, beyond the context of the American artists, dealers, critics, and collectors who made up Rothko's art world, such paintings were often received with skepticism. They were seen by many as incomprehensible—lacking both technical skill and recognizable subject matter, two criteria that were part of the general public's

definition of art at the time. Abstract paintings soon inspired a popular retort: "That's not art; my child could do it!" Interestingly enough, Rothko saw in the childlike character of his own paintings one of the qualities that made them works of art. Children, he said, "put forms, figures, and views into pictorial arrangements, employing out of necessity most of the rules of optical **perspective** and geometry but without the knowledge that they are employing them." He characterized his own art as childlike, as "an attempt to recapture the freshness and naiveté of childish vision." In part because they are carefully crafted by an established artist who provided these kinds of intellectual justifications for their character and appearance, Rothko's abstract paintings are broadly considered works of art and are treasured possessions of major museums across the globe.

Works of art, however, do not always have to be created by individuals who perceive themselves as artists. Nor are all works produced for an art market surrounded by critics and collectors ready to explain, exhibit, and disperse them, ideally to prestigious museums. Such is the case with this quilt (**FIG. Intro-2**), made by Martha Knowles and Henrietta Thomas a century before Rothko's painting. Their work is similarly composed of blocks of color, and like Rothko, they produced their visual effect by arranging these flat chromatic shapes carefully and regularly on a rectangular field. But this quilt was not meant to hang on the wall of an art museum. It is the social product of a friendship, intended as an intimate gift, presented to a loved one for use in her home. An inscription on the quilt itself makes this clear—"From M.A. Knowles to her

Intro-2 • Martha Knowles and Henrietta Thomas
MY SWEET SISTER EMMA
1843. Cotton quilt, 8'11" × 9'1" (2.72 × 2.77 m). International Quilt Studies Center, University of Nebraska, Lincoln, Nebraska.

This book contains much more than paintings and textiles. Within these pages you will also encounter sculpture, vessels, books, jewelry, tombs, chairs, photographs, architecture, and more. But as with Rothko's *Magenta, Black, Green, on Orange (No. 3/No. 13)* (see FIG. Intro–1) and Knowles and Thomas's *My Sweet Sister Emma* (see FIG. Intro–2), criteria have been used to determine which works are selected for inclusion in a book titled *Art History*. Architecture presents an interesting case.

Buildings meet functional human needs by enclosing human habitation or activity. Many works of architecture, however, are considered "exceptional" because they transcend functional demands by manifesting distinguished architectural design or because they embody in important ways the values and goals of the culture that built them. Such buildings are usually produced by architects influenced, like painters, by great works and traditions from the past. In some cases they harmonize with, or react to, their natural or urban surroundings. For such reasons, they are discussed in books on the history of art.

Typical of such buildings is the church of Nôtre-Dame-du-Haut in Ronchamp, France, designed and constructed between 1950 and 1955

by Swiss architect Charles-Edouard Jeanneret, better known by his pseudonym, Le Corbusier. This building is the product of a significant historical moment, rich in international cultural meaning. A pilgrimage church on this site had been destroyed during World War II, and the creation here of a new church symbolized the end of a devastating war, embodying hopes for a brighter global future. Le Corbusier's design—drawing on sources that ranged from Algerian mosques to imperial Roman villas, from crab shells to airplane wings—is sculptural as well as architectural. It soars at the crest of a hill toward the sky but at the same time seems solidly anchored in the earth. And its coordination with the curves of the natural landscape complement the creation of an outdoor setting for religious ceremonies (to the right in the figure) to supplement the church interior that Le Corbusier characterized as a "container for intense concentration." In fact, this building is so renowned today as a monument of modern architecture, that the bus-loads of pilgrims who arrive at the site are mainly architects and devotees of architectural history.

Intro–3 • Le Corbusier
NÔTRE-DAME-DU-HAUT
Ronchamp, France. 1950–1955.

Sweet Sister Emma, 1843." Thousands of such friendship quilts were made by women during the middle years of the nineteenth century for use on beds, either to provide warmth or as a covering spread. Whereas quilts were sometimes displayed to a broad and enthusiastic audience of producers and admirers at competitions held at state and county fairs, they were not collected by art museums or revered by artists until relatively recently.

In 1971, at the Whitney Museum in New York—an establishment bastion of the art world in which Rothko moved and

worked—art historians Jonathan Holstein and Gail van der Hoof mounted an exhibition entitled "Abstract Design in American Quilts," demonstrating the artistic affinity we have already noted in comparing the way Knowles and Thomas, like Rothko, create abstract patterns with fields of color. Quilts were later accepted—or perhaps "**appropriated**"—as works of art and hung on the walls of a New York art museum because of their visual similarities with the avant-garde, abstract works of art created by establishment, New York artists.

Art historian Patricia Mainardi took the case for quilts one significant step further in a pioneering article of 1973 published in *The Feminist Art Journal*. Entitled, "Quilts: The Great American Art," her argument was rooted not only in the aesthetic affinity of quilts with the esteemed work of contemporary abstract painters, but also in a political conviction that the definition of art had to be broadened. What was at stake here was historical veracity. Mainardi began, "Women have always made art. But for most women, the arts highest valued by male society have been closed to them for just that reason. They have put their creativity instead into the needlework arts, which exist in fantastic variety wherever there are women, and which in fact are a universal female art, transcending race, class, and national borders." She argued for the inclusion of quilts within the history of art to give deserved attention to the work of women artists who had been excluded from discussion because they created textiles and because they worked outside the male-dominated professional structures of the art world—because they were women. Quilts now hang as works of art on the walls of museums and appear with regularity in books that survey the history of art.

As these two examples demonstrate, definitions of art are rooted in cultural systems of value that are subject to change. And as they change, the list of works considered by art historians is periodically revised. Determining what to study is a persistent part of the art historian's task.

WHAT IS ART HISTORY?

There are many ways to study or appreciate works of art. Art history represents one specific approach, with its own goals and its own methods of assessment and interpretation. Simply put, art historians seek to understand the meaning of art from the past within its original cultural contexts, both from the point of view of its producers—artists, architects, and patrons—as well as from the point of view of its consumers—those who formed its original audience. Coming to an understanding of the cultural meaning of a work of art requires detailed and patient investigation on many levels, especially with art that was produced long ago and in societies distinct from our own. This is a scholarly rather than an intuitive exercise. In art history, the work of art is seen as an embodiment of the values, goals, and aspirations of its time and place of origin. It is a part of culture.

Art historians use a variety of theoretical perspectives and a host of interpretive strategies to come to an understanding of works of art within their cultural contexts. But as a place to begin, the work of art historians can be divided into four types of investigation:

1. assessment of physical properties,
2. analysis of visual or formal structure,
3. identification of subject matter or conventional symbolism, and
4. integration within cultural context.

ASSESSING PHYSICAL PROPERTIES

Of the methods used by art historians to study works of art, this is the most objective, but it requires close access to the work itself. Physical properties include shape, size, materials, and technique. For instance, many pictures are rectangular (e.g., see FIG. Intro–1), but some are round (see page xxv, FIG. C). Paintings as large as Rothko's require us to stand back if we want to take in the whole image, whereas some paintings (see page xxiv, FIG. A) are so small that we are drawn up close to examine their detail. Rothko's painting and Knowles and Thomas's quilt are both rectangles of similar size, but they are distinguished by the materials from which they are made—oil paint on canvas versus cotton fabric joined by stitching. In art history books, most physical properties can only be understood from descriptions in captions, but when we are in the presence of the work of art itself, size and shape may be the first thing we notice. To fully understand **medium** and technique, however, it may be necessary to employ methods of scientific analysis or documentary research to elucidate the practices of artists at the time when and place where the work was created.

ANALYZING FORMAL STRUCTURE

Art historians explore the visual character that artists bring to their works—using the materials and the techniques chosen to create them—in a process called **formal analysis**. On the most basic level, it is divided into two parts:

- assessing the individual visual elements or formal vocabulary that constitute pictorial or sculptural communication, and
- discovering the overall arrangement, organization, or structure of an image, a design system that art historians often refer to as **composition**.

THE ELEMENTS OF VISUAL EXPRESSION Artists control and vary the visual character of works of art to give their subjects and ideas meaning and expression, vibrancy and persuasion, challenge or delight (see "A Closer Look," page xxiv). For example, the motifs, objects, figures, and environments within paintings can be sharply defined by line (see FIGS. Intro–2, Intro–4), or they can be suggested by a sketchier definition (see FIGS. Intro–1, Intro–5). Painters can simulate the appearance of three-dimensional form through **modeling** or shading (see FIG. Intro–4 and page xxv, FIG. C), that is, by describing the way light from a single source will highlight one side of a solid while leaving the other side in shadow. Alternatively, artists can avoid any strong sense of three-dimensionality by emphasizing patterns on a surface rather than forms in space (see FIG. Intro–1 and page xxiv, FIG. A). In addition to revealing the solid substance of forms through modeling, dramatic lighting can also guide viewers to specific areas of a picture (see page xxiv, FIG. B), or it can be lavished on every aspect of a picture to reveal all its detail and highlight the vibrancy of its color (see page xxv, FIG. D). Color itself can be muted or intensified, depending on the mood artists want to create or the tastes and expectations of their audiences.

LINE

A. Carpet Page from the Lindisfarne Gospels
From Lindisfarne, England. c. 715–720. Ink and tempera on vellum, 13⅜″ × 9⁷⁄₁₆″ (34 × 24 cm). British Library, London. Cotton MS Nero D.IV fol. 26v

Every element in this complicated painting is sharply outlined by abrupt barriers between light and dark or between one color and another; there are no gradual or shaded transitions. Since the picture was created in part with pen and ink, the linearity is a logical extension of medium and technique. And although line itself is a "flattening" or two-dimensionalizing element in pictures, a complex and consistent system of overlapping gives the linear animal forms a sense of shallow but carefully worked-out three-dimensional relationships to one another.

LIGHT

B. Georges de la Tour *The Education of the Virgin*
c. 1650. Oil on canvas, 33″ × 39½″ (83.8 × 100.4 cm). The Frick Collection, New York.

The source of illumination is a candle depicted within the painting. The young girl's upraised right hand shields its flame, allowing the artist to demonstrate his virtuosity in painting the translucency of human flesh.

Since the candle's flame is partially concealed, its luminous intensity is not allowed to distract from those aspects of the painting most brilliantly illuminated by it—the face of the girl and the book she is reading.

View the Closer Look for visual elements of pictorial expression: line, light, form, and color on myartslab.com

FORM

C. Michelangelo
The Holy Family
(Doni Tondo)
c. 1503. Oil and
tempera on panel,
diameter 3′11¼″
(1.2 m). Galleria
degli Uffizi,
Florence.

The complex overlapping of
their highly three-dimensionalized
bodies conveys the somewhat
contorted spatial positioning
and relationship of these
three figures.

Through the use of modeling
or shading—a gradual
transition from lights to
darks—Michelangelo
imitates the way solid forms
are illuminated from a single
light source—the side
closest to the light source is
bright while the other side is
cast in shadow—and gives a
sense of three-dimensional
form to his figures.

The actual three-dimensional
projection of the sculpted heads
in medallions around the frame—
designed for this painting by
Michelangelo himself—heightens the
effect of fictive three-dimensionality in
the figures painted on its flat surface.

In a technique called **foreshortening**,
the carefully calculated angle of the
Virgin's elbow makes it seem to
project out toward the viewer.

Junayd chose to flood every aspect of his painting
with light, as if everything in it were illuminated from
all sides at once. As a result, the emphasis here
is on jewel-like color. The vibrant tonalities and
dazzling detail of the dreamy landscape are not
only more important than the simulation of three-
dimensional forms distributed within a consistently
described space; they actually upstage the human
drama taking place against a patterned, tipped-up
ground in the lower third of the picture.

COLOR

**D. Junayd *Humay and Humayun*,
from a manuscript of the *Divan*
of Kwaju Kirmani**
Made in Baghdad, Iraq. 1396.
Color, ink, and gold on paper,
12⅝″ × 9⁷⁄₁₆″ (32 × 24 cm).
British Library, London.
MS Add. 18113, fol. 31r

Thus, artists communicate with their viewers by making choices in the way they use and emphasize the elements of visual expression, and art-historical analysis seeks to reveal how artists' decisions bring meaning to a work of art. For example, in two paintings of women with children (see FIGS. Intro-4, Intro-5), Raphael and Renoir work with the same visual elements of line, form, light, and color in the creation of their images, but they employ these shared elements to differing expressive ends. Raphael concentrates on line to clearly differentiate each element of his picture as a separate form. Careful modeling describes these outlined forms as substantial solids surrounded by space. This gives his subjects a sense of clarity, stability, and grandeur. Renoir, on the other hand, foregrounds the flickering of light and the play of color as he downplays the sense of three-dimensionality in individual forms. This gives his image a more ephemeral, casual sense. Art historians pay close attention to such variations in the use of visual elements—the building blocks of artistic expression—and use visual analysis to characterize the expressive effect of a particular work, a particular artist, or a general period defined by place and date.

COMPOSITION When art historians analyze composition, they focus not on the individual elements of visual expression but on the overall arrangement and organizing design or structure of a work of art. In Raphael's **MADONNA OF THE GOLDFINCH** (FIG. Intro-4), for example, the group of figures has been arranged in a triangular shape and placed at the center of the picture. Raphael emphasized this central weighting by opening the clouds to reveal a

patch of blue in the middle of the sky, and by flanking the figural group with lacelike trees. Since the Madonna is at the center and since the two boys are divided between the two sides of the triangular shape, roughly—though not precisely—equidistant from the center of the painting, this is a bilaterally symmetrical composition: on either side of an implied vertical line at the center of the picture, there are equivalent forms on left and right, matched and balanced in a mirrored correspondence. Art historians refer to such an implied line—around which the elements of a picture are organized—as an **axis**. Raphael's painting has not only a vertical, but also a horizontal axis, indicated by a line of demarcation between light and dark—as well as between degrees of color saturation—in the terrain of the landscape. The belt of the Madonna's dress is aligned with this horizontal axis, and this correspondence, taken with the coordination of her head with the blue patch in the sky, relates her harmoniously to the natural world in which

Intro-4 • Raphael **MADONNA OF THE GOLDFINCH (MADONNA DEL CARDELLINO)**
1506. Oil on panel, 42″ × 29½″ (106.7 × 74.9 cm). Galleria degli Uffizi, Florence.

The vibrant colors of this important work were revealed in the course of a careful, ten-year restoration, completed only in 2008.

Intro-5 • Auguste Renoir **MME. CHARPENTIER AND HER CHILDREN** 1878. Oil on canvas, 60½″ × 74⅞″ (153.7 × 190.2 cm). Metropolitan Museum of Art, New York.

she sits, lending a sense of stability, order, and balance to the picture as a whole.

The main axis in Renoir's painting of **MME. CHARPENTIER AND HER CHILDREN** (**FIG. Intro-5**) is neither vertical, nor horizontal, but diagonal, running from the upper right to the lower left corner of the painting. All major elements of the composition are aligned along this axis—dog, children, mother, and the table and chair that represent the most complex and detailed aspect of the setting. The upper left and lower right corners of the painting balance each other on either side of the diagonal axis as relatively simple fields of neutral tone, setting off and framing the main subjects between them. The resulting arrangement is not bilaterally symmetrical, but blatantly asymmetrical, with the large figural mass pushed into the left side of the picture. And unlike Raphael's composition, where the spatial relationship of the figures and their environment is mapped by the measured placement of elements that become increasingly smaller in scale and fuzzier in definition as they recede into the background, the relationship of Renoir's figures to their spatial environment is less clearly defined as they recede into the background along the dramatic diagonal axis. Nothing distracts us from the bold informality of this family gathering.

Both Raphael and Renoir arrange their figures carefully and purposefully, but they follow distinctive compositional systems that communicate different notions of the way these figures interact with each other and the world around them. Art historians pay special attention to how pictures are arranged because composition is one of the principal ways artists charge their paintings with expressive meaning.

IDENTIFYING SUBJECT MATTER

Art historians have traditionally sought subject matter and meaning in works of art with a system of analysis that was outlined by Erwin Panofsky (1892–1968), an influential German scholar who was expelled from his academic position by the Nazis in 1933 and spent the rest of his career of research and teaching in the United States. Panofsky proposed that when we seek to understand the subject of a work of art, we derive meaning initially in two ways:

- First we perceive what he called "natural subject matter" by recognizing forms and situations that we know from our own experience.
- Then we use what he called "**iconography**" to identify the conventional meanings associated with forms and figures as bearers of narrative or symbolic content, often specific to a particular time and place.

Some paintings, like Rothko's abstractions and Knowles and Thomas's quilt, do not contain subjects drawn from the world around us, from stories, or from conventional symbolism, but Panofsky's scheme remains a standard method of investigating

The study and identification of conventional themes, motifs, and symbols to elucidate the subject matter of works of art.

These grapes sit on an imported, Italian silver *tazza*, a luxury object that may commemorate northern European prosperity and trade. This particular object recurs in several of Peeters's other still lifes.

An image of the artist herself appears on the reflective surface of this pewter tankard, one of the ways that she signed her paintings and promoted her career.

Luscious fruits and flowers celebrate the abundance of nature, but because these fruits of the earth will eventually fade, even rot, they could be moralizing references to the transience of earthly existence.

These coins, including one minted in 1608–1609, help focus the dating of this painting. The highlighting of money within a still life could reference the wealth of the owner—or it could subtly allude to the value the artist has crafted here in paint.

Detailed renderings of insects showcased Peeters's virtuosity as a painter, but they also may have symbolized the vulnerability of the worldly beauty of flowers and fruit to destruction and decay.

This knife—which appears in several of Peeters's still lifes—is of a type that is associated with wedding gifts.

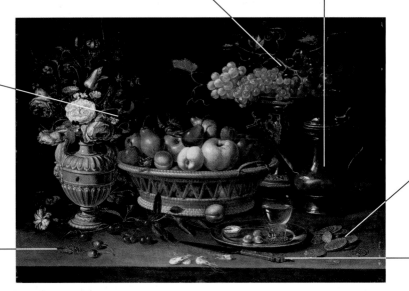

A. Clara Peeters Still Life with Fruit and Flowers
c. 1612. Oil on copper, 25⅕″ × 35″ (64 × 89 cm). Ashmolean Museum, Oxford.

Quince is an unusual subject in Chinese painting, but the fruit seems to have carried personal significance for Zhu Da. One of his friends was known as the Daoist of Quince Mountain, a site in Hunan Province that was also the subject of a work by one of his favorite authors, Tang poet Li Bai.

The artist's signature reads "Bada Shanren painted this," using a familiar pseudonym in a formula and calligraphic style that the artist ceased using in 1695.

This red block is a seal with an inscription drawn from a Confucian text: "Teaching is half of learning." This was imprinted on the work by the artist as an aspect of his signature, a symbol of his identity within the picture, just as the reflection and inscribed knife identify Clara Peeters as the painter of her still life.

B. Zhu Da (Bada Shanren) Quince (Mugua)
1690. Album leaf mounted as a hanging scroll; ink and colors on paper, 7⅞″ × 5¾″ (20 × 14.6 cm). Princeton University Art Museum.

View the Closer Look for iconography on myartslab.com

meaning in works of art that present narrative subjects, portray specific people or places, or embody cultural values with iconic imagery or allegory.

NATURAL SUBJECT MATTER We recognize some things in works of visual art simply by virtue of living in a world similar to that represented by the artist. For example, in the two paintings by Raphael and Renoir just examined (see FIGS. Intro–4, Intro–5), we immediately recognize the principal human figures in both as a woman and two children, boys in the case of Raphael's painting, girls in Renoir's. We can also make a general identification of the animals: a bird in the hand of Raphael's boys, and a pet dog under one of Renoir's girls. And natural subject matter can extend from an identification of figures to an understanding of the expressive significance of their postures and facial features. We might see in the boy who snuggles between the knees of the woman in Raphael's painting, placing his own foot on top of hers, an anxious child seeking the security of physical contact with a trusted caretaker—perhaps his mother—in response to fear of the bird he reaches out to touch. Many of us have seen insecure children take this very pose in response to potentially unsettling encounters.

The closer the work of art is in both time and place to our own situation temporally and geographically, the easier it sometimes is to identify what is represented. But although Renoir painted his picture over 125 years ago in France, the furniture in the background still looks familiar, as does the book in the hand of Raphael's Madonna, painted five centuries before our time. But the object hanging from the belt of the scantily clad boy at the left in this painting will require identification for most of us. Iconographic investigation is necessary to understand the function of this form.

ICONOGRAPHY Some subjects are associated with conventional meanings established at a specific time or place; some of the human figures portrayed in works of art have specific identities; and some of the objects or forms have symbolic or allegorical meanings in addition to their natural subject matter. Discovering these conventional meanings of art's subject matter is called iconography. (See "A Closer Look," opposite.)

For example, the woman accompanied in the outdoors by two boys in Raphael's *Madonna of the Goldfinch* (see FIG. Intro–4) would have been immediately recognized by members of its intended early sixteenth-century Florentine audience as the Virgin Mary. Viewers would have identified the naked boy standing between her knees as her son Jesus, and the boy holding the bird as Jesus' cousin John the Baptist, sheathed in the animal skin garment that he would wear in the wilderness and equipped with a shallow cup attached to his belt, ready to be used in baptisms. Such attributes of clothing and equipment are often critical in making iconographic identifications. The goldfinch in the Baptist's hand was at this time and place a symbol of Christ's death on the cross, an allegorical implication that makes the Christ Child's retreat

into secure contact with his mother—already noted on the level of natural subject matter—understandable in relation to a specific story. The comprehension of conventional meanings in this painting would have been almost automatic among those for whom it was painted, but for us, separated by time and place, some research is necessary to recover associations that are no longer part of our everyday world.

Although it may not initially seem as unfamiliar, the subject matter of Renoir's 1878 portrait of *Mme. Charpentier and her Children* (see FIG. Intro–5) is in fact even more obscure. There are those in twenty-first-century American culture for whom the figures and symbols in Raphael's painting are still recognizable and meaningful, but Marguérite-Louise Charpentier died in 1904, and no one living today would be able to identify her based on the likeness Renoir presumably gave to her face in this family portrait commissioned by her husband, the wealthy and influential publisher Georges Charpentier. We need the painting's title to make that identification. And Mme. Charpentier is outfitted here in a gown created by English designer Charles Frederick Worth, the dominant figure in late nineteenth-century Parisian high fashion. Her clothing was a clear attribute of her wealth for those who recognized its source; most of us need to investigate to uncover its meaning. But a greater surprise awaits the student who pursues further research on her children. Although they clearly seem to our eyes to represent two daughters, the child closest to Mme. Charpentier is actually her son Paul, who at age 3, following standard Parisian bourgeois practice, has not yet had his first haircut and still wears clothing comparable to that of his older sister Georgette, perched on the family dog. It is not unusual in art history to encounter situations where our initial conclusions on the level of natural subject matter will need to be revised after some iconographic research.

INTEGRATION WITHIN CULTURAL CONTEXT
Natural subject matter and iconography were only two of three steps proposed by Panofsky for coming to an understanding of the meaning of works of art. The third step he labeled "**iconology**," and its aim is to interpret the work of art as an embodiment of its cultural situation, to place it within broad social, political, religious, and intellectual contexts. Such integration into history requires more than identifying subject matter or conventional symbols; it requires a deep understanding of the beliefs and principles or goals and values that underlie a work of art's cultural situation as well as the position of an artist and patron within it.

In "A Closer Look" (opposite), the subject matter of two **still life** paintings (pictures of inanimate objects and fruits or flowers taken out of their natural contexts) is identified and elucidated, but to truly understand these two works as bearers of cultural meaning, more knowledge of the broader context and specific goals of artists and audiences is required. For example, the fact that Zhu Da (1626–1705) became a painter was rooted more in the political than the artistic history of China at the middle of the seventeenth century. As a member of the imperial family of the Ming dynasty, his life of privilege was disrupted when the Ming were overthrown during the Manchu conquest of China in 1644. Fleeing for his life, he sought refuge in a Buddhist monastery, where he wrote poetry and painted. Almost 40 years later, in the aftermath of a nervous breakdown (that could have been staged to avoid retribution for his family background), Zhu Da abandoned his monastic life and developed a career as a professional painter, adopting a series of descriptive pseudonyms—most notably Bada Shanren ("mountain man of eight greatnesses") by which he is most often known today. His paintings are at times saturated with veiled political commentary; at times they seek to accommodate the expectations of collectors to assure their marketability; and in paintings like the one illustrated here (see page xxviii, FIG. B), the artist seems to hark back to the contemplative, abstract, and spontaneous paintings associated with great Zen masters such as Muqi (c. 1201–after 1269), whose calligraphic pictures of isolated fruits seem almost like acts of devotion or detached contemplations on natural forms, rather than the works of a professional painter.

Clara Peeters's still life (see page xxviii, FIG. A), on the other hand, fits into a developing Northern European painting tradition within which she was an established and successful professional, specializing in portrayals of food and flowers, fruit and reflective objects. Still-life paintings in this tradition could be jubilant celebrations of the abundance of the natural world and the wealth of luxury objects available in the prosperous mercantile society of the Netherlands. Or they could be moralizing "**vanitas**" paintings, warning of the ephemeral meaning of those worldly possessions, even of life itself. But this painting has also been interpreted in a more personal way. Because the type of knife that sits in the foreground near the edge of the table was a popular wedding gift, and since it is inscribed with the artist's own name, some have suggested that this still life could have celebrated Peeters's marriage. Or this could simply be a witty way to sign her picture. It certainly could be personal and at the same time participate in the broader cultural meaning of still-life paintings. Mixtures of private and public meanings have been proposed for Zhu Da's paintings as well. Some have seen the picture of quince illustrated here (see page xxviii, FIG. B) as part of a series of allegorical "self-portraits" that extend across his career as a painter. Art historians frequently reveal multiple meanings when interpreting single works. Art often represents complex cultural and personal situations.

A CASE STUDY: ROGIER VAN DER WEYDEN'S PHILADELPHIA *CRUCIFIXION*

The basic, four-part method of art historical investigation and interpretation just outlined and explored may become clearer when its extended use is traced in relation to one specific work of art. A particularly revealing subject for such a case study is a seminal and somewhat perplexing painting now in the Philadelphia Museum of Art—the **CRUCIFIXION WITH THE VIRGIN AND ST. JOHN THE EVANGELIST** (FIG. Intro-6) by Rogier van der Weyden (c. 1400–1464), a Flemish artist who will be featured in Chapter 19. Each of the four levels of art-historical inquiry reveals important information about this painting, information that has been used by art historians to reconstruct its relationship to its artist, its audience, and its broader cultural setting. The resulting interpretation is rich, but also complex. An investigation this extensive will not be possible for all the works of art in the following chapters, where the text will focus only on one or two facets of more expansive research. Because of the amount and complexity of information involved in a thorough art-historical interpretation, it is sometimes only in a second reading that we can follow the subtleties of its argument, after the first reading has provided a basic familiarity with the work of art, its conventional subjects, and its general context.

PHYSICAL PROPERTIES

Perhaps the most striking aspect of this painting's physical appearance is its division into two separate tall rectangular panels, joined by a frame to form a coherent, almost square composition. These are oak panels, prepared with chalk to form a smooth surface on which to paint with mineral pigments suspended in oil. A technical investigation of the painting in 1981 used infrared reflectography to reveal a very sketchy under-drawing beneath the surface of the paint, proving to the investigators that this painting is almost entirely the work of Rogier van der Weyden himself. Famous and prosperous artists of this time and place employed many assistants to work in large production workshops, and they would make detailed under-drawings to ensure that assistants replicated the **style** of the master. But in cases where the masters themselves intended to execute the work, only summary compositional outlines were needed. Modern technical investigation of Rogier's painting also used **dendrochronology** (the dating of wood based on the patterns of the growth rings) to date the oak panels and consequently the painting itself, now securely situated near the end of the artist's career, c. 1460.

The most recent restoration of the painting—during the early 1990s by Mark Tucker, Senior Conservator at the Philadelphia Museum of Art—returned it, as close as possible, to current views of its original fifteenth-century appearance (see "De-restoring and Restoring Rogier van der Weyden's *Crucifixion*," page xxxii). This project included extensive technical analysis of almost every aspect of the picture, during which a critical clue emerged, one that may lead to a sharper understanding of its original use. X-rays revealed dowel holes and plugs running in a horizontal line about one-fourth of the way up from the bottom across the entire expanse of the two-panel painting. Tucker's convincing research suggests that the dowels would have attached these two panels to the backs of wooden boxes that contained sculptures in a complex work of art that hung over the altar in a fifteenth-century church.

Intro-6 • Rogier van der Weyden **CRUCIFIXION WITH THE VIRGIN AND ST. JOHN THE EVANGELIST**
c. 1460. Oil on oak panels, 71″ × 73″ (1.8 × 1.85 m). John G. Johnson Collection, Philadelphia Museum of Art.

FORMAL STRUCTURE

The visual organization of this two-part painting emphasizes both connection and separation. It is at the same time one painting and two. Continuing across both panels is the strip of midnight blue sky and the stone wall that constricts space within the picture to a shallow corridor, pushing the figures into the foreground and close to the viewer. The shallow strip of mossy ground under the two-figure group in the left panel continues its sloping descent into the right panel, as does the hem of the Virgin's ice-blue garment. We look into this scene as if through a window with a mullion down the middle and assume that the world on the left continues behind this central strip of frame into the right side.

On the other hand, strong visual forces isolate the figures within their respective panels, setting up a system of "compare and contrast" that seems to be at the heart of the painting's design. The striking red cloths that hang over the wall are centered directly behind the figures on each side, forming internal frames that highlight them as separate groups and focus our attention back and forth between them rather than on the pictorial elements that unite their environments. As we begin to compare the two sides,

Ever since Rogier van der Weyden's strikingly asymmetrical, two-panel rendering of the *Crucifixion* (see FIG. Intro–6) was purchased by Philadelphia lawyer John G. Johnson in 1906 for his spectacular collection of European paintings, it has been recognized not only as one of the greatest works by this master of fifteenth-century Flemish painting, but as one of the most important European paintings in North America. Soon after the Johnson Collection became part of the Philadelphia Museum of Art in 1933, however, this painting's visual character was significantly transformed. In 1941, the museum employed freelance restorer David Rosen to work on the painting. Deciding that Rogier's work was seriously marred by later overpainting and disfigured by the discoloration of old varnish, he subjected the painting to a thorough cleaning. He also removed the strip of dark blue paint forming the sky above the wall at the top—identifying it as an eighteenth-century restoration—and replaced it with gold leaf to conform with remnants of gold in this area that he assessed as surviving fragments of the original background. Rosen's restoration of Rogier's painting was uncritically accepted for almost half a century, and the gold background became a major factor in the interpretations of art historians as distinguished as Erwin Panofsky and Meyer Schapiro.

In 1990, in preparation for a new installation of the work, Rogier's painting received a thorough technical analysis by Mark Tucker, the museum's Senior Conservator. There were two startling discoveries:

- The dark blue strip that had run across the top of the picture before Rosen's intervention was actually original to the painting. Remnants of paint left behind in 1941 proved to be the same azurite blue that also appears in the clothing of the Virgin, and in no instance did the traces of gold discovered in 1941 run under aspects of the original paint surface. Rosen had removed Rogier's original midnight blue sky.

- What Rosen had interpreted as disfiguring varnish streaking the wall and darkening the brilliant cloths of honor hanging over it were actually Rogier's careful painting of lichens and water stains on the stone and his overpainting on the fabric that had originally transformed a vermillion undercoat into deep crimson cloth.

In meticulous work during 1992–1993, Tucker cautiously restored the painting based on the evidence he had uncovered. Neither the lost lichens and water stains nor the toning crimson overpainting of the hangings were replaced, but a coat of blue-black paint was laid over Rosen's gold leaf at the top of the panels, taking care to apply the new layer in such a way that should a later generation decide to return to the gold leaf sky, the midnight tonalities could be easily removed. That seems an unlikely prospect. The painting as exhibited today comes as close as possible to the original appearance of Rogier's *Crucifixion*. At least we think so.

---

it becomes increasingly clear that the relationship between figures and environment is quite distinct on each side of the divide.

The dead figure of Christ on the cross, elevated to the very top of the picture, is strictly centered within his panel, as well as against the cloth that hangs directly behind him. The grid of masonry blocks and creases in the cloth emphasizes his rectilinear integration into a system of balanced, rigid regularity. His head is aligned with the cap of the wall, his flesh largely contained within the area defined by the cloth. His elbows mark the juncture of the wall with the edge of the hanging, and his feet extend just to the end of the cloth, where his toes substitute for the border of fringe they overlap. The environment is almost as balanced. The strip of dark sky at the top is equivalent in size to the strip of mossy earth at the bottom of the picture, and both are visually bisected by centered horizontals—the cross bar at the top and the alignment of bone and skull at the bottom. A few disruptions to this stable, rectilinear, symmetrical order draw the viewers' attention to the panel at the left: the downward fall of the head of Christ, the visual weight of the skull, the downturn of the fluttering loin cloth, and the tip of the Virgin's gown that transgresses over the barrier to move in from the other side.

John and Mary merge on the left into a single figural mass that could be inscribed into a half-circle. Although set against a rectilinear grid background comparable to that behind Jesus, they contrast with, rather than conform to, the regular sense of order. Their curving outlines offer unsettling unsteadiness, as if they are toppling to the ground, jutting into the other side of the frame. This instability is reinforced by their postures. The projection of Mary's knee in relation to the angle of her torso reveals that she is collapsing into a curve, and the crumpled mass of drapery circling underneath her only underlines her lack of support. John reaches out to catch her, but he has not yet made contact with her body. He strikes a stance of strident instability without even touching the ground, and he looks blankly out into space with an unfocused expression, distracted from, rather than concentrating on, the task at hand. Perhaps he will come to his senses and grab her. But will he be able to catch her in time, and even then support her, given his unstable posture? The moment is tense; the outcome is unclear. But we are moving into the realm of natural subject matter. The poignancy of this concentrated portrayal seems to demand it.

ICONOGRAPHY

The subject of this painting is among the most familiar themes in the history of European art. The dead Jesus has been crucified on the cross, and two of his closest associates—his mother and John, one of his disciples—mourn his loss. Although easily recognizable, the austere and asymmetrical presentation is unexpected. More usual is an earlier painting of this subject by the same artist, **CRUCIFIXION TRIPTYCH WITH DONORS AND SAINTS** (**FIG. Intro–7**), where he situates the crucified Christ at the center

Intro-7 • Rogier van der Weyden **CRUCIFIXION TRIPTYCH WITH DONORS AND SAINTS**
c. 1440. Oil on wooden panels, 39¾″ × 55″ (101 × 140 cm). Kunsthistorisches Museum, Vienna.

of a symmetrical arrangement, the undisputed axial focus of the composition. The scene unfolds here within an expansive landscape, populated with a wider cast of participants, each of whom takes a place with symmetrical decorum on either side of the cross. Because most crucifixions follow some variation on this pattern, Rogier's two-panel portrayal (see FIG. Intro-6) in which the cross is asymmetrically displaced to one side, with a spare cast of attendants relegated to a separately framed space, severely restricted by a stark stone wall, requires some explanation. As does the mysterious dark world beyond the wall, and the artificial backdrop of the textile hangings.

This scene is not only austere and subdued; it is sharply focused, and the focus relates it to the specific moment in the story that Rogier decided to represent. The Christian Bible contains four accounts of Jesus' crucifixion, one in each of the four Gospels. Rogier took two verses in John's account as his painting's text (John 19:26–27), cited here in the Douai-Reims literal English translation (1582, 1609) of the Latin Vulgate Bible that was used by Western European Christians during the fifteenth century:

> When Jesus therefore had seen his mother and the disciple standing whom he loved, he saith to his mother: Woman, behold thy son. After that, he saith to the disciple: Behold thy mother. And from that hour, the disciple took her to his own.

Even the textual source uses conventions that need explanation, specifically the way the disciple John is consistently referred to in this Gospel as "the disciple whom Jesus loved." Rogier's painting, therefore, seems to focus on Jesus' call for a newly expanded relationship between his mother and a beloved follower. More specifically, he has projected us slightly forward in time to the moment when John needs to respond to that call—Jesus has died; John is now in charge.

There are, however, other conventional iconographic associations with the crucifixion that Rogier has folded into this spare portrayal. Fifteenth-century viewers would have understood the skull and femur that lie on the mound at the base of the cross as the bones of Adam—the first man in the Hebrew Bible account of creation—on whose grave Jesus' crucifixion was believed to have taken place. This juxtaposition embodied the Christian belief that Christ's sacrifice on the cross redeemed believers from the death that Adam's original sin had brought to human existence.

Mary's swoon and presumed loss of consciousness would have evoked another theological idea, the *co-passio*, in which Mary's anguish while witnessing Jesus' suffering and death was seen as a parallel passion of mother with son, both critical for human salvation. Their connection in this painting is underlined visually by the similar bending of their knees, inclination of their heads, and closing of their eyes. They even seem to resemble each other in facial likeness, especially when compared to John.

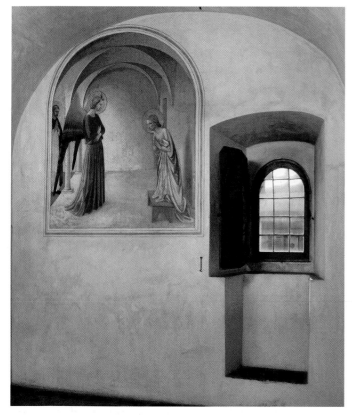

Intro-8 • VIEW OF A MONK'S CELL IN THE MONASTERY OF SAN MARCO, FLORENCE
Including Fra Angelico's fresco of the *Annunciation*. c. 1438–1445.

CULTURAL CONTEXT

In 1981 art historian Penny Howell Jolly published an interpretation of Rogier's Philadelphia *Crucifixion* as the product of a broad personal and cultural context. In addition to building on the work of earlier art historians, she pursued two productive lines of investigation to explain the rationale for this unusually austere presentation:

- the prospect that Rogier was influenced by the work of another artist, and
- the possibility that the painting was produced for an institutional context that called for a special mode of visual presentation and a particular iconographic focus.

FRA ANGELICO AT SAN MARCO We know very little about the life of Rogier van der Weyden, but we do know that in 1450, when he was already established as one of the principal painters in northern Europe, he made a pilgrimage to Rome. Either on his way to Rome, or during his return journey home, he stopped off in Florence and saw the **altarpiece**, and presumably also the frescos, that Fra Angelico (c. 1400–1455) and his workshop had painted during the 1440s at the monastery of San Marco. The evidence of Rogier's contact with Fra Angelico's work is found in a work Rogier painted after he returned home, based on a panel of the San Marco altarpiece. For the Philadelphia *Crucifixion*,

however, it was Fra Angelico's devotional frescos on the walls of the monks' individual rooms (or cells) that seem to have had the greatest impact (**FIG. Intro-8**). Jolly compared the Philadelphia *Crucifixion* with a scene of the Mocking of Christ at San Marco to demonstrate the connection (**FIG. Intro-9**). Fra Angelico presented the sacred figures with a quiet austerity that recalls Rogier's unusual composition. More specific parallels are the use of an expansive stone wall to restrict narrative space to a shallow foreground corridor, the description of the world beyond that wall as a dark sky that contrasts with the brilliantly illuminated foreground, and the use of a draped cloth of honor to draw attention to a narrative vignette from the life of Jesus, to separate it out as an object of devotion.

THE CARTHUSIANS Having established a possible connection between Rogier's unusual late painting of the crucifixion and frescos by Fra Angelico that he likely saw during his pilgrimage to Rome in 1450, Jolly reconstructed a specific context of patronage and meaning within Rogier's own world in Flanders that could explain why the paintings of Fra Angelico would have had such an impact on him at this particular moment in his career.

During the years around 1450, Rogier developed a personal and professional relationship with the monastic order of

Intro-9 • Fra Angelico MOCKING OF CHRIST WITH THE VIRGIN MARY AND ST. DOMINIC
Monastery of San Marco, Florence. c. 1441–1445.

Intro-10 • DETAIL OF FIG. Intro-6 SHOWING PART OF THE LEFT WING

individual dormitory rooms of Carthusian monks. The reference in this painting to the *co-passio* of the Virgin provides supporting evidence since this theological idea was central to Carthusian thought and devotion. The *co-passio* was even reflected in the monks' own initiation rites, during which they re-enacted and sought identification with both Christ's sacrifice on the cross and the Virgin's parallel suffering.

In Jolly's interpretation, the religious framework of a Carthusian setting for the painting emerges as a personal framework for the artist himself, since this *Crucifixion* seems to be associated with important moments in his own life—his religious pilgrimage to Rome in 1450 and the initiation of his oldest son as a Carthusian monk at about the same time. Is it possible that the sense of loss and separation that Rogier evoked in his portrayal of a poignant moment in the life of St. John (**FIG. Intro-10**) could have been especially meaningful to the artist himself at the time this work was painted?

A CONTINUING PROJECT The final word has not been spoken in the interpretation of this painting. Mark Tucker's recent work on the physical evidence revealed by x-ray analysis points toward seeing these two panels as part of a large sculptured altarpiece. Even if this did preclude the prospect that it is the **panel painting** Rogier donated to the chapel of St. Catherine at Hérrines, it does not negate the relationship Jolly drew with Fra Angelico, nor the Carthusian context she outlined for the work's original situation. It simply reminds us that our historical understanding of works such as this will evolve when new evidence about them emerges.

As the history of art unfolds in the ensuing chapters of this book, it will be important to keep two things in mind as you read the characterizations of individual works of art and the larger story of their integration into the broader cultural contexts of those who made them and those for whom they were initially made. Art-historical interpretations are built on extended research comparable to that we have just summarily surveyed for Rogier van der Weyden's Philadelphia *Crucifixion*. But the work of interpretation is never complete. Art history is a continuing project, a work perpetually in progress.

the Carthusians, and especially with the Belgian Charterhouse (or Carthusian monastery) of Hérrines, where his oldest son was invested as a monk in 1450. Rogier gave money to Hérrines, and texts document his donation of a painting to its chapel of St. Catherine. Jolly suggested that the Philadelphia *Crucifixion* could be that painting. Its subdued colors and narrative austerity are consistent with Carthusian aesthetic attitudes, and the walled setting of the scene recalls the enclosed gardens that were attached to the

THINK ABOUT IT

I.1 Analyze the composition of one painting illustrated in this Introduction.

I.2 Characterize the difference between natural subject matter and iconography, focusing your discussion on a specific work of art.

I.3 What are the four separate steps proposed here for characterizing the methods used by art historians to interpret works of art? Characterize the cultural analysis in step four by showing the way it expands our understanding of one of the still lifes in the Closer Look.

I.4 What aspect of the case study of Rogier van der Weyden's Philadelphia *Crucifixion* was especially interesting to you? Why? How did it broaden your understanding of what you will learn in this course?

✔—**Study** and review on myartslab.com

18–1 • Ambrogio Lorenzetti **FRESCOS OF THE SALA DEI NOVE (OR SALA DELLA PACE)**
Palazzo Pubblico, Siena, Italy. 1338–1339. Length of long wall about 46′ (14 m).

Read the document related to the frescos in the Palazzo Pubblico on myartslab.com

Fourteenth-Century Art in Europe

In 1338, the Nine—a council of merchants and bankers that governed Siena as an oligarchy—commissioned frescos from renowned Sienese painter Ambrogio Lorenzetti (c. 1295–c. 1348) for three walls in the chamber within the Palazzo Pubblico where they met to conduct city business. This commission came at the moment of greatest prosperity and security since the establishment of their government in 1287.

Lorenzetti's frescos combine allegory with panoramic landscapes and cityscapes to visualize and justify the beneficial effects of the Sienese form of government. The moral foundation of the rule of the Nine is outlined in a complicated allegory in which seated personifications (far left in FIG. 18–1) of Concord, Justice, Peace, Strength, Prudence, Temperance, and Magnanimity, not only diagram good governance but actually reference the Last Judgment in a bold assertion of the relationship between secular rule and divine authority. This tableau contrasts with a similar presentation of bad government, where Tyranny is flanked by the personified forces that keep tyrants in power—Cruelty, Treason, Fraud, Fury, Division, and War. A group of scholars would have devised this complex program of symbols and meanings; it is unlikely that Lorenzetti would have known the philosophical works that underlie them. Lorenzetti's fame, however, and the wall paintings' secure position among the most remarkable surviving mural programs of the period, rests on the other part of this ensemble—the effects of good and bad government in city and country life (see FIG. 18–15).

Unlike the tableau showing the perils of life under tyrannical rule, the panoramic view of life under good government—which in this work of propaganda means life under the rule of the Nine—is well preserved. A vista of fourteenth-century Siena—identifiable by the cathedral dome and tower peeking over the rooftops in the background—showcases carefree life within shops, schools, taverns, and worksites, as the city streets bustle with human activity. Outside, an expansive landscape highlights agricultural productivity.

Unfortunately, within a decade of the frescos' completion, life in Siena was no longer as stable and carefree. The devastating bubonic plague visited in 1348—Ambrogio Lorenzetti himself was probably one of the victims—and the rule of the Nine collapsed in 1355. But this glorious vision of joyful prosperity preserves the dreams and aspirations of a stable government, using some of the most progressive and creative ideas in fourteenth-century Italian art, ideas we will see developed at the very beginning of the century, and whose history we will trace over the next two centuries through the Renaissance.

LEARN ABOUT IT

18.1 Compare and contrast the Florentine and Sienese styles of narrative painting as exemplified by Giotto and Duccio.

18.2 Investigate the Bible stories that were the subject of fourteenth-century sacred art, as well as the personal and political themes highlighted in secular art.

18.3 Assess the close connections between works of art and their patrons in fourteenth-century Europe.

18.4 Explore the production of small-scale works, often made of precious materials and highlighting extraordinary technical virtuosity, that continues from the earlier Gothic period.

((•—Listen to the chapter audio on myartslab.com

MAP 18–1 • EUROPE IN THE FOURTEENTH CENTURY

Following its outbreak in the Mediterranean in 1347, the Black Death swept across the European mainland over the next four years.

FOURTEENTH-CENTURY EUROPE

Literary luminaries Dante, Petrarch, Boccaccio, Chaucer, and Christine de Pizan (see "A New Spirit in Fourteenth-Century Literature," opposite) and the visionary painters Giotto, Duccio, Jean Pucelle, and Master Theodoric participated in a cultural explosion that swept through fourteenth-century Europe, and especially Italy. The poet Petrarch (1304–1374) was a towering figure in this change, writing his love lyrics in Italian, the language of everyday life, rather than Latin, the language of ceremony and high art. Similarly, the deeply moving murals of Florentine painter Giotto di Bondone (c. 1277–1337) were rooted in his observation of the people around him, giving the participants in sacred narratives both great dignity and striking humanity, thus making them familiar, yet new, to the audiences that originally experienced them. Even in Paris—still the artistic center of Europe as far as refined taste and technical sophistication were concerned—the painter Jean Pucelle began to show an interest in experimenting with established conventions.

For Petrarch and his contemporaries, the essential qualifications for a writer were an appreciation of Greek and Roman authors and an ability to observe the people living around them. Although fluent in Latin, they chose to write in the language of their own time and place—Italian, English, French. Leading the way was Dante Alighieri (1265–1321), who wrote *The Divine Comedy*, his great summation of human virtue and vice, and ultimately human destiny, in Italian, establishing his daily vernacular as worthy to express great literary themes.

Francesco Petrarca, called simply Petrarch (1304–1374), raised the status of secular literature with his sonnets to his unattainable beloved, Laura, his histories and biographies, and his writings on the joys of country life in the Roman manner. Petrarch's imaginative updating of Classical themes in a work called *The Triumphs*—which examines the themes of Chastity triumphant over Love, Death over Chastity, Fame over Death, Time over Fame, and Eternity over Time—provided later Renaissance poets and painters with a wealth of allegorical subject matter.

More earthy, Giovanni Boccaccio (1313–1375) perfected the art of the short story in *The Decameron*, a collection of amusing and moralizing tales told by a group of young Florentines who moved to the countryside to escape the Black Death. With wit and sympathy, Boccaccio presents the full spectrum of daily life in Italy. Such secular literature, written in Italian as it was then spoken in Tuscany, provided a foundation for fifteenth-century Renaissance writers.

In England, Geoffrey Chaucer (c. 1342–1400) was inspired by Boccaccio to write his own series of stories, *The Canterbury Tales*, told by pilgrims traveling to the shrine of St. Thomas à Becket (1118?–1170) in Canterbury. Observant and witty, Chaucer depicted the pretensions and foibles, as well as the virtues, of humanity.

Christine de Pizan (1364–c. 1431), born in Venice but living and writing at the French court, became an author out of necessity when she was left a widow with three young children and an aged mother to support. Among her many works are a poem in praise of Joan of Arc and a history of famous women—including artists—from antiquity to her own time. In *The Book of the City of Ladies*, she defended women's abilities and argued for women's rights and status.

These writers, as surely as Giotto, Duccio, Peter Parler, and Master Theodoric, led the way into a new era.

Changes in the way that society was organized were also under way, and an expanding class of wealthy merchants supported the arts as patrons. Artisan guilds—organized by occupation—exerted quality control among members and supervised education through an apprenticeship system. Admission to the guild came after examination and the creation of a "masterpiece"—literally, a piece fine enough to achieve master status. The major guilds included cloth finishers, wool merchants, and silk manufacturers, as well as pharmacists and doctors. Painters belonged to the pharmacy guild, perhaps because they used mortars and pestles to grind their colors. Their patron saint, Luke, who was believed to have painted the first image of the Virgin Mary, was also a physician—or so they thought. Sculptors who worked in wood and stone had their own guild, while those who worked in metals belonged to another. Guilds provided social services for their members, including care of the sick and funerals for the deceased. Each guild had its patron saint, maintained a chapel, and participated in religious and civic festivals.

Despite the cultural flourishing and economic growth of the early decades, by the middle of the fourteenth century much of Europe was in crisis. Prosperity had fostered population growth, which began to exceed food production. A series of bad harvests compounded this problem with famine. To make matters worse, a prolonged conflict known as the Hundred Years' War (1337–1453) erupted between France and England. Then, in mid century, a lethal plague known as the Black Death swept across Europe (**MAP 18-1**), wiping out as much as 40 percent of the population. In spite of these catastrophic events, however, the strong current of cultural change still managed to persist through to the end of the century and beyond.

ITALY

As great wealth promoted patronage of art in fourteenth-century Italy, artists began to emerge as individuals, in the modern sense, both in their own eyes and in the eyes of patrons. Although their methods and working conditions remained largely unchanged from the Middle Ages, artists in Italy contracted freely with wealthy townspeople and nobles as well as with civic and religious bodies. Perhaps it was their economic and social freedom that encouraged ambition and self-confidence, individuality and innovation.

FLORENTINE ARCHITECTURE AND METALWORK

The typical medieval Italian city was a walled citadel on a hilltop. Houses clustered around the church and an open city square. Powerful families added towers to their houses, both for defense and as expressions of family pride. In Florence, by contrast, the ancient Roman city—with its axial rectangular plan and open city squares—formed the basis for civic layout. The cathedral stood northeast of the ancient forum and a street following the Roman plan connected it with the Piazza della Signoria, the seat of the government.

THE PALAZZO DELLA SIGNORIA The Signoria (ruling body, from *signore*, meaning "Lord") that governed Florence met

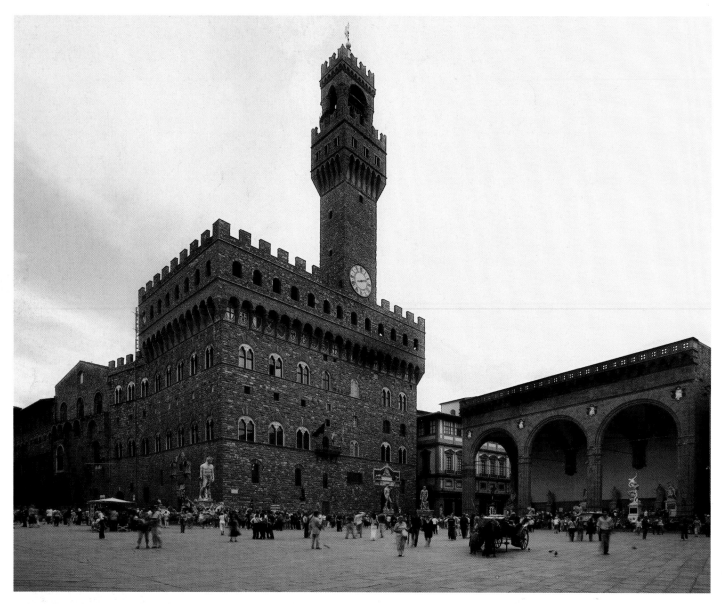

18-2 • PIAZZA DELLA SIGNORIA WITH PALAZZO DELLA SIGNORIA (TOWN HALL) 1299–1310, AND LOGGIA DEI LANZI (LOGGIA OF THE LANCERS), 1376–1382
Florence.

in the **PALAZZO DELLA SIGNORIA**, a massive fortified building with a bell tower 300 feet tall (**FIG. 18-2**). The building faces a large square, or piazza, which became the true center of Florence. The town houses around the piazza often had benches along their walls to provide convenient public seating. Between 1376 and 1382, master builders Benci di Cione and Simone Talenti constructed a huge **loggia** or covered open-air corridor at one side—now known as the Loggia dei Lanzi (Loggia of the Lancers)—to provide a sheltered locale for ceremonies and speeches.

THE BAPTISTERY DOORS In 1330, Andrea Pisano (c. 1290–1348) was awarded the prestigious commission for a pair of gilded bronze doors for Florence's Baptistery of San Giovanni, situated directly in front of the cathedral. (Andrea's "last" name means "from Pisa," and he was not related to Nicola and Giovanni

Pisano.) The doors were completed within six years and display 20 scenes from the **LIFE OF ST. JOHN THE BAPTIST** (the San Giovanni to whom the baptistery is dedicated) set above eight personifications of the Virtues (**FIG. 18-3**). The overall effect is two-dimensional and decorative: a grid of 28 rectangles with repeated quatrefoils filled by the graceful, patterned poses of delicate human figures. Within the quatrefoil frames, however, the figural compositions create the illusion of three-dimensional forms moving within the described spaces of natural and architectural worlds.

The scene of John baptizing a multitude (**FIG. 18-4**) takes place on a shelflike stage created by a forward extension of the rocky natural setting, which also expands back behind the figures into a corner of the quatrefoil frame. Composed as a rectangular group, the gilded figures present an independent mass of modeled forms. The illusion of three-dimensionality is enhanced by the

18–3 • Andrea Pisano LIFE OF ST. JOHN THE BAPTIST
South doors, baptistery of San Giovanni, Florence. 1330–1336. Gilded bronze, each panel 19¼″ × 17″
(48 × 43 cm). Frame, Ghiberti workshop, mid 15th century.

The bronze vine scrolls filled with flowers, fruits, and birds on the lintel and jambs framing the door
were added in the mid fifteenth century.

way the curving folds of their clothing wrap around their bodies. At the same time, their graceful gestures and the elegant fall of their drapery reflect the soft curves and courtly postures of French Gothic art.

FLORENTINE PAINTING

Florence and Siena, rivals in so many ways, each supported a flourishing school of painting in the fourteenth century. Both grew out of local thirteenth-century painting traditions and engendered individual artists who became famous in their own time. The Byzantine influence—the *maniera greca* ("Greek style")—continued to provide models of dramatic pathos and narrative iconography, as well as stylized features including the use of gold for drapery folds and striking contrasts of highlights and shadows in the modeling of individual forms. By the end of the fourteenth century, the painter and commentator Cennino Cennini (see "Cennino

Cennini on Panel Painting," page 546) would be struck by the accessibility and modernity of Giotto's art, which, though it retained traces of the *maniera greca*, was moving toward the depiction of a lifelike, contemporary world anchored in solid, three-dimensional forms.

CIMABUE In Florence, this stylistic transformation began a little earlier than in Siena. About 1280, a painter named Cenni di Pepi (active c. 1272–1302), better known by his nickname "Cimabue," painted a panel portraying the **VIRGIN AND CHILD ENTHRONED** (FIG. 18-5), perhaps for the main altar of the church of Santa Trinità in Florence. At over 12 feet tall, this enormous painting set a new precedent for monumental altarpieces. Cimabue surrounds the Virgin and Child with angels and places a row of Hebrew Bible prophets beneath them. The hierarchically scaled figure of Mary holds the infant Jesus in her lap. Looking out at the viewer while gesturing toward her son as the path to salvation, she adopts a formula popular in Byzantine iconography since at least the sixth century (see FIG. 8–14).

Mary's huge throne, painted to resemble gilded bronze with inset enamels and gems, provides an architectural framework for the figures. Cimabue creates highlights on the drapery of Mary, Jesus, and the angels with thin lines of gold, as if to capture their divine radiance. The viewer seems suspended in space in front of the image, simultaneously looking down on the projecting elements of the throne and Mary's lap, while looking straight ahead at the prophets at the base of the throne and the angels at each side. These spatial ambiguities, the subtle asymmetries within the centralized composition, the Virgin's engaging gaze, and the individually conceived faces of the old men give the picture a sense of life and the figures a sense of presence. Cimabue's ambitious attention to spatial volumes, his use of delicate modeling in light and shade to simulate three-dimensional form, and his efforts to give naturalistic warmth to human figures had an impact on the future development of Florentine painting.

18–5 • Cimabue VIRGIN AND CHILD ENTHRONED
Most likely painted for the high altar of the church of Santa Trinità, Florence. c. 1280. Tempera and gold on wood panel, 12'7" × 7'4" (3.53 × 2.2 m). Galleria degli Uffizi, Florence.

👁 **Watch** a video about the egg tempera process on myartslab.com

GIOTTO DI BONDONE According to the sixteenth-century chronicler Giorgio Vasari, Cimabue discovered a talented shepherd boy, Giotto di Bondone (active c. 1300–1337), and taught him to paint; "not only did the young boy equal the style of his master, but he became such an excellent imitator of nature that he completely banished that crude Greek [i.e., Byzantine] style and revived the modern and excellent art of painting, introducing good drawing from live natural models, something which had not been done for more than two hundred years" (Vasari, translated by Bondanella and Bondanella, p. 16). After his training, Giotto

may have collaborated on murals at the prestigious church of St. Francis in Assisi. We know he worked for the Franciscans in Florence and absorbed facets of their teaching. St. Francis's message of simple, humble devotion, direct experience of God, and love for all creatures was gaining followers throughout western Europe, and it had a powerful impact on thirteenth- and fourteenth-century Italian literature and art.

Compared to Cimabue's *Virgin and Child Enthroned*, Giotto's altarpiece of the same subject (**FIG. 18-6**), painted about 30 years later for the church of the Ognissanti (All Saints) in Florence,

18-6 • Giotto di Bondone VIRGIN AND CHILD ENTHRONED
Most likely painted for the high altar of the church of the Ognissanti (All Saints), Florence. 1305–1310. Tempera and gold on wood panel, 10′8″ × 6′8¼″ (3.53 × 2.05 m). Galleria degli Uffizi, Florence.

The two techniques used in mural painting are *buon* ("true") *fresco* ("fresh"), in which water-based paint is applied on wet plaster, and *fresco secco* ("dry"), in which paint is applied to a dry plastered wall. The two methods can be used on the same wall painting.

The advantage of *buon fresco* is its durability. A chemical reaction occurs as the painted plaster dries, which bonds the pigments into the wall surface. In *fresco secco*, by contrast, the color does not become part of the wall and tends to flake off over time. The chief disadvantage of *buon fresco* is that it must be done quickly without mistakes. The painter plasters and paints only as much as can be completed in a day, which explains the Italian term for each of these sections: **giornata**, or a day's work. The size of a *giornata* varies according to the complexity of the painting within it. A face, for instance, might take an entire day, whereas large areas of sky can be painted quite rapidly. In Giotto's Scrovegni Chapel, scholars have identified 852 separate *giornate*, some worked on concurrently within a single day by assistants in Giotto's workshop.

In medieval and Renaissance Italy, a wall to be frescoed was first prepared with a rough, thick undercoat of plaster known as the *arriccio*. When this was dry, assistants copied the master painter's composition onto it with reddish-brown pigment or charcoal. The artist made any necessary adjustments. These underdrawings, known as **sinopia**, have an immediacy and freshness that are lost in the finished painting. Work proceeded in irregularly shaped *giornate* conforming to the contours of major figures and objects. Assistants covered one section at a time with a fresh, thin coat of very fine plaster—the *intonaco*—over

the *sinopia*, and when this was "set" but not dry, the artist worked with pigments mixed with water, painting from the top down so that drips fell on unfinished portions. Some areas requiring pigments such as ultramarine blue (which was unstable in *buon fresco*), as well as areas requiring gilding, would be added after the wall was dry using the *fresco secco* technique.

arriccio

sinopia drawing

water-based paint on damp intonaco

wall

intonaco layer

buon fresco

---

exhibits greater spatial consistency and sculptural solidity while retaining some of Cimabue's conventions. The position of the figures within a symmetrical composition reflects Cimabue's influence. Gone, however, are Mary's modestly inclined head and the delicate gold folds in her drapery. Instead, light and shadow play gently across her stocky form, and her action—holding her child's leg instead of pointing him out to us—seems less contrived. This colossal Mary overwhelms her slender Gothic tabernacle of a throne, where figures peer through openings and haloes overlap faces. In spite of the hierarchic scale and the formal, enthroned image and flat, gold background, Giotto has created the sense that these are fully three-dimensional beings, whose plainly draped, bulky bodies inhabit real space. The Virgin's solid torso is revealed by her thin tunic, and Giotto's angels are substantial solids whose foreshortened postures project from the foreground toward us, unlike those of Cimabue, which stay on the surface along lateral strips composed of overlapping screens of color.

Although he was trained in the Florentine tradition, many of Giotto's principal works were produced elsewhere. After a sojourn in Rome during the last years of the thirteenth century, he was called to Padua in northern Italy soon after 1300 to paint frescos (see "*Buon Fresco*," above) for a new chapel being constructed at the site of an ancient Roman arena—explaining why it is usually

referred to as the Arena Chapel. The chapel was commissioned by Enrico Scrovegni, whose family fortune was made through the practice of usury—which at this time meant charging interest when loaning money, a sin so grave that it resulted in exclusion from the Christian sacraments. Enrico's father, Regibaldo, was a particularly egregious case (he appears in Dante's *Inferno* as the prototypical usurer), but evidence suggests that Enrico followed in his father's footsteps, and the building of the Arena Chapel next to his new palatial residence seems to have been conceived at least in part as a penitential act, part of Enrico's campaign not only to atone for his father's sins, but also to seek absolution for his own. He was pardoned by Pope Benedict XI (pontificate 1303–1304).

That Scrovegni called two of the most famous artists of the time—Giotto and Giovanni Pisano (see FIG. 17-36)—to decorate his chapel indicates that his goals were to express his power, sophistication, and prestige, as well as to atone for his sins. The building itself has little architectural distinction. It is a simple, barrel-vaulted room that provides broad walls, a boxlike space to showcase Giotto's paintings (FIG. 18-7). Giotto covered the entrance wall with the *Last Judgment* (not visible here), and the sanctuary wall with three highlighted scenes from the life of Christ. The Annunciation spreads over the two painted architectural frameworks on either side of the high arched opening into the sanctuary itself.

18-7 • Giotto di Bondone **SCROVEGNI (ARENA) CHAPEL, VIEW TOWARD EAST WALL**
Padua. 1305–1306. Frescos.

View the Closer Look for the Scrovegni Chapel on myartslab.com

Below this are, to the left, the scene of Judas receiving payment for betraying Jesus, and, to the right, the scene of the Visitation, where the Virgin, pregnant with God incarnate, embraces her cousin Elizabeth, pregnant with John the Baptist. The compositions and color arrangement of these two scenes create a symmetrical pairing that encourages viewers to relate them, comparing the ill-gotten financial gains of Judas (a rather clear reference to Scrovegni usury) to the miraculous pregnancy that brought the promise of salvation.

Giotto subdivided the side walls of the chapel into framed pictures. A dado of faux-marble and allegorical **grisaille** (monochrome paintings in shades of gray) paintings of the Virtues and Vices support vertical bands painted to resemble marble inlay into which are inserted painted imitations of carved medallions. The central band of medallions spans the vault, crossing a brilliant, lapis-blue, star-spangled sky in which large portrait disks float like glowing moons. Set into this framework are three horizontal bands of rectangular narrative scenes from the life of the Virgin and her parents at the top, and Jesus along the middle and lower registers,

constituting together the primary religious program of the chapel.

Both the individual scenes and the overall program display Giotto's genius for distilling complex stories into a series of compelling moments. He concentrates on the human dimensions of the unfolding drama—from touches of anecdotal humor to expressions of profound anguish—rather than on its symbolic or theological weight. His prodigious narrative skills are apparent in a set of scenes from Christ's life on the north wall (**FIG. 18-8**). At top left Jesus performs his first miracle, changing water into wine at the wedding feast at Cana. The wine steward—looking very much like the jars of new wine himself—sips the results. To the right is the Raising of Lazarus, where boldly modeled and individualized figures twist in space. Through their postures and gestures they react to the human drama by pleading for Jesus' help, or by expressing either astonishment at the miracle or revulsion at the smell of death. Jesus is separated from the crowd. His transforming gesture is highlighted against the dark blue of the background, his profile face locked in communication with the similarly isolated

18-8 • Giotto di Bondone **MARRIAGE AT CANA, RAISING OF LAZARUS, LAMENTATION, AND RESURRECTION/NOLI ME TANGERE**

North wall of Scrovegni (Arena) Chapel, Padua. 1305–1306. Fresco, each scene approx. 6′5″ × 6′ (2 × 1.85 m).

Lazarus, whose eyes—still fixed in death—let us know that the miracle is just about to happen.

On the lower register, where Jesus' grief-stricken followers lament over his dead body, Giotto conveys palpable human suffering, drawing viewers into a circle of personal grief. The stricken Virgin pulls close to her dead son, communing with mute intensity, while John the Evangelist flings his arms back in convulsive despair and others hunch over the corpse. Giotto has linked this somber scene—much as he linked the scene of Judas' pact and the Visitation across the sanctuary arch—to the mourning of Lazarus on the register above through the seemingly continuous diagonal implied by the sharply angled hillside behind both scenes and by the rhyming repetition of mourners in each scene—facing in opposite directions—who throw back their arms to express their emotional state. Viewers would know that the mourning in both

scenes is resolved by resurrection, portrayed in the last picture in this set.

Following traditional medieval practice, the fresco program is full of scenes and symbols like these that are intended to be contemplated as coordinated or contrasting juxtapositions. What is new here is the way Giotto draws us into the experience of these events. This direct emotional appeal not only allows viewers to imagine these scenes in relation to their own life experiences; it also embodies the new Franciscan emphasis on personal devotion rooted in empathetic responses to sacred stories.

One of the most gripping paintings in the chapel is Giotto's portrayal of the **KISS OF JUDAS**, the moment of betrayal that represents the first step on Jesus' road to the Crucifixion (**FIG. 18–9**). Savior and traitor are slightly off-center in the near foreground. The expansive sweep of Judas' strident yellow cloak—the same outfit he

18-9 • Giotto di Bondone **KISS OF JUDAS**
South wall of Scrovegni (Arena) Chapel, Padua. 1305–1306. Fresco, 6'6¾" × 6'7⅞" (2 × 1.85 m).

wore at the scene of his payment for the betrayal on the strip of wall to the left of the sanctuary arch—almost completely swallows Christ's body. Surrounding them, faces glare from all directions. A bristling array of weapons radiating from the confrontation draws attention to the encounter between Christ and Judas and documents the militarism of the arresting battalion. Jesus stands solid, a model of calm resolve that recalls his visual characterization in the Resurrection of Lazarus, and forms a striking foil to the noisy and chaotic aggression that engulfs him. Judas, in simian profile, purses his lips for the treacherous kiss that will betray Jesus to his captors, setting up a mythic confrontation of good and evil. In a subplot to the left, Peter lunges forward to sever the ear of a member of the arresting retinue. They are behind another broad sweep of fabric, this one extended by an ominous figure seen from behind and completely concealed except for the clenched hand that pulls at Peter's mantle. Indeed, a broad expanse of cloth and lateral gestures creates a barrier along the picture plane—as if to protect viewers from the compressed chaos of the scene itself. Rarely has this poignant event been visualized with such riveting power.

SIENESE PAINTING

Like their Florentine rivals, Sienese painters were rooted in thirteenth-century pictorial traditions, especially those of Byzantine art. Sienese painting emphasized the decorative potential of narrative painting, with brilliant, jewel-like colors and elegantly posed figures. For this reason, some art historians consider Sienese art more conservative than Florentine art, but we will see that it has its own charm, and its own narrative strategies.

DUCCIO DI BUONINSEGNA Siena's foremost painter was Duccio di Buoninsegna (active 1278–1318), whose creative synthesis of Byzantine and French Gothic sources transformed the tradition in which he worked. Between 1308 and 1311, Duccio and his workshop painted a huge altarpiece commissioned for Siena Cathedral and known as the **MAESTÀ** ("Majesty") (**FIG. 18-10**). Creating this altarpiece—assembled from many wood panels bonded together before painting—was an arduous undertaking. The work was not only large—the central panel alone was 7 by 13 feet—but it had to be painted on both sides since it could

18–10 • Duccio di Buoninsegna
CONJECTURAL RECONSTRUCTION
OF THE FRONT (A) AND BACK (B)
OF THE MAESTÀ ALTARPIECE
Made for Siena Cathedral. 1308–1311.
Tempera and gold on wood, main front
panel 7′ × 13′ (2.13 × 4.12 m).

Read the document related to
Duccio's *Maestà* on myartslab.com

18-11 • Duccio di Buoninsegna
RAISING OF LAZARUS
From the predella of the back of the *Maestà* altarpiece (lower right corner of FIG. 18–10B), made for Siena Cathedral. 1308–1311. Tempera and gold on wood, 17⅛″ × 18¼″ (43.5 × 46.4 cm). Kimbell Art Museum, Fort Worth, Texas.

be seen from all directions when installed on the main altar at the center of the sanctuary.

Because the *Maestà* was dismantled in 1771, its power and beauty can only be imagined from scattered parts, some still in Siena but others elsewhere. FIGURE 18-10A is a reconstruction of how the front of the original altarpiece might have looked. It is dominated by a large representation of the Virgin and Child in Majesty (thus its title of *Maestà*), flanked by 20 angels and ten saints, including the four patron saints of Siena kneeling in the foreground. Above and below this lateral tableau were small narrative scenes from the last days of the life of the Virgin (above) and the infancy of Christ (spread across the predella). An inscription running around the base of Mary's majestic throne places the artist's signature within an optimistic framework: "Holy Mother of God, be thou the cause of peace for Siena and life to Duccio because he painted thee thus." This was not Duccio's first work for the cathedral. In 1288, he had designed a stunning stained-glass window portraying the Death, Assumption, and Coronation of the Virgin for the huge circular opening in the east wall of the sanctuary. It would have hovered over the installed *Maestà* when it was placed on the altar in 1311.

On the back of the *Maestà* (FIG. 18-10B) were episodes from the life of Christ, focusing on his Passion. Sacred narrative unfolds in elegant episodes enacted by graceful figures who seem to dance their way through these stories while still conveying emotional content. Characteristic of Duccio's narrative style is the scene of the **RAISING OF LAZARUS** (FIG. 18-11). Lyrical figures enact the event with graceful decorum, but their highly charged glances and expressive gestures—especially the bold reach of Christ—convey a strong sense of dramatic urgency that contrasts with the tense stillness that we saw in Giotto's rendering of this same moment of confrontation (see FIG. 18-8). Duccio's shading of drapery, like his modeling of faces, faithfully describes the figures' three-dimensionality, but the crisp outlines of the jewel-colored shapes created by their clothing, as well as the sinuous continuity of folds and gestures, generate rhythmic patterns crisscrossing the surface. Experimentation with the portrayal of space extends from the receding rocks of the mountainous landscape to carefully studied interiors, here the tomb of Lazarus whose heavy door was removed by the straining hug of a bystander to reveal the shrouded figure of Jesus' resurrected friend, propped up against the door jamb.

Duccio's rendering of the **BETRAYAL OF JESUS** (FIG. 18-12) is more expansive, both pictorially and temporally, occupying one of the broadest panels in the altarpiece (see FIG. 18-10B, lower center) and encompassing within this one composition several moments in the sequential narrative of its subject matter. The tableau is centered and stabilized by the frontal figure of Jesus, whose dark mantle with its sinuous gold trim stands out from the densely packed, colorful crowd of figures surrounding him. Judas approaches from the left to identify Jesus; although the heads of betrayer and betrayed touch in this moment, Duccio avoids the psychological power of Giotto's face-to-face confrontation in the Scrovegni chapel (see FIG. 18-9). Flanking Duccio's stable, packed central scene of betrayal, are two subsequent moments in the story, each pulling our attention away from the center and toward the sides. To the left, with a forceful stride and dynamic gesture, the apostle Peter lunges to sever the ear of a member of the arresting party, while on the other side of the composition a group of fearful apostles rushes gracefully but with united resolve to escape the central scene, abandoning Jesus to his fate. Within the complexity of this broad, multi-figure, continuous narrative, Duccio manages to express—through the postures and facial expressions of his figures—the emotional charge of these pivotal moments in the narrative of Christ's Passion. At the same time, he creates a dazzling picture, as rich in color and linear elegance as it is faithful to the human dimensions of the situations it portrays.

The enthusiasm with which citizens greeted a great painting or altarpiece like the *Maestà* demonstrates the power of images as well as the association of such magnificent works with the glory of the city itself. According to a contemporary account, on December 20, 1311, the day that Duccio's altarpiece was carried from his workshop to the cathedral, all the shops were shut, and everyone in the city participated in the procession, with "bells ringing joyously, out of reverence for so noble a picture as is this" (Holt, p. 69).

SIMONE MARTINI The generation of painters who followed Duccio continued to paint in the elegant style he established, combining the evocation of three-dimensional form with a graceful continuity of linear pattern. One of Duccio's most successful and innovative followers was Simone Martini (c. 1284–1344), whose paintings were in high demand throughout Italy, including in Assisi where he covered the walls of the St. Martin Chapel with frescos between 1312 and 1319. His most famous work, however, was commissioned in 1333 for the cathedral of his native Siena, an altarpiece of the **ANNUNCIATION** flanked by two saints (**FIG. 18-13**) that he painted in collaboration with his brother-in-law, Lippo Memmi.

18-12 • Duccio di Buoninsegna BETRAYAL OF JESUS
From the back of the *Maestà* altarpiece (lower center of FIG. 18-10B), made for Siena Cathedral. 1308–1311.
Tempera and gold on wood, 22½″ × 40″ (57.2 × 101.6 cm). Museo dell'Opera del Duomo, Siena.

Il Libro dell' Arte (*The Book of Art*) of Cennino Cennini (c. 1370–1440) is a compendium of Florentine painting techniques from about 1400 that includes step-by-step instructions for making panel paintings, a process also used in Sienese paintings of the same period.

The wood for the panels, he explains, should be fine-grained, free of blemishes, and thoroughly seasoned by slow drying. The first step in preparing such a panel for painting was to cover its surface with clean white linen strips soaked in a **gesso** made from gypsum, a task, he tells us, best done on a dry, windy day. Gesso provided a ground, or surface, on which to paint, and Cennini specified that at least nine layers should be applied. The gessoed surface should then be burnished until it resembles ivory. Only then could the artist sketch the composition of the work with charcoal made from burned willow twigs. At this point, advised Cennini, "When you have finished drawing your figure, especially if it is in a very valuable [altarpiece], so that you are counting on profit and reputation from it, leave it alone for a few days, going back to it now and then to look it over and improve it wherever it still needs something. When it seems to you about right (and bear in mind that you may copy and examine things done by other good masters; that it is no shame to

you) when the figure is satisfactory, take the feather and rub it over the drawing very lightly, until the drawing is practically effaced" (Cennini, trans. Thompson, p. 75). At this point, the final design would be inked in with a fine squirrel-hair brush. Gold leaf, he advises, should be affixed on a humid day, the tissue-thin sheets carefully glued down with a mixture of fine powdered clay and egg white on the reddish clay ground called bole. Then the gold is burnished with a gemstone or the tooth of a carnivorous animal. Punched and incised patterning should be added to the gold leaf later.

Fourteenth- and fifteenth-century Italian painters worked principally in tempera paint, powdered pigments mixed with egg yolk, a little water, and an occasional touch of glue. Apprentices were kept busy grinding pigments and mixing paints, setting them out for more senior painters in wooden bowls or shell dishes.

Cennini outlined a detailed and highly formulaic painting process. Faces, for example, were always to be done last, with flesh tones applied over two coats of a light greenish pigment and highlighted with touches of red and white. The finished painting was to be given a layer of varnish to protect it and intensify its colors.

📖 **Read** the document related to Cennino Cennini on myartslab.com

18–13 • Simone Martini and Lippo Memmi ANNUNCIATION Made for Siena Cathedral. 1333. Tempera and gold on wood, 10′ × 8′9″ (3 × 2.67 m). Galleria degli Uffizi, Florence.

18–14 • AERIAL VIEW OF THE CAMPO IN SIENA WITH THE PALAZZO PUBBLICO (CITY HALL INCLUDING ITS TOWER) FACING ITS STRAIGHT SIDE
Siena. Palazzo Pubblico 1297–c. 1315; tower 1320s–1340s.

The smartly dressed figure of Gabriel—the extended flourish of his drapery behind him suggesting he has just arrived, and with some speed—raises his hand to address the Virgin. The words of his message are actually incised into the gold-leafed gesso of the background, running from his opened mouth toward the Virgin's ear: *Ave gratia plena dominus tecum* (Luke 1:28: "Hail, full of grace, the Lord is with thee"). Seemingly frightened—at the very least startled—by this forceful and unexpected celestial messenger, Mary recoils into her lavish throne, her thumb inserted into the book she had been reading to safeguard her place, while her other hand pulls at her clothing in an elegant gesture of nobility ultimately deriving from the courtly art of thirteenth-century Paris (see Solomon, second lancet from the right in FIGURE 17–11).

AMBROGIO LORENZETTI The most important civic structure in Siena was the **PALAZZO PUBBLICO** (**FIG. 18–14**), the town hall which served as the seat of government, just as the Palazzo della Signoria did in rival Florence (see FIG. 18–2). There are similarities between these two buildings. Both are designed as strong, fortified structures sitting on the edge of a public piazza; both have a tall tower, making them visible signs of the city from a considerable distance. The Palazzo Pubblico was constructed from 1297 to c. 1315, but the tower was not completed until 1348, when the bronze bell, which rang to signal meetings of the ruling council, was installed.

The interior of the Palazzo Pubblico was the site of important commissions by some of Siena's most famous artists. In c. 1315, Simone Martini painted a large mural of the Virgin in Majesty surrounded by saints—clearly based on Duccio's recently installed *Maestà*. Then, in 1338, the Siena city council commissioned Ambrogio Lorenzetti to paint frescos for the council room of the Palazzo known as the Sala dei Nove (Chamber of the Nine) or Sala della Pace (Chamber of Peace) on the theme of the contrast between good and bad government (see FIG. 18–1).

Ambrogio painted the results of both good and bad government on the two long walls. For the expansive scene of **THE EFFECTS OF GOOD GOVERNMENT IN THE CITY AND IN THE COUNTRY**, and in tribute to his patrons, Ambrogio created an idealized but recognizable portrait of the city of Siena and its immediate environs (**FIG. 18-15**). The cathedral dome and the distinctive striped campanile are visible in the upper left-hand corner; the streets are filled with the bustling activity of productive citizens who also have time for leisurely diversions. Ambrogio shows the city from shifting viewpoints so we can see as much as possible, and renders its inhabitants larger in scale than the buildings around them so as to highlight their activity. Featured in the foreground is a circle of dancers—probably a professional troupe of male entertainers masquerading as women as part of a spring festival—and above them, at the top of the painting, a band of masons stand on exterior scaffolding constructing the wall of a new building.

The Porta Romana, Siena's gateway leading to Rome, divides the thriving city from its surrounding countryside. In this panoramic landscape painting, Ambrogio describes a natural world marked by agricultural productivity, showing activities of all seasons simultaneously—sowing, hoeing, and harvesting. Hovering above the gate that separates city life and country life is a woman clad in a wisp of transparent drapery, a scroll in one hand and a miniature gallows complete with a hanged man in the other. She represents Security, and her scroll bids those coming to the city to enter without fear because she has taken away the power of the guilty who would harm them.

The world of the Italian city-states—which had seemed so full of promise in Ambrogio Lorenzetti's *Good Government* fresco—was transformed as the middle of the century approached into uncertainty and desolation by a series of natural and societal disasters. In 1333, a flood devastated Florence, followed by banking failures in the 1340s, famine in 1346–1347, and epidemics of the bubonic plague, especially virulent in the summer of 1348, just a few years after Ambrogio's frescos were completed. Some art historians have traced the influence of these calamities on the visual arts at the middle of the fourteenth century (see "The Black Death," page 550). Yet as dark as those days must have seemed to the men and women living through them, the strong currents of cultural and artistic change initiated earlier in the century would persist. In a relatively short span of time, the European Middle Ages gave way in Florence to a new movement that would blossom in the Italian Renaissance.

FRANCE

At the beginning of the fourteenth century, the royal court in Paris was still the arbiter of taste in western Europe, as it had been in the days of King Louis IX (St. Louis). During the Hundred Years' War, however, the French countryside was ravaged by armed struggles and civil strife. The power of the nobility, weakened significantly by warfare, was challenged by townsmen, who took advantage of new economic opportunities that opened up in the wake of the conflict. As centers of art and architecture, the duchy of Burgundy, England, and, for a brief golden moment, the court of Prague began to rival Paris.

French sculptors found lucrative new outlets for their work—not only in stone, but in wood, ivory, and precious metals, often decorated with enamel and gemstones—in the growing demand among wealthy patrons for religious art intended for homes as well as churches. Manuscript painters likewise created lavishly illustrated books for the personal devotions of the wealthy and powerful. And

18-15 • Ambrogio Lorenzetti THE EFFECTS OF GOOD GOVERNMENT IN THE CITY AND IN THE COUNTRY
Sala dei Nove (also known as Sala della Pace), Palazzo Pubblico, Siena, Italy. 1338–1339. Fresco, total length about 46′ (14 m).

architectural commissions focused on exquisitely detailed chapels or small churches, often under private patronage, rather than on the building of grand cathedrals funded by Church institutions.

MANUSCRIPT ILLUMINATION

By the late thirteenth century, private prayer books became popular among wealthy patrons. Because they contained special prayers to be recited at the eight canonical devotional "hours" between morning and night, an individual copy of one of these books came to be called a **Book of Hours**. Such a book included everything the lay person needed for pious practice—psalms, prayers and offices of the Virgin and other saints (such as the owners' patron or the patron of their home church), a calendar of feast days, and sometimes prayers for the dead. During the fourteenth century, a richly decorated Book of Hours was worn or carried like jewelry, counting among a noble person's most important portable possessions.

THE BOOK OF HOURS OF JEANNE D'ÉVREUX Perhaps at their marriage in 1324, King Charles IV gave his 14-year-old queen, Jeanne d'Évreux, a tiny Book of Hours—it fits easily when open within one hand—illuminated by Parisian painter Jean Pucelle (see "A Closer Look," page 551). This book was so precious to the queen that she mentioned it and its illuminator specifically in her will, leaving this royal treasure to King Charles V. Pucelle painted the book's pictures in *grisaille*—monochromatic painting in shades of gray with only delicate touches of color. His style clearly derives from the courtly mode established in Paris at the time of St. Louis, with its softly modeled, voluminous draper-

ies gathered loosely and falling in projecting diagonal folds around tall, elegantly posed figures with carefully coiffed curly hair, broad foreheads, and delicate features. But his conception of space, with figures placed within coherent, discrete architectural settings, suggests a firsthand knowledge of contemporary Sienese art.

Jeanne appears in the initial *D* below the Annunciation, kneeling in prayer before a lectern, perhaps using this Book of Hours to guide her meditations, beginning with the words written on this page: *Domine labia mea aperies* (Psalm 51:15: "O Lord, open thou my lips"). The juxtaposition of the praying Jeanne's portrait with a scene from the life of the Virgin Mary suggests that the sacred scene is actually a vision inspired by Jeanne's meditations. The young queen might have identified with and sought to feel within herself Mary's joy at Gabriel's message. Given what we know of Jeanne's own life story and her royal husband's predicament, it might also have directed the queen's prayers toward the fulfillment of his wish for a male heir.

In the Annunciation, Mary is shown receiving the archangel Gabriel in a Gothic building that seems to project outward from the page toward the viewer, while rejoicing angels look on from windows under the eaves. The group of romping youths at the bottom of the page at first glance seems to echo the angelic jubilation. Folklorists have suggested, however, that the children are playing "froggy in the middle" or "hot cockles," games in which one child was tagged by the others. To the medieval viewer, if the game symbolized the mocking of Christ or the betrayal of Judas, who "tags" his friend, it would have evoked a darker mood by referring to the picture on the other page of this opening, foreshadowing Jesus' imminent death even as his life is beginning.

⬜●─┤ **Read** the document related to *The Effects of Good Government in the City and in the Country* on myartslab.com

A deadly outbreak of the bubonic plague, known as the Black Death after the dark sores that developed on the bodies of its victims, spread to Europe from Asia, both by land and by sea, in the middle of the fourteenth century. At least half the urban population of Florence and Siena—some estimate 80 percent—died during the summer of 1348, probably including the artists Andrea Pisano and Ambrogio Lorenzetti. Death was so quick and widespread that basic social structures crumbled in the resulting chaos; people did not know where the disease came from, what caused it, or how long the pandemic would last.

Mid-twentieth-century art historian Millard Meiss proposed that the Black Death had a significant impact on the development of Italian art in the middle of the fourteenth century. Pointing to what he saw as a reactionary return to hieratic linearity in religious art, Meiss theorized that artists had retreated from the rounded forms that had characterized the work of Giotto to old-fashioned styles, and that this artistic change reflected a growing reliance on traditional religious values in the wake of a disaster that some interpreted as God's punishment of a world in moral decline.

An altarpiece painted in 1354–1357 by Andrea di Cione, nicknamed Orcagna ("Archangel"), under the patronage of Tommaso Strozzi—the so-called Strozzi Altarpiece (**FIG. 18–16**)—is an example of the sort of paintings that led Meiss to his interpretation. This painting's otherworldly vision is dominated by a central figure of Christ, presumably enthroned, but without any hint of an actual seat, evoking the image of the judge at the Last Judgment, outside time and space. The silhouetted outlines of the standing and kneeling saints emphasize surface over depth; the gold expanse of floor beneath them does not offer any reassuring sense of spatial recession to contain them and their activity. Throughout, line and color are more prominent than form.

Recent art historians have stepped back from Meiss's contextual explanation of stylistic change. Some have pointed out logical relationships between style and subject in the works Meiss cites; others have seen in them a mannered outgrowth of current style rather than a reversion to an earlier style; still others have discounted the underlying notion that stylistic change is connected with social situations. But there is a clear relationship of works such as the Strozzi Altarpiece with death and judgment, sanctity and the promise of salvation—themes also suggested in the narrative scenes on the **predella** (the lower zone of the altarpiece): Thomas Aquinas's ecstasy during Mass, Christ's miraculous walk on water to rescue Peter, and the salvation of Emperor Henry II because of a pious donation. While these are not uncommon scenes in sacred art, it is easy to see a relationship between their choice as subject matter here and the specter cast by the Black Death over a world that had just imagined its prosperity in pathbreaking works of visual art firmly rooted in references to everyday life (see FIG. 18–15).

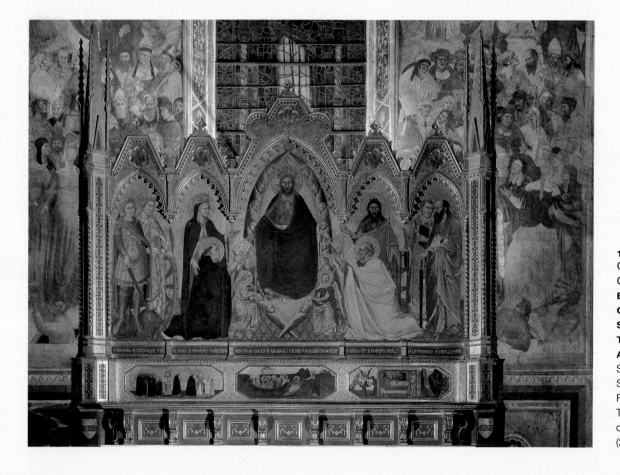

18–16 • Andrea di Cione (nicknamed Orcagna) **ENTHRONED CHRIST WITH SAINTS, FROM THE STROZZI ALTARPIECE**
Strozzi Chapel, Santa Maria Novella, Florence. 1354–1357. Tempera and gold on wood, 9′ × 9′8″ (2.74 × 2.95 m).

Read the document related to the Black Death on myartslab.com

A CLOSER LOOK | The Hours of Jeanne d'Évreux

by Jean Pucelle, Two-Page Opening with the Kiss of Judas and the Annunciation.
Paris. c. 1324–1328. *Grisaille* and color on vellum, each page 3⅝″ × 2⁷⁄₁₆″ (9.2 × 6.2 cm).
Metropolitan Museum of Art, New York. The Cloisters Collection (54.1.2), fols. 15v–16r

In this opening Pucelle juxtaposes complementary scenes drawn from the Infancy and Passion of Christ, placed on opposing pages, in a scheme known as the Joys and Sorrows of the Virgin. The "joy" of the Annunciation on the right is paired with the "sorrow" of the betrayal and arrest of Christ on the left.

Christ sways back gracefully as Judas betrays him with a kiss. The S-curve of his body mirrors the Virgin's pose on the opposite page, as both accept their fate with courtly decorum.

The prominent lamp held aloft by a member of the arresting battalion informs the viewer that this scene takes place at night, in the dark.

The angel who holds up the boxlike enclosure where the Annunciation takes place is an allusion to the legend of the miraculous transportation of this building from Nazareth to Loreto in 1294.

Christ reaches casually down to heal Malchus, the assistant of the high priest whose ear Peter had just cut off in angry retaliation for his participation in the arrest of Jesus.

Scenes of secular amusements from everyday life, visual puns, and off-color jokes appear at the bottom of many pages of this book. Sometimes they relate to the themes of the sacred scenes above them. These comic knights riding goats may be a commentary on the lack of valor shown by the soldiers assaulting Jesus, especially if this wine barrel conjured up for Jeanne an association with the Eucharist.

The candle held by the cleric who guards the "door" to Jeanne's devotional retreat, as well as the rabbit emerging from its burrow in the marginal scene, are sexually charged symbols of fertility that seem directly related to the focused prayers of a child bride required to produce a male heir.

View the Closer Look for the Hours of Jeanne d'Évreux on myartslab.com

Fourteenth-century Paris was renowned for more than its goldsmiths (see FIG. 18–20). Among the most sumptuous and sought-after Parisian luxury products were small chests assembled from carved ivory plaques that were used by wealthy women to store jewelry or other personal treasures. The entirely secular subject matter of these chests explored romantic love. Indeed, they seem to have been courtship gifts from smitten men to desired women, or wedding presents offered by grooms to their brides.

A chest from around 1330–1350, now in the Walters Museum (FIGS. 18–17, 18–18, 18–19), is one of seven that have survived intact; there are fragments of a dozen more. It is a delightful and typical example. Figural relief covers five exterior sides of the box: around the perimeter and on the hinged top. The assembled panels were joined by metal hardware—strips, brackets, hinges, handles, and locks—originally

wrought in silver. Although some chests tell a single romantic story in sequential episodes, most, like this one, anthologize scenes drawn from a group of stories, combining courtly romance, secular allegory, and ancient fables.

On the lid of the Walters casket (see FIG. 18–18), jousting is the theme. Spread over the central two panels, a single scene catches two charging knights in the heat of a tournament, while trumpeting heralds call the attention of spectators, lined up above in a gallery to observe this public display of virility. The panel at right mocks the very ritual showcased in the middle panels by pitting a woman against a knight, battling not with lances but with a long-stemmed rose (symbolizing sexual surrender) and an oak bough (symbolizing fertility). Instead of observing these silly goings-on, however, the spectators tucked into the upper architecture pursue their own amorous flirtations. Finally, in the scene on the left,

knights use crossbows and a catapult to hurl roses at the Castle of Love, while Cupid returns fire with his seductive arrows.

On the front of the chest (see FIG. 18–17), generalized romantic allegory gives way to vignettes from a specific story. At left, the long-bearded Aristotle teaches the young Alexander the Great, using exaggerated gestures and an authoritative text to emphasize his point. Today's lesson is a stern warning not to allow the seductive power of women to distract the young prince from his studies. The subsequent scene, however, pokes fun at his eminent teacher, who has become so smitten by the wiles of a young beauty named Phyllis that he lets her ride him around like a horse, while his student observes this farce, peering out of the castle in the background. The two scenes at right relate to an eastern legend of the fountain of youth, popular in medieval Europe. A line of bearded elders approaches the fountain

18-17 • SMALL IVORY CHEST WITH SCENES FROM COURTLY ROMANCES
Made in Paris. c. 1330–1350. Elephant ivory with modern iron mounts, height 4½″ (11.5 cm), width 9¹¹⁄₁₆″ (24.6 cm), depth 4⅞″ (12.4 cm). The Walters Art Museum, Baltimore.

from the left, steadied by their canes. But after having partaken of its transforming effects, two newly rejuvenated couples, now nude, bathe and flirt within the fountain's basin. The man first in line for treatment, stepping up to climb into the fountain, looks suspiciously like the figure of the aging Aristotle, forming a link between the two stories on the casket front.

Unlike royal marriages of the time, which were essentially business contracts based on political or financial exigencies, the romantic love of the aristocratic wealthy involved passionate devotion. Images of gallant knights and their coy paramours, who could bring intoxicating bliss or cruelly withhold their love on a whim, captured the popular Gothic imagination. They formed the principal subject matter on personal luxury objects, not only chests like this, but mirror backs, combs, writing tablets, even ceremonial saddles. And these stories evoke themes that still captivate us since they reflect notions of desire and betrayal, cruel rejection and blissful folly, at play in our own romantic conquests and relationships to this day. In this way they allow us some access to the lives of the people who commissioned and owned these precious objects, even if we ourselves are unable to afford them.

18–18 • ATTACK ON THE CASTLE OF LOVE
Top of the chest in FIG. 18–17.

18–19 • TRISTAN AND ISEULT AT THE FOUNTAIN; CAPTURE OF THE UNICORN
Left short side of the chest in FIG. 18–17.

Two other well-known medieval themes are juxtaposed on this plaque from the short side of the ivory chest. At left, Tristan and Iseult have met secretly for an illicit romantic tryst, while Iseult's husband, King Mark, tipped off by an informant, observes them from a tree. But when they see his reflection in a fountain between them, they alter their behavior accordingly, and the king believes them innocent of the adultery he had (rightly) suspected. The medieval bestiary ("book of beasts") claimed that only a virgin could capture the mythical unicorn, which at right lays his head, with its aggressively phallic horn, into the lap of just such a pure maiden so that the hunter can take advantage of her alluring powers over the animal to kill it with his phallic counterpart of its horn, a large spear.

18–20 • VIRGIN AND CHILD
c. 1324–1339. Silver gilt and enamel, height 27⅛" (69 cm).
Musée du Louvre, Paris.

METALWORK AND IVORY

Fourteenth-century French sculpture is intimate in character. Religious subjects became more emotionally expressive; objects became smaller and demanded closer scrutiny from the viewer. In the secular realm, tales of love and valor were carved on luxury items to delight the rich (see "An Ivory Chest with Scenes of Romance," page 552). Precious materials—gold, silver, and ivory—were preferred.

THE VIRGIN AND CHILD FROM SAINT-DENIS

A silver-gilt image of a standing **VIRGIN AND CHILD** (**FIG. 18-20**) is a rare survivor that verifies the acclaim that was accorded fourteenth-century Parisian goldsmiths. An inscription on the base documents the statue's donation to the abbey church of Saint-Denis in 1339 and the donor's name, the same Queen Jeanne d'Évreux whose Book of Hours we have just examined. In a style that recalls the work of artist Jean Pucelle in that Book of Hours, the Virgin holds Jesus in her left arm with her weight on her left leg, standing in a graceful, characteristically Gothic S-curve pose. Mary originally wore a crown, and she still holds a large enameled and jeweled *fleur-de-lis*—the heraldic symbol of royal France—which served as a reliquary container for strands of Mary's hair. The Christ Child, reaching out tenderly to caress his mother's face, is babylike in both form and posture. On the base, minuscule statues of prophets stand on projecting piers to separate 14 enameled scenes from Christ's Infancy and Passion, reminding us of the suffering to come. The apple in the baby's hand carries the theme further with its reference to Christ's role as the new Adam, whose sacrifice on the cross—medieval Christians believed—redeemed humanity from the first couple's fall into sin when Eve bit into the forbidden fruit.

ENGLAND

Fourteenth-century England prospered in spite of the ravages of the Black Death and the Hundred Years' War with France. English life at this time is described in the brilliant social commentary of Geoffrey Chaucer in the *Canterbury Tales* (see "A New Spirit in Fourteenth-Century Literature," page 533). The royal family, especially Edward I (r. 1272–1307)—the castle builder—and many of the nobles and bishops were generous patrons of the arts.

EMBROIDERY: OPUS ANGLICANUM

Since the thirteenth century, the English had been renowned for pictorial needlework, using colored silk and gold threads to create images as detailed as contemporary painters produced in manuscripts. Popular throughout

Europe, the art came to be called *opus anglicanum* ("English work"). The popes had more than 100 pieces in the Vatican treasury. The names of several prominent embroiderers are known, but in the thirteenth century no one surpassed Mabel of Bury St. Edmunds, who created both religious and secular articles for King Henry III (r. 1216–1272).

THE CHICHESTER-CONSTABLE CHASUBLE This *opus anglicanum* liturgical vestment worn by a priest during Mass (**FIG. 18-21**) was embroidered c. 1330–1350 with images formed by subtle gradations of colored silk. Where gold threads were laid and couched (tacked down with colored silk), the effect resembles the burnished gold-leaf backgrounds of manuscript illuminations.

The Annunciation, the Adoration of the Magi, and the Coronation of the Virgin are set in cusped, crocketed ogee (S-shape) arches, supported on animal-head corbels and twisting branches sprouting oak leaves with seed-pearl acorns. Because the star and crescent moon in the Coronation of the Virgin scene are heraldic emblems of Edward III (r. 1327–1377), perhaps he or a family member commissioned this luxurious vestment.

During the celebration of the Mass, especially as the priest moved, *opus anglicanum* would have glinted in the candlelight amid treasures on the altar. Court dress was just as rich and colorful, and at court such embroidered garments proclaimed the rank and status of the wearer. So heavy did such gold and bejeweled garments become that their wearers often needed help to move.

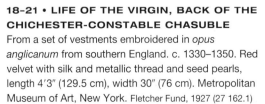

18-21 • LIFE OF THE VIRGIN, BACK OF THE CHICHESTER-CONSTABLE CHASUBLE
From a set of vestments embroidered in *opus anglicanum* from southern England. c. 1330–1350. Red velvet with silk and metallic thread and seed pearls, length 4′3″ (129.5 cm), width 30″ (76 cm). Metropolitan Museum of Art, New York. Fletcher Fund, 1927 (27 162.1)

ARCHITECTURE

In the later years of the thirteenth century and early years of the fourteenth, a distinctive and influential Gothic architectural style, popularly known as the "Decorated style," developed in England. This change in taste has been credited to Henry III's ambition to surpass St. Louis, who was his brother-in-law, as a royal patron of the arts.

THE DECORATED STYLE AT EXETER One of the most complete Decorated-style buildings is **EXETER CATHEDRAL**. Thomas of Witney began construction in 1313 and remained master mason from 1316 to 1342. He supervised construction of the nave and redesigned upper parts of the choir. He left the towers of the original Norman cathedral but turned the interior into a dazzling stone forest of colonnettes, moldings, and vault ribs (**FIG. 18-22**). From piers formed by a cluster of colonnettes rise multiple moldings that make the arcade seem to ripple. Bundled colonnettes spring from sculptured foliate corbels (brackets that project from a wall) between the arches and rise up the wall to support conical clusters of 13 ribs that meet at the summit of the vault, a modest 69 feet above the floor. The basic structure here is the four-part vault with intersecting cross-ribs, but the designer added additional ribs, called tiercerons, to create a richer linear pattern. Elaborately carved **bosses** (decorative knoblike elements) signal the point where ribs meet along the ridge of the vault. Large bar-tracery clerestory windows illuminate the 300-foot-long nave. Unpolished gray marble shafts, yellow sandstone arches, and a white French stone, shipped from Caen, add subtle gradations of color to the upper wall.

Detailed records survive for the building of Exeter Cathedral, documenting work over the period from 1279 to 1514, with only two short breaks. They record where masons and carpenters were housed (in a hostel near the cathedral) and how they were paid (some by the day with extra for drinks, some by the week, some for each finished piece); how materials were acquired and transported (payments for horseshoes and fodder for the horses); and, of course, payments for the building materials (not only stone and wood but rope for measuring and parchment on which to draw forms for the masons). The bishops contributed generously to the building funds. This was not a labor only of love.

Thomas of Witney also designed the intricate, 57-foot-high bishop's throne (at right in FIGURE 18-22), constructed by Richard de Galmeton and Walter of Memburg, who led a team of a dozen carpenters. The

18-22 • INTERIOR, EXETER CATHEDRAL

Devon, England. Thomas of Witney, choir, 14th century and bishop's throne, 1313–1317; Robert Lesyngham, east window, 1389–1390.

canopy resembles embroidery translated into wood, with its maze of pinnacles, bursting with leafy crockets and tiny carved animals and heads. To finish the throne in splendor, Master Nicolas painted and gilded the wood. When the bishop was seated on his throne wearing embroidered vestments like the Chichester-Constable Chasuble (see FIG. 18-21), he must have resembled a golden image in a shrine—more a symbol of the power and authority of the Church than a specific human being.

THE PERPENDICULAR STYLE AT EXETER During years following the Black Death, work at Exeter Cathedral came to a standstill. The nave had been roofed but not vaulted, and the windows had no glass. When work could be resumed, tastes had changed. The exuberance of the Decorated style gave way to an austere style in which rectilinear patterns and sharp angular shapes replaced intricate curves, and luxuriant foliage gave way to simple stripped-down patterns. This phase is known as the Perpendicular style.

In 1389–1390, well-paid master mason Robert Lesyngham rebuilt the great east window (see FIG. 18-22, far wall), designing its tracery in the new Perpendicular style. The window fills the east wall of the choir like a glowing altarpiece. A single figure in each light stands under a tall painted canopy that flows into and blends with the stone tracery. The Virgin with the Christ Child stands in the center over the high altar, with four female saints at the left and four male saints on the right, including St. Peter, to whom the church is dedicated. At a distance, the colorful figures silhouetted against the silver *grisaille* glass become a band of color, conforming to and thus reinforcing the rectangular pattern of the mullions and transoms. The combination of *grisaille*, silver-oxide stain (staining clear glass with shades of yellow or gold), and colored glass produces a glowing wall and casts a cool, silvery light over the nearby stonework.

Perpendicular architecture heralds the Renaissance style in its regularity, its balanced horizontal and vertical lines, and its plain wall or window surfaces. When Tudor monarchs introduced Renaissance art into the British Isles, builders were not forced to rethink the form and structure of their buildings; they simply changed the ornament from the pointed cusps and crocketed arches of the Gothic style to the round arches and columns and capitals of Roman Classicism. The Perpendicular style itself became an English architectural vernacular. It has even been popular in the United States, especially for churches and college buildings.

THE HOLY ROMAN EMPIRE

By the fourteenth century, the Holy Roman Empire existed more as an ideal fiction than a fact. The Italian territories had established their independence, and in contrast to England and France, Germany had become further divided into multiple states with powerful regional associations and princes. The Holy Roman emperors, now elected by Germans, concentrated on securing the fortunes of their families. They continued to be patrons of the arts, promoting local styles.

MYSTICISM AND SUFFERING

The by-now-familiar ordeals of the fourteenth century—famines, wars, and plagues—helped inspire a mystical religiosity in Germany that emphasized both ecstatic joy and extreme suffering. Devotional images, known as *Andachtsbilder* in German, inspired worshipers to contemplate Jesus' first and last hours, especially during evening prayers, or vespers, giving rise to the term *Vesperbild* for the image of Mary mourning her son. Through such religious exercises, worshipers hoped to achieve understanding of the divine and union with God.

VESPERBILD In this well-known example (**FIG. 18-23**), blood gushes from the hideous rosettes that form the wounds of an emaciated and lifeless Jesus who teeters improbably on the lap of his

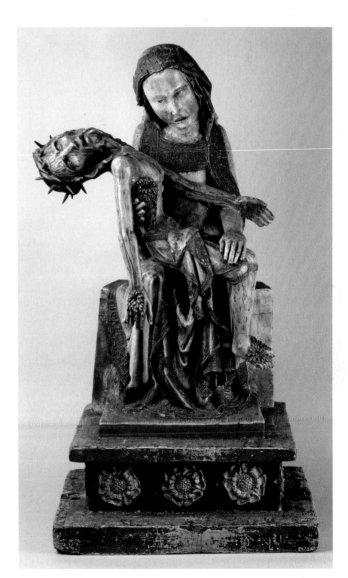

18-23 • VESPERBILD (PIETÀ)
From the Middle Rhine region, Germany. c. 1330. Wood and polychromy, height 34½″ (88.4 cm). Landesmuseum, Bonn.

hunched-over mother. The Virgin's face conveys the intensity of her ordeal, mingling horror, shock, pity, and grief. Such images took on greater poignancy since they would have been compared, in the worshiper's mind, to the familiar, almost ubiquitous images of the young Virgin mother holding her innocent and loving baby Jesus.

THE HEDWIG CODEX The extreme physicality and emotion-alism of the *Vesperbild* finds parallels in the actual lives of some medieval saints in northern Europe. St. Hedwig (1174–1243), married at age 12 to Duke Henry I of Silesia and mother of his seven children, entered the Cistercian convent of Trebniz (in modern Poland) on her husband's death in 1238. She devoted the rest of her life to caring for the poor and seeking to emulate the suffering of Christ by walking barefoot in the snow. As described in her *vita* (biography), she had a particular affection for a small ivory statue of the Virgin and Child, which she carried with her at all times, and which "she often took up in her hands to envelop it in love, so that out of passion she could see it more often and through the seeing could prove herself more devout, inciting her to even greater love of the glorious Virgin. When she once blessed the sick with this image they were cured immediately" (translation from Schleif, p. 22). Hedwig was buried clutching the statue, and when her tomb was opened after her canonization in 1267, it was said that although most of her body had deteriorated, the fingers that still gripped the beloved object had miraculously not decayed.

A picture of Hedwig serves as the frontispiece (**FIG. 18-24**) of a manuscript of her *vita* known as the Hedwig Codex, commissioned

18-24 • ST. HEDWIG OF SILESIA WITH DUKE LUDWIG I OF LIEGNITZ-BRIEG AND DUCHESS AGNES
Dedication page of the Hedwig Codex. 1353. Ink and paint on parchment, 13⁷⁄₁₆″ × 9¾″ (34 × 25 cm). The J. Paul Getty Museum, Los Angeles. MS. Ludwig XI 7, fol. 12v

in 1353 by one her descendants, Ludwig I of Liegnitz-Brieg. Duke Ludwig and his wife, Agnes, are shown here kneeling on either side of St. Hedwig, dwarfed by the saint's architectural throne and her own imposing scale. With her prominent, spidery hands, she clutches the famous ivory statue, as well as a rosary and a prayer book, inserting her fingers within it to maintain her place as if our arrival had interrupted her devotions. She has draped her leather boots over her right wrist in a reference to her practice of removing them to walk in the snow. Hedwig's highly volumetric figure stands in a swaying pose of courtly elegance derived from French Gothic, but the fierce intensity of her gaze and posture are far removed from the mannered graciousness of the smiling angel of Reims (see statue at far left in FIG. 17-14), whose similar gesture and extended finger are employed simply to grasp his drapery and assure its elegant display.

THE SUPREMACY OF PRAGUE

Charles IV of Bohemia (r. 1346–1378) was raised in France, and his admiration for the French king Charles IV was such that he changed his own name from Wenceslas to Charles. He was officially crowned king of Bohemia in 1347 and Holy Roman Emperor in 1355. He established his capital in Prague, which, in the view of his contemporaries, replaced Constantinople as the "New Rome." Prague had a great university, a castle, and a cathedral overlooking a town that spread on both sides of a river joined by a stone bridge, a remarkable structure itself.

choir

nave

18-25 • Heinrich and Peter Parler PLAN AND INTERIOR OF THE CHURCH OF THE HOLY CROSS, SCHWÄBISCH GMÜND
Germany. Begun in 1317 by Heinrich Parler; choir by Peter Parler begun in 1351; vaulting completed 16th century.

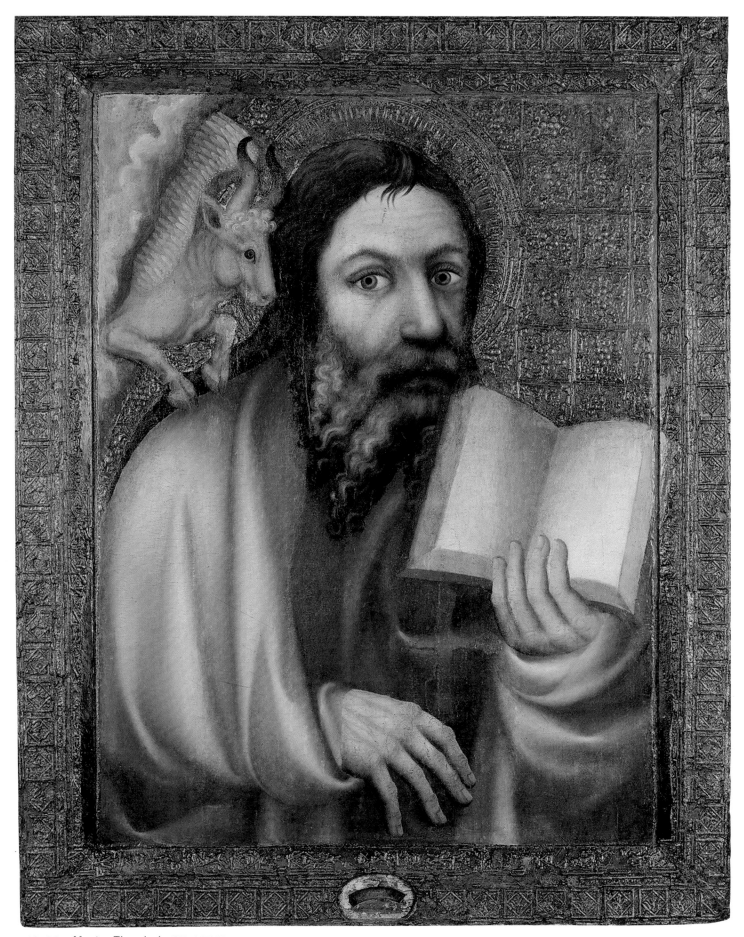

18–26 • Master Theodoric ST. LUKE
Holy Cross Chapel, Karlstejn Castle, near Prague. 1360–1364. Paint and gold on panel, 45¼″ × 37″ (115 × 94 cm).

When Pope Clement VI made Prague an archbishopric in 1344, construction began on a new cathedral in the Gothic style—to be named for St. Vitus. It would also serve as the coronation church and royal pantheon. But the choir was not finished for Charles's first coronation, so he brought Peter Parler from Swabia to complete it.

THE PARLER FAMILY In 1317, Heinrich Parler, a former master of works on Cologne Cathedral, designed and began building the church of the Holy Cross in Schwäbisch Gmünd, in southwest Germany. In 1351, his son Peter (c. 1330–1399), the most brilliant architect of this talented family, joined the workshop. Peter designed the choir (**FIG. 18-25**) in the manner of a hall church whose triple-aisled form was enlarged by a ring of deep chapels between the buttresses. The contrast between Heinrich's nave and Peter's choir (seen clearly in the plan of FIGURE 18-25) illustrates the increasing complexity of rib patterns covering the vaults, which emphasizes the unity of interior space rather than its division into bays.

Called by Charles IV to Prague in 1353, Peter turned the unfinished St. Vitus Cathedral into a "glass house," adding a vast clerestory and glazed triforium supported by double flying buttresses, all covered by net vaults that created a continuous canopy over the space. Because of the success of projects such as this, Peter and his family became the most successful architects in the Holy Roman Empire. Their concept of space, luxurious decoration, and intricate vaulting dominated central European architecture for three generations.

MASTER THEODORIC At Karlstejn Castle, a day's ride from Prague, Charles IV built another chapel, covering the walls with gold and precious stones as well as with paintings. There were 130 paintings of the saints serving as reliquaries, with relics inserted into their frames. Master Theodoric, the court painter, provided drawings on the wood panels, and he painted about 30 images himself. Figures are crowded into—even extend over—their frames, emphasizing their size and power. Master Theodoric was head of the Brotherhood of St. Luke, and the way that his painting of **ST. LUKE** (**FIG. 18-26**), patron saint of painters, looks out at the viewer has suggested to scholars that this may be a self-portrait. His personal style combined a preference for substantial bodies, oversized heads and hands, dour and haunted faces, and soft, deeply modeled drapery, with a touch of grace derived from the French Gothic style. The chapel, consecrated in 1365, so pleased the emperor that in 1367 he gave the artist a farm in appreciation of his work.

Prague and the Holy Roman Empire under Charles IV had become a multicultural empire where people of different religions (Christians and Jews) and ethnic heritages (German and Slav) lived side by side. Charles died in 1378, and without his strong central government, political and religious dissent overtook the empire. Jan Hus, dean of the philosophy faculty at Prague University and a powerful reforming preacher, denounced the immorality he saw in the Church. He was burned at the stake, becoming a martyr and Czech national hero. The Hussite Revolution in the fifteenth century ended Prague's—and Bohemia's—leadership in the arts.

THINK ABOUT IT

18.1 Compare and contrast Giotto's and Duccio's renderings of the biblical story of Christ's Raising of Lazarus (FIGS. 18–8, 18–11).

18.2 Discuss Ambrogio Lorenzetti's engagement with secular subject matter in his frescos for Siena's Palazzo Pubblico (FIG. 18–15). How did these paintings relate to their sociopolitical context?

18.3 Discuss the circumstances surrounding the construction and decoration of the Scrovegni (Arena) Chapel, with special attention to its relationship to the life and aspirations of its patron.

18.4 Choose one small work of art in this chapter that is crafted from precious materials with exceptional technical skill. Explain how it was made and how it was used. How does the work of art relate to its cultural and social context?

CROSSCURRENTS

FIG. 16–26

FIG. 18–20

Depictions of the Virgin Mary holding the infant Jesus represent a continuing theme in the history of European Christian art, developed early on, and continuing to this day. Describe the relationship between the mother and child in these two examples. Characterize the difference in artistic style. How does the choice of medium contribute to the distinction between them? How were they used?

✔—**Study** and review on myartslab.com

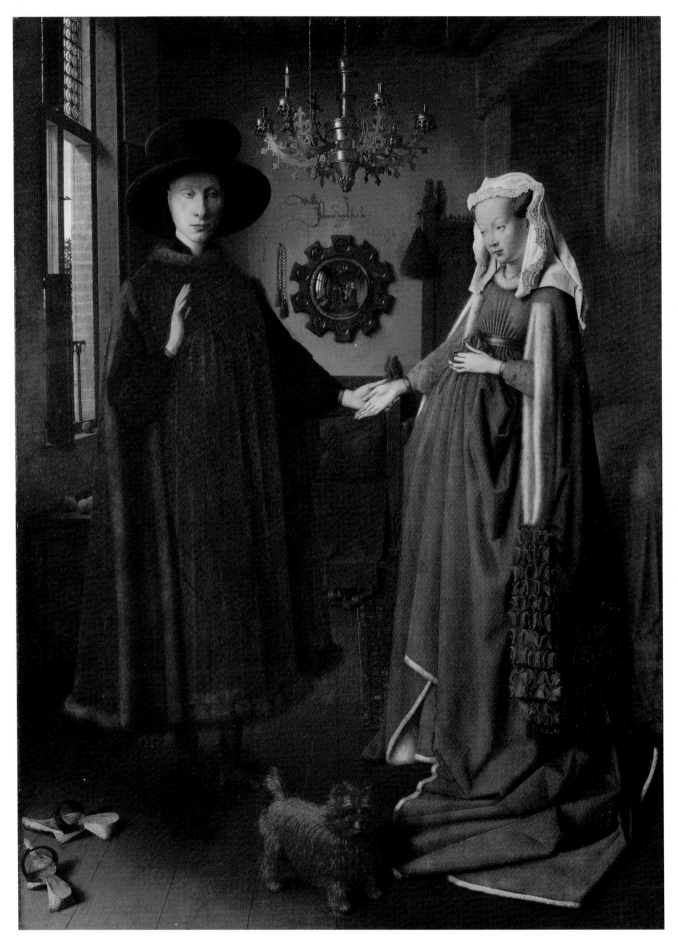

19–1 • Jan van Eyck DOUBLE PORTRAIT OF GIOVANNI ARNOLFINI AND HIS WIFE
1434. Oil on wood panel, 33″ × 22½″ (83.8 × 57.2 cm). The National Gallery, London.

Fifteenth-Century Art in Northern Europe

Fifteenth-century Europe saw the emergence of wealthy merchants whose rise to power was fueled by individual accomplishment, rather than hereditary succession within noble families. Certainly Giovanni Arnolfini—the pasty gentleman with the extravagant hat in this double portrait (FIG. 19–1)—earned, rather than inherited, the right to have himself and his wife recorded by renowned artist Jan van Eyck. It was the wealth and connections he made as an Italian cloth merchant providing luxury fabrics to the Burgundian court that put him in the position to commission such a precious picture, in which both patron and painter are identified with conspicuous clarity. Giovanni's face looks more like a personal likeness than anything we have seen since ancient Rome, and not only did Jan van Eyck inscribe his name above the convex mirror ("Jan van Eyck was here, 1434") but his personal painting style also carries the stamp of authorship. The doll-like face of the woman standing next to Giovanni is less individualized. Has she lifted her skirt over her belly so she can follow Giovanni, who has taken her by the hand? Or are most modern observers correct in assuming that she is pregnant? This painting is full of mysteries.

The precise identity of the couple is still open to scholarly debate. And is this a wedding, a betrothal, or perhaps security for a shady financial deal? Recently it has been interpreted as a memorial to a beloved wife lost to death, perhaps in childbirth. Only the wealth of the couple is beyond dispute. They are surrounded by luxury objects: lavish bed hangings, sumptuous chandelier, precious oriental carpet, rare oranges, not to mention their extravagant clothing. The man wears a fur-lined, silk velvet *heuque* (sleeveless overgarment). The woman's gown not only employs more costly wool fabric than necessary to cover her slight body; the elaborate cutwork decoration and white fur lining of her sleeves is an ostentatious indicator of cost. In fact, the painting itself—probably hung in the couple's home—was an object of considerable value.

Even within its secular setting, however, the picture resonated with sacred meaning. The Church still provided spiritual grounding for men and women of the Renaissance. The crystal prayer beads hanging next to the convex mirror imply the couple's piety, and the mirror itself—a symbol of the all-seeing eye of God—is framed with a circular cycle of scenes from Christ's Passion. A figure of St. Margaret—protector of women in childbirth—is carved at the top of a post in the highbacked chair beside the bed, and the perky *Affenpinscher* in the foreground may be more than a pet. Dogs served as symbols of fidelity and also have funerary associations, but choosing a rare, ornamental breed for inclusion here may have been yet another opportunity to express wealth.

LEARN ABOUT IT

19.1 Analyze how Flemish painters gave scrupulous attention to describing the textures and luminosity of objects in the natural world and in domestic interiors, as well as having an extraordinary interest in evoking human likeness in portraits.

19.2 Uncover the complex symbolic meanings that saturated both settings and subjects of northern European paintings.

19.3 Explore the ways in which northern European paintings of the fifteenth century captured in concrete form the spiritual visions of their meditating donors.

19.4 Investigate the emergence of printing as a major pictorial medium.

((•—Listen to the chapter audio on myartslab.com

THE NORTHERN RENAISSANCE

Revitalized civic life and economic growth in the late fourteenth century gave rise to a prosperous middle class that supported scholarship, literature, and the arts. Their patronage resulted in the explosion of learning and creativity that we call the Renaissance (French for "rebirth")—a term that was assigned to this period by later historians.

A major manifestation of the Renaissance in northern Europe was a growing and newly intense interest in the natural world manifested in the close observation and detailed recording of nature. Artists depicted birds, plants, and animals with breathtaking descriptive accuracy. They applied the same scrutiny to people and objects, modeling forms with light and shadow to give them the semblance of three-dimensionality. These carefully described subjects were situated into spatial settings, applying an intuitive perspective system by diminishing their scale as they receded into the distance. In the portrayal of landscapes—which became a northern specialty—artists used atmospheric perspective in which distant elements appear increasingly indistinct and less colorful as they approach the background. The sky, for instance, becomes paler near the horizon and the distant landscape turns bluish-gray.

One aspect of the desire for accurate visual depictions of the natural world was a new interest in individual personalities. Fifteenth-century portraits have an astonishingly lifelike quality, combining careful—sometimes seemingly unflattering—surface description with an uncanny sense of vitality. Indeed, the individual becomes important in every sphere. More names of artists survive from the fifteenth century, for example, than in the entire span from the beginning of the Common Era to the year 1400, and some artists begin regularly to sign their work.

The new power of cities in Flanders and the greater Netherlands (present-day Belgium, Luxembourg, and the Netherlands) (**MAP 19–1**) provided a critical tension and balance with the traditional powers of royalty and the Church. Increasingly, the urban lay public sought to express personal and civic pride by sponsoring secular architecture, sculptured monuments, or paintings directed toward the community. The commonsense values of the merchants formed a solid underpinning for the Northern Renaissance, but their influence remained intertwined with the continuing power of the Church and the royal and noble courts. Giovanni Arnolfini's success at commerce and negotiation provided the funding for his extraordinary double portrait (see FIG. 19–1), but he was able to secure the services of Jan van Eyck only with the cooperation of the duke of Burgundy.

ART FOR THE FRENCH DUCAL COURTS

The dukes of Burgundy (controlling present-day east-central France, Belgium, Luxembourg, and the Netherlands) were the most powerful rulers in northern Europe for most of the fifteenth century. Their domain encompassed not only Burgundy itself but also the Flemish and Netherlandish centers of finance and trade, including the thriving cities of Ghent, Bruges, Tournai, and Brussels. The major seaport, Bruges, was the commercial center of northern Europe, rivaling the Italian city-states of Florence, Milan, and Venice as an economic hub. In the late fourteenth century, Burgundian Duke Philip the Bold (r. 1363–1404) had acquired territory in the Netherlands—including the politically desirable region of Flanders—by marrying the daughter of the Flemish count. Though dukes Philip the Bold of Burgundy, Jean of Berry, and Louis of Anjou were brothers of King Charles V of France, their interests rarely coincided. Even the threat of a common enemy, England, during the Hundred Years' War was not a strong unifying factor, since Burgundy and England were often allied because of common financial interests in Flanders.

While the French king held court in Paris, the dukes held even more splendid courts in their own cities. The dukes of Burgundy and Berry (central France), not the king in Paris, were the real arbiters of taste. Especially influential was Jean, duke of Berry, who commissioned many works from Flemish and Netherlandish painters in the fashionable International Gothic style.

This new, composite style emerged in the late fourteenth century from the multicultural papal court in Avignon in southern France, where artists from Italy, France, and Flanders worked side by side. The International Gothic style became the prevailing manner of late fourteenth-century Europe. It is characterized by slender, gracefully posed figures whose delicate features are framed by masses of curling hair and extraordinarily complex headdresses. Noble men and women wear rich brocaded and embroidered fabrics and elaborate jewelry. Landscape and architectural settings are miniaturized; however, details of nature—leaves, flowers, insects, birds—are rendered in nearly microscopic detail. Spatial recession is represented by rising tiled floors in rooms that are open to view like stage sets, by fanciful mountains and meadows with high horizon lines, and by progressive diminution in the size of receding objects and by atmospheric perspective. Artists and patrons preferred light, bright colors and a liberal use of gold in manuscript and panel paintings, tapestries, and polychromed sculpture. International Gothic was so appealing that it endured well into the fifteenth century.

PAINTING AND SCULPTURE FOR THE CHARTREUSE DE CHAMPMOL

One of Philip the Bold's most lavish projects was the Carthusian monastery, or *chartreuse* ("charterhouse"), at Champmol, outside Dijon, his Burgundian capital city. Land was acquired in 1377 and 1383, and construction began in 1385. The monastic church was intended to house the family's tombs, and the monks were expected to pray continuously for the souls of Philip and his family. Carthusian monasteries were particularly expensive to maintain because Carthusian monks did not provide for themselves by farming or other physical work but were dedicated exclusively to prayer and solitary meditation.

MAP 19–1 •
FIFTEENTH-
CENTURY
NORTHERN
EUROPE

The dukes of
Burgundy—whose
territory included much
of present-day Belgium
and Luxembourg, the
Netherlands, and eastern
France—became the
cultural and political
leaders of western
Europe. Their major
cities of Bruges (Belgium)
and Dijon (France)
were centers of art
and industry as well
as politics.

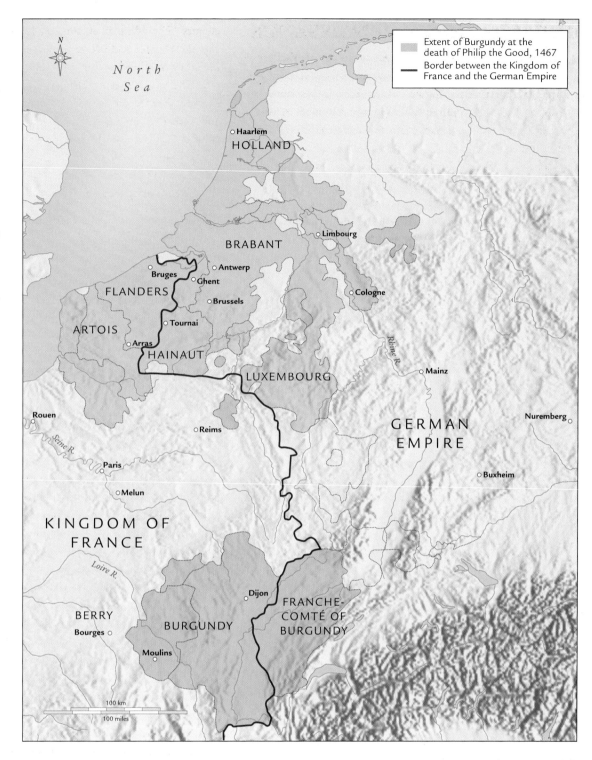

MELCHIOR BROEDERLAM The duke ordered a magnificent carved and painted altarpiece (see "Altars and Altarpieces," page 566) for the Chartreuse de Champmol. The interior of the altarpiece, carved and gilded by Jacques de Baerze, depicts scenes of the Crucifixion flanked by the Adoration of the Magi and the Entombment. The exteriors of the protective shutters of this triptych were covered not by carvings but by two paintings by Melchior Broederlam (active 1381–1410) showing scenes from the life of the Virgin and the infancy of Christ (**FIG. 19–2**).

Broederlam situates his closely observed, International-Style figures within fanciful miniature architectural and landscape settings. His lavish use of brilliantly seductive colors foregrounds one of the features that made International Gothic so popular.

The archangel Gabriel greets Mary while she is at prayer. She sits in a Gothic room with a back door leading into the dark interior of a Romanesque rotunda that symbolizes the Temple of Jerusalem as a repository of the Old Law. According to legend, Mary was an attendant in the Temple prior to her marriage to

The altar in a Christian church symbolizes both the table of Jesus' Last Supper and the tombs of Christ and the saints. As a table, the altar is the site where priests celebrate Mass. And as a tomb, it traditionally contained a relic before the Reformation, placed in a reliquary on the altar, beneath the floor on which the altar rests, or even enclosed within the altar itself.

Altarpieces are painted or carved constructions placed at the back of or behind the altar so that altar and altarpiece appear visually to be joined. By the fifteenth century, important altarpieces had evolved into large and elaborate architectural structures filled with images and protected by movable wings that function like shutters. An altarpiece can sit on a base, called a predella. A winged altarpiece can be a diptych, in which two panels are hinged together; a **triptych**, in which two wings fold over a center section, forming a diptych when closed; or a **polyptych**, consisting of many panels.

diptych   triptych   altar and polyptych altarpiece

Joseph. The tiny enclosed garden and conspicuous pot of lilies are symbols of Mary's virginity. In International Gothic fashion, both the interior and exterior of the building are shown, and the floors are tilted up at the back to give clear views of the action. Next, in the Visitation, just outside the temple walls, the now-pregnant Mary greets her older cousin Elizabeth, who will soon give birth to John the Baptist.

On the right shutter is the Presentation in the Temple. Mary and Joseph have brought the newborn Jesus to the Temple for his redemption as a first-born son and for Mary's purification, where Simeon takes the baby in his arms to bless him (Luke 2:25–32). At the far right, the Holy Family flees to Egypt to escape King Herod's order that all Jewish male infants be killed. The family travels along treacherous terrain similar to that in the Visitation scene, where a path leads the viewers' eyes up from the foreground and into the distance along a rising ground plane. Broederlam has created a sense of light and air around his solid figures. Anecdotal details drawn from the real world are scattered throughout the pictures—a hawk flies through the golden sky, the presented baby looks anxiously back at his mother, and Joseph drinks from a flask and carries the family belongings in a satchel over his shoulder on the journey to Egypt. The statue of a pagan god, visible at the upper right, breaks and tumbles from its pedestal as the Christ Child approaches. A new era dawns and a new religion replaces the old, among both Jews and gentiles.

CLAUS SLUTER Flemish sculptor Jean de Marville (active 1366–1389) initially directed the decoration of the Chartreuse, and when he died in 1389, he was succeeded by his talented assistant Claus Sluter (c. 1360–1406), from Haarlem, in Holland. Sluter's distinctive work survives in a monumental **WELL OF MOSES** carved for the main cloister (**FIG. 19-3**), begun in 1395 and left unfinished at Sluter's death.

The design of this work was complex. A pier rose from the water to support a large free-standing figure of Christ on the cross, mourned by the Virgin Mary, Mary Magdalen, and John the Evangelist. Forming a pedestal for this Crucifixion group at the viewers' eye level are life-size stone figures from the Hebrew Bible who Christians believe foretold the coming of Christ: Moses, David, and the prophets Jeremiah, Zachariah, Daniel, and Isaiah. This concept may have been inspired by contemporary mystery plays, in which prophets foretell and explain events of Christ's Passion. Sluter's patriarchs and prophets are distinct individuals, physically and psychologically. Moses' sad old eyes blaze out from a memorable face entirely covered with a fine web of wrinkles. Even his horns are wrinkled. (These horns are traditional attributes based on a mistranslation of Exodus 34:29–35 in the Latin Vulgate Bible, where the rays of light radiating from Moses' face become horns.) A mane of curling hair and beard cascades over his heavy shoulders and chest, and an enormous cloak envelops his body. Beside him stands David, in the voluminous robes of a medieval king, the very personification of nobility.

19-2 • Melchior Broederlam ANNUNCIATION, VISITATION, PRESENTATION IN THE TEMPLE, AND FLIGHT INTO EGYPT

Exterior of the wings of the altarpiece of the Chartreuse de Champmol. 1393–1399. Oil on wood panel, 5′5¾″ × 4′1¼″ (1.67 × 1.25 m). Musée des Beaux-Arts, Dijon.

Sluter looked at human figures in new ways—as a weighty mass defined by voluminous drapery that lies in deep folds and falls in horizontal arcs and cascading lines—both concealing and revealing the body, creating strong highlights and shadows. With the vigorous, imposing, and highly individualized figures of the Well of Moses, Sluter abandoned the idealized faces, elongated figures, and vertical drapery of International Gothic for particularized description and the broad horizontal movement of forms. He retained, however, the detailed naturalism and rich colors (now almost lost but revealed in recent cleaning) and surfaces still preferred by his patrons.

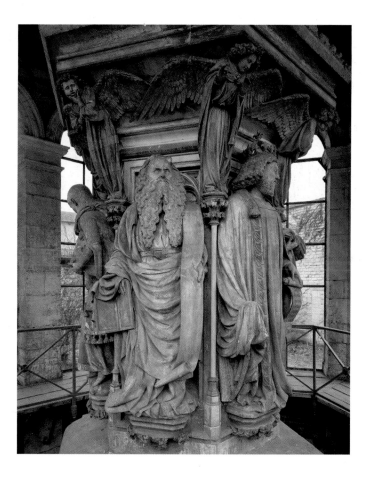

19-3 • Claus Sluter WELL OF MOSES, DETAIL OF MOSES AND DAVID

The Chartreuse de Champmol, Dijon, France. 1395–1406. Limestone with traces of paint, height of figures about 5′8″ (1.69 m).

The sculpture's original details included metal used for buckles and even eyeglasses. It was also painted: Moses wore a gold mantle with a blue lining over a red tunic; David's gold mantle had a painted lining of ermine, and his blue tunic was covered with gold stars and wide bands of ornament.

Since most formal apprenticeships were not open to them, medieval and Renaissance women artists typically learned to paint from their husbands and fathers. Noblewomen, who were often educated in convents, also learned to draw, paint, and embroider. One of the earliest examples of a signed work by a woman is in a tenth-century Spanish manuscript of the Apocalypse illustrated by an artist named Ende (see FIG. 15–11), who describes herself as "painter and servant of God." In the twelfth century, a German nun named Guda not only signed her work but also included a self-portrait (see FIG. 16–34).

Examples proliferate during the later Middle Ages. In the fourteenth century, Jeanne de Montbaston and her husband, Richart, worked together as book illuminators under the auspices of the University of Paris. After Richart's death, Jeanne maintained the workshop and, following the custom of the time, was sworn in as a *libraire* (publisher) by the university in 1353. Bourgot, the daughter of the miniaturist Jean le Noir, illuminated books for King Charles V of France and Duke Jean of Berry. In the fifteenth century, women could be admitted to guilds in the Flemish towns of Ghent, Bruges, and Antwerp.

In a French edition of a book by the Italian author Boccaccio entitled *Concerning Famous Women*, there is a picture of Thamyris, an artist of antiquity, at work in her studio (FIG. 19–4). She appears in fifteenth-century dress, painting an image of the Virgin and Child. At the right, an assistant grinds and mixes her colors. In the foreground, her brushes and paints are laid out neatly and conveniently on a table.

19–4 • PAGE WITH THAMYRIS
From Giovanni Boccaccio's *De Claris Mulieribus* (*Concerning Famous Women*). 1402. Ink and tempera on vellum, 14″ × 9½″ (35.5 × 24 cm). Bibliothèque Nationale, Paris.

MANUSCRIPT ILLUMINATION

Besides religious texts, wealthy patrons treasured richly illuminated secular writings such as herbals (encyclopedias of plants), health manuals, and works of history and literature. A typical manuscript page (see FIG. 19–4) might have leafy tendrils framing the text, decorated opening initials, and perhaps a small inset picture. Only the most lavish books would have full-page miniature paintings, set off with frames. The pictures in these books are conceived as windows looking into rooms or out onto landscapes with distant horizons.

THE LIMBOURG BROTHERS Among the finest Netherlandish painters at the beginning of the century were three brothers—Paul, Herman, and Jean Limbourg—their "last" name referring to their home region. At this time people generally did not have

family names in the modern sense, but were known instead by their first names, often followed by a reference to their place of origin, parentage, or occupation.

About 1404, the Limbourg brothers entered the service of avid bibliophile Duke Jean of Berry (1340–1416), for whom they produced their most impressive surviving work, the so-called **TRÈS RICHES HEURES** (Very Sumptuous Book of Hours), between 1411 and 1416 (FIGS. 19–5, 19–6). A Book of Hours, in addition to containing prayers and readings used in daily devotion, also included a calendar of holy days. The Limbourgs created full-page illustrations for the calendar in the *Très Riches Heures*, with subjects including both peasant labors and aristocratic pleasures of each month in a framed lower field, while elaborate calendar devices, with the chariot of the sun and the zodiac symbols, fill a

**19-5 • Paul, Herman, and Jean Limbourg FEBRUARY: LIFE
IN THE COUNTRY, TRÈS RICHES HEURES**
1411–1416. Colors and ink on parchment, 11⅜″ × 8¼″ (29 × 21 cm).
Musée Condé, Chantilly, France.

View the Closer Look for *February: Life in the Country* on
myartslab.com

semicircular area on the upper part of the page. Like most European artists of the time, the Limbourgs showed the laboring classes in a light acceptable to aristocrats—that is, happily working for the nobles' benefit or displaying an uncouth lifestyle for aristocratic amusement. At times, however, the peasants seem to be enjoying the pleasures of their leisure moments.

In the February page (see FIG. 19-5), farm folks relax cozily before a blazing fire. Although many country people at this time lived in hovels, this farm looks comfortable and well maintained, with timber-framed buildings, a row of beehives, a sheepfold, and tidy woven wattle fences. In the distance are a village and church. Within this scene, although all are much lower in social standing than the duke himself, there is a hierarchy of class. Largest in scale and most elegantly dressed is the woman closest to us, perhaps the owner of the farm, who carefully lifts her overgarment, balancing it daintily with both hands as she warms herself. She shares her

**19-6 • Paul, Herman, and Jean Limbourg JANUARY: THE
DUKE OF BERRY AT TABLE, TRÈS RICHES HEURES**
1411–1416. Colors and ink on parchment, 11⅜″ × 8¼″ (29 × 21 cm).
Musée Condé, Chantilly, France.

fire with a couple, smaller because farther in the background, who wear more modest clothing and are considerably less well behaved, especially the uncouth man, who exposes himself as he lifts his clothing to take advantage of the fire's warmth.

One of the most remarkable aspects of this painting is the way it conveys the feeling of cold winter weather: the leaden sky and bare trees, the soft snow and huddled sheep, the steamy breath of the bundled-up worker blowing on his hands, and the comforting smoke curling from the farmhouse chimney. The artists employ several International Gothic conventions: the high placement of the **horizon line**, the small size of trees and buildings in relation to people, and the cutaway view of the house showing both interior and exterior. The muted palette is sparked with touches of yellowish-orange, blue, and patches of bright red, including the man's turban at the lower left. Scale relationships seem consistent with our experience in the natural world since as the landscape recedes, the size of figures and buildings diminishes progressively in stages from foreground to middle ground to background.

19-7 • Mary of Burgundy Painter MARY AT HER DEVOTIONS, HOURS OF MARY OF BURGUNDY
Before 1482. Colors and ink on parchment, size of image 7½″ × 5¼″ (19.1 × 13.3 cm). Österreichische Nationalbibliothek, Vienna.

by 5¼ inches, earthly reality and a religious vision have been rendered equally tangible (**FIG. 19-7**). The painter conjures up a complex pictorial space. We look not only through the "window" of the illustration's frame but through another window in the wall of the room depicted in the foreground of the painting. The artist shows real virtuosity in representing these worlds. Spatial recession leads the viewer into the far reaches of the church interior, past the Virgin and the gilded altarpiece in the sanctuary to two people conversing in the far distance. The filmy veil covering Mary of Burgundy's steeple headdress is exquisitely described, as is the transparency of the glass vase, and the distinctive bull's eye glass (circular panes whose center "lump" was formed by the glassblower's pontil) filling the foreshortened, open window.

Mary of Burgundy appears twice. She is seated in the foreground by a window, reading from, or contemplating a picture within, her Book of Hours, held carefully and protected by a lush green cloth, perhaps from the diminutive dog cuddled into her lap. She appears again in the background, within the representation of the personal vision inspired by her private meditations. A glorious Gothic church may form the setting for her vision, but it results not from attendance at Mass nor from the direction of a priestly advisor. She experiences it in private, a reward for her personal faith. Christians were encouraged in this period to imagine themselves participating in biblical stories and sacred events so as to feel within bodies and souls the experiences of the protagonists. Secluded in her private space, and surrounded by devotional aids on the window ledge—book, rosary, and symbolic flowers (carnations symbolized the nails of the Crucifixion, the irises Mary's sorrow)—it seems that Mary of Burgundy is doing just that. In her vision, she kneels with attendants and angels in front of a gracefully human Virgin and Child.

TEXTILES

In the fifteenth and sixteenth centuries, the best European tapestries came from Flanders. Major weaving centers at Brussels, Tournai, and Arras produced intricately woven wall hangings for royal and aristocratic patrons across Europe, important church officials including the pope, and even town councils. Among the most common subjects were foliage and flower patterns, scenes from the lives of the saints, and themes from Classical mythology and history, such as the Battle of Troy seen hanging on the walls of Duke Jean of Berry's reception room (see **FIG. 19-6**). Tapestries provided both insulation and luxurious decoration for the stone walls of castle halls, churches, and municipal buildings, and because they were much more expensive than wall or panel paintings, they also showed off the owners' wealth. Since they were portable, many were included in aristocratic baggage as courts moved from residence to residence.

The price of a tapestry depended on the artists involved, the work required, and the materials used. Rarely was a fine, commissioned series woven only with wool; instead, tapestry producers enhanced the weaving with silk, and with silver and gold threads

In contrast, the illustration for the other winter month—January—depicts an aristocratic household (see **FIG. 19-6**). The duke of Berry himself sits behind a table laden with food and rich tableware, presiding over his New Year's feast and surrounded by servants and allies. His chamberlain invites smartly dressed courtiers to greet the duke (the words written overhead say "approach"), who is himself singled out visually by the red cloth of honor with his heraldic arms—swans and the lilies of France—hanging over him and by a large fire screen that circles his head like a secular halo. Tapestries with battle scenes cover the walls. Such luxury objects attest to the wealth and lavish lifestyle of this great patron of the arts, a striking contrast to the farm life that will be revealed in February when turning to the next page in the book.

THE MARY OF BURGUNDY PAINTER One of the finest painters of Books of Hours later in the century was an artist known as the Mary of Burgundy Painter—so called because he painted a Book of Hours for Mary of Burgundy (1457–1482), only child of Charles the Bold. Within a full-page miniature in a book only 7½

19–8 • UNICORN IS FOUND AT THE FOUNTAIN
From the Hunt of the Unicorn tapestry series. c. 1495–1505. Wool, silk, and silver- and gilt-wrapped thread
(13–21 warp threads per inch), 12′1″ × 12′5″ (3.68 × 3.78 m). Metropolitan Museum of Art, New York.
Gift of John D. Rockefeller Jr., The Cloisters Collection, 1937 (37.80.2)

that must have glittered on the walls of princely residences, especially at night, illuminated by flickering lamps or candles. Because silver and gold threads were made of silk wrapped with real silver and gold, people later burned many tapestries to retrieve the precious materials. As a result, few royal tapestries in France survived the French Revolution. If a greater percentage had survived, these luxurious and monumental textile wall paintings would surely figure more prominently in the history of art.

THE UNICORN TAPESTRY Tapestries were often produced in series. One of the best known is the Hunt of the Unicorn series from c. 1500. Four of the seven surviving hangings present scenes of people and animals set against a dense field of trees and flowers, with a distant view of a castle, as in the **UNICORN IS FOUND AT THE FOUNTAIN (FIG. 19–8)**. The unusually fine condition of the tapestry allows us to appreciate its rich colors and the subtlety in modeling the faces, the tonal variations in the animals' fur, and even the depiction of reflections in the water. The technical skill of its weavers is astonishing.

In tapestry, designs are woven directly into the fabric. The Unicorn tapestries seem to have been woven on huge, horizontal looms, where weavers interwove fine weft yarn of wool and silk—dyed in a multitude of colors from the creative combination of three vegetal dyes—onto the parallel strands of the coarser wool warp. Weavers worked from behind what would be the front surface of the finished tapestry, following the design on a full-scale cartoon laid on the floor under the loom. They could only see the actual effect of their work by checking the front with mirrors. Making a tapestry panel this large was a collaborative effort that required the organizational skills of a talented production manager and five or six weavers working side by side on a single loom. What is so extraordinary about their work is the skillful way they created curving lines—since the tapestry process is based on a rectilinear network of threads, curves have be simulated—and the lighting effects of shading and reflections, which require using yarn in the same hue with a multitude of values.

The subject of this series concerns the unicorn, a mythical horselike animal with a single long twisted horn and said to be supernaturally swift; it could only be captured by a virgin, to whom it came willingly. Thus, the unicorn became both a symbol of the Incarnation (Christ is the unicorn captured by the Virgin Mary) and also a metaphor for romantic love (see FIG. 18–19). The capture and killing of the unicorn was also equated with Christ's death on the cross to save humanity.

The natural world represented so splendidly in this tapestry also has potential symbolic meaning. For instance, lions represented valor, faith, courage, and mercy, and even—because they were thought to breathe life into their cubs—the Resurrection of Christ. The stag is another Resurrection symbol (it sheds and grows its antlers) and a protector against poisonous serpents and evil in general. Even today we see rabbits as symbols of fertility, and dogs of fidelity. Many of the easily identifiable flowers and trees also carry both religious and secular meaning. There is a strong theme of marriage: the strawberry is a common symbol of sexual love; the pansy means remembrance; and the periwinkle, a cure for spiteful feelings and jealousy. The trees include oak for fidelity, beech for nobility, holly for protection against evil, hawthorn for the power of love, and pomegranate and orange for fertility.

COPE OF THE ORDER OF THE GOLDEN FLEECE Surviving vestments of the Order of the Golden Fleece are remarkable examples of Flemish textiles. The Order of the Golden Fleece was an honorary fraternity founded by Duke Philip the Good of Burgundy in 1430 with 23 knights chosen for their moral character and bravery. Religious services were an integral part of the order's meetings, and opulent liturgical and clerical objects were created for the purpose.

The surface of the sumptuous cope (cloak) in **FIGURE 19-9** is divided into compartments filled with the standing figures of saints. At the top of the neck edge, as if presiding over the company, is an enthroned figure of Christ, flanked along the front edge by

19-9 • COPE OF THE ORDER OF THE GOLDEN FLEECE
Flemish. Mid 15th century. Cloth with gold and colored silk embroidery, 5′4⁹⁄₁₆″ × 10′9⁵⁄₁₆″ (1.64 × 3.3 m). Imperial Treasury, Vienna.

Whereas Italian artists favored tempera, using it almost exclusively for panel painting until the end of the fifteenth century (see "Cennino Cennini on Panel Painting," page 546), Flemish artists preferred oil paints, in which powdered pigments are suspended in linseed—and occasionally walnut—oil. They exploited the potential of this medium during the fifteenth century with a virtuosity that has never been surpassed.

Tempera had to be applied in a very precise manner because it dried almost as quickly as it was laid down. Shading was restricted to careful overlying strokes in graded tones ranging from white and gray to dark brown and black. Because tempera is opaque—light striking its surface does not penetrate to lower layers of color and reflect back—the resulting surface is **matte**, or dull, taking on a sheen only with burnishing or an overlay of varnish.

On the other hand, oil paint is a viscous medium which takes much longer to dry, and while it is still wet changes can be made easily. Once applied, the paint has time to smooth out during the drying process, erasing traces of individual brushstrokes on the surface of the finished panel. Perhaps even more importantly, oil paint is translucent when applied in very thin layers, called glazes. Light striking a surface built up of glazes penetrates to the lower layers and is reflected back, creating the appearance of an interior glow. These luminous effects enabled artists to capture jewel-like colors and the varying effects of light on changing textures, enhancing the illusion that viewers are looking at real objects rather than their painted imitation.

So brilliant was Jan van Eyck's use of oil paint that he was credited by Giorgio Vasari with inventing the medium. Actually, it had been in use since at least the twelfth century, when it is described in Theophilus Presbyter's *De diversis artibus* (see "Stained-Glass Windows," page 501).

👁—[**Watch** a video about the processes of oil painting and grinding oil paint on myartslab.com

---

scholar-saints in their studies. The embroiderers worked with great precision to match the illusionistic effects of contemporary Flemish painting. The particular stitch used here is known as couching. Gold threads are tacked down using unevenly spaced colored silk threads to create images and an iridescent effect.

PAINTING IN FLANDERS

A strong economy based on the textile industry and international trade provided stability and money for a Flemish efflorescence in the arts. Civic groups, town councils, and wealthy merchants were important patrons in the Netherlands, where the cities were self-governing and largely independent of landed nobility. Guilds oversaw nearly every aspect of their members' lives, and high-ranking guild members served on town councils and helped run city governments. Even experienced artists who moved from one city to another usually had to work as assistants in a local workshop until they met the requirements for guild membership.

Throughout most of the fifteenth century, Flemish art and artists were greatly admired across Europe. Artists from abroad studied Flemish works, and their influence spread even to Italy. Only at the end of the fifteenth century did a pervasive preference for Netherlandish painting give way to a taste for the new styles of art and architecture developing in Italy.

THE FOUNDERS OF THE FLEMISH SCHOOL

Flemish panel painters preferred using an oil medium rather than the tempera paint that was standard in the works of Italian artists. Since it was slow to dry, oil paint provided flexibility, and it had a luminous quality (see "Oil Painting," above). Like manuscript illuminations, Flemish panel paintings provided a window onto a scene rendered with keen attention to describing individual features—people, objects, or aspects of the natural world—with consummate skill.

THE MASTER OF FLÉMALLE Some of the earliest and most outstanding exponents of the new Flemish style were painters in the workshop of an artist known as the Master of Flémalle, identified by some art historians as Robert Campin (active 1406–1444). About 1425–1430, these artists painted the triptych now known as the **MÉRODE ALTARPIECE**, after its later owners (**FIG. 19-10**). Its relatively small size—slightly over 2 feet tall and about 4 feet wide with the wings open—suggests that it was probably made for a small private chapel.

The Annunciation of the central panel is set in a Flemish home and incorporates common household objects, many invested with symbolic religious meaning. The lilies in the **majolica** (glazed earthenware) pitcher on the table, for example, often appear in Annunciations to symbolize Mary's virginity. The hanging water pot in the background niche refers to Mary's purity and her role as the vessel for the Incarnation of God. What seems at first to be a towel hung over the prominent, hinged rack next to the niche may be a tallis (Jewish prayer shawl). Some art historians have referred to these as "hidden" or "disguised" symbols because they are treated as a normal part of the setting, but their routine religious meanings would have been obvious to the intended audience.

Some have interpreted the narrative episode captured in the central panel as the moment immediately following Mary's acceptance of her destiny. A rush of wind riffles the book pages and snuffs the candle (the flame, symbolic of God's divinity, extinguished at the moment he takes human form) as a tiny figure of Christ carrying a cross descends on a ray of light. Having accepted the miracle of the Incarnation (God assuming human form), Mary reads her Bible while sitting humbly on the footrest of the long bench. Her

19–10 • Workshop of the Master of Flémalle MÉRODE ALTARPIECE (TRIPTYCH OF THE ANNUNCIATION) (OPEN)

c. 1425–1430s. Oil on wood panel, center 25¼″ × 24⅞″ (64.1 × 63.2 cm); each wing approx. 25⅜″ × 10¾″ (64.5 × 27.6 cm). Metropolitan Museum of Art, New York. The Cloisters Collection, 1956 (56.70)

In the late nineteenth century, this triptych was associated with a group of stylistically related works and assigned to an artist called the Master of Flémalle, who was subsequently identified by some art historians as a documented artist named Robert Campin. Recently, however, experts have questioned this association and proposed that the triptych we now see was the work of several artists working within the workshop that created the stylistic cluster. Current opinion holds that the *Annunciation* was initially created as an independent panel, and shortly afterward expanded into a triptych with the addition of the side panels under the patronage of the donor in the foreground at left. Finally, some time later in the 1430s, the figure of his wife was added behind him, presumably on the occasion of his marriage.

View the Closer Look for the Mérode Altarpiece on myartslab.com

position becomes a symbol of her submission to God's will. Other art historians have proposed that the scene represents the moment just prior to the Annunciation. In this view, Mary is not yet aware of Gabriel's presence, and the rushing wind is the result of the angel's rapid entry into the room, where he appears before her, half kneeling and raising his hand in salutation.

In the left wing of the triptych, the donors—presumably a married couple—kneel in an enclosed garden, another symbol of Mary's virginity, before the open door of the house where the Annunciation is taking place, implying that the scene is a vision engendered by their faithful meditations, comparable to the vision we have already seen in the Hours of Mary of Burgundy (see FIG. 19-7). Such presentations, very popular with Flemish patrons, allowed those who commissioned a religious work to appear in the same space and time, and often on the same scale, as religious figures. The donors' eyes, which seem oddly unfocused, are directed not outward but inward, intent on the spiritual exercise of imagining their own presence within this sacred narrative.

On the right wing, Joseph is working in his carpentry workshop. A prosperous Flemish city is exquisitely detailed in the view through

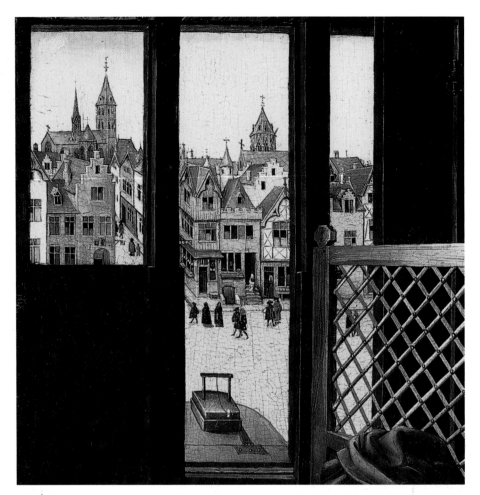

19–11 • Workshop of the Master of Flémalle **A FLEMISH CITY**
Detail of the right wing of the Mérode Altarpiece (FIG. 19–10).

the shop window, with people going about their daily business (**FIG. 19–11**). Even here there is religious symbolism. On the windowsill of Joseph's shop is a mousetrap (another sits on the workbench next to him), which fifteenth-century viewers would understand as a reference to Christ as the bait in a trap set by God to catch Satan. Joseph is drilling holes in a small board used as a drainboard for making wine, calling to mind the Eucharist and Christ's Passion.

The complex and consistent treatment of light in the Mérode Altarpiece represents a major preoccupation of Flemish painters. The strongest illumination comes from an unseen source at the upper left in front of the **picture plane** (the picture's front surface) as if sunlight were entering through the opened front of the room. More light comes from the rear windows, and a few painted, linear rays come from the round window at left, a symbolic vehicle for the Christ Child's descent. Jesus seems to slide down the rays of light linking God with Mary, carrying the cross of human salvation over his shoulder. The light falling on the Virgin's lap emphasizes this connection, and the transmission of the symbolic light through a transparent panel of glass (which remains intact) recalls the virginal nature of Jesus' conception.

JAN VAN EYCK In 1425, Jan van Eyck (active 1420s–1441) became court painter to Duke Philip the Good of Burgundy (r. 1419–1467), who was the uncle of the king of France and one of the most sophisticated men in Europe. Philip made Jan one of his confidential employees and even sent him on a diplomatic mission to Portugal, charged with painting a portrait of a prospective bride for himself. The duke alluded to Jan's remarkable technical skills in a letter of 1434–1435, saying that he could find no other painter equal to his taste or so excellent in art and science. So brilliant was Jan's use of oil glazes that he was mistakenly credited with the invention of **oil painting** (see "Oil Painting," page 573).

Jan's 1433 portrait of a **MAN IN A RED TURBAN** (**FIG. 19–12**) projects a particularly strong sense of personality, and the signed and dated frame also bears Jan's personal motto—"As I can, [but not as I would]"—in Greek letters at the top. Since these letters also form an anagram of his own name, most scholars see this painting as a self-portrait in which physical appearance seems recorded in a magnifying mirror. We see the stubble of a day's growth of beard on his chin and cheeks, and every carefully described wrinkle around the artist's eyes, reddened from the strain of his work,

19-12 • Jan van Eyck MAN IN A RED TURBAN
1433. Oil on wood panel, 13⅛″ × 10¼″ (33.3 × 25.8 cm). National Gallery, London.

sunlight coming through the window of the very chapel where it was meant to be installed. Jan's painting is firmly grounded in the terrestrial world even when he is rendering a visionary subject.

The Ghent altarpiece may have been Jan's most famous painting during his lifetime, but his best-known painting today is a distinctive double portrait of a couple identified as a Giovanni Arnolfini and his wife (see FIG. 19-1). Early interpreters saw this fascinating work as a wedding or betrothal. Above the mirror on the back wall (FIG. 19-13), the artist inscribed the words: *Johannes de eyck fuit hic 1434* ("Jan van Eyck was here 1434"). More normal as a signature would have been, "Jan van Eyck made this," so the words "was here" might suggest that Jan served as a witness to a matrimonial episode portrayed in the painting. Jan is not the only witness recorded in the painting. The convex mirror between the figures reflects not only the back of the couple but a front view of two visitors standing in the doorway, entering the room. Perhaps one of them is the artist himself.

New research has complicated the developing interpretation of this painting by revealing that the Giovanni Arnolfini traditionally identified as the man in this painting married his wife Giovanna Cenami only in 1447, long after the date on the wall and Jan van Eyck's own death. One scholar has proposed that the picture is actually a prospective portrait of Giovanni and Giovanna's marriage in the future, painted in 1434 to secure the early transfer of the dowry from her father to her future husband. Others have more recently suggested the man portrayed here is a different Giovanni Arnolfini, accompanied either by his putative second wife or a memorial portrait of his first wife, Costanza Trenta, who died the year before this picture was painted, perhaps in childbirth. The true meaning of this fascinating masterpiece may remain a mystery, but it is doubtful that scholars will stop trying to solve it.

and reflecting light that seems to emanate from our own space. That same light source gives the inscriptions the *trompe l'oeil* sense of having been engraved into the frame, heightening the illusionistic wizardry of Jan's painting. Is Jan looking out directly at us, or are we seeing his reflection in a mirror?

In his lifetime, one of the most famous works of Jan van Eyck was a huge polyptych with a very complicated and learned theological program that he (perhaps in collaboration with his brother Hubert) painted for a chapel in what is now the Cathedral of St. Bavo in Ghent (see "The Ghent Altarpiece," page 578). The three-dimensional mass of the figures, the voluminous draperies as well as their remarkable surface realism, and the scrupulous attention to the luminous details of textures as variable as jewels and human flesh, are magnificent examples of Jan's artistic wizardry. He has carefully controlled the lighting within this multi-panel ensemble to make it appear that the objects represented are illuminated by

ROGIER VAN DER WEYDEN Little as we know about Jan van Eyck, we know even less about the life of Rogier van der Weyden (c. 1400–1464). Not a single existing work of art bears his name. He may have studied under the Master of Flémalle, but the relationship is not altogether clear. Having first established himself in 1432 as an independent master in Tournai, Rogier maintained at the peak of his career a large workshop in Brussels, where he was the official city painter, attracting apprentices and shop assistants from as far away as Italy. To establish the stylistic characteristics of Rogier's art, scholars have turned to a painting of the **DEPOSITION** (FIG. 19-16), an altarpiece commissioned by

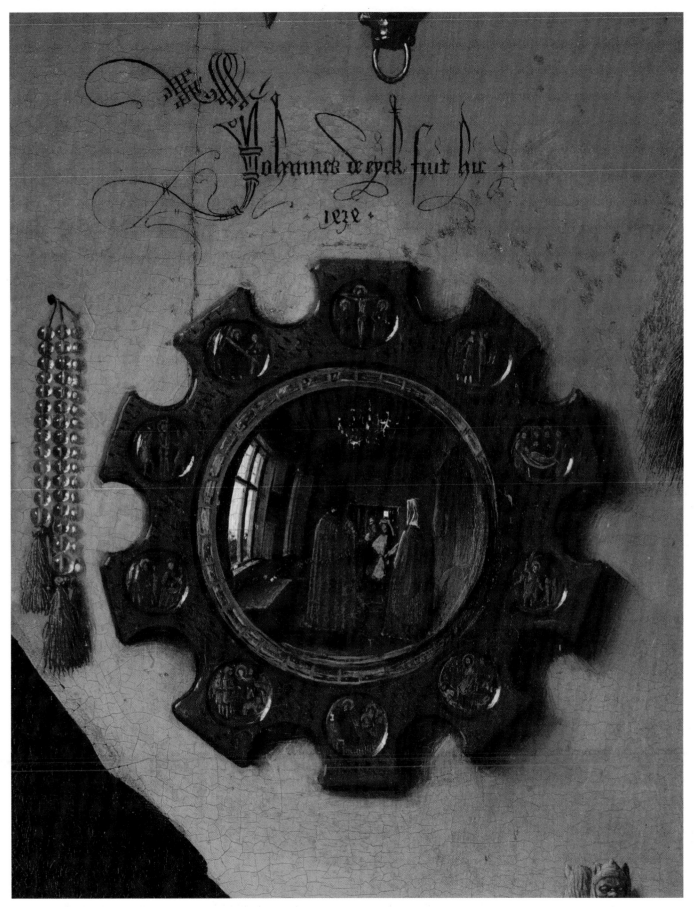

19–13 • Jan van Eyck DETAIL OF MIRROR AND SIGNATURE IN A DOUBLE PORTRAIT OF GIOVANNI ARNOLFINI AND HIS WIFE (FIG. 19–1)
1434. Oil on wood panel. The National Gallery, London.

An inscription on the frame of the Ghent Altarpiece seems to identify both Jan and Hubert van Eyck as its artists: "The painter Hubert van Eyck, greater than whom no one was found, began [this work]; and Jan, his brother, second in art, having carried through the task at the expense of Jodocus Vyd, invites you by this verse, on the sixth of May [1432], to look at what has been done."

Many art historians believe Hubert began this altarpiece, and after his death in 1426, Jan completed it, when free of ducal responsibilities in 1430–1432. Others believe the entire painting was produced by Jan and his workshop, Hubert perhaps being responsible for the frame. At least commission and situation are clear. Jodocus Vijd, who appears with his wife Isabella Borluut on the outside of the polyptych's two shutters—both visible only when the altarpiece is closed—commanded the work. One of a wealthy family of financiers, Jodocus was a city official in Ghent—holding an office comparable to mayor in 1433–1434—and the altarpiece was part of a renovation he funded in the family chapel at the parish church of St. John (now the Cathedral of St. Bavo). He also endowed daily Masses in the chapel for the couple's salvation, and that of their ancestors.

When the altarpiece was closed (FIG. 19–14), the exterior of the shutters displayed the striking likenesses of the donor couple kneeling to face painted statues of SS. John the Baptist (patron of Ghent) and John the Evangelist (patron of this church) that recall those on Sluter's *Well of Moses* (see FIG. 19–3). Above this row is an expansive rendering of the Annunciation—whose somber color scheme coordinates with the *grisaille* statues painted below—situated in an upstairs room that looks out over a panoramic cityscape. As in Simone Martini's Annunciation altarpiece (see FIG. 18–13), the words that issue from Gabriel's mouth ("Hail, full of grace, the Lord is with thee") appear on the painting's surface, and here there is Mary's response as well ("Behold the handmaid of the Lord"), only it is painted upside down since it is directed to God, who hovers above her head as the dove of the Holy Spirit. Prophets and sibyls perch in the irregular compartments at the top, unfurling scrolls recording their predictions of Christ's coming.

When the shutters were opened (FIG. 19–15) on Sundays and feast days, the mood changed. The effect is no longer muted, but rich in both color and implied sound. Dominating the altarpiece by size, central location, and brilliant color is the enthroned, red-robed figure of God, wearing the triple papal crown, with an earthly crown at his feet, and flanked by the Virgin Mary and John the Baptist, each holding an open book. To either side are first angel musicians and then Adam and Eve, represented as lifelike nudes. Adam seems to have been painted from a model, from whom Jan reproduced even the "farmer's

19-14 • Jan and Hubert (?) van Eyck GHENT ALTARPIECE (CLOSED), ANNUNCIATION WITH DONORS
Completed 1432. Oil on panel, height 11'5" (3.48 m). Cathedral of St. Bavo, Ghent.

tan" of his hands and face. Eve displays clear features of the female anatomy; the pigmented line running downward from her navel appears frequently during pregnancy. Each of the three themes of the upper register—God with Mary and John, musical angels, and Adam and Eve—is set in a distinct space: the holy trio in a golden shrine, angels against a blue sky, Adam and Eve in shallow stone niches.

The five lower panels present a unified field. A vast landscape with meadows, woods, and distant cities is set against a continuous horizon. A diverse array of saints—apostles, martyrs, confessors, virgins, hermits, pilgrims, warriors, judges—assembles to adore the Lamb of God as described in the book of Revelation. The Lamb stands on an altar, blood flowing into a chalice, ultimately leading to the fountain of life.

The Ghent altarpiece became a famous work of art almost as soon as it was completed. To celebrate Duke Philip the Good's visit to the city in 1458, citizens of Ghent welcomed him with *tableaux vivants* (living pictures) of its scenes. German artist Albrecht Dürer traveled to Ghent to see the altarpiece in 1521. During the French occupation of Flanders in 1794 it was transferred to Paris (returned in 1815), and during World War II it was confiscated by the Nazis. It is now displayed within a secure glass case in the baptismal chapel of the church for which it was made.

19–15 • Jan and Hubert (?) van Eyck GHENT ALTARPIECE (OPEN), ADORATION OF THE MYSTIC LAMB
Completed 1432. Oil on panel, 11′5¾″ × 15′1½″ (3.5 × 4.6 m). Cathedral of St. Bavo, Ghent.

Read the document related to Jan van Eyck and the Ghent Altarpiece on myartslab.com

19–16 • Rogier van der Weyden DEPOSITION
From an altarpiece commissioned by the crossbowmen's guild, Louvain, Belgium. Before 1443, possibly c. 1435–1438.
Oil on wood panel, 7′2⅝″ × 8′7⅛″ (2.2 × 2.62 m). Museo del Prado, Madrid.

View the Closer Look for the *Deposition* on myartslab.com

the Louvain crossbowmen's guild (crossbows can be seen in the tracery painted in the upper corners) sometime before 1443, the date of the earliest known copy of it by another artist.

The Deposition was a popular theme in the fifteenth century because of its potential for dramatic, personally engaging portrayal. Rogier sets the act of removing Jesus' body from the cross on the shallow stage of a gilt wooden box, just like the case of a carved and painted altarpiece. The ten solid, three-dimensional figures, however, are not simulations of polychromed wood carving, but near life-size renderings of actual human figures who seem to press forward into the viewers' space, allowing them no escape from the forceful expressions of heartrending grief. Jesus' friends seem palpably real, with their portraitlike faces and scrupulously described contemporary dress, as they tenderly and sorrowfully remove his body from the cross for burial. Jesus' corpse dominates the center of the composition, drooping in a languid curve, framed

by jarringly thin, angular arms. His pose is echoed by the rhyming form of the swooning Virgin. It is as if mother and son share in the redemptive passion of his death on the cross, encouraging viewers to identify with them both, or to join their assembled companions in mourning their fate. Although united by sorrow, the mourning figures react in personal ways, from the intensity of Mary Magdalen at far right, wringing her hands in anguish, to John the Evangelist's blank stare at left, lost in grief as he reaches to support the collapsing Virgin. The anguish of the woman behind him, mopping her tear-soaked eyes with the edge of her veil, is almost unbearably poignant.

Rogier's choice of color and pattern balances and enhances his composition. The complexity of the gold brocade worn by Joseph of Arimathea, who offered his new tomb for the burial, and the contorted pose and vivid dress of Mary Magdalen increase the visual impact of the right side of the panel to counter the pictorial weight of the larger number of figures at the left. The palette contrasts subtle, slightly muted colors with brilliant expanses of blue and red, while white accents focus the viewers' attention on the main subjects. The whites of the winding cloth and the tunic of the youth on the ladder set off Jesus' pale body, as the white turban and shawl emphasize the ashen face of Mary.

Another work by Rogier, painted at about the same time as the Deposition, is both quieter and more personal. It represents the evangelist St. Luke executing a preparatory drawing in silverpoint for a painting of the Virgin and Child who seem to have materialized to pose for him (**FIG. 19-17**). The painting is based on a legend with origins in sixth-century Byzantium of a miraculous appearance of the Virgin and Child to Luke so he could record their appearance and pass on his authentic witness to his Christian followers. Rogier's version takes place in a carefully defined interior space that opens onto a garden, and from there into a distant vista of urban life before dissolving into the countryside through which a winding river guides our exploration all the way to the horizon. The Virgin is preoccupied with a routine maternal activity. Her baby has pulled away from her breast, producing a smile and flexing his hand—familiar gestures of actual babies during nursing. The good mother and happy baby are observed by Luke, who, half-kneeling, captures the

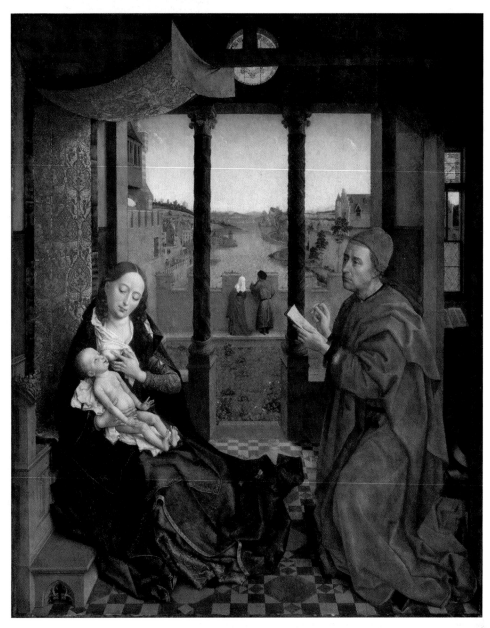

19-17 • Rogier van der Weyden **ST. LUKE DRAWING THE VIRGIN AND CHILD**
c. 1435–1440. Oil and tempera on wood panel, 54¼″ × 43⅝″ (137.7 × 110.8 cm).
Museum of Fine Arts, Boston.

scene in a silverpoint sketch, a common preliminary step used by fifteenth-century Flemish painters in the planning of their paintings, especially portraits. And the portraitlike quality of Luke's face here has led scholars to propose that this image of a saint is a self-portrait of its artist.

Art historians have traditionally interpreted this painting in two ways. Some see it—especially if it is a self-portrait—as a document of Rogier's sense of his own profession. They see him distancing himself and his fifteenth-century Flemish colleagues from identification with the laboring artisans of the Middle Ages, and staking a claim for his special role as an inspired creator who recorded sacred visions in valuable, individualistic works of art. The notion of Rogier's own identification with Luke in this painting is supported by the fact that later artists emulated his composition

in creating their own self-portraits as the century progressed. But other art historians, proposing that this painting was created for the chapel of the guildhall of the painters in Brussels (the evidence is suggestive but unclear), have interpreted it as a claim for the importance of the painters' profession because it is rooted in saintly legend. Perhaps this extraordinary picture was both self-fashioning and professional propaganda. But it was also a devotional image. Luke's tenuous, half-kneeling posture, and his dreamy, introspective gaze certainly remind us that one of the tasks of painters in this period was to create inspiring pictures of religious visions that are also materialized by meticulous references to the real world. This most certainly is that. (For another painting by Rogier van der Weyden, see FIG. Intro-6, and its discussion in the Introduction.)

PAINTING AT MID CENTURY: THE SECOND GENERATION

The extraordinary accomplishments of the Master of Flémalle, Jan van Eyck, and Rogier van der Weyden attracted many followers in Flanders. The work of this second generation of Flemish painters may have been simpler, more direct, often easier to understand than that of their predecessors, but they produced extraordinary works of great emotional power. They were in large part responsible for the rapid spread of the Flemish style throughout Europe.

PETRUS CHRISTUS Among the most interesting of these painters was Petrus Christus (active 1444–c. 1475/1476), who became a citizen of Bruges in 1444 and signed and dated six paintings in a career that extended over three decades.

In 1449, Christus painted a portrait of a goldsmith, serving two well-dressed customers in his shop (see "A Closer Look," opposite). A halo around the head of the seated figure—not originally a part of the painting—was removed by restorers in 1993. This coincided with a reevaluation of the subject matter of the work, now seen as a vocational portrait of an actual goldsmith, rather than an image of St. Eloi, patron saint of goldsmiths, set in the present. Both finished products and raw materials of the jeweler's trade sit on the shelves behind the goldsmith: containers, rings, brooches, a belt buckle, a string of beads, pearls, gemstones, coral, and crystal cylinders. A betrothal belt curls across the counter. Such a combination of objects suggests that the painting expresses the hope for health and well-being for the couple who may be in the process of procuring rings for their upcoming marriage.

As in Jan van Eyck's double portrait, a convex mirror extends the viewer's field of vision, in this instance to the street outside, where two men appear. One is stylishly dressed in red and black, and the other holds a falcon, another indication of high status. Whether or not the reflected image has symbolic meaning, the mirror would have had practical value in a goldsmith's shop, allowing him to observe the approach of potential customers to the counter outside his shop window.

DIERIC BOUTS Dieric Bouts (active c. 1444–1475) is best known among Flemish painters as a storyteller, and he exercised those skills in a series of large altarpieces, with narrative scenes drawn from the life of Christ and the lives of the saints. But he also created more intimate pictures, such as this tender rendering of the **VIRGIN AND CHILD**, just 8½ inches tall (**FIG. 19-18**). Even it evokes a story. Mary holds her baby securely, using both of her plain, strong hands to surround completely the lower part of his body. The baby reaches across his mother's chest and around her neck, pulling himself closer to press his face next to hers, cheek to cheek, nose to nose, mouth to mouth, eyes locked together, forming a symmetrical system that links them in pattern and almost melds them into a single mirrored form. It is as if a fifteenth-century St. Luke had captured a private moment

19-18 • Dieric Bouts VIRGIN AND CHILD
c. 1455–1460. Oil on wood panel, 8½″ × 6½″ (21.6 × 16.5 cm).
Metropolitan Museum of Art, New York.

between the Virgin and Child—a dimpled mother and baby looking very much like the actual people in the artist's world—during their miraculous appearance to sit as his model (compare **FIG. 19-17**). The concept is actually not so far-fetched. Bouts's painting is modeled after a fourteenth-century Italian image in the cathedral of Cambrai that in the fifteenth century was believed to have been painted by St. Luke himself.

HUGO VAN DER GOES Hugo van der Goes (c. 1440–1482), dean of the painters' guild in Ghent (1468–1475), united the intellectual prowess of Jan van Eyck with the emotional sensitivity of Rogier van der Weyden to create an entirely new personal style. Hugo's major work was an exceptionally large altarpiece, more than 8 feet tall, of the Nativity (**FIG. 19-19**), commissioned by Tommaso Portinari, head of the Medici bank in Bruges. Painted probably between 1474 and 1476, the triptych was sent to Florence and installed in 1483 in the Portinari family chapel, where it had a noticeable impact on Florentine painters.

Tommaso, his wife Maria Baroncelli, and their three oldest children are portrayed kneeling in prayer on the side panels of the

A CLOSER LOOK | *A Goldsmith in his Shop*

by Petrus Christus. 1449. Oil on oak panel, 38⅝″ × 33½″ (98 × 85 cm).
Metropolitan Museum of Art, New York. Robert Lehman Collection, 1975. 1975.1.110

The coat of arms of the dukes of Guelders hangs from a chain around this man's neck, leading some to speculate that the woman, who is the more active of the pair, is Mary of Guelders, niece of Duke Philip the Good, who married King James II of the Scots the same year this picture was painted.

Goldsmiths were expected to perform all their transactions, including the weighing of gold, in public view to safeguard against dishonesty. Here the scales tip toward the couple, perhaps an allusion to the scales of the Last Judgment, which always tip to the side of the righteous.

Three types of coins rest on the shop counter: "florins" from Mainz, "angels" from English King Henry VI's French territories, and "riders" minted under Philip the Good. Such diversity of currency could show the goldsmith's cosmopolitanism, or they could indicate his participation in money changing, since members of that profession belonged to the same guild as goldsmiths.

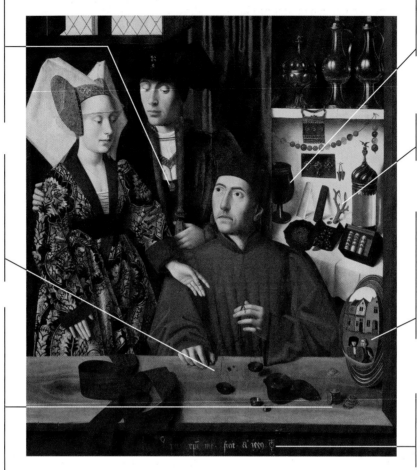

This coconut cup was supposed to neutralize poison. The slabs of porphyry and rock crystal were "touchstones," used to test gold and precious stones.

The red coral and serpents' tongues (actually fossilized sharks' teeth) were intended to ward off the evil eye.

Two men, one with a falcon on his arm, are reflected in the obliquely placed mirror as they stand in front of the shop. The edges of the reflection catch the red sleeve of the goldsmith and the door frame, uniting the interior and exterior spaces and drawing the viewer into the painting.

The artist signed and dated his work in a bold inscription that appears just under the tabletop at the bottom of the painting: "Master Petrus Christus made me in the year 1449."

View the Closer Look for *A Goldsmith in his Shop* on myartslab.com

wing interiors. On the left wing, looming larger than life behind Tommaso and his son Antonio, are their name saints—SS. Thomas and Anthony of Egypt. Since the younger son, Pigello, born in 1474, was apparently added after the original composition was set, his saintly counterpart is lacking. On the right wing, Maria and her daughter Margherita are presented by SS. Mary Magdalen and Margaret.

The theme of the altarpiece is the Nativity as told by Luke (2:10–19). The central panel represents the Adoration of the newborn Christ Child by Mary and Joseph, a host of angels, and the shepherds who have rushed in from the fields. In the middle ground of the wings are additional scenes. Winding their way through the winter landscape are two groups headed for Bethlehem. On the left wing, Mary and Joseph travel there to take part in a census. Near term in her pregnancy, Mary has dismounted from her donkey and staggers, supported by Joseph. On the right wing, a servant of the three Magi, who are coming to honor the awaited Savior, asks directions from a peasant.

Hugo paints meadows and woods meticulously, and he used atmospheric perspective to approximate distance in the landscape. He shifts figure size hierarchically for emphasis: The huge figures of Joseph, Mary, and the shepherds are the same size as the patron saints on the wings, in contrast to the much smaller Portinari family and still smaller angels. Hugo also uses light, as well as the gestures and gazes of the figures, to focus our eyes on the center panel where the mystery of the Incarnation takes place. Instead of lying swaddled in a manger or in his mother's arms, Jesus rests naked and vulnerable on the barren ground. Rays of light emanate from his body. This image was based on the visionary writing of the medieval Swedish mystic St. Bridget (who composed her work c. 1360–1370), which describes Mary kneeling to adore the Christ Child immediately after giving birth.

19-19 • Hugo van der Goes PORTINARI ALTARPIECE (OPEN) c. 1474–1476. Tempera and oil on wood panel; center 8′3½″ × 10′ (2.53 × 3.01 m), wings each 8′3½″ × 4′7½″ (2.53 × 1.41 m). Galleria degli Uffizi, Florence.

As in the work of Jan van Eyck, aspects of the setting of this painting are infused with symbolic meaning. In the foreground, the wheatsheaf refers both to the location of the event at Bethlehem, which in Hebrew means "house of bread," and to the Eucharistic Host, which represents the body of Christ. The majolica albarello is decorated with vines and grapes, alluding to the Eucharistic wine, which represents the blood of Christ. It holds a red lily for Christ's blood and three irises—white for purity and purple for Christ's royal ancestry. The seven blue columbines in the glass vessel remind the viewer of the Virgin's future sorrows, and scattered on the ground are violets, symbolizing humility. But Hugo's artistic vision transcends such formal religious symbolism. For example, the shepherds, who stand in unaffected awe before the miraculous event, are among the most sympathetically rendered images of common people to be found in the art of any period, and the portraits of the Portinari children are unusually sensitive renderings of the delicate features of youthful faces.

HANS MEMLING The artist who seems to summarize and epitomize painting in Flanders during the second half of the fifteenth century is German-born Hans Memling (c. 1435–1494). Memling combines the intellectual depth and virtuoso rendering of his predecessors with a delicacy of feeling and exquisite grace, a "prettiness" that made his work exceptionally popular. Memling may have worked in Rogier van der Weyden's Brussels workshop in the 1460s, but soon after Rogier's death in 1464, Memling moved to Bruges, where he developed an international clientele that supported a thriving workshop. He also worked for local patrons.

In 1487, the 24-year-old Maarten van Nieuwenhove (1463–1500), member of a powerful political family in Bruges (he would himself become mayor of Bruges in 1497), commissioned from Memling a diptych that combined a meticulously detailed portrait with a visionary apparition of the Virgin and Child, presented as a powerful fiction of their physical encounter in Maarten's own home (**FIG. 19-20**). This type of devotional diptych was a specialty of Rogier van der Weyden, but Memling transforms the type into something more intimate by placing it in a domestic setting. An expensively outfitted figure of Maarten appears in the right wing of the diptych, seen from an oblique angle, hands folded in prayer. He seems caught in a moment of introspection inspired by personal devotions—his Book of Hours lies still open on the table in front of him. The window just over his shoulder holds a stained-glass rendering of his name saint, Martin, in the top pane, while a recognizable landmark in Bruges can be seen through the opening below. The Virgin and Child on the adjacent panel are presented frontally, and the strong sense of specific likeness characterizing Maarten's portrait has given way to an idealized delicacy and grace in the visage of the Virgin that complements the extravagance of her clothing. Although she does not seem to be focusing on him, a completely nude Jesus stretches out on the silk pillow in front of her; she stabilizes him with one hand and offers him an apple with the other. This seems a clear reference to their roles as the new Adam and Eve, ready to redeem the sin brought into the world by the first couple. The stained glass behind them is filled with heraldry, devices, and a motto associated with Maarten's family.

Memling's construction of a coherent interior space for these figures is both impressive and meaningful. We are looking through two windows into a rectangular room containing this devotional group. The pillow under the Christ Child casts a shadow, painted on the lower frame of the left panel, to intensify the illusion, and the Virgin's scarlet mantle extends under the division between the two wings of the diptych to reappear on Maarten's side of the painting underneath his Book of Hours. This mantle not only connects the two sides of the painting spatially but also relates Maarten's devotional exercise and the apparition of the Virgin and Child. This relationship is also documented with a device already familiar to us in paintings by Jan van Eyck (see FIG. 19–13) and Petrus Christus (see "A Closer Look," page 583). On the shadowy back wall, over the Virgin's right shoulder and set against the closed shutters of a window, is a convex mirror that reflects the backs of both Maarten and Mary, bearing visual witness to their presence together within his domestic space and undoing the division between them that is endemic to the diptych format. Maarten's introspective gaze signals that for him the encounter is internal and spiritual, but Memling transforms Maarten's private devotion into a concrete public statement that promotes an image of his piety and freezes him in perpetual prayer. We bear witness to his vision as an actual event.

EUROPE BEYOND FLANDERS

Flemish art—its complex symbolism and visionary meaning, its coherent configurations of atmospheric space, its luminous colors and sensuous surface textures—delighted wealthy patrons and well-educated courtiers both inside and outside Flanders. At first, Flemish artists worked in foreign courts or their works were commissioned and exported abroad. Flemish manuscripts, tapestries, altarpieces, and portraits appeared in palaces and chapels throughout Europe. Soon regional artists traveled to Flanders to learn oil-painting techniques and practice emulating the Flemish style. By

19–20 • Hans Memling DIPTYCH OF MAARTEN VAN NIEUWENHOVE
1487. Oil on wood panel, each panel (including frames) 20½″ × 16¼″ (52 × 41.5 cm). Hans Memling Museum, Musea Brugge, Sint-Jans Hospital, Bruges.

the end of the fifteenth century, distinctive regional variations of Flemish art could be found throughout Europe, from the Atlantic Ocean to the Danube.

FRANCE

The centuries-long struggle for power and territory between France and England continued well into the fifteenth century. When King Charles VI of France died in 1422, England claimed the throne for the king's 9-month-old grandson, Henry VI of England. The plight of Charles VII, the late French king's son, inspired Joan of Arc to raise an army to return him to the throne. Thanks to Joan's efforts, Charles was crowned at Reims in 1429. Although Joan was burned at the stake in 1431, the revitalized French forces drove the English from French lands. In 1461, Louis XI succeeded his father, Charles VII, as king of France. Under his rule the French royal court again became a major source of patronage for the arts.

JEAN FOUQUET The leading court artist of fifteenth-century France, Jean Fouquet (c. 1425–1481), was born in Tours and may have trained in Paris as an illuminator and in Bourges in the workshop of Jacob de Littemont, Flemish court painter to Charles VII. He was part of a French delegation to Rome in 1446–1448, but by mid century he had established a workshop in Tours and was a renowned painter. Fouquet drew from contemporary Italian Classicism, especially in rendering architecture, and he was also strongly influenced by Flemish illusionism. He painted pictures of Charles VII, the royal family, and courtiers; he also illustrated manuscripts and designed tombs.

Among the court officials who commissioned paintings from Fouquet was Étienne Chevalier, treasurer of France under Charles VII. Fouquet painted a diptych for him that was installed over the tomb of Chevalier's wife Catherine Budé (d. 1452) in the church of Notre-Dame in Melun (**FIG. 19-21**). Chevalier appears in the left panel, kneeling in prayer with clasped hands and an introspective, meditative gaze within an Italianate palace, accompanied by his name saint Stephen (Étienne in French). Fouquet describes the courtier's ruddy features with a mirrorlike precision that is reminiscent of Flemish art. He is expensively dressed in a heavy red wool garment lined with fur, and his "bowl cut" represents the latest fashion in Parisian coiffure. St. Stephen's features convey a comparable sense of likeness and sophistication. A deacon in the Early Christian church in Jerusalem, Stephen was the first Christian martyr, stoned to death for defending his beliefs. Here he wears the fifteenth-century liturgical vestments of a deacon and carries a large stone on a closed Gospel book as evidence of his martyrdom. A trickle of blood can be seen on his tonsured head (male members of religious orders shaved the tops of their heads as a sign of humility). Placing his arm around Étienne Chevalier's back, the saint seems to be introducing the treasurer to the Virgin and Child in the adjacent panel.

19-21 • Jean Fouquet ÉTIENNE CHEVALIER AND ST. STEPHEN, VIRGIN AND CHILD
The Melun Diptych. c. 1452–1455. Oil on oak panel. Left wing: 36½″ × 33½″ (92.7 × 85.5 cm), Staatliche Museen zu Berlin, Preussischer Kulturbesitz, Gemäldegalerie; right wing: 37¼″ × 33½″ (94.5 × 85.5 cm), Koninklijk Museum voor Schone Kunsten, Antwerp, Belgium.

The Virgin and Child, however, exist in another world. A supernatural vision unfolds here as the queen of heaven is enthroned surrounded by red and blue seraphim and cherubim, who form a tapestrylike background. Even the Virgin seems a celestial being, conceived by Fouquet as a hybrid of careful description and powerful abstraction. Her fashionable, tightly waisted bodice has been unlaced so she can present her spherical breast to a substantial, seated baby, who points across the juncture between the two wings of the diptych to acknowledge Chevalier. According to tradition, Fouquet gave this image of the Virgin the features of the king's much loved and respected mistress, Agnès Sorel, who died in 1450. The original frame that united these two panels—now divided between two museums—into a diptych is lost, but among the fragments that remain is a stunning medallion self-portrait that served as the artist's signature.

JEAN HEY, THE MASTER OF MOULINS Perhaps the greatest French follower of Jean Fouquet is an artist who for many years was known as the Master of Moulins after a large triptych he painted at the end of the fifteenth century under the patronage of Duke Jean II of Bourbon, for the Burgundian Cathedral of Moulins. This triptych combines the exuberance of Flemish attention to brilliant color and the differentiation of surface texture with a characteristically French air of reserved detachment. Recently the work of this artist has been associated with the name Jean Hey, a painter of Flemish origin, who seems to have been trained in the workshop of Hugo van der Goes, but who pursued his career at the French court.

This charming portrait (**FIG. 19–22**)—which may have been one half of a devotional diptych comparable to that painted by Memling for Maarten van Nieuwenhove (see FIG. 19–20)—portrays Margaret of Austria (1480–1530), daughter of Emperor Maximilian I, who had been betrothed to the future French king Charles VIII (r. 1483–1498) at age 2 or 3 and was being brought up at the French court. She would return home to her father in 1493 after Charles decided to pursue another, more politically expedient marriage (after two political marriages of her own, the widowed Margaret would eventually become governor of the Habsburg Netherlands), but Hey captures her at a tender moment a few years before those troubled times. She kneels in front of a strip of wall between two windows that open onto a lush country landscape, fingering the pearl beads of her rosary. Details of her lavish velvet and ermine outfit not only proclaim her wealth but provide the clues to her identity—the *Cs* and *Ms* embroidered on her collar signal her betrothal to Charles and the ostentatious *fleur-de-lis* pendant set with large rubies and pearls proclaims her affiliation with the French court. But it is the delicacy and sweet vulnerability of this 10-year-old girl that are most arresting. They recall Hugo van der Goes's sensitivity to the childlike qualities of the young members of donor families (see FIG. 19–19) and provide one strong piece of evidence for ascribing Hey's training to the workshop of this Flemish master.

19–22 • Jean Hey (The Master of Moulins) PORTRAIT OF MARGARET OF AUSTRIA
c. 1490. Oil on wood panel, 12⅞″ × 9⅛″ (32.7 × 23 cm). Metropolitan Museum of Art, New York. Robert Lehman Collection

FLAMBOYANT ARCHITECTURE The great age of cathedral building that had begun in the second half of the twelfth century was essentially over by the end of the fourteenth century, but growing urban populations needed houses, city halls, guildhalls, and more parish churches. It was in buildings such as these that late Gothic architecture took form in a style we call "Flamboyant" because of its repeated, twisted, flamelike tracery patterns. Late Gothic masons covered their buildings with increasingly elaborate, complex, and at times playful architectural decoration. Like painters, sculptors also turned to describing the specific nature of the world around them, and they covered capitals and moldings with ivy, hawthorn leaves, and other vegetation, not just the conventional acanthus motifs inherited from the Classical world.

The **CHURCH OF SAINT-MACLOU** in Rouen, which was begun after a fund-raising campaign in 1432 and dedicated in 1521, is an outstanding and well-preserved example of Flamboyant Gothic (**FIG. 19–23**) probably designed by the Paris architect Pierre Robin. A projecting porch bends to enfold the façade of the church in a screen of tracery. Sunlight on the flame-shape openings casts ever-changing shadows across the intentionally complex surface. **Crockets**—small, knobby leaflike ornaments that line the

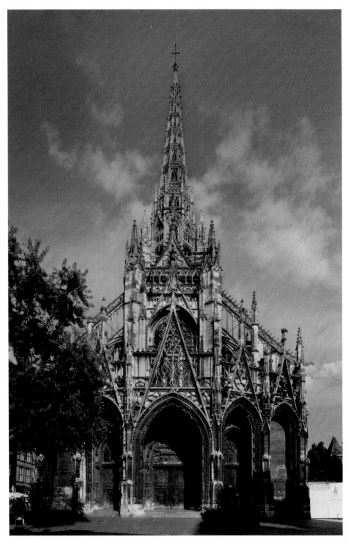

19-23 • Pierre Robin (?) CHURCH OF SAINT-MACLOU, ROUEN
Normandy, France. West façade, 1432–1521; façade c. 1500–1514.

Present-day Germany and Switzerland were situated within the Holy Roman Empire, a loose confederation of primarily German-speaking states. Artisan guilds grew powerful and trade flourished under the auspices of the Hanseatic League, an association of cities and trading outposts, stimulating a strengthening of the merchant

courtyard

19-24 • PLAN (A) AND INTERIOR COURTYARD (B) OF JACQUES COEUR HOUSE
Bourges, France. 1443–1451.

steep gables and slender buttresses—break every defining line. In the Flamboyant style, decoration sometimes disguises structural elements with an overlay of tracery and ornament in geometric and natural shapes, all to dizzying effect.

The house of Jacques Coeur, a fabulously wealthy merchant in Bourges, reflects the popularity of the Flamboyant style for secular architecture (**FIG. 19-24**). Built at great expense between 1443 and 1451, it survives almost intact, although it has been stripped of its rich furnishings. The rambling, palatial house is built around an irregular open courtyard, with spiral stairs in octagonal towers giving access to the upper-floor rooms. Tympana over doors indicate the function of the rooms within; for example, over the door to the kitchen a cook stirs the contents of a large bowl. Among the carved decorations are puns on the patron's surname, Coeur (meaning "heart" in French). The house was also Jacques Coeur's place of business, so it had large storerooms for goods and a strongroom for treasure.

19-25 • Konrad Witz MIRACULOUS DRAFT OF FISHES
From an altarpiece for the Cathedral of St. Peter, Geneva, Switzerland. 1444. Oil on wood panel,
4′3″ × 5′1″ (1.29 × 1.55 m). Musée d'Art et d'Histoire, Geneva.

class. The Fugger family, for example, began their spectacular rise from simple textile workers and linen merchants to bankers for the Habsburgs and the popes.

KONRAD WITZ Germanic fifteenth-century artists worked in two very different styles. Some, clustered around Cologne, continued the International Gothic style with increased prettiness, softness, and sweetness of expression. Other artists began an intense investigation and detailed description of the physical world. The major exponent of the latter style was Konrad Witz (active 1434–1446). A native of Swabia in southern Germany, Witz moved to Basel (in present-day Switzerland), where he found a rich source of patronage in the Church.

Witz's last large commission before his early death in 1446 was an altarpiece dedicated to St. Peter for the cathedral of Geneva, signed and dated to 1444. In one of its scenes—the **MIRACU-LOUS DRAFT OF FISHES** (**FIG. 19-25**)—Jesus appears posthumously to his disciples as they fish on the Sea of Galilee and Peter

leaps from the boat to greet him. But Witz sets the scene on the Lake of Geneva, with the distinctive dark mountain (the Mole) rising on the north shore and the snow-covered Alps shining in the distance. Witz records every nuance of light and water—the rippling surface, the reflections of boats, figures, and buildings, even the lake bottom. Peter's body and legs, visible through the water, are distorted by the refraction. It is one of the earliest times in European art that an artist captures both the appearance and the spirit of nature.

MICHAEL PACHER In Germanic lands, patrons preferred altarpieces that featured polychromed wood carvings rather than the large ensembles of panel paintings that we saw in Flanders (for example, "The Ghent Altarpiece," page 578). One of the greatest artists working in this tradition was painter and sculptor Michael Pacher (1435–1498), based in Bruneck, now in the Italian Alps. In 1471, Benedict Eck, abbot of Mondsee, commissioned from Pacher for the pilgrimage church of St. Wolfgang a grand high

19–26 • Michael Pacher
ST. WOLFGANG ALTARPIECE
Church of St. Wolfgang, Austria. 1471–1481. Carved, painted, and gilt wood; wings are oil on wood panel.

altarpiece that is still installed in its original church setting (**FIG. 19-26**). The surviving contract specifies materials and subject matter and even documents the cost—1,200 Hungarian florins—but sets no time limit for its completion. Pacher and his shop worked on it for ten years.

When it is open (as in FIG. 19-26), a dizzyingly complicated sculptural ensemble aligns up the middle, flanked by four large panel paintings portraying scenes from the life of the Virgin on the opened shutters. Both the design and execution were supervised by Pacher, but many other artists collaborated with him on the actual carving and painting. In the main scene, the wood carvings create a vision in Paradise where Christ crowns his mother as the queen of heaven, flanked by imposing images of local saints. The use of soft wood facilitated deep undercutting and amazing detail in the rendering of these figures, and the elaborate polychromy and gold leaf sheathed them in a shimmering finish that glitters in the changing patterns of natural light or the flickering glow of candles. It must have been an otherworldly sight.

19-27 • THE BUXHEIM ST. CHRISTOPHER
Mid 15th century. Hand-colored woodcut, 11⅜″ × 8⅛″ (28.85 × 20.7 cm).
Courtesy of the Director and Librarian, the John Rylands University Library, the
University of Manchester, England.

The Latin text reads, "Whenever you look at the face of St. Christopher, you will not die a terrible death that day."

THE GRAPHIC ARTS

Printmaking emerged in Europe at the end of the fourteenth century with the development of printing presses and the increased local manufacture and wider availability of paper. The techniques used by printmakers during the fifteenth century were woodcut and engraving (see "Woodcuts and Engravings on Metal," page 592). **Woodblocks** cut in relief had long been used to print designs on cloth, but only in the fifteenth century did the printing of images and texts on paper and the production of books in multiple copies of a single edition, or version, begin to replace the copying of each book by hand. Both hand-written and printed books were often illustrated, and printed images were sometimes hand-colored.

SINGLE SHEETS

Large quantities of single-sheet prints were made using woodcut and engraving techniques in the early decades of the fifteenth century. Often artists drew the images for professional woodworkers to cut from the block.

THE BUXHEIM ST. CHRISTOPHER Devotional images were sold as souvenirs to pilgrims at holy sites. **THE BUXHEIM ST. CHRISTOPHER** was found in the Carthusian monastery of Buxheim, in southern Germany, glued to the inside of the back cover of a manuscript (**FIG. 19-27**). St. Christopher, patron saint of travelers and protector from the plague, carries the Christ Child across the river. His efforts are witnessed by a monk holding out a light to guide him to the monastery door, but ignored by the hardworking millers on the opposite bank. Both the cutting of

19-27 • THE BUXHEIM ST. CHRISTOPHER
Mid 15th century. Hand-colored woodcut, 11⅜″ × 8⅛″ (28.85 × 20.7 cm).
Courtesy of the Director and Librarian, the John Rylands University Library, the University of Manchester, England.

the block and the quality of the printing are very high. Lines vary in width to strengthen major forms. Delicate lines are used for inner modeling (facial features) and short parallel lines to indicate shadows (the inner side of draperies). The date 1423, which is cut into the block, was once thought to identify this print as among the earliest to survive. Recent studies have determined that the date refers to some event, and the print is now dated at mid century.

MARTIN SCHONGAUER Engraving may have originated with goldsmiths and armorers, who recorded their work by rubbing lampblack into the engraved lines and pressing paper over the plate. German artist Martin Schongauer (c. 1435–1491), who learned engraving from his goldsmith father, was an immensely skillful printmaker who excelled both in drawing and in the difficult technique of shading from deep blacks to faintest grays using only line. In **THE TEMPTATIONS OF ST. ANTHONY**, probably engraved during the 1470s (**FIG. 19-28**), Schongauer illustrated the original biblical meaning of temptation as a physical assault

19-28 • Martin Schongauer THE TEMPTATIONS OF ST. ANTHONY
c. 1470–1480. Engraving, 12¼″ × 9″ (31.1 × 22.9 cm).
Metropolitan Museum of Art, New York. Rogers Fund, 1920 (20.5.2)

Woodcuts are made by drawing on the smooth surface of a block of fine-grained wood, then cutting away all the areas around the lines with a sharp tool called a gouge, leaving the lines in high relief. When the block's surface is inked and a piece of paper pressed down hard on it, the ink on the relief areas transfers to the paper to create a reverse image. The effects can be varied by making thicker and thinner lines, and shading can be achieved by placing the lines closer or farther apart. Sometimes the resulting black-and-white images were then painted by hand.

Engraving on metal requires a technique called **intaglio**, in which the lines are cut into the plate with tools called gravers or **burins**. The engraver then carefully burnishes the plate to ensure a clean, sharp image. Ink is applied over the whole plate and forced down into the lines, then the plate's surface is carefully wiped clean of the excess ink. When paper and plate are held tightly together by a press, the ink in the recessed lines transfers to the paper.

Woodblocks and metal plates could be used repeatedly to make nearly identical images. If the lines of the block or plate wore down, the artists could repair them. Printing large numbers of identical prints of a single version, called an edition, was usually a team effort in a busy workshop. One artist would make the drawing. Sometimes it was drawn directly on the block or plate with ink, in reverse of its printed direction, sometimes on paper to be transferred in reverse onto the plate or block by another person, who then cut the lines. Others would ink and print the images.

In the illustration of books, the plates or blocks would be reused to print later editions and even adapted for use in other books. A set of blocks or plates for illustrations was a valuable commodity and might be sold by one workshop to another. Early in publishing, there were no copyright laws, and many entrepreneurs simply had their workers copy book illustrations onto woodblocks and cut them for their own publications.

Watch a video about the process of woodcut on myartslab.com

rather than a subtle inducement. Wildly acrobatic, slithery, spiky demons lift Anthony up off the ground to torment and terrify him in midair. The engraver intensified the horror of the moment by condensing the action into a swirling vortex of figures beating, scratching, poking, tugging, and no doubt shrieking at the stoical saint, who remains impervious to all, perhaps because of his power to focus inwardly on his private meditations.

PRINTED BOOKS

The explosion of learning in Europe in the fifteenth century encouraged experiments in faster and cheaper ways of producing books than by hand-copying them. The earliest printed books were block books, for which each page of text, with or without illustrations, was cut in relief on a single block of wood. Movable-type printing, in which individual letters could be arranged and locked together, inked, and then printed onto paper, was first achieved in Europe in the workshop of Johann Gutenberg in Mainz, Germany. More than 40 copies of Gutenberg's Bible, printed around 1455, still exist. As early as 1465, two German printers were working in Italy, and by the 1470s there were presses in France, Flanders, Holland, and Spain. With the invention of this fast way to make a number of identical books, the intellectual and spiritual life of Europe—and with it the arts—changed forever.

THE NUREMBERG CHRONICLE The publication of the *Nuremberg Chronicle* by prosperous Nuremberg printer Anton Koburger was the culmination of his complicated collaboration with scholars, artists, and investors, in an early capitalist enterprise that is a landmark in the history of printed books. The text of this history of the world was compiled by physician and scholar Hartmann Schedel, drawing from the work of colleagues and the extensive holdings of his private library. When Koburger set out to publish Schedel's compilation, he sought financial support from Sebald Schregel and his brother-in-law Sebastian Kammermaister, who had a proven record of patronage in book publishing. He also contracted in the 1480s with artists Michael Wolgemut and Wilhelm Pleydenwurff to produce the woodcut illustrations and in 1491 to work on the layout.

The *Nuremberg Chronicle* was published in 1493 in an edition of 2,500. Woodcut illustrations—1,809 in total—were dispersed throughout the book, spreading across the width of whole pages or tucked into the text along either margin. Those interested in purchasing the book could obtain it in Latin or German, on parchment or on paper, bound or unbound, as it came from the press or tinted with color. It seems fitting that the only instance of a double-page picture—filling the entire expanse of an opening with text restricted to headings and labels—is a

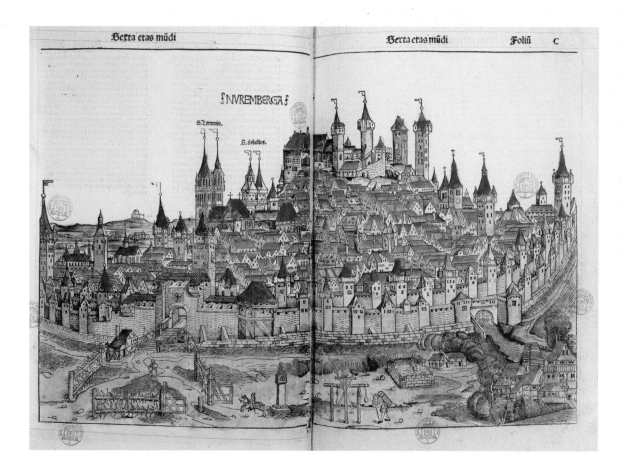

Berta etas mûdi   Berta etas mûdi   Foliũ   C

§ NVREMBERGA §

S. Lanniis.

S. Sebolbus.

19-29 • Michael Wolgemut, Wilhelm Pleydenwurff, and workshop **THE CITY OF NUREMBERG** *Nuremberg Chronicle*, published by Anton Koberger in 1493. Woodcut within a printed book, hand-colored after printing, each page 18½" × 12¾" (47 × 32.4 cm). Bibliothèque Mazarine, Paris.

panoramic view of the city of Nuremberg where this collaborative enterprise was centered (**FIG. 19-29**). Illustrated here is a view of this expansive cityscape in a copy of the book that was originally owned by a bibliophile who could afford to have the woodcuts hand-painted with color to enhance the appearance of this proud Renaissance city's portrait. As we will see, Nuremberg was the site of significant artistic developments in the sixteenth century as well.

THINK ABOUT IT

19.1 Explain how oil-painting technique allowed fifteenth-century Flemish painters to achieve unprecedented descriptive effects in their work. Support your answer by discussing one specific work in this chapter.

19.2 Discuss the symbolic meanings that fifteenth-century viewers would have comprehended in the objects contained in the domestic environment of either the Mérode Altarpiece (FIG. 19–10) or the Arnolfini double portrait (FIG. 19–1).

19.3 How have fifteenth-century northern paintings been characterized as devotional visions of the patrons who are portrayed within them? Use a specific work discussed in this chapter as the focus of your answer.

19.4 Why did printmaking become a major pictorial medium in northern Europe during the fifteenth century? Choose a work discussed in this chapter and explain how it supports your answer.

CROSSCURRENTS

FIG. 18–13

FIG. 19–10

These two paintings portray the same subject. Both were used as altarpieces. But they were painted by artists working in different places and trained in different traditions. Characterize the differences in style and narrative presentation. How are these features related to the cultural context of each?

✓—⌷ **Study** and review on myartslab.com

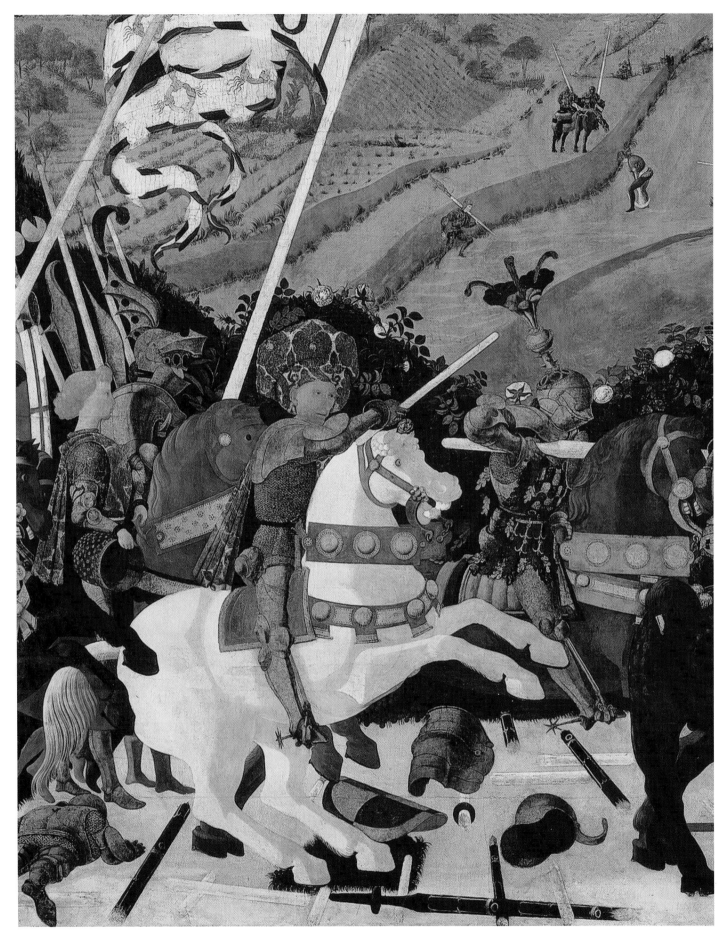

20–1 • Paolo Uccello NICCOLÒ DA TOLENTINO LEADING THE CHARGE
Detail from *The Battle of San Romano* (FIG. 20–24), 1438–1440. Tempera on wood panel. National Gallery, London.

Renaissance Art in Fifteenth-Century Italy

This ferocious but bloodless battle seems to take place in a dream, but it depicts a historical event (**FIG. 20-1**). Under an elegantly fluttering banner, the Florentine general Niccolò da Tolentino leads his men against the Sienese at the Battle of San Romano, which took place on June 1, 1432. The battle rages across a shallow stage defined by the debris of warfare arranged in a neat pattern on a pink ground and backed by blooming hedges. In the center foreground, Niccolò holds aloft a baton of command, the sign of his authority. His bold gesture—together with his white horse and outlandish, though quite fashionable, crimson and gold damask hat— ensures that he dominates the scene. His knights charge into the fray, and when they fall, like the soldier at the lower left, they join the many broken lances on the ground—all arranged in conformity with the new mathematical depiction of receding space called **linear perspective**, posed to align with the implied lines that would converge at a single point on the horizon.

An eccentric Florentine painter nicknamed Paolo Uccello ("Paul Bird") created the panel painting (see FIG. 20-24) from which the detail in FIGURE 20-1 is taken. It is one of three related panels—now separated, hanging in major museums in Florence, London, and Paris—commissioned by Lionardo Bartolini Salimbeni (1404–1479), who led the Florentine governing Council of Ten during the war against Lucca and Siena. Uccello's remarkable accuracy when depicting armor from the 1430s, heraldic banners, and even fashionable fabrics and crests surely would have appealed to Lionardo's civic pride. The hedges of oranges, roses, and pomegranates—all ancient fertility symbols—suggest that Lionardo might have commissioned the paintings at the time of his wedding in 1438. Lionardo and his wife, Maddalena, had six sons, two of whom inherited the paintings.

According to a complaint brought by Damiano, one of the heirs, Lorenzo de' Medici, the powerful *de facto* ruler of Florence, "forcibly removed" the paintings from Damiano's house. They were never returned, and Uccello's masterpieces are recorded in a 1492 inventory as hanging in the Medici palace. Perhaps Lorenzo, who was called "the Magnificent," saw Uccello's heroic pageant as a trophy more worthy of a Medici merchant prince. We will certainly discover that princely patronage was a major factor in the genesis of the Italian Renaissance as it developed in Florence during the early years of the fifteenth century.

LEARN ABOUT IT

20.1 Examine how sculptors were instrumental in the early development of the Italian Renaissance by increasing the lifelike qualities of human figures and drawing inspiration from ancient Roman sculpture.

20.2 Explore how an interest in scientific investigation blossomed into the development and use of linear perspective throughout fifteenth-century Italian painting.

20.3 Assess the role of wealthy merchants and *condottieri* in driving the development of Renaissance art and architecture.

20.4 Consider how the new focus on artistic competition and individual achievement created a climate for innovative and ambitious works.

(((•─[**Listen** to the chapter audio on myartslab.com

HUMANISM AND THE ITALIAN RENAISSANCE

By the end of the Middle Ages, the most important Italian cultural centers lay north of Rome in the cities of Florence, Milan, and Venice, and in the smaller duchies of Mantua, Ferrara, and Urbino. Both political power and artistic patronage were dominated by wealthy families: the Medici in Florence, the Montefeltro in Urbino, the Gonzaga in Mantua, the Visconti and Sforza in Milan, and the Este in Ferrara (**MAP 20–1**). Cities grew in wealth and independence as people migrated from the countryside in unprecedented numbers. As in northern Europe, commerce became increasingly important. Money conferred status, and a shrewd business or political leader could become very powerful. The period saw the rise of mercenary armies led by entrepreneurial (and sometimes brilliant) military commanders called *condottieri*, who owed allegiance only to those who paid them well; their employer might be a city-state, a lord, or even the pope. Some *condottieri*, like Niccolò da Tolentino (see FIG. 20–1), became rich and famous. Others, like Federico da Montefeltro (see FIG. 20–31), were lords or dukes themselves, with territories of their own in need of protection. Patronage of the arts was an important public activity with political overtones. As one Florentine merchant, Giovanni Rucellai, succinctly noted, he supported the arts "because they serve the glory of God, the honour of the city, and the commemoration of myself" (cited in Baxandall, p. 2).

The term Renaissance (French for "rebirth") was only applied to this period by later historians. However, its origins lie in the thought of Petrarch and other fourteenth-century Italian writers, who emphasized the power and potential of human beings for great individual accomplishment. These Italian humanists also looked back at the thousand years extending from the disintegration of the Western Roman Empire to their own day and determined that the achievements of the Classical world were followed by what they perceived as a period of decline—a "middle" or "dark" age. They proudly saw their own era as a third age characterized by a revival or rebirth ("renaissance"), when humanity began to emerge from what they erroneously saw as intellectual and cultural stagnation to appreciate once more the achievement of the ancients and the value of rational, scientific investigation. They looked to the accomplishments of the Classical past for inspiration and instruction, and in Italy this centered on the heritage of ancient Rome. They sought the physical and literary records of the ancient world—assembling libraries, collecting sculpture and fragments of architecture, and beginning archaeological investigations. Their aim was to live a rich, noble, and productive life—usually within the framework of Christianity, but always adhering to a school of philosophy as a moral basis.

Artists, like the humanists, turned to Classical antiquity for inspiration, emulating what they saw in ancient Roman sculpture and architecture, even as they continued to fulfill commissions for predominantly Christian subjects and buildings. But from the secular world a number of home furnishings such as birth trays and marriage chests have survived, richly painted with allegorical and mythological themes (see "The Morelli–Nerli Wedding Chests," page 616). Patrons began to collect art for their personal enjoyment.

Like Flemish artists, Italian painters and sculptors increasingly focused their attention on rendering the illusion of physical reality. They did so in a more analytical way than the northerners. Rather than seeking to describe the detailed visual appearance of nature through luminosity and textural differentiation, Italian artists aimed at achieving lifelike but idealized weighty figures set within a rationally configured space organized through strict adherence to a mathematical system called linear perspective, which achieved the illusion of a measured and continuously receding space (see "Renaissance Perspective," page 610).

FLORENCE

In seizing Uccello's battle painting (see FIG. 20–1), Lorenzo de' Medici was asserting the role his family had come to expect to play in the history of Florence. The fifteenth century witnessed the rise of the Medici from among the most successful of a newly rich middle class (primarily merchants and bankers) to become the city's virtual rulers. Unlike the hereditary aristocracy, the Medici emerged from obscure roots to make their fortune in banking; from their money came their power.

The competitive Florentine atmosphere that had fostered mercantile success and civic pride also cultivated competition in the arts and encouraged an interest in ancient literary texts. This has led many to consider Florence the cradle of the Italian Renaissance. Under Cosimo the Elder (1389–1464), the Medici became leaders in intellectual and artistic patronage. They sponsored philosophers and other scholars who wanted to study the Classics, especially the works of Plato and his followers, the Neoplatonists. Neoplatonism distinguished between the spiritual (the ideal or Idea) and the physical (Matter) and encouraged artists to represent ideal figures. But it was writers, philosophers, and musicians—and not artists—who dominated the Medici Neoplatonic circle. Architects, sculptors, and painters learned their craft in apprenticeships and were therefore considered manual laborers. Nevertheless, interest in the ancient world rapidly spread from the Medici circle to visual artists, who gradually began to see themselves as more than laborers. Florentine society soon recognized their best works as achievements of a very high order.

Although the Medici were the *de facto* rulers, Florence was considered a republic. The Council of Ten (headed for a time by Salimbeni, who commissioned Uccello's *Battle of San Romano*) was a kind of constitutional oligarchy where wealthy men formed the government. At the same time, the various guilds wielded tremendous power; guild membership was a prerequisite for holding government office. Consequently, artists could look to the Church and the state—the city government and the guilds—as well as private individuals for patronage, and these patrons expected the

MAP 20-1 • FIFTEENTH-CENTURY ITALY

Powerful families divided the Italian peninsula into city-states: the Medici in Florence, the Visconti and Sforza in Milan, the Montefeltro in Urbino, the Gonzaga in Mantua, and the Este in Ferrara. After 1420, the popes ruled Rome, while in the south Naples and Sicily were French and then Spanish (Aragonese) territories. Venice maintained its independence as a republic.

artists to reaffirm and glorify their achievements with works that were not only beautiful but intellectually powerful.

ARCHITECTURE

The defining civic project of the early years of the fifteenth century was the completion of Florence Cathedral with a magnificent dome over the high altar. The construction of the cathedral had begun in the late thirteenth century and had continued intermittently during the fourteenth century. As early as 1367, builders had envisioned a very tall dome to span the huge interior space of the crossing, but they lacked the engineering know-how to construct it. When interest in completing the cathedral revived, around 1407, the technical solution was proposed by a young sculptor-turned-architect, Filippo Brunelleschi.

20-2 • Filippo Brunelleschi **DOME OF FLORENCE CATHEDRAL (SANTA MARIA DEL FIORE)**
1420–1436; lantern completed 1471.

👁 **Watch** an architectural simulation about Brunelleschi's dome on myartslab.com

20-3 • SCHEMATIC DRAWING OF FLORENCE CATHEDRAL
The separate, central-plan building in front of the façade is the baptistery. Adjacent to the façade is a tall tower designed by Giotto in 1334.

FILIPPO BRUNELLESCHI Filippo Brunelleschi (1377–1446) achieved what many considered impossible: He solved the problem of the dome of Florence Cathedral. Brunelleschi had originally trained as a goldsmith (see "The Competition Reliefs," page 603). To further his education, he traveled to Rome to study ancient Roman sculpture and architecture, and it was on his return to Florence that he tackled the dome. After the completion of a tall octagonal drum in 1412, Brunelleschi designed the dome itself in 1417, and it was built between 1420 and 1436 (**FIGS. 20-2, 20-3**). A revolutionary feat of engineering, the dome is a double shell of masonry 138 feet across. The octagonal outer shell is supported on eight large and 16 lighter ribs. Instead of using a costly and even dangerous scaffold and centering, Brunelleschi devised a system in which temporary wooden supports were cantilevered out from the drum. He moved these supports up as building progressed. As the dome was built up course by course, each portion of the structure reinforced the next one. Vertical marble ribs interlocked with horizontal sandstone rings, connected and reinforced with iron rods and oak beams. The inner and outer shells were linked internally by a system of arches. When completed, this self-buttressed unit required no external support to keep it standing.

An oculus (round opening) in the center of the dome was surmounted by a lantern designed in 1436. After Brunelleschi's death, this crowning structure, made up of Roman architectural forms, was completed by another Florentine architect, Michelozzo di Bartolomeo (1396–1472). The final touch—a gilt-bronze ball by Andrea del Verrocchio—was added in 1468–1471 (but replaced in 1602 with a smaller one).

Other commissions came quickly after the cathedral dome project established Brunelleschi's fame. From about 1418 until his death in 1446, Brunelleschi was involved in a series of influential projects. In 1419, he designed a foundling hospital for the city (see "The Foundling Hospital," page 600). Between 1419 and 1423, he built the elegant Capponi Chapel in the church of Santa Felicità (see **FIG. 21-29**). For the Medicis' parish church of San Lorenzo, he designed and built a centrally planned sacristy (a room where ritual attire and vessels are kept), from 1421 to 1428, and also conceived plans for a new church.

Brunelleschi's **SAN LORENZO** has a basilican plan with a long nave flanked by side aisles that open into shallow lateral chapels (**FIG. 20-4**). A short transept and square crossing lead to a square sanctuary flanked by additional chapels opening off the transept. Brunelleschi based his mathematically regular plan on a square module—a basic unit of measure that could be multiplied or

20-4 • Filippo Brunelleschi (continued by Michelozzo di Bartolomeo) **INTERIOR (A) AND PLAN (B) OF CHURCH OF SAN LORENZO, FLORENCE**
c. 1421–1428; nave (designed 1434?) 1442–1470.

In 1419, the guild of silk manufacturers and goldsmiths (Arte della Seta) in Florence undertook a significant public service: It established a large public orphanage and commissioned the brilliant young architect Filippo Brunelleschi to build it near the church of the Santissima Annunziata (Most Holy Annunciation), which housed a miracle-working painting of the Annunciation, making it a popular pilgrimage site. Completed in 1444, the Foundling Hospital—**OSPEDALE DEGLI INNOCENTI**—was unprecedented in terms of scale and design (**FIG. 20–5**).

Brunelleschi created a building that paid homage to traditional forms while introducing features that we associate with the Italian Renaissance style. Traditionally, a charitable foundation's building had a portico open to the street to provide shelter, and Brunelleschi built an arcade of striking lightness and elegance,

using smooth round columns and richly carved capitals—his own interpretation of the Classical Corinthian order. Although we might initially assume that the sources for this arcade lay in the Roman architecture of Classical antiquity, columns were not actually used in antiquity to support free-standing arcades, only to support straight architraves. In fact, it was local Romanesque architecture that was the source for Brunelleschi's graceful design. It is the details of capitals and moldings that bring an air of the antique to this influential building.

The underlying mathematical basis for Brunelleschi's design—traced to the same Pythagorean proportional systems that were believed to create musical harmony—creates a distinct sense of harmony in this graceful arcade. Each bay encloses a cube of space defined by the 10-*braccia* (20-foot) height of the columns and the diameter of the arches.

Domical vaults, half again as high as the columns, cover the cubes. The bays at the end of the arcade are slightly larger than the rest, creating a subtle frame for the composition. Brunelleschi defined the perfect squares and semicircles of his building with dark gray stone (*pietra serena*) against plain white walls. His training as a goldsmith and sculptor (see "The Competition Reliefs," page 603) served him well as he led his artisans to carve crisp, elegantly detailed capitals and moldings for the covered gallery.

A later addition to the building seems eminently suitable: About 1487, Andrea della Robbia, who had inherited the family ceramics firm and its secret **glazing** formulas from his uncle Luca, created for the spandrels between the arches glazed terra-cotta medallions (**FIG. 20–6**) that signified the building's function. Molds were used in the ceramic workshop to facilitate the production of the series of similar

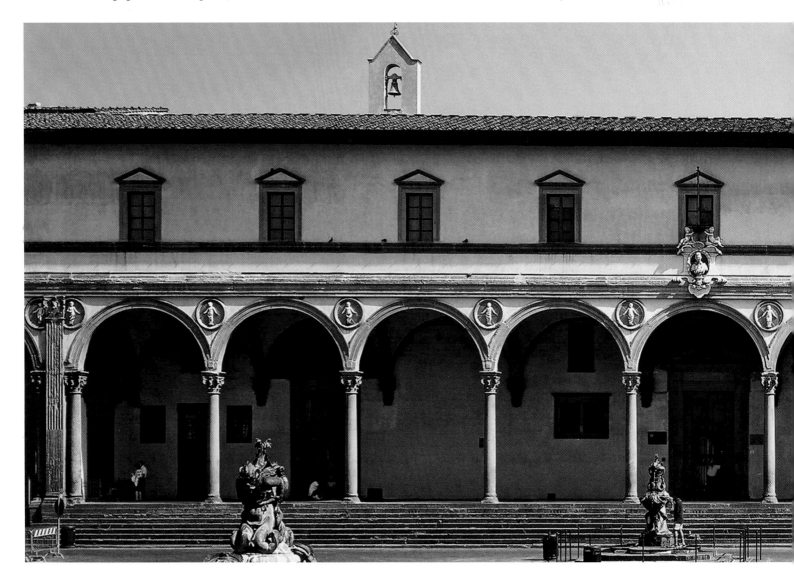

babies in swaddling clothes that float at the center of each medallion. The molded terra-cotta forms were covered with a tin glaze to make the sculptures both weatherproof and decorative, and the baby-blue ceramic backgrounds—a signature color for the della Robbia family workshop—makes them seem to float as celestial apparitions. This is not altogether inappropriate. Although they clearly refer to the foundlings (*innocenti*) cared for in the hospital, they are also meant to evoke the "innocent" baby boys martyred by King Herod in his attempt to rid his realm of the potential rival the Magi had journeyed to venerate (Matthew 2:16).

Andrea della Robbia's adorable ceramic babies—which remain among the most beloved images of the city of Florence—seem to lay claim to the human side of Renaissance humanism, reminding viewers that the city's wealthiest guild cared for the most helpless members of society. Perhaps the Foundling Hospital spoke to fifteenth-century Florentines of an increased sense of social responsibility. Or perhaps, by so publicly demonstrating social concerns, the wealthy guild that sponsored it solicited the approval and support of the lower classes in the cut-throat power politics of the day.

20-6 • Andrea della Robbia INFANT IN SWADDLING CLOTHES (ONE OF THE HOLY INNOCENTS MASSACRED BY HEROD)
Ospedale degli Innocenti (Foundling Hospital), Florence. 1487. Glazed terra cotta.

20-5 • Filippo Brunelleschi OSPEDALE DEGLI INNOCENTI (FOUNDLING HOSPITAL), FLORENCE
Designed 1419; begun under Brunelleschi's direct supervision 1421–1427; construction continued into the 1440s.

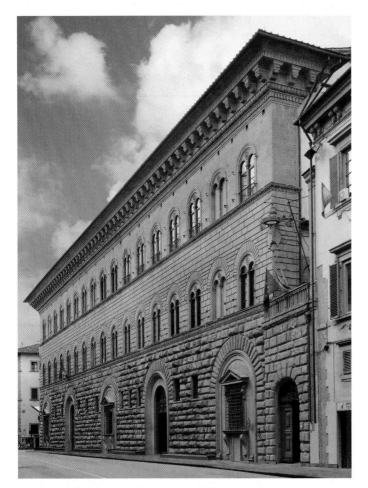

20–7 • Attributed to Michelozzo di Bartolomeo FAÇADE, PALAZZO MEDICI-RICCARDI, FLORENCE
Begun 1446 (the view shown here includes a two-bay extension constructed during the 18th century).

For the palace site, Cosimo de' Medici the Elder chose the Via de' Gori at the corner of the Via Larga, the widest city street at that time. Despite his practical reasons for constructing a large residence and the fact that he chose simplicity and austerity over grandeur in the exterior design, his detractors commented and gossiped. As one exaggerated, "[Cosimo] has begun a palace which throws even the Colosseum at Rome into the shade."

THE MEDICI PALACE Brunelleschi may have been involved in designing the nearby Medici Palace (now known as the Palazzo Medici-Riccardi) in 1446. According to Giorgio Vasari, the sixteenth-century artist and theorist who wrote the first modern history of art, Cosimo de' Medici the Elder rejected Brunelleschi's model for the **palazzo** as too grand (any large house was called a *palazzo*—"palace"). Many now attribute the design of the building to Michelozzo. The austere exterior (**FIG. 20-7**) was in keeping with the Florentine political climate and concurrent religious attitudes, imbued with the Franciscan ideals of poverty and charity. Like many other European cities, Florence had sumptuary laws, which forbade ostentatious displays of wealth—but they were often ignored. For example, private homes were supposed to be limited to a dozen rooms, but Cosimo acquired and demolished 20 small houses to provide the site for his new residence. His house was more than a dwelling place; it was his place of business, his company headquarters. The palazzo symbolized the family and established its proper place in the Florentine social hierarchy.

Huge in scale—each story is more than 20 feet high—the building is marked by harmonious proportions and elegant, Classically inspired details. On one side, the ground floor originally opened through large, round arches onto the street, creating in effect a loggia that provided space for the family business. These arches were walled up in the sixteenth century and given windows designed by Michelangelo. The large, **rusticated** stone blocks—that is, blocks with their outer faces left rough—facing the lower story clearly set it off from the upper two levels. In fact, all three stories are distinguished by stone surfaces that vary from sculptural at the ground level to almost smooth dressed stone on the third floor.

The builders followed the time-honored tradition of placing rooms around a central courtyard. Unlike the plan of the house of Jacques Coeur (see FIG. 19-24), however, the **PALAZZO MEDICI-RICCARDI COURTYARD** is square in plan with rooms arranged symmetrically (**FIG. 20-8**). Round arches on slender columns form a continuous arcade under an enclosed second story. Disks

divided and applied to every element of the design, creating a series of clear, harmonious spaces. Architectural details, all in a Classical style, were carved in **pietra serena**, a gray Tuscan sandstone that became synonymous with Brunelleschi's interiors. Below the plain clerestory with its unobtrusive openings, the arches of the nave arcade are carried on tall, slender Corinthian columns made even taller by the insertion of an impost block between the column capital and the springing of the round arches—one of Brunelleschi's favorite details. Flattened architectural moldings in *pietra serena* repeat the arcade in the outer walls of the side aisles, and each bay is covered by its own shallow domical vault. Brunelleschi's rational approach, clear sense of order, and innovative incorporation of Classical motifs inspired later Renaissance architects, many of whom learned from his work firsthand by completing his unfinished projects.

20-8 • COURTYARD WITH SGRAFFITO DECORATION, PALAZZO MEDICI-RICCARDI, FLORENCE
Begun 1446.

In 1401, the building supervisors of the baptistery of Florence Cathedral decided to commission a new pair of bronze doors, funded by the powerful wool merchants' guild. Instead of choosing a well-established sculptor with a strong reputation, a competition was announced for the commission. This prestigious project would be awarded to the artist who demonstrated the greatest talent and skill in executing a trial piece: a bronze relief representing Abraham's sacrifice of Isaac (Genesis 22:1–13) composed within the same Gothic quatrefoil framework used in Andrea Pisano's first set of bronze doors for the baptistery, made in the 1330s (see FIG. 18–3). The narrative subject was full of dramatic potential. Abraham, commanded by God to slay his beloved son Isaac as a burnt offering, has traveled to the mountains for the sacrifice. Just as he is about to slaughter Isaac, an angel appears, commanding him to save his son and substitute a ram tangled in the bushes behind him.

Two competition panels have survived, those submitted by the presumed finalists—Filippo Brunelleschi and Lorenzo Ghiberti, both young artists in their early twenties. Brunelleschi's composition (FIG. 20–9) is rugged and explosive, marked by raw dramatic intensity. At the right, Abraham lunges forward, grabbing his son by the neck, while the angel swoops energetically to stay his hand just as the knife is about to strike. Isaac's awkward pose embodies his fear and struggle. Ghiberti's version (FIG. 20–10) is quite different, suave and graceful rather than

powerful and dramatic. Poses are controlled and choreographed; the harmonious pairing of son and father contrasts sharply with the wrenching struggle in Brunelleschi's rendering. And Ghiberti's Isaac is not a stretched, scrawny youth, but a fully idealized Classical figure exuding calm composure.

Brunelleschi's biographer, Antonio di Tuccio Manetti, claimed that the competition ended in a tie, and that when the committee decided to split the commission between the two young artists, Brunelleschi withdrew. It is possible, however, that the cloth merchants actually chose Ghiberti to make the doors. They might have preferred the suave elegance of his figural composition. Perhaps they liked the prominence of elegantly disposed swags of cloth, reminders of the source of their patronage and prosperity. But they also could have been swayed by the technical superiority of Ghiberti's relief. Unlike Brunelleschi, Ghiberti cast background and figures mostly as a single piece, making his bronze stronger, lighter, and less expensive to produce. The finished doors—installed in the baptistery in 1424—were so successful that Ghiberti was commissioned to create another set (see FIG. 20–16), his most famous work, hailed by Michelangelo as the "Gates of Paradise." Brunelleschi would refocus his career on buildings rather than bronzes, becoming one of the most important architects of the Italian Renaissance (see FIGS. 20–2, 20–3, 20–4, 20–5).

20-9 • Filippo Brunelleschi SACRIFICE OF ISAAC
1401–1402. Bronze with gilding, 21″ × 17½″ (53 × 44 cm) inside molding. Museo Nazionale del Bargello, Florence.

20-10 • Lorenzo Ghiberti SACRIFICE OF ISAAC
1401–1402. Bronze with gilding, 21″ × 17½″ (53 × 44 cm) inside molding. Museo Nazionale del Bargello, Florence.

bearing the Medici arms surmount each arch in a frieze decorated with swags in **sgraffito** work (decoration produced by scratching through a darker layer of plaster or glaze). Such classicizing elements, inspired by the study of Roman ruins, gave the great house an aura of dignity and stability that enhanced the status of its owners. The Medici Palace inaugurated a new fashion for monumentality and regularity in residential Florentine architecture. Wealthy Florentine families soon emulated it in their own houses.

SCULPTURE

The new architectural language inspired by ancient Classical forms was accompanied by a similar impetus in sculpture. By 1400, Florence had enjoyed internal stability and economic prosperity for over two decades. However, until 1428, the city and its independence were challenged by two great anti-republican powers: the duchy of Milan and the kingdom of Naples. In an atmosphere of wealth and civic patriotism, Florentines turned to commissions that would express their self-esteem and magnify the importance of their city. A new attitude toward realism, space, and the Classical past set the stage for more than a century of creativity. Sculptors led the way.

ORSANMICHELE In 1339, 14 of Florence's most powerful guilds had been commissioned to fill the ground-floor niches that decorated the exterior of **ORSANMICHELE**—a newly completed loggia that served as a grain market—with sculpted images of their patron saints (**FIG. 20–11**). By 1400, only three had fulfilled this assignment. In the new climate of republicanism and civic pride, the government pressured the guilds to furnish their niches with statuary. In the wake of this directive, Florence witnessed a dazzling display of sculpture produced by the most impressive local practitioners, including Nanni di Banco, Lorenzo Ghiberti, and Donatello, each of whom took responsibility for filling three niches.

In about 1409, Nanni di Banco (c. 1385–1421), son of a sculptor in the Florence Cathedral workshop, was commissioned by the stonecarvers' and woodworkers' guild (to which he himself belonged) to produce **THE FOUR CROWNED MARTYRS** (**FIG. 20–12**). According to tradition, these third- or fourth-century Christian martyrs were sculptors, executed for refusing to make an image of a pagan Roman god for Emperor Diocletian. Although the architectural setting is Gothic in style, Nanni's figures—with their solid bodies, heavy, form-revealing togas, noble hair and beards, and portraitlike features—reveal his interest in ancient Roman sculpture, particularly portraiture (see **FIG. 6-22**). They stand as a testimony to this sculptor's role in the Florentine revival of interest in antiquity.

The saints convey a new spatial relationship to the building and to the viewer. They stand in a semicircle, with feet and drapery protruding beyond the floor of the niche and into the viewer's space. The saints appear to be four

20-11 • EXTERIOR VIEW OF ORSANMICHELE SHOWING SCULPTURE IN NICHES
Florence. Begun 1337.

At street level, Orsanmichele was constructed originally as an open loggia (similar to the Loggia dei Lanzi in FIG. 18–2); in 1380 the spaces under the arches were filled in. In this view of the southeast corner, appearing on the receding wall to the left is first (in the foreground on the corner pier) Donatello's *St. George*, then, Nanni di Banco's *Four Crowned Martyrs*. However, the sculptures seen in this photograph are modern replicas; the originals have been removed to museums for safekeeping.

individuals interacting within their own world, but a world that opens to engage with passing pedestrians (see FIG. 20–11). The relief panel below the niche shows the four sculptors at work, embodied with a similar solid vigor. Nanni deeply undercut both figures and objects to cast shadows that enhance the illusion of three-dimensionality.

Donatello (Donato di Niccolò di Betto Bardi, c. 1386/1387–1466) also received three commissions for the niches at Orsanmichele during the first quarter of the century. Like Nanni, a member of the guild of stonecarvers and woodworkers, he worked

20–13 • Donatello **ST. GEORGE**
Formerly in Orsanmichele, Florence. 1417–1420. Marble, height 6′5″ (1.95 m). Museo Nazionale del Bargello, Florence.

20–12 • Nanni di Banco **THE FOUR CROWNED MARTYRS**
c. 1409–1417. Marble, height of figures 6′ (1.83 m). Photographed *in situ* before removal of the figures to the Museo di Orsanmichele, Florence.

in both media, as well as in bronze. During a long and productive career, he developed into one of the most influential and distinguished figures in the history of Italian sculpture, approaching each commission as if it were the opportunity for a new experiment. One of Florence's lesser guilds—the armorers and swordmakers—called on Donatello to carve a majestic and self-assured **ST. GEORGE** for their niche (**FIG. 20–13**). As originally conceived, the saint would have been a standing advertisement for their trade, carrying a metal sword in his right hand and probably wearing a metal helmet and sporting a scabbard, all now lost. The figure has remarkable presence, even without his accessories. St. George stands in solid contrapposto, legs braced to support his armor-heavy torso, the embodiment of alertness and courage. He seems to stare out into our world, perhaps surveying his most famous adversary—a dragon that was holding a princess captive—lurking unsettlingly in the space behind us. With his wrinkled brow and determined expression, he is tense, alert, focused, if perhaps also slightly worried. Donatello's complex psychological characterization of this warrior-saint particularly impressed Donatello's contemporaries, not least among them his potential patrons.

For the base of the niche, Donatello carved a remarkable shallow relief showing St. George slaying the dragon and saving the princess, a well-known part of his story. The contours of the foreground figures are slightly undercut to emphasize their mass, while the landscape and architecture are in progressively lower relief until they are barely incised rather than carved, an ingenious emulation of the painters' technique of atmospheric perspective. This is also a pioneering example of linear perspective (see "Renaissance Perspective," page 610), in which the orthogonals converge on the figure of the saint himself, using this burgeoning representational system not only to simulate spatial recession but also to provide narrative focus.

DONATELLO Donatello's long career as a sculptor in a broad variety of media established him as one of the most successful and admired sculptors of the Italian Renaissance. He excelled in part because of his attentive exploration of human emotions and expression, as well as his ability to solve the technical problems posed by various media—from lost-wax casting in bronze and carved marble to polychromed wood. In a bronze **DAVID**, he produced the first life-size, free-standing nude since antiquity (**FIG. 20–14**), and in his portrait of the soldier Erasmo da Narni, one of the first life-size bronze equestrian portraits of the Renaissance (see **FIG. 20–15**).

Since nothing is known about the circumstances of its creation, the *David* has been the subject of continuing inquiry and speculation. Although the statue clearly draws on the Classical tradition of heroic nudity, the meaning of this sensuous, pre-pubescent boy in a jaunty laurel-trimmed shepherd's hat and boots has long piqued interest. Some art historians have stressed an overt homoeroticism, especially in the openly effeminate conception of David and the way a wing from the helmet on Goliath's severed head caresses the young hero's inner thigh. Others have seen in David's angular pose and boyish torso a sense that he is poised between childish interests and adult responsibility, an image of improbable heroism. David was a potent political image in Florence, a symbol of the citizens' resolve to oppose tyrants regardless of their superior power, since virtue brings divine support and preternatural strength, and we will see other Florentine Renaissance renderings of this biblical hero. Indeed, an inscription engraved into the base where the sculpture

20–14 • Donatello DAVID
c. 1446–1460(?). Bronze, height 5′2¼″ (1.58 m). Museo Nazionale del Bargello, Florence.

This sculpture is first recorded as being in the courtyard of the Medici Palace in 1469, where it stood on a base inscribed with these lines:

The victor is whoever defends the fatherland.
All-powerful God crushes the angry enemy.
Behold, a boy overcomes the great tyrant.
Conquer, O citizens!

👁 **Watch** a video about the process of lost-wax casting on myartslab.com once stood suggests that it could have celebrated the Florentine triumph over the Milanese in 1425, a victory that brought resolution to a quarter-century struggle with despots and helped give Florence a vision of itself as a strong, virtuous republic.

In 1443, Donatello was probably called to Padua to execute an **EQUESTRIAN STATUE (FIG. 20-15)** to commemorate the Paduan general of the Venetian army, Erasmo da Narni, nicknamed "Gattamelata" (meaning "Honeyed Cat"—a reference to his mother, Melania Gattelli). If any image could be said to characterize the self-made men of the Italian Renaissance, surely it would be those of the *condottieri*—the brilliant generals such as Gattamelata and Niccolò da Tolentino (see FIG. 20-1) who organized the armies and fought for any city-state willing to pay for their services. As guardians for hire, they were tough, opportunistic mercenaries. But they also subscribed to an ideal of military and civic virtue.

Horsemanship was more than a necessary skill for the *condottieri*. The horse, a beast of enormous brute strength, symbolized animal passions, and skilled horsemanship demonstrated physical and intellectual control—self-control, as well as control of the animal—the triumph of the intellect, of "mind over matter."

Donatello's sources for this statue were surviving Roman bronze equestrian portraits, notably the famous image of Marcus Aurelius (see FIG. 6-57), which the sculptor certainly knew from his stay in Rome, as well as the famous set of Roman bronze horses installed on the façade of St. Mark's Cathedral in Venice. Viewed from a distance, Donatello's man–animal juggernaut, installed on a high marble base in front of the church of Sant'Antonio in Padua, seems capable of thrusting forward at the first threat. Seen up close, however, the man's sunken cheeks, sagging jaw, ropy neck, and stern but sad expression suggest a warrior grown old and tired from the constant need for military vigilance and rapid response.

THE GATES OF PARADISE The bronze doors that Lorenzo Ghiberti (1381?–1455) produced for the Florentine Baptistery after winning his famous competition with Brunelleschi in 1401 (see "The Competition Reliefs," page 603) were such a success that in 1425 he was awarded the commission for yet another set of bronze doors for the east side of the Baptistery, facing the doors of the cathedral; his first set of doors was moved to the north side. The new door panels, funded by the wool manufacturers' guild, were a significant conceptual leap from the older schemes of 28 small scenes employed for Ghiberti's earlier doors and those of Andrea Pisano in the fourteenth century (see FIG. 18-3). Ghiberti departed entirely from the old arrangement, producing a set of ten scenes from the Hebrew Bible—from the Creation

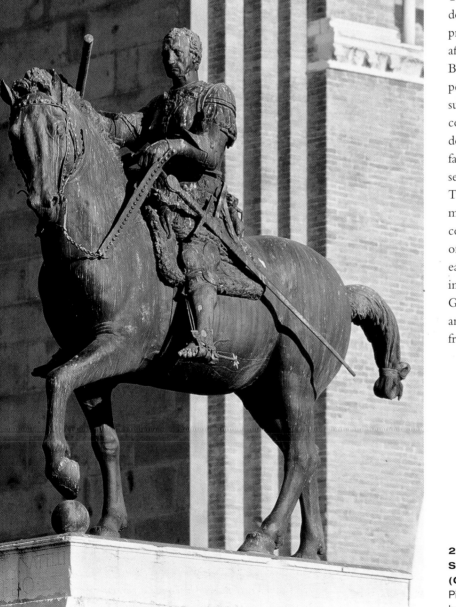

20-15 • Donatello EQUESTRIAN STATUE OF ERASMO DA NARNI (GATTAMELATA)
Piazza del Santo, Padua. 1443–1453. Bronze, height approx. 12′2″ (3.71 m).

to the reign of Solomon—composed in rectangular fields, like a set of framed paintings. Michelangelo reportedly said that the results, installed in 1452, were worthy of the **"GATES OF PARADISE"**—the name by which they are now commonly known (**FIG. 20–16**).

Ghiberti organized the space in the ten square reliefs either by a system of linear perspective with obvious orthogonal lines (see "Renaissance Perspective," page 610) or more intuitively by a series of arches or rocks or trees charting the path into the distance. Foreground figures are grouped in the lower third of each panel, while the other figures decrease gradually in size to map their positioning in deep space. The use of a system of perspective, with clearly differentiated background and foreground, also helped Ghiberti combine a series of related events, separated by narrative time, within a single pictorial frame.

The story of **JACOB AND ESAU** (Genesis 25 and 27) fills the center panel of the left door. Ghiberti creates a coherent and measurable space peopled by graceful, idealized figures (**FIG. 20–17**). He pays careful attention to one-point perspective in laying out the architectural setting. Squares in the pavement establish the receding lines of the orthogonals that seem to converge on a central vanishing point under the loggia, while towering arches overlap and gradually diminish in size from foreground to background to define the receding space above the figures. The story unfolds in a series of individual episodes and begins in the background. On the rooftop (upper right) Rebecca stands, listening as God warns of her unborn sons' future conflict; under the left-hand arch she gives birth to the twins. The adult Esau sells his rights as oldest son to his brother Jacob, and when he goes hunting (center right), Rebecca and Jacob plot against him. Finally, in the right foreground, Jacob receives Isaac's blessing, while in the center, Esau faces his father. Ghiberti's portrayal of the scene relates more closely to developments in painting than to contemporary sculpture. Ghiberti not only signed his work, but also included his self-portrait in the medallion beside the lower right-hand corner of this panel.

20–17 • Lorenzo Ghiberti JACOB AND ESAU, PANEL OF THE "GATES OF PARADISE" (EAST BAPTISTERY DOORS)
Formerly on the Baptistery of San Giovanni, Florence. c. 1435. Gilded bronze, 31¼″ (79 cm) square. Museo dell'Opera del Duomo, Florence.

20–16 • Lorenzo Ghiberti "GATES OF PARADISE" (EAST BAPTISTERY DOORS)
Formerly on the Baptistery of San Giovanni, Florence. 1425–1452. Gilt bronze, height 15′ (4.57 m). Museo dell'Opera del Duomo, Florence.

The door panels, commissioned by the wool manufacturers' guild, depict ten scenes from the Hebrew Bible beginning with the Creation in the upper left panel. The murder of Abel by his brother, Cain, follows in the upper right panel, succeeded in the same left–right paired order by the Flood and the drunkenness of Noah, Abraham sacrificing Isaac, the story of Jacob and Esau, Joseph sold into slavery by his brothers, Moses receiving the Tablets of the Law, Joshua and the fall of Jericho, David and Goliath, and finally Solomon and the queen of Sheba. Ghiberti placed his own portrait as a signature in the frame at the lower right corner of the Jacob and Esau panel. He wrote in his *Commentaries* (c. 1450–1455): "I strove to imitate nature as clearly as I could, and with all the perspective I could produce, to have excellent compositions with many figures."

PAINTING

Wealthy patrons commissioned murals and large altarpieces for their local churches and smaller panel paintings for their houses and private chapels. Artists experienced in fresco were in great demand and traveled widely to execute wall and ceiling decorations. At first the Italians showed little interest in oil painting, for the most part using tempera even for their largest works. But, in the last decades of the century, oil painting became popular in Venice.

MASACCIO Even though his brief career lasted less than a decade, Tommaso di Ser Giovanni di Mone Cassai (1401–1428/1429?), nicknamed "Masaccio" (meaning "Big Tom"), established a new direction in Florentine painting, much as Giotto had a century earlier. He did this by integrating monumental and consistently scaled figures into rational architectural and natural settings using linear perspective. The chronology of Massaccio's works is uncertain, but his fresco of the **TRINITY** in the church of Santa Maria Novella in Florence must have been painted around 1426, the date on the Lenzi family tombstone that once stood in front of it (**FIGS. 20–19, 20–20**).

Masaccio's fresco was meant to give the illusion of a stone funerary monument and altar table set below a deep **aedicula** (framed niche) in the wall. The effect of looking up into a barrel-vaulted niche was made plausible through precisely rendered linear perspective. The eye level of an adult male viewer standing within

Fifteenth-century Italian artists developed a system known as linear, or mathematical perspective that enabled them to represent three dimensions on a two-dimensional surface, simulating the recession of space in the visible world pictorially in a way they found convincing. The sculptor and architect Filippo Brunelleschi first demonstrated the system about 1420, and the theorist and architect Leon Battista Alberti codified it in 1436 in his treatise *Della Pittura* (*On Painting*).

For Alberti, in one-point linear perspective a picture's surface was conceived as a flat plane that intersected the viewer's field of vision at right angles. This highly artificial concept presumed a viewer standing dead center at a prescribed distance from a work of art. From this single fixed vantage point, everything would appear to recede into the distance at the same rate, following imaginary lines called orthogonals that met at a single **vanishing point** on the horizon. By using orthogonals in concert with controlled diminution of scale as forms move back toward the vanishing point, artists could replicate the optical illusion that things appear to grow smaller, rise higher, and come closer together as they get farther away from us. Linear perspective makes pictorial spaces seem almost like extensions of the viewer's real space, creating a compelling, even exaggerated sense of depth (**FIG. 20–18**).

Linear perspective is not the only way to simulate spatial recession in two-dimensional painting (See "Pictorial Devices for Depicting Recession in Space," page xxiii). In atmospheric perspective, for example, variations in color and clarity convey the feeling of distance when objects and landscape are portrayed less clearly, and colors become grayer, in the background, imitating the natural effects of a loss of clarity and color when viewing things in the distance through an atmospheric haze.

20-18 • Perugino CHRIST GIVING THE KEYS TO ST. PETER, WITH A SCHEMATIC DRAWING SHOWING THE ORTHOGONALS AND VANISHING POINT
Fresco on the right wall of the Sistine Chapel (see FIG. 20–33), Vatican, Rome. 1481. 11′5½″ × 18′8½″ (3.48 × 5.70 m).

Christ Giving the Keys to St. Peter is a remarkable study in linear perspective. The clear demarcation of the paving stones of the piazza provides a network of orthogonal and horizontal lines for the measured placement of the figures. People and buildings become increasingly, and logically, smaller as the space recedes. Horizontally, the composition is divided between the foreground frieze of figures and the widely spaced background buildings, vertically by the open space at the center between Christ and Peter and by the symmetrical architectural forms on either side of this central axis. Perugino's painting is, among other things, a representation of Alberti's ideal city, described in *De re aedificatoria* as having a "temple" (that is, a church) at the very center of a great open space raised on a dais and separate from any other buildings that might obstruct it.

the church determined the horizon line on which the vanishing point was centered, just below the kneeling figures above the altar. And the painting demonstrates not only Masaccio's intimate knowledge of Brunelleschi's perspective experiments (see "Renaissance Perspective," above), but also his architectural style (see FIG. 20-4). The painted architecture is an unusual combination of Classical orders. On the wall surface, Corinthian pilasters support a plain architrave below a cornice, while inside the niche Renaissance variations on Ionic columns support framing arches at the front and rear of the barrel vault. The "source" of the consistent illumination of the architecture lies in front of the picture, casting reflections on the coffers, or sunken panels, of the ceiling.

The figures are organized in a measured progression through space. At the near end of the recessed, barrel-vaulted space is the Trinity—Jesus on the cross, the dove of the Holy Spirit poised in downward flight above his tilted halo, and God the Father, who stands behind to support the cross from his elevated perch on a high platform. As in many scenes of the Crucifixion, Jesus is flanked by the Virgin Mary and John the Evangelist, who contemplate the scene on either side of the cross. Mary gazes calmly out at us, her raised hand drawing our attention to the Trinity. Members of the Lenzi family kneel in front of the pilasters—thus closer to us than the Crucifixion; the red robes of the male donor signify that he was a member of the governing council of Florence. Below these donors, in an open sarcophagus, is a skeleton, a grim reminder of the Christian belief that since death awaits us all, our only hope is redemption and the promise of life in the hereafter, rooted in Christ's sacrifice on the cross. The inscription above the skeleton reads: "I was once that which you are, and what I am you also will be."

20–20 • SECTION DIAGRAM OF THE ILLUSIONISTIC SPATIAL WORLD PORTRAYED IN MASACCIO'S TRINITY
After Gene Brucker, *Florence: The Golden Age*, Berkeley, 1998.

horizon

picture plane

viewing point

20-21 • Masaccio THE EXPULSION OF ADAM AND EVE FROM PARADISE

Brancacci Chapel, church of Santa Maria del Carmine, Florence. c. 1427. Fresco, 7′ × 2′11″ (214 × 90 cm).

Cleaning and restoration of the Brancacci Chapel paintings revealed the remarkable speed and skill with which Masaccio worked. He painted Adam and Eve in four *giornate* (each *giornata* of fresh plaster representing a day's work). Working from the top down and left to right, he painted the angel on the first day; on the second day, the portal; Adam on the third day; and Eve on the fourth.

THE BRANCACCI CHAPEL Masaccio's brief career culminated in the frescos he painted on the walls of the Brancacci Chapel in the church of Santa Maria del Carmine in Florence. Reproduced here are two of the best-known scenes: **THE EXPULSION OF ADAM AND EVE FROM PARADISE** (FIG. 20-21) and **THE TRIBUTE MONEY** (FIG. 20-22). In *The Expulsion*, he presented Adam and Eve as monumental nude figures, combining his studies of the human figure with an intimate knowledge of ancient Roman sculpture. In contrast to Flemish painters, who sought to record every visible detail of a figure's surface (compare Adam and Eve from FIG. 19-15), Masaccio focused on the mass of the bodies formed by the underlying bone and muscle structure, and a single light source emphasizes their tangibility with modeled forms and cast shadows. Departing from earlier interpretations of the event that emphasized wrongdoing and the fall from grace, Masaccio concerns himself with the psychological impact of shame on these first humans, who have been cast out of paradise mourning and protesting, thrown naked into the world.

In *The Tribute Money* (see FIG. 20-22), Masaccio portrays an incident from the life of Jesus that highlights St. Peter (Matthew 17:24–27), to whom this chapel was dedicated. In the central scene a tax collector (dressed in a short red tunic and seen from behind) asks Peter (in the left foreground with the short gray beard) if Jesus pays the Jewish temple tax (the "tribute money" of the title). Set against the stable backdrop of a semicircular block of apostolic observers, a masterful series of dynamic diagonals in the postures and gestures of the three main figures interlocks them in a compositional system that imbues their interaction with a sense of tension calling out for resolution. Jesus instructs Peter to "go to the sea, drop in a hook, and take the first fish that comes up," which Peter does at the far left. In the fish's mouth is a coin, which Peter gives to the tax collector at the far right. The tribute story was especially significant for Florentines because in 1427, to raise money for defense against military aggression, the city enacted a graduated tax, based on the value of people's personal property.

The Tribute Money is particularly remarkable for its early use of both linear and atmospheric perspective to integrate figures, architecture, and landscape into a consistent whole. Jesus, and the apostles surrounding him, form a clear central focus, from which the landscape seems to recede naturally into the far distance. To foster this illusion, Masaccio used linear perspective in the depiction of the house, and then reinforced it by diminishing the sizes of the distant barren trees and reducing the size of the crouching Peter at far left. The central vanishing point established by the orthogonals of the house corresponds with the head of Jesus.

The cleaning of the painting in the 1980s revealed that it was painted in 32 *giornate* (a *giornata* is a section of fresh plaster that could be prepared and painted in a single day; see *"Buon Fresco,"* page 539). The cleaning also uncovered Masaccio's subtle use of color to create atmospheric perspective in the distant landscape, where mountains fade from grayish-green to grayish-white and the houses and trees on their slopes are loosely sketched to simulate

20-22 • Masaccio THE TRIBUTE MONEY
Brancacci Chapel, church of Santa Maria del Carmine, Florence. c. 1427. Fresco, 8′1″ × 19′7″ (2.46 × 6 m).

View the Closer Look for *The Tribute Money* on myartslab.com

the lack of clear definition when viewing things in the distance through a haze. Green leaves were painted on the branches *al secco* (meaning "on the dry plastered wall").

As in *The Expulsion*, Masaccio modeled the foreground figures here with bold highlights and long shadows on the ground toward the left, giving a strong sense of volumetric solidity and implying a light source at the far right, as if the scene were lit by the actual window in the rear wall of the Brancacci Chapel. Not only does the lighting give the forms sculptural definition; the colors vary in tone according to the strength of the illumination. Masaccio used a wide range of hues—pale pink, mauve, gold, blue-green, seafoam-green, apple-green, peach—and a sophisticated shading technique using contrasting colors, as in Andrew's green robe which is shaded with red instead of darker green. The figures of Jesus and the apostles originally had gold-leaf haloes, several of which have flaked off. Rather than silhouette the heads against consistently flat gold circles (e.g. see FIG. 10–12), however, Masaccio conceived of haloes as gold disks hovering in space above each head that moved with the heads as they moved, and he foreshortened them depending on the angle from which each head is seen.

Some stylistic innovations take time to be fully accepted, and Masaccio's innovative depictions of volumetric solidity, consistent lighting, and spatial integration—though they clearly had an impact on his immediate successors—were perhaps best appreciated by a later generation of painters. Many important sixteenth-century Italian artists, including Michelangelo, studied and sketched Masaccio's Brancacci Chapel frescos, as they did Giotto's work in the Scrovegni Chapel. In the meantime, painting in Florence after Masaccio's death developed along somewhat different lines.

PAINTING IN FLORENCE AFTER MASACCIO

The tradition of covering walls with frescos continued uninterrupted through the fifteenth century. Between 1438 and 1445, Fra Angelico's decoration of the Dominican monastery of San Marco in Florence was one of the most extensive projects.

FRA ANGELICO Guido di Piero da Mugello (c. 1395/1400–1455), earned his nickname "Fra Angelico" ("Angelic Brother") through his piety as well as his painting: in 1984, he was beatified, the first step toward sainthood. Fra Angelico is first documented painting in Florence in 1417–1418, and he remained an active painter after taking vows as a Dominican monk in nearby Fiesole between 1418 and 1421.

Between 1438 and 1445, in the monastery of San Marco, Fra Angelico and his assistants—probably working under the patronage of Cosimo de' Medici—created paintings to inspire meditation in each monk's cell (44 in all; see FIGS. Intro-8, Intro-9), in the chapter house (meeting room), and even in the corridors (hallways). At the top of the stairs in the north corridor, where the monks passed frequently on their way to their individual cells, Fra Angelico painted a serene picture of the **ANNUNCIATION (FIG. 20-23)**. To describe the quiet, measured space where the demure archangel greets the unassuming, youthful Mary, Fra Angelico used linear perspective with striking sensitivity, extending the monks'

20–23 • Fra Angelico
ANNUNCIATION
North dormitory corridor, monastery of San Marco, Florence. c. 1438–1445. Fresco, 7'1" × 10'6" (2.2 × 3.2 m).

The shadowed vault of the portico is supported by a wall on one side and by slender Ionic and Corinthian columns on the other, a new building technique used by Brunelleschi (see FIG. 20–5).

stairway and corridor outward into an imagined portico and garden beside the Virgin's home. The slender, graceful figures wear quietly flowing draperies and assume modest poses. Natural light falling from the left models their forms gently, casting an almost supernatural radiance over their faces and hands. This is a sacred vision rendered in a contemporary setting, welcoming the monks to the most intimate areas of the monastery and preparing them for their private meditations. The line of Latin text running along the bottom of the picture directs the monks, "As you revere this figure of the intact Virgin while passing before it, beware lest you omit to say a Hail Mary."

UCCELLO At mid century, when Fra Angelico was still painting his radiant visions of Mary and Jesus in the monastery of San Marco, other artists explored different directions. Thoroughly conversant with the theories of Brunelleschi and Alberti, they had mastered the techniques (and tricks) of depicting figures in a constructed architectural space. Paolo Uccello devoted himself with

20–24 • Paolo Uccello **THE BATTLE OF SAN ROMANO**
1438–1440. Tempera on wood panel, approx. 6' × 10'6" (1.82 × 3.2 m). National Gallery, London.

20–25 • Andrea del Castagno THE LAST SUPPER

Refectory, convent of Sant'Apollonia, Florence. 1447. Fresco, width approx. 16′ × 32′ (4.6 × 9.8 m).

Castagno worked quickly, completing this huge mural in at most 32 days.

special fervor to the study of linear perspective (**FIG. 20-24**; see also **FIG. 20-1**). In his biographies of Italian artists, Vasari described Uccello as a man so obsessed with the science of perspective that he neglected his painting, his family, and even his pet birds (his *uccelli*). According to Vasari, Uccello's wife complained that he sat up drawing all night and when she called to him to come to bed he would say, "Oh, what a sweet thing this perspective is!" (Vasari, trans. Bondanella and Bondanella, p. 83).

CASTAGNO Andrea del Castagno (c. 1417/19–1457) is best known for a fresco of **THE LAST SUPPER** painted for a convent of Benedictine nuns in 1447 (**FIG. 20-25**). The subject was often painted in monastic refectories (dining halls) to remind the monks or nuns of Christ's Last Supper with his first followers and encourage them to see their daily gatherings for meals almost as a sacramental act rooted in this biblical tradition. Here Castagno has not portrayed the scene in the biblical setting of an "upper room." Rather, the humble house of the original account has become a great palace with sumptuous marble revetment. The most brilliantly colored and wildly patterned marble panel frames the off-center heads of Christ and Judas to focus viewers on the most important part of the picture. Judas takes his traditional position on the viewer's side of the table, separated from the other apostles. Equally conventional is the seemingly sleeping figure of St. John, head collapsed onto the tabletop (John 13:23). The lines of floor tiles, ceiling rafters, and paneled walls draw viewers into the scene, notably the nuns who would have seen the painting as an extension of their own dining hall. At first, the lines

of the orthogonals seem perfectly logical, but close examination reveals that only the lines of the ceiling converge to a single point. Two windows light the painting's room from the direction of the actual refectory windows, further unifying the two spaces.

FRA FILIPPO LIPPI During the middle of the fifteenth century, portraiture comes into its own as a major artistic form in Italy, and among the most extraordinary—if enigmatic—examples is this **PORTRAIT OF A WOMAN AND MAN** (**FIG. 20-27**), an early work of Fra Filippo Lippi (c. 1406–1469). This painting is also the earliest surviving double portrait of the Italian Renaissance. Lippi grew up as an orphan in the Carmelite church where Masaccio had painted frescos in the Brancacci Chapel, and art historians have stressed the impact this work had on Lippi's development as an artist. But although he may have absorbed Masaccio's predilection for softly rounded forms situated in carefully mapped spaces, in Lippi's hands these artistic tools became the basis for pictures that often ask more questions than they answer, by stressing outline at the same time as form, and by creating complex and often confusing spatial systems.

The emphasis in this double portrait is squarely on the woman. She is spotlighted in the foreground, sharply profiled against a window that serves as an unsettling internal frame, not big enough to contain her. This window opens onto a vista, clearly a fragment of a larger world, but one that highlights an orthogonal to emphasize a spatial recession only partially revealed. The woman blocks most of this vista with her shining visage and sumptuous costume—notably its embroidered velvet, fur lining, and luminous

The palazzos of wealthy Florentine families housed not only panels painted with portraits or Madonnas; they were also appointed with massive pieces of elaborate furniture. Constructed of richly carved wood that was gilded and often covered with paintings, these household objects were not a minor sideline, but a central feature of the fifteenth-century Florentine art world. Some of the most impressive surviving examples of Renaissance furniture are great chests—called **cassoni**—that were used to store clothing and other precious personal objects in a couple's bedroom. They were frequently commissioned in pairs on the occasion of a wedding.

Marriages between members of wealthy Florentine families were not the result of romantic connections between two young people. They were political alliances and economic transactions that involved the transfer of capital and the exchange of gifts as displays of wealth. In preparation for such high-class marriages, husbands refurbished their living quarters in the family palazzo where they would bring a bride into the household. We have a detailed accounting of the extent of work, as well as the required expenditure, when 30-year-old Lorenzo di Matteo Morelli prepared his apartments for the arrival of his young bride, Vaggia di Tanai Nerli, after their marriage in 1472. His commissioning of a pair of *cassoni*—one for him and one for Vaggia—represented almost two-thirds of the entire cost of redecoration. Fortunately, the two chests still survive (**FIG. 20–26**). They are among the most important and best-preserved Renaissance *cassoni* that have come down to us, especially since they still maintain the original backboard—called a *spalliera*—that was produced concurrent with and hung on the wall directly behind the chests when they were placed in Lorenzo's bedroom. The lion's feet on which the chests now stand are modern additions, and the *spalliera* was originally hung as one continuous painting above both *cassoni*, not two separate panels mounted behind each lid as in the current configuration. Otherwise these chests give a strong sense of their original appearance.

Like most Renaissance *cassoni*, Lorenzo's chest is painted with pictures drawn from stories that extol moral virtues, and reflect some of their values and glories on Lorenzo himself. The long painted scene on the front tells the story of ancient Roman hero Marcus Furius Camillus' defeat of the Gauls as he

chases them out of Rome. On the *spalliera*, *trompe l'oeil* curtains part to reveal the scene of another Roman hero defending a bridge against insurmountable odds. Presumably Lorenzo wanted to be seen as a heroic descendant of such illustrious Romans—strong, brave, and triumphant. The scenes portrayed on Vaggia's chest (like Lorenzo's, identified by her coat of arms) challenge her to care for the children she is expected to produce and practice the virtues of temperance, prudence, and patience that were valued in Florentine patrician brides.

The Morelli–Nerli *cassoni* passed from Lorenzo to his son, and they remained in the Morelli family at least until 1680, maybe into the nineteenth century, when they first appeared together in the art market. Elaborate Renaissance furniture became coveted items in the homes of wealthy art collectors in late nineteenth-century Europe and America, where the new owners doubtless saw themselves as worthy successors to the wealthy and powerful merchants who had commissioned them at the height of the Italian Renaissance.

20-26 • Jacopo del Sellaio, Biagio d'Antonio (painters), and Zanobi di Domenico (woodworker) **CASSONE MADE FOR THE MARRIAGE OF LORENZO DI MATTEO MORELLI AND VAGGIA DI TANAI NERLI (ONE OF A SET OF TWO)**

1472. Tempera and gold on wood, chest 83½″ × 75″ × 30″ (212 × 193 × 76.2 cm). The Samuel Courtauld Trust, The Courtauld Gallery, London. (F.1947.LF.4)

20-27 • Fra Filippo Lippi PORTRAIT OF A WOMAN AND MAN (ANGIOLA DI BERNARDO SAPITI AND LORENZO DI RANIERI SCOLARI?)
c. 1435–1445. Tempera on wood panel, 25¼″ × 16½″ (64.1 × 41.9 cm). Metropolitan Museum of Art, New York.

Some art historians have seen in the sumptuousness of this woman's costume an indication that she is a newlywed, outfitted in the extravagant clothing and jewelry presented to her by her husband at the time of their marriage, especially since the pearls sewn with gold threads into the embroidery on her sleeve spell out the word lealtà, meaning "loyalty." Florentine law prevented a woman from wearing such ostentatious expressions of wealth—especially the jewelry—more than three years after her marriage.

pearls. There is no engagement with the viewer and little sense of likeness. And it is not at all clear where or to what she directs her attention, especially since the gaze of the man in the background does not meet hers. He is even more of a mystery. We see only a masklike sliver of his profile—capped by the red *berretta* that signals his high status—although the substantiality of his face is reinforced by the strong shadow it casts against the window casement through which he looks. Unlike the woman, who clasps her inert hands in front of her as if to highlight her rings, this man fidgets with his

fingers, perhaps to draw our attention to the heraldic device below him that may identify him as a member of the Scolari family. This could be a double portrait of Lorenzo di Ranieri Scolari and Angiola di Bernardo Sapiti, who married in 1436 and welcomed a son in 1444. But what does the painting say about them? Does it commemorate their marriage, celebrate the birth of their child, or memorialize one of their deaths? All have been proposed by art historians as an explanation for this innovative double portrait, but it remains a puzzle to be pondered. Could that pondering be the point of the picture?

ITALIAN ART IN THE SECOND HALF OF THE FIFTEENTH CENTURY

In the second half of the fifteenth century, the ideas and ideals of artists like Brunelleschi, Donatello, and Masaccio began to spread from Florence to the rest of Italy, as artists who had trained or worked in Florence traveled to other cities to work, carrying the style with them. Northern Italy embraced the new Classical ideas swiftly, especially in the ducal courts at Urbino and Mantua. Venice and Rome also emerged as innovative art centers in the last quarter of the century.

URBINO

Under Federico da Montefeltro, Urbino developed into a thriving artistic center. A new palace was under construction, and prominent architects and artists were brought into the court to make the new princely residence a showcase of ducal splendor.

THE PALACE AT URBINO Construction of the palace had been under way for about 20 years in 1468 when Federico hired Luciano Laurana (c. 1420/1425–1479) to direct the work. Among Laurana's major contributions to the palace were closing the courtyard with a fourth wing and redesigning the courtyard façades (**FIG. 20-28**). The result is a superbly rational solution to the problems created in courtyard design by the awkward juncture of the arcades at the four corners. The ground-level portico on each side has arches supported by columns, but piers embellished with pilasters bridge the corner angles. This arrangement avoided the awkward visual effect of two arches springing from a single column (see FIG. 20-8) and gave the corner a greater sense of stability. A variation of the composite capital (a Corinthian capital with added Ionic volutes) was used, perhaps for the first time, on the ground level. Corinthian pilasters flank the windows in the story above, forming divisions that repeat the bays of the portico. (The two low upper stories were added later.) The plain architrave was engraved with inscriptions lauding Federico's many virtues, added when the count became duke of Urbino in 1476.

The interior of the Urbino palace likewise reflected its patron's embrace of new Renaissance ideas and interest in Classical antiquity, seen in carved marble fireplaces and window and door surrounds. In creating luxurious home furnishings and interior decorations for sophisticated clients such as Federico, Italian artists found freedom to experiment with new subjects, treatments, and techniques. Among these was the creation of remarkable **trompe l'oeil** ("fool-the-eye") effects using scrupulously applied linear perspective and foreshortening in **intarsia** (wood inlay) decoration. An extraordinary example is on the walls of Federico da Montefeltro's **STUDIOLO**, or study, a room for private conversation and the owner's collection of fine books and art objects (**FIG. 20-29**). The work, probably done by the architect and woodworker Giuliano da Maiano (1432–1490), carries the date 1476.

20-29 • Giuliano da Maiano (?) **STUDIOLO OF FEDERICO DA MONTEFELTRO**
Ducal palace, Urbino. 1476.
Intarsia, height 7′3″ (2.21 m).

The elaborate scenes in the small room are created entirely of wood inlaid on flat surfaces. Each detail is rendered with convincing illusionism: pilasters, carved cupboards with latticed doors, niches with statues, paintings, and built-in tables. Prominent in the decorative scheme is the prudent and industrious squirrel, a Renaissance symbol of the ideal ruler: in other words, of Federico da Montefeltro. A large "window" looks out onto an elegant marble loggia with a distant view of the countryside through its arches; and the shelves, cupboards, and tables are filled with all manner of fascinating things—scientific instruments, books, even the duke's armor hanging like a suit in a closet.

PIERO DELLA FRANCESCA Federico brought the artist Piero della Francesca (c. 1415–1492) to Urbino. Piero had worked in Florence in the 1430s before settling in his native Borgo San Sepolcro, a Tuscan hill town under papal control. He knew current art theory and art practice—including Brunelleschi's system of spatial illusion and linear perspective, Masaccio's powerful modeling of forms and atmospheric perspective, and Alberti's theoretical treatises. Piero was one of the few practicing artists who also wrote his own books of theory. Not surprisingly, in his treatise on perspective he emphasized the geometry and the volumetric construction of forms and spaces that were so apparent in his own work.

20–30 • Piero della Francesca BAPTISM OF CHRIST
c. 1450. Tempera on wood panel, 66″ × 45¾″ (1.67 × 1.16 m). National Gallery, London.

The three angels standing in a cluster at left, partially overlapped by the foreground tree, have been interpreted as an emblem of concord—representing the rapprochement reached between the Roman and Byzantine Christian churches in 1439 at the Council of Florence. Another reference to this council has been seen in the exotic costumes of the figures in the far background. Since the accord reached at the council was very short-lived, this interpretation would move the date of the painting into the early 1440s rather than the 1450s.

These characteristic features of Piero's painting are marvelously apparent in a serene image of the **BAPTISM OF CHRIST** that has become one of Piero's signature works (**FIG. 20–30**). It was commissioned by the Graziani family, probably during the 1450s, for the priory of San Giovanni Battista in Borgo San Sepolchro. The central figure of Christ dominates the painting, standing in a shallow stream of glassy water under a tree of manicured regularity. Christ's legs and the sleek tree trunk set up a series of emphatically upright forms, one of many formal relationships that reverberate both across the picture's surface and into its carefully measured space. Feet and ankles rotate across the lower quarter of the painting, providing a clear and well-distributed sense of grounding for the figural composition, while the radically foreshortened dove (Holy Spirit), John's baptismal dish, and the clouds create a rhythmic line of horizontals that adds stability above and creates a staccato rhythm that merges foreground and background on the painting's surface. The mirrored profiles and gestures of the outside angel and the baptizing John provide an internal frame for the central action. Such carefully crafted formal

20–31 • Piero della Francesca BATTISTA SFORZA AND FEDERICO DA MONTEFELTRO
c. 1474. Oil on wood panel, each 18½″ × 13″ (47 × 33 cm). Galleria degli Uffizi, Florence.

Battista Sforza died in 1472 at age 26, shortly after the birth of her ninth child, a son who would one day be duke. We are told that Federico was disconsolate. Some arranged aristocratic marriage alliances blossomed into loving partnerships, and it seems that one such was memorialized in this double portrait.

correspondences infuse this picture with an air of beatific calm and peaceful stasis—a stillness suggesting that nothing will ever change, no one will ever move in this frozen moment within a story that, for Christian believers, actually changed everything.

Piero traveled widely—to Rome, to the Este court in Ferrara, and especially to Urbino. In about 1474, he painted the portraits of **FEDERICO DA MONTEFELTRO** and his recently deceased wife, **BATTISTA SFORZA** (**FIG. 20-31**). The small panels resemble Flemish painting in their detail and luminosity, their record of surfaces and textures, and their vast landscapes. But in traditional Italian fashion, figures are portrayed in strict profile, disengaged psychologically from the viewer. The profile format also allowed for an accurate recording of Federico's likeness without emphasizing two disfiguring scars—the loss of his right eye from a lance blow and his broken nose. His good left eye is shown, and the angular profile of his nose might easily be merely a distinctive family trait. Typically, Piero emphasized the underlying geometry of

the forms. Dressed in the most elegant fashion (Federico wears his red ducal robe and Battista's jewels are meticulously recorded), they are silhouetted against a panoramic landscape. These are the hills around Urbino, seemingly dissolving into infinity through an atmospheric perspective as subtle and luminous as in any Flemish panel painting. Piero used another northern European device in the harbor view just in front of Federico, where the water narrows into a river that leads us into the distant landscape (see FIG. 19-17). He would have had contact in Urbino with the Flemings who were also working there.

MANTUA

Ludovico Gonzaga, the marquis of Mantua, ruled a territory that lies on the north Italian plain between Venice and Milan. Like Federico, he made his fortune as a *condottiere*. Ludovico was schooled by humanist teachers and created a court where humanist ideas flourished in art as well as in literature.

20-32 • Andrea Mantegna TWO VIEWS OF THE CAMERA PICTA, DUCAL PALACE, MANTUA

1465–1474. Fresco, diameter of false oculus 8'9" (2.7 m); room 26'6" square (8 m square).

MANTEGNA Working at Ludovico's court was Andrea Mantegna (1431–1506), a painter trained in Padua and profoundly influenced by the sculptor Donatello, who arrived in Padua in 1443 and worked there for a decade. Mantegna learned the Florentine system of linear perspective and pushed to their limits experiments in radically foreshortened forms and dramatic spatial recessions. He went to work for Ludovico Gonzaga in 1460, and he continued to work for the Gonzaga family for the rest of his life.

Perhaps his finest works are the frescos of the **CAMERA PICTA** ("Painted Room"), a tower chamber in Ludovico's palace, which Mantegna decorated between 1465 and 1474 (**FIG. 20-32**). Around the walls the family—each member seemingly identified by a portrait likeness—receives in landscapes and in loggias the return of Ludovico's son, Cardinal Francesco Gonzaga. On the domed ceiling, the artist painted a *tour de force* of radical perspective in a technique called *di sotto in sù* ("from below upwards"). The room appears to be open to a cloud-filled sky through a large oculus in a simulated marble- and mosaic-covered vault. On each side of a precariously balanced planter, four young women—one an African, outfitted in an exotic turban—peer over a marble balustrade into the room below, while a fourth looks dreamily upward. Joined by a large peacock, several putti play around the balustrade, three standing on the interior ledge of a cornice, unprotected by the balustrade, toes projecting into space but seemingly oblivious to the danger of their perch. This ceiling began a long tradition of illusionistic ceiling painting that culminated in the extravagant and explosive ceilings of Baroque churches (see Chapter 23).

ROME

Rome's development into a Renaissance center of the arts was greatly enhanced when Pope Sixtus IV called to the city in the early 1480s a group of young Florentine and Umbrian artists to decorate the walls of his newly built chapel (1479–1481), now named the **SISTINE CHAPEL** after him (**FIG. 20-33**). Botticelli and Ghirlandaio were among the most famous artists summoned to the chapel to paint, but many art historians believe that Perugino was the supervising artist in charge of the project.

PERUGINO Pietro Vannucci, called "Perugino" (c. 1445–1523), was originally from near the town of Perugia in Umbria (thus the nickname), and he worked for a while in Florence, but by 1479 he was in Rome. Two years later, he was working on the Sistine murals. One of his contributions, *Christ Giving the Keys to St. Peter* (foreground painting at lower right in FIG. 20-33; also FIG. 20-18), portrayed the event that provided biblical support for the supremacy of papal authority (Matthew 16:19). In a light-filled piazza in which banded paving stones provide a geometric

20-33 • VIEW OF THE SISTINE CHAPEL SHOWING PAINTINGS COMMISSIONED FOR THE SIDE WALLS BY POPE SIXTUS IV
Vatican, Rome. At lower right, Perugino's *Christ Giving the Keys to St. Peter*, c. 1480–1482. 11′5½″ × 18′8½″ (3.48 × 5.70 m).

grid for perspectival recession, the figures stand like chess pieces on the squares, scaled to size according to their distance from the picture plane and modeled by a consistent light source from the upper left. Triumphal arches inspired by ancient Rome frame the church and focus attention on the center of the composition, where the vital key is being transferred. The carefully calibrated scene is softened by the subdued colors, the distant idealized landscape and cloudy skies, and the variety of the figures' positions.

FLORENCE

Florence remained a thriving artistic center throughout the fifteenth century. Sculptors continued to explore Classical themes and experiment with the representation of the human form. Florentine painting pursued a love of material opulence, an interest in describing the natural world, and a poetic, mystical spirit, motivated by the patronage of citizens who sought to advertise their wealth and prestige as well as by the religious fervor that arose at the very end of the century.

20-34 • Andrea del Verrocchio DAVID
Commissioned by Lorenzo de' Medici for the Medici Palace. c. 1470–1475. Bronze with gilded details, height 49⅝″ (1.26 m). Museo Nazionale del Bargello, Florence.

VERROCCHIO One of the most prestigious and active workshops in Florence was that of Andrea di Michele Cioni (1435–1488), nicknamed "Verrocchio" ("true eye"). Trained as a goldsmith, but best known for his works as a painter and bronze sculptor, Verrocchio was also a gifted teacher, counting among his pupils Perugino and Leonardo da Vinci. Around 1470, Lorenzo de' Medici commissioned from Verrocchio a bronze statue of David for the Palazzo Medici, the location where Donatello's sculpture of the same subject (see FIG. 20-14) was then displayed. Verrocchio's work (FIG. 20-34) seems to have been conceived as a response to the demure, sleek, but awkwardly boyish nude of his famous predecessor. Verrocchio's triumphant biblical hero is a poised and proud adolescent, modestly clothed and confidently looking out to meet the gaze of the viewer. Although slight, he is equipped with the developing musculature required for the

daunting task—whose accomplishment is signaled by the severed head of his foe, displayed like a trophy between his feet. The careful attention to the textural details of hair and clothing reveal Verrocchio's training as a goldsmith.

POLLAIUOLO Florentine sculptors not only created large-scale figures, but also small works designed to inspire the mind and delight the eye of its private owner. The ambitious and multi-talented Antonio del Pollaiuolo (c. 1431–1498)—goldsmith, embroidery designer, printmaker, sculptor, and painter—who came to work for the Medici family in Florence about 1460, created mostly small bronze sculptures. His **HERCULES AND ANTAEUS** of about 1475 is one of the largest (FIG. 20-35). This study of complex interlocking figures has an explosive energy that can best be appreciated by viewing it from every angle.

20-35 • Antonio del Pollaiuolo HERCULES AND ANTAEUS
c. 1475. Bronze, height with base 18″ (45.7 cm). Museo Nazionale del Bargello, Florence.

20-36 • Antonio del Pollaiuolo
THE BATTLE OF THE NUDES
c. 1465–1470. Engraving, 15⅛″ × 23¼″
(38.3 × 59 cm). Cincinnati Art Museum,
Ohio. Bequest of Herbert Greer French.
1943.118

Statuettes of religious subjects were still popular, but humanist patrons were beginning to collect bronzes of Classical subjects. Many sculptors, especially those trained as goldsmiths, started to cast small copies after well-known ancient works. Some artists also executed original designs *all'antica* ("in the antique style") to appeal to a cultivated humanist taste. Hercules was always a popular figure; as a patron of Florence, he was on the city seal. Among the many courageous acts by which Hercules gained immortality was the slaying of the evil Antaeus in a wrestling match by lifting him off the earth, the source of the giant's great physical power.

An engraving by Pollaiuolo, **THE BATTLE OF THE NUDES** (**FIG. 20-36**), reflects two interests of Renaissance scholars—the study of Classical sculpture and anatomical research. Pollaiuolo may have intended this, his only known—but highly influential—print, as a study in composition involving the human figure in action. The naked men, fighting each other ferociously against a tapestrylike background of foliage, seem to have been drawn from a single model in a variety of poses, many of which were taken from Classical sources. Like the artist's *Hercules and Antaeus*, much of the engraving's fascination lies in its depiction of the muscles of the male body reacting under tension, more impressive than accurate—anatomical accuracy was clearly not the point.

20-37 • Domenico Ghirlandaio **SCENES FROM THE LIFE OF ST. FRANCIS; ALTARPIECE WITH NATIVITY AND ADORATION OF THE SHEPHERDS**
Sassetti Chapel, church of Santa Trinità, Florence. 1483–1486. Fresco, chapel 12′2″ deep × 17′2″ wide (3.7 × 5.25 m).

20-38 • Domenico Ghirlandaio **CONFIRMATION OF THE FRANCISCAN RULE BY POPE HONORIUS III**
Sassetti Chapel, church of Santa Trinità, Florence. 1483–1486. Fresco, width at base 17′2″ (5.25 m).

GHIRLANDAIO The most prolific later fifteenth-century Florentine painting workshop was that of Domenico di Tommaso Bigordi (1449–1494), known as "Ghirlandaio" ("Garland-Maker"), a nickname first adopted by his father, who was a goldsmith noted for his floral wreaths. A skilled storyteller, the younger Ghirlandaio reinterpreted the art of earlier fifteenth-century painters into a visual language of descriptive immediacy and structural clarity.

Among Ghirlandaio's most impressive narrative programs was the fresco cycle of the **LIFE OF ST. FRANCIS**, commissioned by the wealthy manager of the Medici bank, Francesco Sassetti, and painted between 1483 and 1486 on the walls of the Sassetti family burial chapel in the Florentine church of Santa Trinità (**FIG. 20-37**). In the uppermost tier of the paintings (**FIG. 20-38**), Pope Honorius gives a confirmation of the Franciscan order to the kneeling figure of St. Francis, with the Loggia dei Lanzi and the Palazzo della Signoria (see **FIG. 18-2**) in the background. The foreground figures—arranged in a composition that parallels the sacred scene behind them—are portrait likenesses of well-known Florentines. At far right are (from left to right) poet Antonio Pucci, Lorenzo de' Medici, the patron Francesco Sassetti, and his son Federigo, all

of whom seem to be receiving the approaching retinue coming up the stairs at the lower center of the fresco—humanist poet Poliziano leading his pupils, the sons of Lorenzo de' Medici. Just below this scene, in the middle register (see **FIG. 20-37**), a small boy who has fallen from an upper window is resurrected by St. Francis. This miracle is likewise witnessed by contemporary Florentines, including other members of the Sassetti family and Ghirlandaio himself, and the scene takes place in the piazza outside the actual church of Santa Trinità. Ghirlandaio has thus transferred both events from thirteenth-century Rome to contemporary Florence, painting recognizable views of the city and portraits of living Florentines, delighting in local color and anecdotal detail. Perhaps Renaissance painters, like Gothic painters, represented sacred narratives in contemporary settings to emphasize their current relevance, or perhaps they and their patrons simply enjoyed seeing themselves dressed in their finery, witnessing these dramas within the cities of which they were justifiably proud.

The altarpiece Ghirlandaio painted for the Sassetti Chapel portrays the **NATIVITY AND ADORATION OF THE SHEPHERDS** (**FIG. 20-39**). It is still in its original frame, still in the

20–39 • Domenico Ghirlandaio NATIVITY AND ADORATION OF THE SHEPHERDS
Altarpiece in the Sassetti Chapel, church of Santa Trinità, Florence. 1485. Panel, 65¾" square (1.67 m square).

place for which it was painted (see FIG. 20-37). The influence of Hugo van der Goes's Portinari Altarpiece (see FIG. 19-19), which had been placed on the high altar of the church of Sant'Egidio two years earlier, in 1483, is strong. Ghirlandaio's Christ Child also lies on the ground, adored by the Virgin while rugged shepherds kneel at the right. Ghirlandaio even copies some of Hugo's flowers—although here the iris, a symbol of the Passion, springs not from a vase, but from the earth in the lower right corner. But Ghirlandaio highlights references to Classical Rome. First to catch the eye are the two Classical pilasters with Corinthian capitals, one of which is dated by inscription to 1485. The manger is an ancient sarcophagus with an inscription that promises resurrection (as in the fresco directly above the altarpiece where St. Francis is reviving a child); and in the distance a Classical arch inscribed with a reference to the

Roman general Pompey the Great frames the road along which the Magi travel. Weighty, restrained actors replace the psychologically intense figures of Hugo's painting. Ghirlandaio joins a clear foreground, middle ground, and background in part by the road and in part by **aerial perspective**, which creates a seamless transition of color, from the sharp details and primary hues of the Adoration to the soft gray mountains in the distance.

BOTTICELLI Like most artists in the second half of the fifteenth century, Alessandro di Mariano di Vanni Filipepi (1445–1510), called "Botticelli" ("the little barrel," a nickname borrowed from his older brother), painted sculptural figures that were modeled by light from a consistent source and placed in a setting rendered illusionistic by linear perspective. An outstanding portraitist, he, like

20-40 • Sandro Botticelli BIRTH OF VENUS
c. 1484–1486. Tempera and gold on canvas, 5′8⅞″ × 9′1⅞″ (1.8 × 2.8 m). Galleria degli Uffizi, Florence.

Ghirlandaio, often included recognizable contemporary figures among the saints and angels in religious paintings. He worked in Florence, often for the Medici, then was called to Rome in 1481 by Pope Sixtus IV to help decorate the new Sistine Chapel along with Ghirlandaio, Perugino, and other artists.

Botticelli returned to Florence that same year and entered a new phase of his career. Like other artists working for patrons steeped in Classical scholarship and humanistic thought, he was exposed to philosophical speculations on beauty—as well as to the examples of ancient art in his employers' collections. For the Medici, Botticelli produced secular paintings of mythological subjects inspired by ancient works and by contemporary Neoplatonic thought. Art historian Michael Baxandall has shown that these works were also patterned on the slow movements of fifteenth-century Florentine dance, in which figures acted out their relationships to one another in public performances that would have influenced the thinking and viewing habits of both painters and their audience.

The overall appearance of Botticelli's *Primavera*, or *Spring* (see "A Closer Look," page 628), recalls Flemish tapestries (see FIG. 19-8), which were very popular in Italy at the time. And its subject—like the subjects of many tapestries—is a highly complex **allegory** (a symbolic illustration of a concept or principle), interweaving Neoplatonic ideas with esoteric references to Classical sources. In simple terms, Neoplatonic philosophers and poets conceived Venus, the goddess of love, as having two natures. The first ruled over earthly, human love and the second over universal, divine love. In this way the philosophers could argue that Venus was a Classical equivalent of the Virgin Mary. *Primavera* was painted at the time of the wedding of Lorenzo di Pierfrancesco de' Medici and Semiramide d'Appiano in 1482. The theme suggests love and fertility in marriage, and the painting can be read as a lyrical wish for a similar fecundity in the union of Lorenzo and Semiramide—a sort of highly refined fertility dance.

Several years later, some of the same mythological figures reappeared in Botticelli's **BIRTH OF VENUS** (FIG. 20-40), in which the central image represents the Neoplatonic idea of divine love in the form of a nude Venus based on an antique statue type known as the "modest Venus" that ultimately derives from Praxiteles' *Aphrodite of Knidos* (see FIG. 5-53). Botticelli's Classical goddess of love and beauty, born of sea foam, averts her eyes from our gaze as she floats ashore on a scallop shell, carefully arranging her hands and hair to hide—but actually drawing attention to—her sexuality. Indeed, she is an arrestingly alluring figure, set within a graceful composition organized by Botticelli's characteristically decorative, almost calligraphic use of line. Blown by the wind—Zephyr (with his love, the nymph Chloris)—Venus arrives at her earthly home. She is welcomed by a devotee who offers her a garment embroidered with flowers. The circumstances of this commission are uncertain. It is painted on canvas, which suggests that it may have been a banner or a painted tapestrylike wall hanging.

Botticelli's later career was apparently affected by a profound spiritual crisis. While the artist was creating his mythologies for the Medici, a Dominican monk, Fra Girolamo Savonarola (active in Florence 1490–1498), was preaching impassioned sermons denouncing the worldliness of Florence. Many Florentines reacted with orgies of self-recrimination, and processions of weeping penitents wound through the streets. Botticelli, too, may have fallen into a state of religious fervor. In a dramatic gesture of repentance, he burned many of his earlier paintings and began to produce highly emotional pictures pervaded by an intense religiosity.

A CLOSER LOOK | *Primavera*

by Sandro Botticelli, c. 1482. Tempera on wood panel.
6′8″ × 10′4″ (2.03 × 3.15 m). Galleria degli Uffizi, Florence.

Mercury, the sign for the month of May, disperses the winter clouds with his caduceus. This staff, wound about with serpents, became a symbol for the medical profession. The name Medici means "doctors."

Venus, clothed in contemporary costume and crowned with a marriage wreath, appears in her role as the goddess of wedded love. The presence of both Venus and Mercury may be an astrological reference; prominent Neoplatonist Marsilio Ficino told Lorenzo de Pierfrancesco de' Medici that these planets were aligned in his horoscope.

The setting of the painting is a grove of orange trees. These hold a double meaning—both suggestive of Venus' Garden of the Hesperides, with its golden fruit, and perhaps an allusion to the Medici, whose coat of arms featured golden orbs.

This three-figure grouping tells a story. Zephyrus, the west wind, is accosting the virgin nymph Chloris, identifiable from the roses pouring out of her mouth. Once Zephyrus makes her his bride, Chloris is transformed into the goddess Flora, the elaborately dressed personification of spring at the front of the group.

The gold flames decorating Mercury's garment are also an attribute of St. Lawrence, the namesake of Lorenzo di Pierfrancesco de' Medici, for whom this painting was made. The laurel tree (*laurus* in Latin) behind Zephyrus also alludes to Lorenzo's name.

The Three Graces symbolize ideal female virtues—Chastity, Beauty, Love. Venus' son Cupid—the embodiment of romantic desire—playfully aims his arrow at them.

So accurate is their representation, 138 of the 190 flowering plants depicted in the painting have been identified. Almost all grow in the neighborhood of Florence between the months of March and April, and most carry symbolic associations with love and marriage.

Flora scatters flowers held in a fold of her dress at the level of her womb, equating the fecundity brought about by changing seasons with female procreative fertility.

View the Closer Look for *Primavera* on myartslab.com

VENICE

In the last quarter of the fifteenth century, Venice emerged as a major Renaissance art center. Ruled as an oligarchy (government by a select few) with an elected duke (*doge* in the Venetian dialect), the city government was founded at the end of the Roman Empire and survived until the Napoleonic era. In building their city, the Venetians had turned marshes into a commercial seaport, and they saw the sea as a resource, not a threat. They depended on naval power and on the natural defense of their lagoons rather than city walls. Venice turned toward the east, especially after the crusaders' conquest of Constantinople in 1204, designing the church of St. Mark as a great Byzantine building sheathed in mosaics (see FIG. 8–24A). In addition to its long history of painting and sculpture, Venice excelled in the arts of textiles and jewelry, gold and enamel, glass and mosaic, fine printing and bookbinding.

VENETIAN PALACES Venice was a city of waterways with few large public spaces. Even palaces had only small interior courtyards and tiny gardens, and were separated by narrow alleys. Their façades overlooked the canals, permitting owners to project on these major thoroughfares the large portals, windows, and loggias that proclaimed their importance through the lavishness of their residences—a sharp contrast to the fortresslike character of most Florentine town houses (see FIG. 20–7). But, as with the Florentine great houses, Venetian owners combined in these structures a place of business with a dwelling.

The **CA D'ORO** (House of Gold), home of the wealthy nobleman Marino Contarini, has a splendid front with three superimposed loggias facing the Grand Canal (**FIG. 20–41**). The house was constructed between 1421 and 1437, and its asymmetrical elevation is based on a traditional Byzantine plan. A wide central hall ran from front to back all the way through the building to a small inner courtyard with a well and garden. An outside stair led to the main floor on the second level. The entrance on the canal permitted goods to be delivered directly into the warehouse that constituted the ground floor. The principal floor, on the second level, had a salon and reception room opening on the richly decorated loggia. It was filled with light from large windows, and more light reflected off the polished terrazzo floor. Private family rooms

filled the upper stories. Contarini's instructions to his contractors and workers specified that the façade was to be painted with white enamel and ultramarine blue and that the red stones in the patterned wall should be oiled to make them even brighter. Details of carving, such as coats of arms and balls on the crest at the roofline, were to be gilded. Beautiful as the palace is today, in the fifteenth and sixteenth centuries it must have been truly spectacular.

THE BELLINI BROTHERS The domes of the church of St. Mark dominated the city center, and the rich colors of its glowing mosaics captured painters' imaginations. Perhaps it was their love of color that encouraged the Venetian painters to embrace the oil medium for both panel and canvas painting.

The most important Venetian artists of this period were two brothers: Gentile (c. 1429–1507) and Giovanni (c. 1430–1516) Bellini, whose father, Jacopo (c. 1400–1470), had also been a central figure in Venetian art. Andrea Mantegna became part of this circle when he married Jacopo's daughter in 1453.

Gentile Bellini celebrated the daily life of the city in large, lively narratives, such as the **PROCESSION OF THE RELIC OF THE TRUE CROSS BEFORE THE CHURCH OF ST. MARK** (**FIG. 20–42**). Every year on the feast of St. Mark (April 25), the Confraternity of St. John the Evangelist carried the miracle-working relic of the True Cross in a procession through the square in front of the church. Bellini's painting of 1496 depicts an event that had occurred in 1444: the miraculous recovery of a sick child whose father (the man in red kneeling to the right of the relic) prayed for help as the relic passed by. Gentile has rendered the cityscape with great attention to detail. The mosaic-encrusted Byzantine

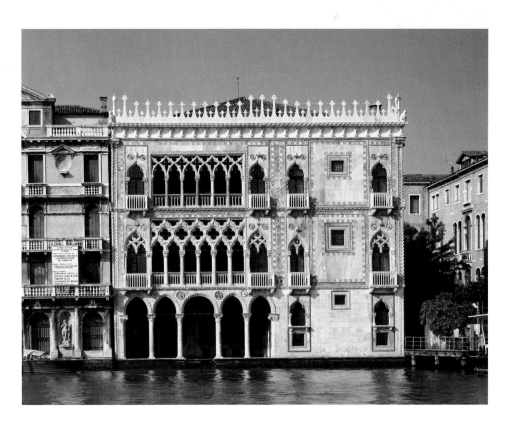

20-41 • CA D'ORO (CONTARINI PALACE), VENICE
1421–1437.

Cathedral of St. Mark (see FIG. 8-24A) forms a backdrop for the procession, and the doge's palace and base of the bell tower can be seen at the right. The gold reliquary is carried under a canopy, surrounded by marchers with giant candles, led by a choir and followed at the far right by the doge and other officials. Gentile's procession serves as a reminder that fifteenth-century piazzas and buildings were sites of ritual ceremony, and it was in moments such as this that they were brought to life.

Gentile's brother Giovanni amazed and attracted patrons with his artistic virtuosity for almost 60 years. The **VIRGIN AND CHILD ENTHRONED WITH SS. FRANCIS, JOHN THE BAPTIST, JOB, DOMINIC, SEBASTIAN, AND LOUIS OF TOULOUSE** (FIG. 20-43), painted about 1478 for the chapel of the Hospital of San Giobbe (St. Job), exhibits a dramatic perspectival view up into a tunnel vault that leads to an apse. Giovanni may have known his brother-in-law Mantegna's early experiments in radical foreshortening and in the use of a low vanishing point. Here Giovanni positions the vanishing point for the rapidly converging lines of the architecture at bottom center, just above the

20-43 • Giovanni Bellini **VIRGIN AND CHILD ENTHRONED WITH SS. FRANCIS, JOHN THE BAPTIST, JOB, DOMINIC, SEBASTIAN, AND LOUIS OF TOULOUSE**
(Computer reconstruction.) Originally commissioned for the chapel of the Hospital of San Giobbe, Venice. c. 1478. Oil on wood panel, 15′4″ × 8′4″ (4.67 × 2.54 m). Galleria dell'Accademia, Venice. The original frame is in the church of San Giobbe, Venice.

Art historians have given the special name **sacra conversazione** ("holy conversation") to this type of composition that shows saints, angels, and sometimes even the painting's donors in the same pictorial space with the enthroned Virgin and Child. Despite the name, no "conversation" or spoken interaction takes place in a literal sense. Instead, the individuals portrayed are joined in a mystical and eternal communion that occurs outside human time and space.

20-44 • Giovanni Bellini
ST. FRANCIS IN ECSTASY
c. 1470s. Oil and tempera on wood
panel, 49″ × 55⅞″ (125 × 142 cm).
The Frick Collection, New York.

Giovanni Bellini's painting of **ST. FRANCIS IN ECSTASY** (**FIG. 20-44**), also from the 1470s, recalls Flemish painting in the fine detail with which he rendered the natural world. The saint stands bathed in early morning sunlight, his outspread hands displaying his stigmata. Francis had moved to a cave in the barren wilderness in his search for communion with God, but in the world Giovanni creates for him, the fields blossom and flocks of animals graze. The grape arbor over his desk adds to the atmosphere of sylvan delight. Like most of the fifteenth-century religious art we have seen, however, Bellini presents viewers with a natural world saturated in symbolism. Here a relationship between St. Francis and Moses is outlined. The tree symbolizes the burning bush; the stream, the miraculous spring brought forth by Moses. The crane and donkey represent the monastic virtue of patience. The detailed description, luminous palette, and symbolic surroundings suggest Flemish art, but the golden light suffusing the painting is unmistakably Venetian.

floor. His figures stand in a Classical architectural interior with a coffered barrel vault reminiscent of Masaccio's *Trinity* (see FIG. 20-19). The gold mosaic, with its identifying inscription and stylized seraphim (angels of the highest rank), recalls Byzantine art and the long tradition of Byzantine-inspired painting and mosaics produced in Venice.

THINK ABOUT IT

20.1 Explain how one Florentine sculptor discussed in this chapter helped establish the increasing naturalism and growing emulation of Classical models that would be central to the early Italian Renaissance.

20.2 Discuss Masaccio's use of linear perspective in either *The Tribute Money* or *Trinity with the Virgin, St. John the Evangelist, and Donors*. How does he use this technique? Illustrate your points with a comparative reference to a work discussed earlier in this chapter or in a previous chapter.

20.3 Choose a wealthy merchant or *condottiere* and discuss how his patronage fostered the emergence of the Renaissance in fifteenth-century Italy. Make reference to specific works in forming your answer.

20.4 Discuss the 1401 competition to choose an artist to create the bronze doors of the Florence Baptistery. How did the competition affect the careers of the two finalists, Ghiberti and Brunelleschi?

CROSSCURRENTS

FIG. 19–15   FIG. 20–21

Compare the representation of the human nude in these two examples of Renaissance art, one from Flanders and one from Florence. How do these works relate to the character of art in these two parts of Europe in the early fifteenth century? How do they embody the cultural expectations of their time and place?

Study and review on myartslab.com

21–1 • Raphael STANZA DELLA SEGNATURA
Vatican, Rome. Fresco in the left lunette, *Parnassus*; in the right lunette, *The School of Athens*. 1510–1511.

Sixteenth-Century Art in Italy

Two young artists—Raphael and Michelangelo—although rivals in almost every sense, were linked in service to Pope Julius II (pontificate 1503–1513) in the early years of the sixteenth century. Raphael was painting the pope's private library (1509–1511) while, nearby, Michelangelo painted the ceiling of his Sistine Chapel (1508–1512). The pope demanded an art that reflected his imperial vision of a new, worldwide Church based on humanistic ideas, which he would lead as a new St. Peter, founding a second great age of papal dominion. In fulfilling this proud demand, Raphael and Michelangelo, following the lead of Leonardo da Vinci, united Renaissance principles of harmony and balance with a new monumentality based on Classical ideals, and they knit these elements into a dynamic and synthetic whole, rich in color and controlled by cohesive design. Working alongside Leonardo and the architect Donato Bramante, they created a style we call the High Renaissance.

Julius II intended the **STANZA DELLA SEGNATURA**, or Room of the Signature, to be his personal study (**FIG. 21-1**). Raphael sought to create an ideal setting for papal activities, with murals proclaiming that all human knowledge exists under the power of divine wisdom. He organized the mural program itself like a library, separated into divisions of theology, philosophy, poetry, and law. He created pictorial allegories to illustrate each theme. On one wall, churchmen discussing the sacraments represent theology, while across the room ancient philosophers led by Plato and Aristotle debate in the School of Athens. Plato holds his book *Timaeus*, in which creation is seen in terms of geometry, and in which humanity encompasses and explains the universe. Aristotle holds his *Nicomachean Ethics*, a decidedly human-centered book concerned with relations among people. Ancient representatives of the academic curriculum—Grammar, Rhetoric, Dialectic, Arithmetic, Music, Geometry, and Astronomy—surround them. On a window wall, Justice, holding a sword and scales, assigns each his due. Across the room, Poetry and the Arts are represented by Apollo and the Muses, and the poet Sappho reclines against the fictive frame of an actual window. Raphael included his own portrait among the onlookers on the extreme lower right in the *School of Athens* fresco and signed the painting with his initials—a signal that both artists and patrons were becoming increasingly aware of their individual significance.

Raphael achieved a lofty style in keeping with papal ambition—using ideals of Classical grandeur, professing faith in human rationality and perfectibility, and celebrating the power of the pope as God's earthly administrator. But when Raphael died at age 37 on April 6, 1520, the grand moment was already passing: Luther and the Protestant Reformation were challenging papal authority, and the world would never be the same again.

LEARN ABOUT IT

21.1 Compare the emphasis on drawing and clearly structured compositions in the work of Roman and Florentine painters with their Venetian counterparts' exploration of the expressive potential of color and dynamic figural arrangements.

21.2 Examine the architectural creativity lavished on the design of both grand churches and pleasurable retreats to embody themes of wealth and power in sixteenth-century Italy.

21.3 Trace the shift in the artistic center of Italy from Florence to Rome, and recognize the efforts of Pope Julius II to create a new "golden age."

21.4 Explore the intentional subversion of Classical style and decorum in the work of Mannerist artists.

(((•——**Listen** to the chapter audio on myartslab.com

EUROPE IN THE SIXTEENTH CENTURY

The sixteenth century was an age of social, intellectual, and religious ferment that transformed European culture. It was marked by continual warfare triggered by the expansionist ambitions of warring rulers. The humanism of the fourteenth and fifteenth centuries, with its medieval roots and its often uncritical acceptance of the authority of Classical texts, slowly developed into a critical exploration of new ideas, the natural world, and distant lands. Cartographers began to acknowledge the Earth's curvature and the degrees of distance, giving Europeans a more accurate understanding of their place within the world. The printing press sparked an explosion in book production, spreading new ideas through the translation and publication of ancient and contemporary texts, broadening the horizons of educated Europeans and encouraging the development of literacy. Since travel was growing more common, artists and their work became mobile, and the world of art was transformed into a more international community.

At the start of the sixteenth century, England, France, and Portugal were nation-states under strong monarchs. German-speaking central Europe was divided into dozens of principalities, counties, free cities, and small territories. But even states as powerful as Saxony and Bavaria acknowledged the supremacy of the Habsburg Holy Roman Empire—in theory the greatest power in Europe. Charles V, elected emperor in 1519, also inherited Spain, the Netherlands, and vast territories in the Americas. Italy, which was divided into numerous small states, was a diplomatic and military battlefield where, for much of the century, the Italian city-states, Habsburg Spain, France, and the papacy fought each other in shifting alliances. Popes behaved like secular princes, using diplomacy and military force to regain control over central Italy and in some cases to establish family members as hereditary rulers.

The popes' incessant demands for money, to finance the rebuilding of St. Peter's as well as their self-aggrandizing art projects and luxurious lifestyles, aggravated the religious dissent that had long been developing, especially north of the Alps. Early in the century, religious reformers within the established Church challenged beliefs and practices, especially Julius II's sale of indulgences promising forgiveness of sins and assurance of salvation in exchange for a financial contribution to the Church. Because they protested, these northern European reformers came to be called Protestants; their demand for reform gave rise to a movement called the Reformation.

The political maneuvering of Pope Clement VII (pontificate 1523–1534) led to a direct clash with Holy Roman Emperor Charles V. In May 1527, Charles's troops attacked Rome, beginning a six-month orgy of killing, looting, and burning. The Sack of Rome, as it is called, shook the sense of stability and humanistic confidence that until then had characterized the Renaissance, and it sent many artists fleeing from the ruined city. Nevertheless, Charles saw himself as the leader of the Catholic forces—and he was the sole Catholic ally Clement had at the time. In 1530, Clement VII crowned Charles emperor in Bologna.

Sixteenth-century patrons valued artists highly and rewarded them well, not only with generous commissions but sometimes even with high social status. Charles V, for example, knighted the painter Titian. Some painters and sculptors became entrepreneurs and celebrities, selling prints of their works on the side and creating international reputations for themselves. Many artists recorded their activities—professional and private—in diaries, notebooks, and letters that have come down to us. In addition, contemporary writers began to report on the lives of artists, documenting their physical appearance and assessing their individual reputations. In 1550, Giorgio Vasari wrote the first survey of Italian art history (revised and expanded in 1568)—*Lives of the Most Excellent Architects, Painters, and Sculptors*—organized as a series of critical biographies but at its core a work of critical judgment. Vasari also commented on the role of patrons, and argued that art had become more realistic and more beautiful over time, reaching its apex of perfection in his own age. From his characterization developed our notion of this period as the High Renaissance—that is, as a high point in art since the early experiments of Cimabue and Giotto, marked by a balanced synthesis of Classical ideals and a lifelike rendering of the natural world.

During this period, the fifteenth-century humanists' notion of painting, sculpture, and architecture not as manual arts but as liberal (intellectual) arts, requiring education in the Classics and mathematics as well as in the techniques of the craft, became a topic of intense interest. And from these discussions arose the Renaissance formulation—still with us today—of artists as divinely inspired creative geniuses, a step above most of us in their gifts of hand and mind. This idea weaves its way through Vasari's work like an organizing principle. And this newly elevated status to which artists aspired favored men. Although few artists of either sex had access to the humanist education required by the sophisticated, often esoteric, subject matter used in paintings (usually devised by someone other than the artist), women were denied even the studio practice necessary to study and draw from nude models. Furthermore, it was almost impossible for an artist to achieve international status without traveling extensively and frequently relocating to follow commissions—something most women could not do. Still, some European women managed to follow their gifts and establish careers as artists during this period despite the obstacles that blocked their entrance into the profession.

ITALY IN THE EARLY SIXTEENTH CENTURY: THE HIGH RENAISSANCE

Italian art between the mid-1480s and the 1520s has been called the "High Renaissance." As we have already seen with the "High Classical" period in ancient Athens, the term "High Renaissance"

MAP 21-1 • RENAISSANCE AND EARLIER MONUMENTS IN ROME

In addition to situating the principal works of the Roman Renaissance that emerged from Julius II's campaign to revitalize the papal city, this map also locates the surviving works of Roman antiquity that would have been available to the Renaissance artists and architects who masterminded the Classical revival.

encapsulates an art-historical judgment, claiming that what happened in Rome at this time represents a pinnacle of achievement within a longer artistic movement, and that it set standards for the future (**MAP 21-1**). High Renaissance art is characterized by a sense of gravity and decorum, a complex but ordered relationship of individual parts to the whole, and an emulation of the principles artists saw in ancient Classical art. Art historian Sydney Freedberg has stressed the way High Renaissance art fuses the real and the ideal, characterizing Leonardo's *Mona Lisa*, for example, as "a rare perfection between art and reality; an image in which a breathing instant and a composure for all time are held in suspension" (Freedberg, p. 28).

Two important practical developments at the turn of the sixteenth century affected the arts in Italy. Technically, the use of tempera had almost completely given way to the more flexible oil

painting medium; and economically, with increasing commissions from private sources, artists no longer depended so heavily on the patronage of the Church, the court, or civic associations.

THREE GREAT ARTISTS OF THE EARLY SIXTEENTH CENTURY

Florence's renowned artistic tradition attracted a stream of young artists to that city, traveling there to study its many artistic treasures, not least of which were Masaccio's solid, monumental figures, with their eloquent facial features, poses, and gestures, in the Brancacci Chapel paintings. The young Michelangelo's sketches of the chapel frescos document the importance of Masaccio to his developing style. In fact, Leonardo, Michelangelo, and Raphael—the three leading artists of the High Renaissance—all worked early in their careers in Florence, although they soon moved to other centers of patronage and their influence spread well beyond that city, even beyond Italy.

LEONARDO DA VINCI Leonardo da Vinci (1452–1519) was 12 or 13 when his family moved to Florence from the Tuscan village of Vinci. After an apprenticeship in the shop of the Florentine painter and sculptor Andrea del Verrocchio, and a few years on his own, Leonardo traveled to Milan in 1481 or 1482 to work for the ruling Sforza family.

Leonardo spent much of his time in Milan on military and civil engineering projects, including both urban-renewal and fortification plans for the city, but he also created a few key monuments of Renaissance painting. In April 1483, Leonardo contracted with the Confraternity of the Immaculate Conception to paint an altarpiece for their chapel in the church of San Francesco Grande in Milan, a painting now known as **THE VIRGIN OF THE ROCKS** (**FIG. 21-2**). The contract stipulates a painting of the Virgin and Child with angels, but Leonardo added a figure of the young John the Baptist, who balances the composition at the left, pulled into dialogue with his younger cousin Jesus by the long, protective arm of the Virgin. She draws attention to her child by extending her other hand over his head, while the enigmatic figure of the angel—who looks out without actually making eye contact with the viewer—points to the center of interaction. The stable, balanced, pyramidal figural group—a compositional formula that will become a standard feature of High Renaissance Classicism—is set against an exquisitely detailed landscape that dissolves mysteriously into the misty distance.

To assure their dominance in the picture, Leonardo picks out the four figures with spotlights, creating a strong **chiaroscuro** (from the Italian words *chiaro*, meaning "light," and *oscuro*, meaning "dark") that enhances their modeling as three-dimensional forms. This painting is an excellent early example of a specific variant of this technique, called **sfumato** ("smoky"), in which there are subtle, almost imperceptible, transitions between light and dark in shading. *Sfumato* becomes a hallmark of Leonardo's style, although the effect is artificially enhanced in this painting by the yellowing of its thick varnish, which masks the original vibrancy of its color.

At Duke Ludovico Sforza's request, Leonardo painted **THE LAST SUPPER** (**FIGS. 21-3, 21-4**) in the refectory, or dining hall, of the monastery of Santa Maria delle Grazie in Milan between 1495 and 1498. In fictive space defined by a coffered ceiling and four pairs of tapestries that seem to extend the refectory itself into another room, Jesus and his disciples are seated at a long table placed parallel to the picture plane and to the monastic diners who would have been seated in the hall below. In a sense, Jesus' meal with his disciples prefigures the daily gathering of

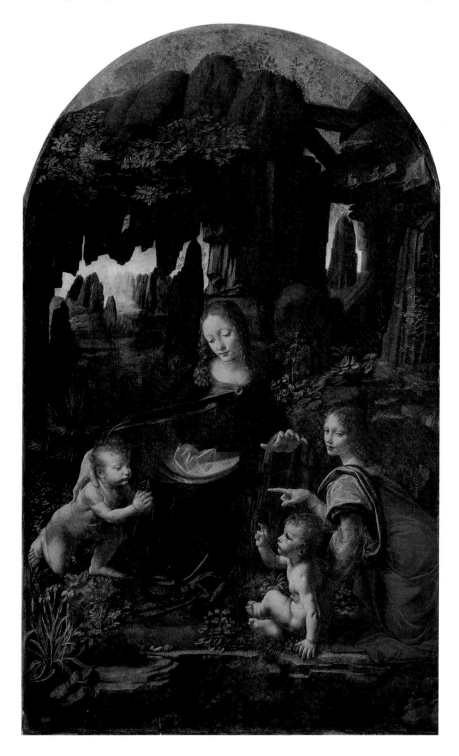

21-2 • Leonardo da Vinci THE VIRGIN OF THE ROCKS
c. 1485. Oil on wood panel (now transferred to canvas), 6′6″ × 4′ (1.9 × 1.2 m). Musée du Louvre, Paris.

21-3 • Leonardo da Vinci THE LAST SUPPER
Refectory of the monastery of Santa Maria delle Grazie, Milan, Italy. 1495–1498. Tempera and oil on plaster, 15′2″ × 28′10″ (4.6 × 8.8 m).

👁—**Watch** a video about Leonardo da Vinci's *The Last Supper* on myartslab.com

21-4 • REFECTORY OF THE MONASTERY OF SANTA MARIA DELLE GRAZIE, SHOWING LEONARDO'S LAST SUPPER
Milan, Italy.

Instead of painting in fresco, Leonardo devised an experimental technique for this mural. Hoping to achieve the freedom and flexibility of painting on wood panel, he worked directly on dry *intonaco*— a thin layer of smooth plaster—with an oil-and-tempera paint for which the formula is unknown. The result was disastrous. Within a short time, the painting began to deteriorate, and by the middle of the sixteenth century its figures could be seen only with difficulty. In the seventeenth century, the monks saw no harm in cutting a doorway through the lower center of the composition. The work has barely survived the intervening period, despite many attempts to halt its deterioration and restore its original appearance. It narrowly escaped complete destruction in World War II, when the refectory was bombed to rubble. The coats of arms at the top are those of patron Ludovico Sforza, duke of Milan (r. 1494–1499), and his wife, Beatrice.

21-5 • Leonardo da Vinci MONA LISA
c. 1503–1506. Oil on wood panel, 30¼″ × 21″ (77 × 53 cm). Musée du Louvre, Paris. (INV. 779)

Read the document related to Leonardo da Vinci on myartslab.com

this local monastic community at mealtimes. The stagelike space recedes from the table to three windows on the back wall, where the vanishing point of the one-point linear perspective lies behind Jesus' head. A stable, pyramidal Jesus at the center is flanked by his 12 disciples, grouped in four interlocking sets of three.

On one level, Leonardo has painted a scene from a story—one that captures the individual reactions of the apostles to Jesus' announcement that one of them will betray him. Leonardo was an acute observer of human behavior, and his art captures human emotions with compelling immediacy. On another level, *The Last Supper* is a symbolic evocation of Jesus' coming sacrifice for the salvation of humankind, the foundation of the institution of the Mass. Breaking with traditional representations of the subject (see FIG. 20-25) to create compositional clarity, balance, and cohesion, Leonardo placed the traitor Judas—clutching his money bags in the shadows—within the first triad to Jesus' right, along with the

young John the Evangelist and the elderly Peter, rather than isolating Judas on the opposite side of the table. Judas, Peter, and John were each to play an essential role in Jesus' mission: Judas set in motion the events leading to Jesus' sacrifice; Peter led the Church after Jesus' death; and John, the visionary, foretold the Second Coming and the Last Judgment in the book of Revelation.

The painting's careful geometry, the convergence of its perspective lines, the stability of its pyramidal forms, and Jesus' calm demeanor at the mathematical center of all the commotion, work together to reinforce the sense of gravity, balance, and order. The clarity and stability of this painting epitomize High Renaissance style.

Leonardo returned to Florence in 1500, after the French, who had invaded Italy in 1494, claimed Milan by defeating Leonardo's Milanese patron, Ludovico Sforza. Perhaps the most famous of his Florentine works is the portrait he painted between about 1503 and 1506 known as the **MONA LISA** (FIG. 21-5). The subject may have been 24-year-old Lisa Gherardini del Giocondo, the wife of a prominent Florentine merchant. Leonardo never delivered the painting and kept it with him for the rest of his life. In a departure from tradition, the young woman is portrayed without jewelry, not even a ring. The solid pyramidal form of her halflength figure—another departure from traditional portraiture, which was limited to the upper torso—is silhouetted against distant hazy mountains, giving the painting a sense of mystery reminiscent of *The Virgin of the Rocks* (see FIG. 21-2). Mona Lisa's facial expression has been called "enigmatic" because her gentle smile—typical of Leonardo's women and angels (see FIG. 21-2)—is not accompanied by the warmth one would expect to see in her eyes, which have boldly shifted to the side to look straight out at the viewer. It is this expressive complexity, and the sense of psychological presence it gives the human face—especially in the context of the masklike detachment that was more characteristic of Renaissance portraiture (compare FIG. 20-31, or even FIG. 21-8)—that makes the innovative *Mona Lisa* so arresting and haunting, even today.

A fiercely debated topic in Renaissance Italy was the question of the relative merits of painting and sculpture. Leonardo insisted on the supremacy of painting as the best and most complete means of creating an illusion of the natural world, while Michelangelo argued for sculpture. Yet in creating a painted illusion, Leonardo considered color to be secondary to the depiction of sculptural volume, which he achieved through his virtuosity in *sfumato*. He also unified his compositions by covering them with a thin, lightly tinted varnish, which enhanced the overall smoky haze. Because early evening light tends to produce a similar effect naturally, Leonardo considered dusk the finest time of day and recommended that painters set up their studios in a courtyard with black walls and a linen sheet stretched overhead to reproduce twilight.

Leonardo's fame as an artist is based on only a few works, for his many interests took him away from painting. Unlike his humanist contemporaries, he was not particularly interested in Classical literature or archaeology. Instead, his passions were

Artists throughout history have turned to geometric shapes and mathematical proportions to seek the ideal representation of the human form. Leonardo, following the first-century BCE Roman architect and engineer Vitruvius, equated the ideal man with both circle and square. Ancient Egyptian artists had laid out square grids as aids to design (see "Egyptian Pictorial Relief," page 64). Medieval artists adapted a variety of figures, from triangles to pentagrams (see "Villard de Honnecourt," page 511).

Vitruvius, in his ten-volume *De architectura* (*On Architecture*), wrote: "For if a man be placed flat on his back, with his hands and feet extended, and a pair of compasses centered at his navel, the fingers and toes of his two hands and feet will touch the circumference of a circle described therefrom. And just as the human body yields a circular outline, so too a square figure may be found from it. For if we measure the distance from the soles of the feet to the top of the head, and then apply that measure to the outstretched arms, the breadth will be found to be the same as the height" (Book III, Chapter 1, Section 3). Vitruvius determined that the ideal body should be eight heads high. Leonardo added his own observations in the reversed writing he always used in his notebooks when he created his well-known diagram for the ideal male figure, called the **VITRUVIAN MAN** (FIG. 21–6).

21–6 • Leonardo da Vinci VITRUVIAN MAN
c. 1490. Ink, 13½″ × 9⅝″ (34.3 × 24.5 cm). Galleria dell'Accademia, Venice.

21-7 • Raphael THE SMALL COWPER MADONNA
c. 1505. Oil on wood panel, 23⅜″ × 17⅝″ (59.5 × 44.1 cm). National Gallery of Art, Washington, DC. Widener Collection (1942.9.57)

In the distance on a hilltop, Raphael has painted a scene he knew well from his childhood, the domed church of San Bernardino, two miles outside Urbino. The church contains the tombs of dukes of Urbino, Federico and Guidobaldo da Montefeltro, and their wives (see FIG. 20-31). Donato Bramante, whose architecture was key in establishing the High Renaissance style, may have designed the church.

mathematics, engineering, and the natural world. He compiled volumes of detailed drawings and notes on anatomy, botany, geology, meteorology, architectural design, and mechanics. In his drawings of human figures, he sought not only the precise details of anatomy but also the geometric basis of perfect proportions (see "The Vitruvian Man," page 639). Leonardo's searching mind is evident in his drawings, not only of natural objects and human beings, but also of machines, so clearly and completely worked out that modern engineers have used them to construct working models. He designed flying machines, a kind of automobile, a parachute, and all sorts of military equipment, including a mobile fortress. His imagination outran his means to bring his creations into being. For one thing, he lacked a source of power other than men and horses. For another, he may have lacked focus and follow-through. His contemporaries complained that he never finished anything and that his inventions distracted him from his painting.

Leonardo returned to Milan in 1508 and lived there until 1513. He also lived for a time in the Vatican at the invitation of Pope Leo X, but there is no evidence that he produced any works of art during his stay. In 1516, he accepted the French king Francis I's invitation to relocate to France as an advisor on architecture, taking the *Mona Lisa*, as well as other important works, with him. He remained at Francis's court until his death in 1519.

RAPHAEL About 1505—while Leonardo was working on the *Mona Lisa*—Raphael (Raffaello Santi or Sanzio, 1483–1520) arrived in Florence from his native Urbino after studying in Perugia with the city's leading artist, Perugino (see FIG. 20-18). Raphael quickly became successful in Florence, especially with small, polished paintings of the Virgin and Child, such as **THE SMALL COWPER MADONNA** (named for a modern owner) of about 1505 (**FIG. 21-7**). Already a superb painter technically, the youthful Raphael shows his indebtedness to his teacher in the delicate tilt of the figures' heads, the brilliant tonalities, and the pervasive sense of serenity. But Leonardo's impact is also evident here in the simple grandeur of these monumental shapes, the pyramidal composition activated by the spiraling movement of the child, and the draperies that cling to the Virgin's substantial form. In other Madonnas from this period, Raphael included the young John the Baptist (see FIG. Intro-4), experimenting with the multiple figure interactions pioneered by Leonardo in *The Virgin of the Rocks* (see FIG. 21-2).

At the same time as he was producing engaging images of elegant Madonnas, Raphael was also painting flawlessly executed portraits of prosperous Florentine patrons. To commemorate the marriage in 1504 of 30-year-old cloth merchant Agnelo Doni to Maddalena Strozzi, the 15-year-old daughter of a powerful banking family, Doni commissioned from Raphael **pendant** portraits of the newlyweds (**FIG. 21-8**). Like Piero della Francesca in his portraits of Battista Sforza and Federico da Montefeltro (see FIG. 20-31), Raphael silhouettes Maddalena and Agnelo against a meticulously described panoramic landscape. But unlike their predecessors, they turn to address the viewer. Agnelo is commanding but casual, leaning his arm on a balustrade to add three-dimensionality to his posture. Maddalena's pose imitates Leonardo's innovative presentation of his subject in the *Mona Lisa* (see FIG. 21-5), which Raphael had obviously seen in progress, but with Maddalena there is no sense of mystery, indeed little psychological presence, and Raphael follows tradition in emphasizing the sumptuousness of her clothing and making ostentatious display of her jewelry. The wisps of hair that escape from her sculpted coiffure are the only hint of human vulnerability.

Raphael left Florence about 1508 for Rome, where Pope Julius II put him to work almost immediately decorating rooms (*stanze*, singular *stanza*) in the papal apartments. In the Stanza della Segnatura (see FIG. 21-1)—the pope's private library—Raphael painted the four branches of knowledge as conceived in the sixteenth century: Religion (the *Disputà*, depicting discussions

21–8 • Raphael AGNELO DONI AND MADDALENA STROZZI
c. 1506. Oil on wood panel, each 24½″ × 17¼″ (63 × 45 cm). Palazzo Pitti, Florence.

These portraits were not the only paintings commissioned by Agnelo Doni to commemorate his upwardly mobile marriage alliance with Maddalena Strozzi. He ordered a tondo portraying the Holy Family from rival artist Michelangelo (see Introduction, "A Closer Look," page xxxi FIG. C). Vasari reports that although the original price for that painting was set at 70 ducats, Doni only sent Michelangelo 40. In order to obtain his painting, the patron eventually had to pay the artist double the original price—140 ducats.

concerning the true presence of Christ in the Eucharistic Host), Philosophy (*The School of Athens*), Poetry (*Parnassus*, home of the Muses), and Law (the Cardinal Virtues under *Justice*).

Raphael's most influential achievement in the papal rooms was *The School of Athens*, painted about 1510–1511 (see "A Closer Look," page 642). Here, the painter seems to summarize the ideals of the Renaissance papacy in a grand conception of harmoniously arranged forms in a rational space, as well as in the calm dignity of the figures that occupy it. If the learned Julius II did not actually devise the subjects, he certainly must have approved them. Greek philosophers Plato and Aristotle take center stage—placed to the right and left of the vanishing point—silhouetted against the sky and framed under three successive barrel vaults. Surrounding Plato and Aristotle are mathematicians, naturalists, astronomers, geographers, and other philosophers, debating and demonstrating their theories with and to onlookers and each other. The scene takes

place in an immense barrel-vaulted interior, flooded with a clear, even light from a single source, and seemingly inspired by the new design for St. Peter's, under construction at the time. The grandeur of the building is matched by the monumental dignity of the philosophers themselves, each of whom has a distinct physical and intellectual presence. The sweeping arcs of the composition are activated by the variety and energy of their poses and gestures, creating a dynamic unity that is a prime characteristic of High Renaissance art.

In 1515, Raphael was commissioned by Pope Leo X (pontificate 1513–1521) to provide designs on themes from the Acts of the Apostles to be woven into tapestries for the strip of blank wall below the fifteenth-century wall paintings of the Sistine Chapel (a surface now decorated with painted simulations of hanging drapery: see FIG. 20-33). For the production of the tapestries, woven in Brussels, Raphael and his large workshop of assistants made

A CLOSER LOOK | *The School of Athens*

by Raphael, fresco in the Stanza della Segnatura, Vatican, Rome.
c. 1510–1511. 19′ × 27′ (5.79 × 8.24 m).

Looking down from niches in the walls are sculptures of Apollo (the god of sunlight, rationality, poetry, music, and the fine arts) and Minerva (the goddess of wisdom and the mechanical arts).

Plato points upward to the realm of ideas and pure forms that were at the center of his philosophy. His pupil Aristotle gestures toward his surroundings, signifying the empirical world that for him served as the basis for understanding.

The figure bent over a slate with a compass is Euclid, the father of geometry. Vasari claimed that Raphael gave this mathematician the portrait likeness of Bramante, the architect whose redesigned St. Peter's was under construction not far from this room and who was also a distant relative of Raphael.

Raphael placed his own portrait in a group that includes the geographer Ptolemy, who holds a terrestrial globe, and the astronomer Zoroaster, who holds a celestial globe.

The brooding figure of Heraclitus, a late addition to the composition, is a portrait of Michelangelo, who was working next door on the ceiling of the Sistine Chapel, and whose monumental figural style is here appropriated (or is it mimicked?) by Raphael. The stonecutter's boots on his feet refer to Michelangelo's self-identification—or Raphael's insistence that he be seen—as a sculptor rather than a painter.

This figure is usually identified as Diogenes the Cynic following Vasari's account of the painting. It is more likely that he is Socrates, however. The cup next to him could refer to his deadly draught of hemlock, and his recumbent position recalls his teaching from his prison bed.

The group of figures gathered around Euclid illustrate the various stages of understanding: literal learning, dawning comprehension, anticipation of the outcome, and assisting the teacher. Raphael received acclaim for his ability to communicate so clearly through the poses and expressions of his figures.

View the Closer Look for *The School of Athens* on myartslab.com full-scale charcoal drawings, then painted over them with color for the weavers to match (see "Raphael's Cartoons for Tapestries in the Sistine Chapel," page 648). Pictorial weaving was the most prestigious and expensive kind of wall decoration. With murals by the leading painters of the fifteenth century above and Michelangelo's work circling over all, Raphael must have felt both honored and challenged. The pope had given him the place of honor among the artists in the papal chapel.

MICHELANGELO'S EARLY WORK Michelangelo Buonarroti (1475–1564) was born in the Tuscan town of Caprese into an impoverished Florentine family that laid a claim to nobility—a claim the artist carefully advanced throughout his life. He grew up in Florence, where at age 13 he was apprenticed to Ghirlandaio

(see FIG. 20-37), in whose workshop he learned the technique of fresco painting and studied drawings of Classical monuments. Soon the talented youth joined the household of Lorenzo the Magnificent, head of the ruling Medici family, where he came into contact with Neoplatonic philosophy and the family's distinguished sculpture collection. After Lorenzo died in 1492, Michelangelo traveled to Venice and Bologna, then returned to Florence.

Michelangelo's major early work at the turn of the century was a marble sculpture of the **PIETÀ**, commissioned by a French cardinal and installed as a tomb monument in Old St. Peter's (**FIG. 21-9**). The theme of the *pietà* (in which the Virgin supports and mourns the dead Jesus in her lap), long popular in northern Europe (see FIG. 18-23), was an unusual theme in Italy at the time. Michelangelo traveled to the marble quarries at Carrara in central Italy

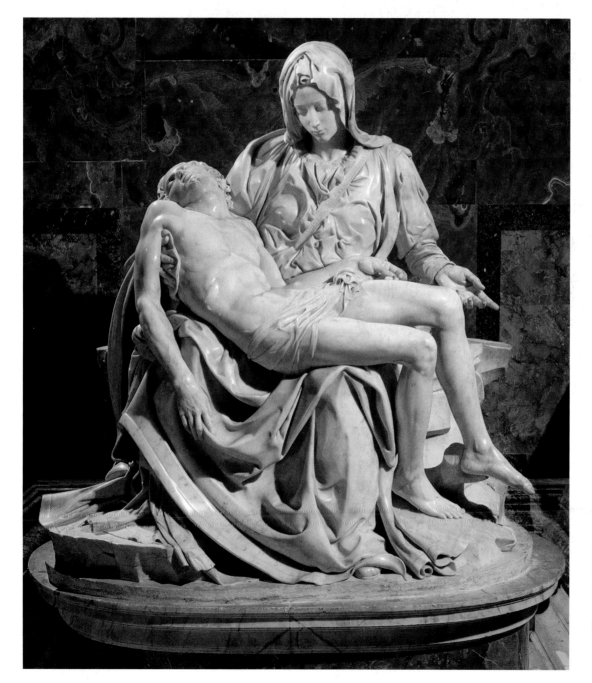

21-9 • Michelangelo
PIETÀ
c. 1500. Marble, height 5′8½″ (1.74 m). St. Peter's, Vatican, Rome.

Read the document related to Michelangelo on myartslab.com to select the block from which to make this large work, a practice he was to continue for nearly all his sculpture. The choice of stone was important to him because he envisioned his sculpture as already existing within the marble, needing only his tools to set it free. Michelangelo was a poet as well as an artist, and later wrote in his Sonnet 15: "The greatest artist has no conception which a single block of marble does not potentially contain within its mass, but only a hand obedient to the mind can penetrate to this image."

Michelangelo's Virgin is a young woman of heroic stature holding the unnaturally smaller, lifeless body of her grown son. Inconsistencies of scale and age are forgotten, however, when contemplating the sweetness of expression, technical virtuosity of the carving, and smooth modeling of the luscious forms. Michelangelo's compelling vision of beauty was meant to be seen up close so that the viewer can look directly into Jesus' face. The 25-year-old artist is said to have slipped into the church at night to sign the statue on a strap across the Virgin's breast after it was finished, answering directly questions that had come up about the identity of its creator.

In 1501, Michelangelo accepted a Florentine commission for a statue of the biblical hero **DAVID** (**FIG. 21-10**), to be placed high atop a buttress of the cathedral. But when it was finished in 1504, the *David* was so admired that the city council instead placed it in the principal city square, next to the Palazzo della Signoria (see FIG. 18-2), the seat of Florence's government. There it stood as a reminder of Florence's republican status, which was briefly reinstated after the expulsion of the powerful Medici oligarchy in 1494. Although in its muscular nudity Michelangelo's *David* embodies the antique ideal of the athletic male nude, the emotional power of its expression and its concentrated gaze are entirely new. Unlike Donatello's bronze *David* (see FIG. 20-14), this is not a triumphant hero with the trophy head of the giant Goliath already under his feet. Slingshot over his shoulder and a rock in his right hand, Michelangelo's *David* knits his brow and stares into space, seemingly preparing himself psychologically for the danger ahead, a mere youth confronting a gigantic experienced warrior. No match for his opponent in experience, weaponry, or physical strength, Michelangelo's powerful *David* stands for the supremacy

21-10 • Michelangelo DAVID
1501–1504. Marble, height 17′ (5.18 m) without pedestal. Galleria dell'Accademia, Florence.

Michelangelo's most famous sculpture was cut from an 18-foot-tall marble block. The sculptor began with a small model in wax, then sketched the contours of the figure as they would appear from the front on one face of the marble. According to his friend and biographer Vasari, Michelangelo then chiseled in from the drawn-on surface, as if making a figure in very high relief. The completed statue took four days to move on tree-trunk rollers down the narrow streets of Florence from the cathedral workshop to its location outside the Palazzo della Signoria (see FIG. 18-2). In 1504, the Florentines gilded the tree stump and added a gilded wreath to the head and a belt of 28 gilt-bronze leaves, since removed. In 1873, the statue was replaced by a copy, and the original was moved into the museum of the Florence Academy.

21-11 • INTERIOR, SISTINE CHAPEL
Vatican, Rome. Built 1475–1481; ceiling painted 1508–1512; end wall, 1536–1541. The ceiling measures 45′ × 128′ (13.75 × 39 m).

of right over might—a perfect emblem for the Florentines, who had recently fought the forces of Milan, Siena, and Pisa, and still faced political and military pressure.

THE SISTINE CHAPEL Despite Michelangelo's contractual commitment to Florence Cathedral for additional statues, in 1505, Pope Julius II, who saw Michelangelo as an ideal collaborator in the artistic aggrandizement of the papacy, arranged for him to come to Rome to work on the spectacular tomb Julius planned for himself. Michelangelo began the tomb project, but two years later the pope ordered him to begin painting the ceiling of the **SISTINE CHAPEL** instead (FIG. 21-11).

Michelangelo considered himself a sculptor, but the strong-minded pope wanted paintings; work began in 1508. Michelangelo

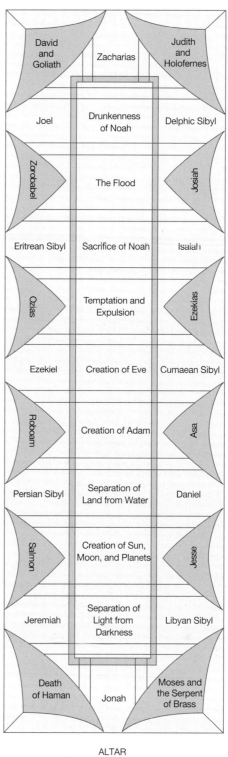

David and Goliath	Zacharias	Judith and Holofernes
Joel	Drunkenness of Noah	Delphic Sibyl
Zorobabel	The Flood	Josiah
Eritrean Sibyl	Sacrifice of Noah	Isaiah
Ozias	Temptation and Expulsion	Ezekias
Ezekiel	Creation of Eve	Cumaean Sibyl
Roboam	Creation of Adam	Asa
Persian Sibyl	Separation of Land from Water	Daniel
Salmon	Creation of Sun, Moon, and Planets	Jesse
Jeremiah	Separation of Light from Darkness	Libyan Sibyl
Death of Haman	Jonah	Moses and the Serpent of Brass

ALTAR

21–12 • Michelangelo SISTINE CHAPEL CEILING WITH DIAGRAM IDENTIFYING SCENES
1508–1512. Fresco.

complained bitterly in a sonnet to a friend: "This miserable job has given me a goiter….The force of it has jammed my belly up beneath my chin. Beard to the sky….Brush splatterings make a pavement of my face…. I'm not a painter." Despite his physical misery as he stood on a scaffold, painting the ceiling just above him, the results were extraordinary, and Michelangelo established a new and remarkably powerful style in Renaissance painting.

Julius's initial order for the ceiling was simple: *trompe l'oeil* coffers to replace the original star-spangled blue decoration. Later he wanted the 12 apostles seated on thrones on the triangular spandrels between the lunettes framing the windows. According to Michelangelo, when he objected to the limitations of Julius's plan, the pope told him to paint whatever he liked. This Michelangelo presumably did, although he was certainly guided by a theological advisor and his plan no doubt required the pope's approval.

In Michelangelo's design, an illusionistic marble architecture establishes a framework for the figures and narrative scenes on the vault of the chapel (**FIG. 21-12**). Running completely around the ceiling is a painted cornice with projections supported by pilasters decorated with "sculptured" *putti*. Between the pilasters are figures of prophets and sibyls (female seers from the Classical world) who

were believed to have foretold Jesus' birth. Seated on the fictive cornice are heroic figures of nude young men called *ignudi* (singular, *ignudo*), holding sashes attached to large gold medallions. Rising behind the *ignudi*, shallow bands of fictive stone span the center of the ceiling and divide it into nine compartments containing successive scenes from Genesis—recounting the Creation, the Fall, and the Flood—beginning over the altar and ending near the chapel entrance. God's earliest acts of creation are therefore closest to the altar, the Creation of Eve at the center of the ceiling, followed by the imperfect actions of humanity: Temptation, Fall, Expulsion from Paradise, and God's eventual destruction of all people except Noah and his family by the Flood. The eight triangular spandrels over the windows, as well as the lunettes crowning them, contain paintings of the ancestors of Jesus.

Perhaps the most familiar scene on the ceiling is the **CREATION OF ADAM** (**FIG. 21-13**), where Michelangelo captures the moment when God charges the languorous Adam—in a pose adapted from the Roman river-god type—with the spark of life. As if to echo the biblical text, Adam's heroic body, outstretched arm, and profile almost mirror those of God, in whose image he has been created. Emerging under God's other arm, and looking across

21-13 • Michelangelo CREATION OF ADAM, SISTINE CHAPEL CEILING
1511–1512. Fresco, 9′2″ × 18′8″ (2.8 × 5.7 m).

The Sistine Chapel was a major focus of papal patronage throughout the Renaissance. The building was constructed in 1475–1481 by Sixtus IV, who also began its painted embellishment by calling a constellation of illustrious artists to Rome in the early 1480s to create a band of framed frescos recounting the life of Moses on one wall and the life of Christ on the other (see FIG. 20–33). Between 1508 and 1512, Michelangelo painted the chapel's ceiling at the behest of Julius II. And soon after he became pope in 1513, Leo X commissioned Raphael to produce ten cartoons (full-size preparatory designs for a work of art executed in another medium) for a lavish set of tapestries portraying scenes from the lives of SS. Peter and Paul that would complete the decorative program on the chapel's lower level. At the time, these would have been considered its most prestigious and expensive works of art. The tapestry program cost Leo X more than five times what Julius II had paid Michelangelo to paint the ceiling. For designing the program and producing the cartoons, however, Raphael only received a sixteenth of the total cost of the tapestries; the expense here involved production more than design.

The cartoons were created in Raphael's workshop between 1515 and 1516. Raphael was clearly the intellect behind the compositions, and he participated in the actual preparation and execution. This was a prestigious commission that would reflect directly on the reputation of the master. But he could not have accomplished this imposing task in a little over a year without the collaboration of numerous assistants working in his thriving workshop. The completed cartoons—first drawn with charcoal on paper (160–170 separate sheets were glued together to form the expanse of a single tapestry) and then overpainted with color—were sent to Brussels, where they were woven into tapestries in the workshop of Pieter van Aelst. The first was complete in 1517, seven were hanging in the chapel for Christmas 1519, and the entire cycle was installed by Leo X's death in 1521.

The process of creation, from design through production, can be charted by examining the tapestry portraying *Christ's Charge to Peter* (John 21:15–17; Matthew 16:17–19) at three stages in its development. We have Raphael's preliminary drawing (**FIG. 21-14**), where models—it is tempting to see these as Raphael's assistants, stripped to their underwear to help the master work out his composition—are posed to enact the moment when Jesus addresses his apostles. This is a preliminary idea for the pose of Christ. In the final cartoon (**FIG. 21-15**), Raphael changes Christ's gesture so that he addresses the kneeling Peter specifically rather than the whole apostolic group; for the patron, this would be an important detail since papal power rested in the belief that Christ had transferred authority to Peter, who was considered the first pope, with subsequent popes inheriting this authority in unbroken succession. Comparison of drawing and cartoon also reveals an important aspect of the design process. The cartoon reverses the figural arrangement of the drawing because in the production process the tapestry would be woven from the back, and if the weavers followed the reversed version of the composition on the cartoon, the resulting tapestry (**FIG. 21-16**) would show the scene in its intended orientation. Comparison of cartoon and tapestry also indicates that the weavers were not required to follow their models slavishly. They have embellished the costume of Christ, perhaps in an attempt to assure that the viewers' attention will be immediately directed to this most important figure in the scene.

After they had been used to create the tapestries hung in the Sistine Chapel, Raphael's cartoons remained in Brussels, where several additional sets of tapestries were made from them—one for Henry VIII of England, another for Francis I of France—before seven surviving cartoons were acquired in 1623 by the future Charles I of England. They remain in the British Royal Collection. The tapestries themselves, although still in the Vatican, are displayed in the museum rather than on the walls of the chapel for which they were originally conceived, as one of the most prestigious artistic projects from the peak of the Roman High Renaissance.

21-14 • Raphael STUDY FOR CHRIST'S CHARGE TO PETER
c. 1515. Red chalk. Royal Library, Windsor Castle.

21–15 • Raphael and assistants CARTOON FOR TAPESTRY PORTRAYING CHRIST'S CHARGE TO PETER

c. 1515–1516. Distemper on paper (now transferred to canvas), 11′1″ × 17′4″ (3.4 × 5.3 m). Lent by Her Majesty the Queen to the Victoria & Albert Museum, London.

21–16 • Shop of Pieter van Aelst, Brussels, after cartoons by Raphael and assistants CHRIST'S CHARGE TO PETER

Woven 1517, installed 1519 in the Sistine Chapel. Wool and silk with silver-gilt wrapped threads. Musei Vaticani, Pinacoteca, Rome.

him in the direction of her future mate, is the robust and energetic figure of Eve before her creation.

MICHELANGELO AT SAN LORENZO After the Medici regained power in Florence in 1512, and Leo X (Giovanni de' Medici) succeeded Julius in 1513, Michelangelo became chief architect for Medici family projects at the church of San Lorenzo in Florence—including a new chapel for the tombs of Lorenzo the Magnificent, his brother Giuliano, and two younger dukes, also named Lorenzo and Giuliano, ordered in 1519 for the so-called New Sacristy (see FIG. 20–4). The older men's tombs were never built to Michelangelo's designs, but the unfinished tombs for the younger relatives were placed on opposite side walls (FIG. 21–17).

Each of the two monuments consists of an idealized portrait of the deceased, who turns to face the family's unfinished ancestral tomb. The men are dressed in a sixteenth-century interpretation of Classical armor and seated in wall niches above pseudo-Classical sarcophagi. Balanced precariously atop the sarcophagi are male and female figures representing the times of day. Their positions would not seem so unsettling had reclining figures of river gods been installed below them, as originally planned, but even so there is a conspicuous tension here between the substantiality of the figures and the limitations imposed on them by their architectural surrounds. In the tomb illustrated here, Michelangelo represents Giuliano as the Active Life, and his sarcophagus figures are allegories of Night and Day. Night at left is accompanied by her symbols: a star and crescent moon on her tiara; poppies, which induce sleep; and an owl under the arch of her leg. The huge mask at her back may allude to Death, since Sleep and Death were said to be the children of Night. Some have seen in this mask that glares out at viewers in the chapel a self-portrait of the artist, serving both as signature and as a way of proclaiming his right to be here because of his long relationship with the family. On the other tomb, Lorenzo, representing the Contemplative Life, is supported by Dawn and Evening.

Concurrent with work on the Medici tombs was the construction of a new library at San Lorenzo. The idea for the library belongs to Cardinal Giulio de' Medici and dates to 1519, but it was only after he was elected Pope Clement VII in 1523 that the money became available to realize it. Michelangelo was commissioned to design and also supervise construction of the new **VESTIBULE** (FIG. 21–18) and reading room and to spare

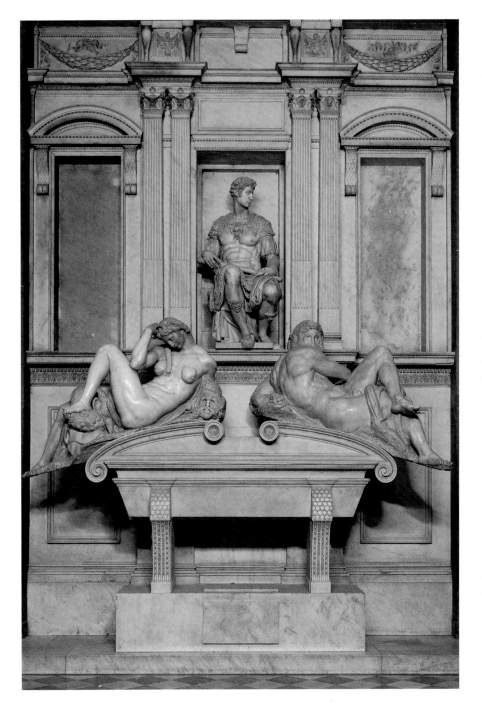

21–17 • Michelangelo TOMB OF GIULIANO DE' MEDICI WITH ALLEGORICAL FIGURES OF NIGHT AND DAY

New Sacristy (Medici Chapel), church of San Lorenzo, Florence. 1519–1534. Marble, height of seated figure approx. 5'10" (1.8 m).

✳ **Explore** the architectural panoramas of the New Sacristy in the church of San Lorenzo on myartslab.com no expense in making them both grand and ambitious. The pope paid keen attention to the library's progress—not, he said, to verify the quality of the design, but because the project had a special interest for him.

Michelangelo coordinated his work within a decorative tradition established at San Lorenzo when Brunelleschi designed the church itself a century earlier (see FIG. 20–4), using stylized architectural elements carved in dark gray *pietra serena*, set against and within a contrasting white wall. However, Michelangelo plays with the Classical architectural etiquette that Brunelleschi had used to create such clarity, harmony, and balance in the nave.

In Michelangelo's vestibule, chunky columns are recessed into rectangular wall niches that can barely contain them. They are crowded and overlapped by the aggressive lateral extension of the pediment over the door. The door itself is broken into parts, sides jutting forward as fluted pilasters that are then partially obscured by the frame around the opening. The three flights of stairs leading up to the reading room almost fill the vestibule, and the central stairs cascade forward forcefully toward visitors, hardly encouraging them to go against the flow and step up. Through their playfulness, these creative combinations of architectural forms draw attention to themselves and their design rather than the function of the building itself or the comfortable accommodation of its users, prime characteristics of the Mannerist architecture then coming into fashion.

Fearing for his life when ongoing political struggles flared up in Florence, Michelango returned to Rome in 1534 and settled permanently. He had left both the Medici Chapel and the library unfinished. In 1557, he sent a plaster model of the library staircase to Florence to assure that its completion conformed to his design. In 1545, his students had assembled the tomb sculptures, including unfinished figures of the times of day, into the composition we see today.

The figures of the dukes are finely finished, but the times of day are notable for their contrasting areas of rough unfinished and polished marble. These are the only unfinished sculptures Michelangelo apparently permitted to be put in place, and we do not know what his reasons were. Specialists in Renaissance art history characterize these works with the word *nonfinito* ("unfinished"), proposing that Michelangelo had begun to view his artistic

21–18 • Michelangelo **VESTIBULE OF THE LAURENTIAN LIBRARY**
Church of San Lorenzo, Florence. Begun 1524; stairway designed 1550s.

creations as symbols of human imperfection. Indeed, Michelangelo's poetry often expressed his belief that humans could achieve perfection only in death.

ARCHITECTURE IN ROME AND THE VATICAN

The election of Julius II as pope in 1503 crystallized a resurgence of papal power, but France, Spain, and the Holy Roman Empire all had designs on Italy. During his ten-year papacy, Julius fought wars and formed alliances to consolidate his power. He also enlisted Bramante, Raphael, and Michelangelo to carry out his vision of a revitalized Rome as the center of a new Christian architecture, inspired by the achievements of their fifteenth-century predecessors as well as the monuments of antiquity. Although most commissions were for churches, opportunities also arose to create urban palaces and country villas.

BRAMANTE Donato Bramante (1444–1514) was born near Urbino and trained as a painter, but turned to architectural design early in his career. About 1481, he became attached to the Sforza court in Milan, where he would have known Leonardo da Vinci. In 1499, Bramante settled in Rome, but work came slowly. The architect was nearing 60 when Julius II asked him to redesign St. Peter's (see "St. Peter's Basilica," opposite) and the Spanish rulers Queen Isabella and King Ferdinand commissioned a small shrine over the spot in Rome where the apostle Peter was believed to have been crucified (**FIG. 21-19**). In this tiny building, known as Il Tempietto ("Little Temple"), Bramante combined his interpretation of the principles of Vitruvius and Alberti from the stepped base, to the Tuscan columns and Doric frieze (Vitruvius had advised that the Doric order be used for temples to gods of particularly forceful character), to the elegant balustrade. The centralized plan and the tall drum supporting a hemispheric dome recall Early Christian shrines built over martyrs' relics, as well as ancient Roman circular temples. Especially notable is the sculptural effect of the building's exterior, with its deep wall niches and sharp contrasts of light and shadow. Bramante's design called for a circular cloister around the church, but the cloister was never built.

ARCHITECTURE, PAINTING, AND SCULPTURE IN NORTHERN ITALY

While Rome was Italy's preeminent arts center at the beginning of the sixteenth century, wealthy and powerful families elsewhere also patronized the arts and letters just as the Montefeltro and Gonzaga had in Urbino and Mantua during the fifteenth century. The architects and painters working for these sixteenth-century patrons created fanciful structures and developed a new colorful, illusionistic painting style. The result was witty, elegant, and finely executed art designed to appeal to the jaded taste of the intellectual elite in cities such as Mantua, Parma, Bologna, and Venice.

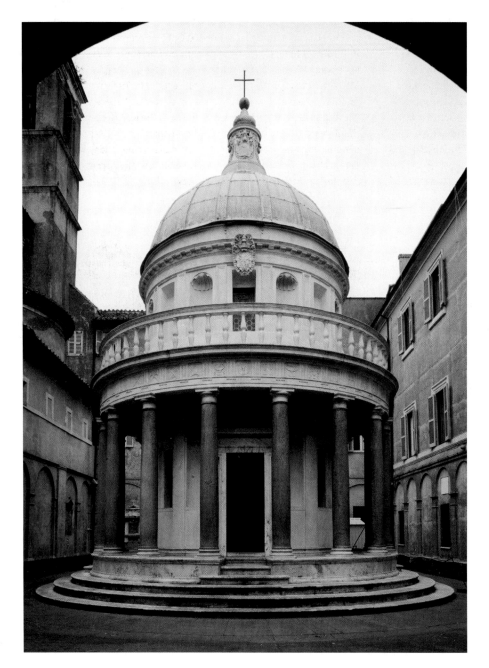

21–19 • Donato Bramante
IL TEMPIETTO, CHURCH OF SAN PIETRO IN MONTORIO
Rome. 1502–1510; dome and lantern were restored in the 17th century.

The history of St. Peter's in Rome is a case study of the effects of individual and institutional demands on the design, construction, and remodeling of a major religious building. The original church—now called Old St. Peter's—was built in the fourth century by Constantine, the first Christian Roman emperor, to mark the grave of the apostle Peter, the first bishop of Rome and therefore considered the first pope. Because the site was so holy, Constantine's architect had to build a structure large enough to hold the crowds of pilgrims who came to visit St. Peter's tomb. To provide a platform for the church, a huge terrace was cut into the side of the Vatican Hill, across the Tiber River from the city. Here Constantine's architect erected a basilica with a new feature, a transept, to allow large numbers of visitors to approach the shrine at the front of the apse. The rest of the church was, in effect, a covered cemetery, carpeted with the tombs of believers who wanted to be buried near the apostle's grave. When it was built, Constantine's basilica, as befitted an imperial commission, was one of the largest buildings in the Roman world (interior length 368 feet, width 190 feet). For more than a thousand years it was the most important pilgrimage site in Europe.

In 1506, Pope Julius II made the astonishing decision to demolish the Constantinian basilica, which had fallen into disrepair, and to replace it with a new building. That anyone, even a pope, should have had the nerve to pull down such a venerated building is an indication of the extraordinary self-assurance of the Renaissance—and of Julius himself. To design and build the new church, the pope appointed Donato Bramante, who envisioned the new St. Peter's as a central-plan building, in the shape of a cross with four arms of equal length, crowned by an enormous dome. This design was intended to emulate the Early Christian tradition of constructing domed and round buildings over the tombs of martyrs, itself derived from the Roman practice of building centrally planned tombs (see "Longitudinal-Plan and Central-Plan Churches," page 225). In Renaissance thinking, the central plan and dome symbolized the perfection of God.

The deaths of pope and architect in 1513 and 1514 put a temporary halt to the project. Successive plans by Raphael, Antonio da Sangallo, and others extended one arm of the cross to provide the church with an extended nave. However, when Michelangelo was appointed architect in 1546, he returned to the centralized plan and simplified Bramante's design to create a single, unified space covered with a hemispherical dome. The dome was finally completed some years after Michelangelo's death by Giacomo della Porta, who retained Michelangelo's basic design but gave the dome a taller profile (see FIG. 21–39).

During the Counter-Reformation, the Catholic Church emphasized congregational worship; as a result, more space was needed to house the congregation and allow for processions. To expand the church—and to make it more closely resemble Old St. Peter's—Pope Paul V in 1606 commissioned the architect Carlo Maderno to change Michelangelo's central plan back once again into a longitudinal plan. Maderno extended the nave to its final length of slightly more than 636 feet and added a new façade, thus completing St. Peter's as we see it is today. Later in the seventeenth century, the sculptor and architect Gianlorenzo Bernini created an elaborate approach to the basilica by surrounding the space in front of it with a great colonnade, like a huge set of arms extended to embrace the faithful as they approach the principal church of Western Christendom.

Old St. Peter's
4th century

Bramante, plan for New St. Peter's
1506

Michelangelo, plan for New St. Peter's
1546–1564

Maderno, plan of St. Peter's Basilica
1607–1612

👁 **Watch** an architectural simulation about St. Peter's Basilica on myartslab.com

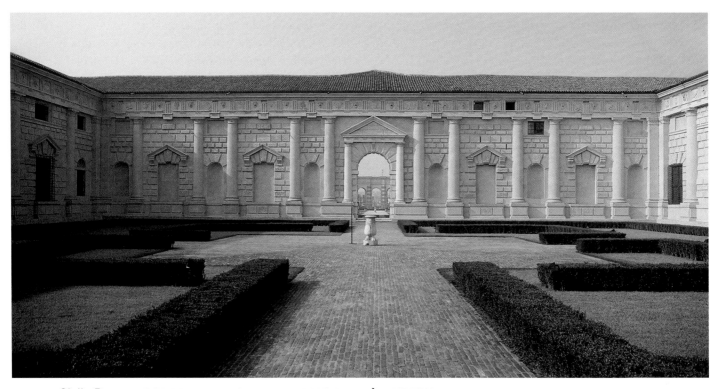

21-20 • Giulio Romano **COURTYARD FAÇADE, PALAZZO DEL TÈ, MANTUA**
1527–1534.

GIULIO ROMANO In Mantua, Federigo II Gonzaga (r. 1519–1540) continued the family tradition of patronage when, in 1524, he lured a Roman follower of Raphael, Giulio Romano (c. 1499–1546), to build him a pleasure palace. Indeed, the Palazzo del Tè (**FIG. 21-20**) devoted more space to gardens, pools, and stables than to rooms for residential living. Since Federigo and his erudite friends would have known Classical orders and proportions, they could appreciate the playfulness with which they are used here. The building is full of visual jokes, such as lintels masquerading as arches and triglyphs that slip sloppily out of place. Like the similar, if more sober, subversions of Classical architectural decorum in Michelangelo's contemporary Laurentian Library (see FIG. 21-18), its sophisticated humor and exquisite craft have been seen as a precursor to Mannerism or as a manifestation of Mannerism itself.

Giulio Romano continued his witty play in the decoration of the two principal rooms. One, dedicated to the loves of the gods, depicted the marriage of Cupid and Psyche. The other room is a remarkable feat of *trompe l'oeil* painting in which the entire building seems to be collapsing around the viewer as the gods defeat

21-21 • Giulio Romano **FALL OF THE GIANTS**
Sala dei Giganti, Palazzo del Tè. 1530–1532. Fresco.

the giants (**FIG. 21-21**). Here, Giulio Romano accepted the challenge Andrea Mantegna had laid down in the Camera Picta of the Gonzaga Palace (see FIG. 20-32), painted for Federigo's grandfather: to dissolve architectural barriers and fantasize a world of playful delight beyond the walls and ceilings. But the Palazzo del Tè was not just fun and games. The unifying themes were love and politics, the former focused on the separate apartments built to house Federigo's mistress, Isabella Boschetti. The palace was constructed in part as a place where they could meet beyond the watchful gaze of her husband. But the decoration also seems to reflect Federigo's dicey alliance with Charles V, who stayed in the palace in 1530

and again in 1532, when the scaffolding was removed from the Sala dei Giganti so the emperor could see the paintings in progress. He must have been impressed with his host's lavish new residence, and doubtless he saw a connection between these reeling paintings and his own military successes.

CORREGGIO At about the same time that Giulio Romano was building and decorating the Palazzo del Tè, in nearby Parma an equally skillful master, Correggio (Antonio Allegri da Correggio, c. 1489–1534), was creating similarly theatrical effects with dramatic foreshortening in Parma Cathedral. Correggio's great work,

21-22 • Correggio ASSUMPTION OF THE VIRGIN
Main dome, interior, Parma Cathedral, Italy. c. 1526–1530. Fresco, diameter of base of dome approx. 36′ (11 m).

securing additional commissions. This particular relief, according to Vasari, was inspired by her own love for a young man, which she got over by carving this panel. Joseph escapes, running, as the partially clad seductress snatches at his cloak. Properzia is the only woman Vasari included in the 1550 edition of *Lives of the Artists*.

VENICE AND THE VENETO

In the sixteenth century the Venetians did not see themselves as rivals of Florence and Rome, but rather as their superiors. Their city was the greatest commercial sea power in the Mediterranean; they had challenged Byzantium and now they confronted the Muslim Turks. Favored by their unique geographical situation—protected by water and controlling sea routes in the Adriatic Sea and the eastern Mediterranean—the Venetians became wealthy and secure patrons of the arts. Their Byzantine heritage, preserved by their conservative tendencies, encouraged an art of rich patterned surfaces emphasizing light and color.

The idealized style and oil-painting technique initiated by the Bellini family in the late fifteenth century (see Chapter 20) were developed further by sixteenth-century Venetian painters. Venetians were the first in Italy to use oils for painting on both wood panel and canvas. Possibly because they were a seafaring people accustomed to working with large sheets of canvas, and possibly because humidity made their walls crack and mildew, the Venetians were also the first to cover walls with large canvas paintings instead of frescos. Because oils dried slowly, errors could be corrected and changes made easily during the work. The flexibility of the canvas support, coupled with the radiance and depth of oil-suspended pigments, eventually made oil on canvas the preferred medium, especially since it was particularly well suited to the rich color and lighting effects favored by Giorgione and Titian, two of the city's major painters of the sixteenth century.

GIORGIONE The career of Giorgione (Giorgio da Castelfranco, c. 1475–1510) was brief—he died from the plague—and most scholars accept fewer than ten paintings as entirely by his hand. But his importance to Venetian painting is critical. He introduced new, enigmatic pastoral themes, known as **poesie** (or "painted poems"), that were inspired by the contemporary literary revival

the **ASSUMPTION OF THE VIRGIN** (**FIG. 21-22**), a fresco painted between about 1526 and 1530 in the cathedral's dome, distantly recalls the illusionism of Mantegna's ceiling in the Gonzaga palace, but Correggio has also assimilated Leonardo da Vinci's use of *sfumato* and Raphael's idealism into his own style. Correggio's *Assumption* is a dazzling illusion—the architecture of the dome seems to dissolve and the forms seem to explode through the building, drawing viewers into the swirling vortex of saints and angels who rush upward amid billowing clouds to accompany the Virgin as she soars into heaven. Correggio's sensual rendering of the figures' flesh and clinging draperies contrasts with the spirituality of the theme (the miraculous transporting of the Virgin to heaven at the moment of her death). The viewer's strongest impression is of a powerful, upward-spiraling motion of alternating cool clouds and warm, alluring figures.

PROPERZIA DE' ROSSI Very few women had the opportunity or inclination to become sculptors. Properzia de' Rossi (c. 1490–1529/30), who lived in Bologna, was an exception. She mastered many arts, including engraving, and was famous for her miniature sculptures, including an entire *Last Supper* carved on a peach pit! She carved several pieces in marble—two sibyls, two angels, and this relief of **JOSEPH AND POTIPHAR'S WIFE**—for the Cathedral of San Petronio in Bologna (**FIG. 21-23**). Vasari wrote that a rival male sculptor prevented her from being paid fairly and from of ancient pastoral verse but defy specific narrative or symbolic interpretation. He is significant above all for his appreciation of nature in landscape painting. His early life and training are undocumented, but his work suggests that he studied with Giovanni Bellini. Perhaps Leonardo da Vinci's subtle lighting system and mysterious, intensely observed landscapes also inspired him.

One of Giorgione's most compelling works, called today **THE TEMPEST** (FIG. 21-24), was painted shortly before his death, potentially in response to personal, private impulses—as with many modern artists—rather than to fulfill the dictates of an external commission. Simply trying to understand what is happening in this enigmatic picture piques our interest. At the right, a woman is seated on the ground, nude except for the end of a long white cloth thrown over her shoulders. Her nudity seems maternal, her sensuality generative rather than erotic, as she nurses the baby, protectively and lovingly embraced at her side. Across the dark, rocky edge of her elevated perch stands a mysterious man, variously interpreted as a German mercenary soldier and as an urban

21-24 • Giorgione THE TEMPEST
c. 1506. Oil on canvas, 32″ × 28¾″ (82 × 73 cm). Galleria dell'Accademia, Venice.

🔍 **View** the Closer Look for *The Tempest* on myartslab.com

21-25 • Giorgione or Titian THE PASTORAL CONCERT OR ALLEGORY ON THE INVENTION OF PASTORAL POETRY
c. 1510. Oil on canvas, 41¼″ × 54¾″ (105 × 136.5 cm). Musée du Louvre, Paris.

dandy wandering in the country. His shadowed head turns in the direction of the woman, but he only appears to have paused for a moment before turning back toward the viewer or resuming his journey along the path. X-rays of the painting show that Giorgione altered the composition while he was still working on the painting—the man replaces a second nude woman, in this case bathing. Between the figures, a spring gushes to feed a lake surrounded by substantial houses, and in the far distance a bolt of lightning splits the darkening sky. Indeed, the artist's attention seems focused as much on the landscape and the unruly elements of nature than on the figures posed within it. Some interpreters have seen in the lake, the verdant ground, the billowing clouds, and the lightning bolt, references to the Classical elements of water, earth, air, and fire.

For a few years before Giorgione's untimely death in 1510, he was associated with Tiziano Vecellio, a painter better known today as Titian (c. 1488–1576). The painting known as **THE PASTORAL**

CONCERT (FIG. 21-25) has been attributed to both of them, although scholarly opinion today favors Titian. As in Giorgione's *The Tempest*, the idyllic, fertile landscape, here bathed in golden, hazy late-afternoon sunlight, seems to be one of the main subjects of the painting. In this mythic world, two men—an aristocratic musician in rich red silks and a barefoot, singing peasant in homespun cloth—turn toward each other, seemingly unaware of the two naked women in front of them. One woman plays a pipe and the other pours water into a well; their swaths of white drapery sliding to the ground enhance rather than hide their nudity. Are they the musicians' muses? Behind the figures, the sunlight illuminates another shepherd and his animals near lush woodland. The painting evokes a golden age of love and innocence recalled in ancient Roman and Italian Renaissance pastoral poetry. In fact, the painting is now interpreted as an allegory on the invention of poetry. Both artists were renowned for painting sensuous female nudes whose bodies seem to glow with an incandescent light, inspired by flesh and blood beauty as much as any source from poetry or art.

TITIAN Titian's early life is obscure. He supposedly began an apprenticeship as a mosaicist, then studied painting under Gentile and Giovanni Bellini, perhaps working later with Giorgione. He certainly absorbed Giorgione's style, and completed at least one of Giorgione's unfinished paintings.

In 1519, Jacopo Pesaro, commander of the papal fleet that had defeated the Turks in 1502, commissioned Titian to commemorate the victory in a votive altarpiece for a side-aisle chapel in the Franciscan church of Santa Maria Gloriosa dei Frari in Venice. Titian worked on the painting for seven years and changed the

21–26 • Titian PESARO MADONNA
1519–1526. Oil on canvas, 16′ × 8′10″ (4.9 × 2.7 m). Side-aisle altarpiece, Santa Maria Gloriosa dei Frari, Venice.

In the sixteenth century, many wealthy women, from both the aristocracy and the merchant class, were enthusiastic patrons of the arts. The Habsburg princesses Margaret of Austria and Mary of Hungary presided over brilliant humanist courts. The marchesa of Mantua, **ISABELLA D'ESTE** (1474–1539; **FIG. 21-27**), became a patron of painters, musicians, composers, writers, and literary scholars. Married to Francesco II Gonzaga at age 15, she had great wealth, and a brilliant mind that made her a successful diplomat and administrator. A true Renaissance woman, her motto was the epitome of rational thinking— "Neither through Hope nor Fear." An avid collector of manuscripts and books, she sponsored the publication of an edition of Virgil while still in her twenties. She also collected ancient art and objects, as well as works by contemporary Italian artists such as Mantegna, Leonardo, Perugino, Correggio, and Titian. Her study in her Mantuan palace was a veritable museum. The walls above the storage and display cabinets were painted in fresco by Mantegna, and the carved wood ceiling was covered with mottoes and visual references to Isabella's impressive literary interests.

21-27 • Titian ISABELLA D'ESTE
1534–1536. Oil on canvas, 40⅛″ × 25³⁄₁₆″ (102 × 64.1 cm). Kunsthistorisches Museum, Vienna.

concept three times before he finally came up with a revolutionary composition—one that complemented the viewer's approach from the left. He created an asymmetrical setting of huge columns on high bases soaring right out of the frame (**FIG. 21-26**). Into this architectural setting, he placed the Virgin and Child on a high throne at one side and arranged saints and the Pesaro family below on a diagonal axis, crossing at the central figure of St. Peter (a reminder of Jacopo's role as head of the papal forces in 1502). The red of Francesco Pesaro's brocade garment and of the banner diagonally across sets up a contrast of primary colors against St. Peter's blue tunic and yellow mantle and the red and blue draperies of the Virgin. St. Maurice (behind the kneeling Jacopo at the left) holds the banner with the papal arms, and a cowering Turkish captive reminds the viewer of the Christian victory. The arresting image of the youth who turns to meet our gaze at lower right guarantees our engagement, and light floods in from above, illuminating not only this and other faces, but also the great columns, where *putti* in the clouds carry a cross. Titian was famous for his mastery of light and color even in his own day, but this altarpiece demonstrates that he also could draw and model as solidly as any Florentine. The perfectly balanced composition, built on color, and on diagonals instead of a vertical and horizontal grid, looks forward to the art of the seventeenth century.

In 1529, Titian, who was well known outside Venice, began a long professional relationship with Emperor Charles V, who vowed to let no one else paint his portrait and ennobled Titian in 1533. The next year Titian was commissioned to paint a portrait of Isabella d'Este (see "Women Patrons of the Arts," above). Isabella was past 60 when Titian portrayed her in 1534–1536, but she asked to appear as she had in her twenties. Titian was able to satisfy her wish by referring to an early portrait by another artist, but he also conveyed the mature Isabella's strength, self-confidence, and energy.

No photograph can convey the vibrancy of Titian's paint surfaces, which he built up in layers of pure colors, chiefly red, white, yellow, and black. A recent scientific study of Titian's paintings revealed that he ground his pigments much finer than had earlier wood-panel painters. The complicated process by which he produced many of his works began with a charcoal drawing on the prime coat of lead white that was used to seal the pores and smooth the surface of the rather coarse Venetian canvas. The artist then

21–28 • Titian "VENUS" OF URBINO
c. 1538. Oil on canvas, 3'11" × 5'5" (1.19 × 1.65 m). Galleria degli Uffizi, Florence.

built up the forms with fine glazes of different colors, sometimes in as many as 10 to 15 layers. Titian had the advantage of working in Venice, the first place to have professional retail "color sellers." These merchants produced a wide range of specially prepared pigments, even mixing their oil paints with ground glass to increase their glowing transparency. Not until the second half of the sixteenth century did color sellers open their shops in other cities.

Paintings of nude reclining women became especially popular in sophisticated court circles, where male patrons could enjoy and appreciate the "Venuses" under the cloak of respectable Classical mythology. Seemingly typical of such paintings is the **"VENUS"** Titian delivered to Guidobaldo della Rovere, duke of Urbino, in spring 1538 (**FIG. 21–28**). Here, we seem to see a beautiful Venetian courtesan, with deliberately provocative gestures, stretching languidly on her couch in a spacious palace, her glowing flesh and golden hair set off by white sheets and pillows. But for its original audience, art historian Rona Goffen has argued, the painting was more about marriage than mythology or seductiveness. The multiple matrimonial references in this work include the pair of *cassoni* (see FIG. 20–26) where servants are removing or storing

the woman's clothing in the background, the bridal symbolism of the myrtle and roses she holds in her hand, and even the spaniel snoozing at her feet—a traditional symbol of fidelity and domesticity, especially when sleeping so peacefully. Titian's picture might be associated with Duke Guidobaldo's marriage in 1534 to the 10-year-old Giulia Verano. Four years later, when this painting arrived, she would have been considered an adult rather than a child bride. It seems to represent not a Roman goddess nor a Venetian courtesan, but a physically and emotionally mature bride welcoming her husband into their lavish bedroom.

MANNERISM

A new style developed in Florence and Rome in the 1520s that some art historians have associated with the death of Raphael and labeled "Mannerism," a word deriving from the Italian *maniera* (meaning "style"). Mannerism developed into an anti-Classical movement in which artificiality, grace, and elegance took priority over the ordered balance and lifelike references that were hallmarks of High Renaissance art. Patrons favored esoteric subjects, displays of extraordinary technical virtuosity, and the pursuit of beauty for its own sake. Painters and sculptors quoted from ancient and modern works of art in the same self-conscious manner that contemporary poets and authors were quoting from ancient and modern literary classics. Architects working in the Mannerist style designed buildings that defied uniformity and balance and used Classical orders in unconventional, even playful, ways.

PAINTING

Painters working in the Mannerist style fearlessly manipulated and distorted accepted formal conventions, creating contrived compositions and irrational spatial environments. Figures take on elongated proportions, complicated artificial poses, enigmatic gestures, and dreamy expressions. The pictures are full of quoted references to the works of illustrious predecessors.

PONTORMO The frescos and altarpiece painted between 1525 and 1528 by Jacopo Carucci da Pontormo (1494–1557) for the 100-year-old **CAPPONI CHAPEL** in the church of Santa Felicità in Florence (**FIG. 21-29**) bear the hallmarks of early Mannerist painting. Open on two sides, Brunelleschi's chapel forms an interior loggia in which frescos on the right-hand wall depict the Annunciation and tondi (circular paintings) on the pendentives under the cupola represent the four evangelists. In the *Annunciation* the Virgin accepts the angel's message but also seems moved by the adjacent vision of her future sorrow, as she turns to see her son's body lowered from the cross in the **DEPOSITION**, portrayed in the altarpiece on the adjoining wall (**FIG. 21-30**).

Pontormo's ambiguous composition in the *Deposition* enhances the visionary quality of the altarpiece. Shadowy ground and cloudy sky give no sense of a specific location, and little sense

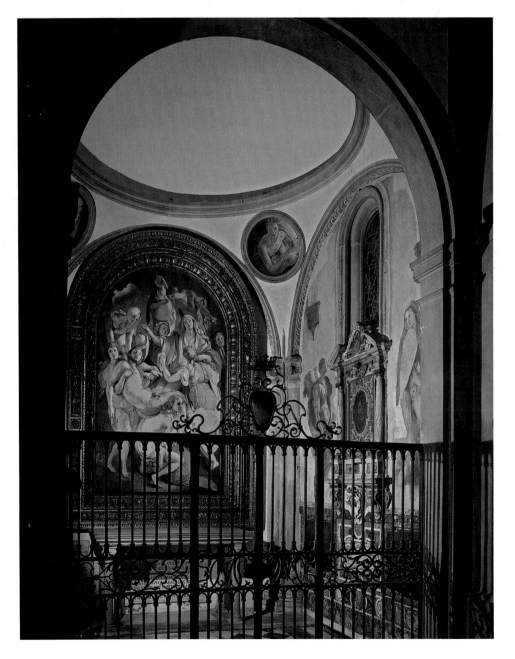

21-29 • CAPPONI CHAPEL, CHURCH OF SANTA FELICITÀ, FLORENCE
Chapel by Filippo Brunelleschi for the Barbadori family, 1419–1423; acquired by the Capponi family, who ordered paintings by Pontormo, 1525–1528.

21–30 • Pontormo DEPOSITION
Altarpiece in Capponi Chapel, church of Santa Felicità, Florence. 1525–1528. Oil and tempera on wood panel, 10′3″ × 6′4″ (3.1 × 1.9 m).

The dreamy-eyed male figure in the background shadows at upper right is a self-portrait of the artist.

of grounding for the figures. Some press forward into the viewer's space, while others seem to levitate or stand precariously on tiptoe. Pontormo chose a moment just after Jesus' removal from the cross, when the youths who have lowered him pause to regain their hold on the corpse, which recalls Michelangelo's Vatican *Pietà* (see FIG. 21-9). Odd poses and drastic shifts in scale charge the scene emotionally, but perhaps most striking is the use of weird colors in odd juxtapositions—baby blue and pink with accents of olive-green, yellow, and scarlet. The overall tone of the picture is set by the unstable youth crouching in the foreground, whose skintight

21-32 • Bronzino **PORTRAIT OF ELEONORA OF TOLEDO AND HER SON GIOVANNI DE' MEDICI**
1545. Oil on wood panel, 45¼″ × 37¾″ (115 × 96 cm). Galleria degli Uffizi, Florence.

21-31 • Parmigianino **MADONNA OF THE LONG NECK**
1534–1540. Oil on wood panel, 7′1″ × 4′4″ (2.16 × 1.32 m). Galleria degli Uffizi, Florence.

Art historian Elizabeth Cropper has noted the visual relationship between the shape of the swelling, tapering-necked, ovoid vessel held by the figure at far left and the form of the figure of the Virgin herself and has proposed that this visual analogy references a sixteenth-century literary conceit that related ideal beauty in women to the slender necks and swelling shapes of antique vessels.

bright pink shirt is shaded in iridescent, pale gray-blue, and whose anxious expression is projected out of the painting, directly at the viewer.

PARMIGIANINO When Parmigianino (Francesco Mazzola, 1503–1540) left his native Parma in 1524 for Rome, the strongest influence on his work was Correggio (see FIG. 21-22). In Rome, however, Parmigianino met Giulio Romano; he also studied the work of Raphael and Michelangelo. What he assimilated developed into a distinctive Mannerist style, calm but strangely unsettling. After the Sack of Rome in 1527, he moved to Bologna and then back to Parma.

Left unfinished at the time of his early death is a disconcerting painting known as the **MADONNA OF THE LONG NECK** (FIG. 21-31). The unnaturally proportioned figure of Mary, whose massive legs and lower torso contrast with her narrow shoulders and long neck and fingers, is presumably seated on a throne, but there is no seat in sight. The languid expanse of the sleeping child recalls the pose of the ashen Christ in a *pietà*; indeed, there is more than a passing resemblance here to Michelangelo's famous sculpture in the Vatican, even to the inclusion of a diagonal band across the Virgin's chest (see FIG. 21-9). The plunge into a deep background to the right reveals a startlingly small St. Jerome, who unrolls a scroll in front of huge white columns from what was to be a temple in the unfinished background, whereas at the left a crowded mass of blushing boys blocks any view into the background. Like Pontormo, Parmigianino presents a well-known image in a challenging manner calculated to intrigue viewers.

BRONZINO About 1522, Agnolo di Cosimo di Mariano Tori (1503–1572), whose nickname of "Bronzino" means "copper-colored" (just as we might call someone "Red"), became Pontormo's pupil and assistant, probably helping with the tondi on the pendentives of the Capponi Chapel (see FIG. 21-29). In 1530, he established his own workshop, though he continued to work with Pontormo on occasional large projects. By 1540, he was court painter to the Medici. Although he produced altarpieces, fresco decorations, and tapestry designs over his long career, he is best known today for his elegant portraits, the focus of his work for Duke Cosimo I de' Medici (r. 1537–1574). Bronzino's virtuosity in rendering costumes and settings, juxtaposed with the masklike quality given to the vacant faces of his subjects, results in cold and formal portraits, but the self-contained demeanor of his subjects admirably conveys their haughtiness and reflects the absolutism of Cosimo's rule.

Typical is an elegantly restrained state portrait of 1545 portraying Cosimo's wife, **ELEONORA OF TOLEDO** (1522–1562) and their second son, Giovanni de' Medici (FIG. 21-32). Bronzino characteristically portrayals this mother and son as aloof and self-assured, their class and connection much more prominent than any sense of individual likeness or personality. In a real sense, this double portrait is an iconic embodiment of dynastic power and an assurance of Medici succession. Giovanni, however, did not succeed his father as duke—that path was taken by his elder brother Francesco. Instead he pursued a fast-tracked career in the Church. Already archbishop of Pisa, in 1560, at age 17, he became a cardinal, only two years before both he and his mother died of malaria.

Bronzino's **ALLEGORY WITH VENUS AND CUPID** is one of the strangest paintings of the sixteenth century (FIG. 21-33). It contains all the formal, iconographical, and psychological characteristics of Mannerist art and could almost stand alone as a summary of the movement. Seven figures, three masks, and a dove interweave in an intricate, claustrophobic formal composition pressed breathlessly into the foreground plane. Taken as individual images, they display the exaggerated poses, graceful forms, polished surfaces, and delicate colors that characterize Mannerist art. But a closer look into this composition uncovers disturbing erotic attachments and bizarre irregularities. The painting's complex allegory and relentless ambiguity probably delighted mid-sixteenth-century courtiers who enjoyed equally sophisticated wordplay and esoteric Classical references, but for us it defies easy explanation. Nothing is quite what it seems.

Venus and her son Cupid engage in an unsettlingly lascivious dalliance, encouraged by a *putto* sauntering in from the right—representing Folly, Jest, or Playfulness—who is about to throw pink roses at them while stepping on a thorny branch that draws blood from his foot. Cupid gently kisses his mother and pinches her erect nipple while Venus snatches an arrow from his quiver, leading some scholars to suggest that the painting's title should be *Venus Disarming Cupid*. Venus holds the golden apple of discord given to her by Paris; her dove conforms to the shape of Cupid's foot without actually touching it, while a pair of masks lying at her feet reiterates the theme of duplicity. An old man, Time or Chronos, assisted by an outraged Truth or Night, pulls back a curtain to expose the couple. Lurking just behind Venus a monstrous serpent—which has the upper body and head of a beautiful young girl and the legs and claws of a lion—crosses her hands to hold a honeycomb and the stinger at the end of her tail. This strange hybrid has been interpreted both as Fraud and Pleasure.

21-33 • Bronzino ALLEGORY WITH VENUS AND CUPID
Mid 1540s. Oil on panel, 57½″ × 46″ (1.46 × 1.16 m). National Gallery, London.
Reproduced by courtesy of the Trustees of the National Gallery, London

View the Closer Look for *Allegory with Venus and Cupid* on myartslab.com

In the shadows to the left, a pale and screaming man tearing at his hair has recently been identified as a victim of syphilis, which raged as an epidemic during this period. The painting could, therefore, be a warning of the dangers of this disease, believed in the sixteenth century to be spread principally by coitus, kissing, and breast feeding, all of which are alluded to in the intertwined Cupid and Venus. But the complexity of the painting makes room for multiple meanings, and deciphering them would be typical of the sorts of games enjoyed by sixteenth-century intellectuals. Perhaps the allegory tells of the impossibility of constant love and the folly of lovers, which becomes apparent across time. Or perhaps it is an allegorical warning of the dangers of illicit sexual liaisons, including the pain, hair loss, and disfiguration of venereal disease. It could be both, and even more. Duke Cosimo commissioned the painting himself and presented it as a diplomatic gift to French King Francis I, who would doubtless have relished its overt eroticism and flawless execution.

SOFONISBA ANGUISSOLA Northern Italy, more than any other part of the peninsula, produced a number of gifted women artists. In the latter half of the sixteenth century, Bologna, for example, boasted some two dozen women painters and sculptors, as well as a number of learned women who lectured at the university. Sofonisba Anguissola (c. 1532–1625), born into a noble

21-35 • Lavinia Fontana **NOLI ME TANGERE**
1581. Oil on canvas, 47⅜″ × 36⅝″ (120.3 × 93 cm). Galleria degli Uffizi, Florence.

family in Cremona (between Bologna and Milan), was unusual in that she was not the daughter of an artist. Her father gave all his children a humanistic education and encouraged them to pursue careers in literature, music, and especially painting. He consulted Michelangelo about Sofonisba Anguissola's artistic talents in 1557, asking for a drawing that she might copy and return to be critiqued. Michelangelo evidently obliged, because her father wrote an enthusiastic letter of thanks.

Anguissola was a gifted portrait painter who also created miniatures, an important aspect of portraiture in the sixteenth century, when people had few means of recording the features of a lover, friend, or family member. Anguissola painted a miniature **SELF-PORTRAIT** holding a medallion, the border of which spells out her name and home town, Cremona (**FIG. 21-34**). The interlaced letters at the center of the medallion pose a riddle; they seem to form a monogram with the first letters of her sisters' names: Minerva, Europa, Elena. Such names are further evidence of the Anguissola family's enthusiasm for the Classics.

In 1560, Anguissola accepted the invitation of the queen of Spain to become a lady-in-waiting and court painter, a post she held for 20 years. Unfortunately, most of her Spanish works were lost in a seventeenth-century palace fire, but a 1582 Spanish inventory described her as "an excellent painter of portraits above all

21-34 • Sofonisba Anguissola **SELF-PORTRAIT**
c. 1552. Oil on parchment on cardboard, 3¼″ × 2½″ (8.3 × 6.4 cm). Museum of Fine Arts, Boston. Emma F. Munroe Fund 60.155

the painters of this time"—extraordinary praise in a court that patronized Titian. After her years at court, she retired to Spanish-controlled Sicily, where she died in her nineties. Anthony Van Dyck met her in Palermo in 1624, where he sketched her and claimed that she was then 96 years old. He wrote that she advised him on positioning the light for her portrait, asking that it not be placed too high because the strong shadows would bring out her wrinkles.

LAVINIA FONTANA Bolognese artist Lavinia Fontana (1552–1614) learned to paint from her father. By the 1570s, her success was so well rewarded that her husband, the painter Gian Paolo Zappi, gave up his own painting career to care for their large family and help his wife with the technical aspects of her work, such as framing. In 1603, Fontana moved to Rome as an official painter to the papal court. She also soon came to the attention of the Habsburgs, who became major patrons.

While still in her twenties, Fontana painted a **NOLI ME TANGERE** (**FIG. 21-35**), where Christ reveals himself for the first time to Mary Magdalen following his Resurrection, warning her not to touch him (John 20:17). Christ's broad-brimmed hat and spade refer to the passage in John's Gospel claiming that Mary Magdalen at first thought Christ was the gardener. In the middle distance Fontana portrays a second version of the Resurrection, where women followers of Christ discover an angel in his empty tomb. This secondary scene's dizzying diagonal plunge into depth is a typical feature of late Mannerist painting in Italy, as are the affected pose of the foreground Christ and the elongated proportions of the Magdalen.

SCULPTURE

Mannerist sculpture—often small in size and made from precious metals—stylizes body forms and foregrounds displays of technical skill in ways that are reminiscent of Mannerist painting.

CELLINI The Florentine goldsmith and sculptor Benvenuto Cellini (1500–1571), who wrote a dramatic—and scandalous—autobiography and a practical handbook for artists, worked in the French court at Fontainebleau. There he made the famous **SALTCELLAR OF KING FRANCIS I** (**FIG. 21-36**),

a table accessory transformed into an elegant sculptural ornament by fanciful imagery and superb execution. In gold and enamel, the Roman sea god Neptune, representing the source of salt, sits next to a tiny boat-shaped container for the seasoning, while a personification of Earth guards the plant-derived pepper, contained in the triumphal arch to her right. Representations of the seasons and the times of day on the base refer to both daily meal schedules and festive seasonal celebrations. The two main figures lean away from each other at impossible angles yet are connected and visually balanced by glance, gestures, and coordinated poses—mirroring each other with one bent and one straight leg. Their supple, elongated bodies and small heads reflect the Mannerist conventions of artists like Parmigianino (see **FIG. 21-31**). Cellini wrote, "I represented the Sea and the Land, both seated, with their legs intertwined just as some branches of the sea run into the land and the land juts into the sea…" (Cellini, *Autobiography*, translated by G. Bull, p. 291).

GIAMBOLOGNA In the second half of the sixteenth century, probably the most influential sculptor in Italy was Jean Boulogne, better known by his Italian names, Giovanni Bologna or Giambologna (1529–1608). Born in Flanders, he settled during the 1550s in Florence, where he worked at the court of Duke Cosimo I de' Medici. He not only influenced and trained a later generation of Italian sculptors; he also spread the Mannerist style to the north through artists who came to study his work.

Although Giambologna's prodigious artistic output included elaborate fountains and many works in bronze—both imposing

21-36 • Benvenuto Cellini SALTCELLAR OF KING FRANCIS I OF FRANCE
1540–1543. Gold and enamel, 10½″ × 13⅛″ (26.67 × 33.34 cm). Kunsthistorisches Museum, Vienna.

Read the document related to Benvenuto Cellini on myartslab.com public monuments and exquisitely rendered statuettes—his most famous sculpture is a monumental marble carving now known as **THE CAPTURE OF A SABINE WOMAN** (FIG. 21-37), a title given to it by a member of the Florentine Academy of Design only after it was finished. Giambologna himself conceived of this composition of three nude figures—spiraling upward in energetic, intertwined torsion—not in relation to any particular subject or story, but as a formal exercise in figural representation and technical virtuosity. In spite of the deep undercutting and projecting gestures, this cohesive column of figures was carved from a single block of marble. Because of the spiraling composition—created by twisting figural cohesion and the projection of dramatic gestures—viewers must walk around the sculpture to explore it; it cannot be fully grasped from any single viewpoint. Grand Duke Francesco I de' Medici installed Giambologna's masterpiece in a place of honor at the front of the Loggia dei Lanzi, where it remains today (see FIG. 18-2).

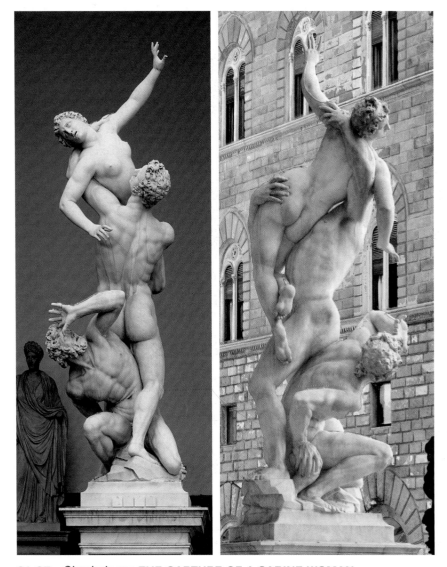

21-37 • Giambologna THE CAPTURE OF A SABINE WOMAN
1581–1582. Marble, height 13′6″ (4.1 m). Loggia dei Lanzi, Florence.

ART AND THE COUNTER-REFORMATION

Pope Clement VII, whose miscalculations had spurred Emperor Charles V to attack and destroy Rome in 1527, also misjudged the threat to the Church and to papal authority posed by the Protestant Reformation. His failure to address the issues raised by the reformers enabled the movement to spread. His successor, Paul III (pontificate 1534–1549), the rich and worldly Roman noble Alessandro Farnese, was the first pope to pursue Church reform in response to the rise of Protestantism. In 1536, he appointed a commission to investigate charges of Church corruption and later convened the Council of Trent (1545–1563) to define Catholic dogma, initiate disciplinary reforms, and regulate the training of clerics.

Pope Paul III also addressed Protestantism through repression and censorship. In 1542, he instituted the Inquisition, a papal office that sought out heretics for interrogation, trial, and sentencing. The enforcement of religious unity extended to the arts. Traditional images of Christ and the saints were sanctioned, but art was scrutinized for traces of heresy and profanity. Guidelines issued by the Council of Trent limited what could be represented in Christian art and led to the destruction of some works. At the same time, art became a powerful weapon of propaganda, especially in the hands of members of the Society of Jesus, a new religious order founded by the Spanish nobleman Ignatius of Loyola (1491–1556) and confirmed by Paul III in 1540. Dedicated to piety, education, and missionary work, the Jesuits, as they are known, spread worldwide and became important leaders of the Counter-Reformation movement and the revival of the Catholic Church.

ART AND ARCHITECTURE IN ROME AND THE VATICAN

To restore the heart of the city of Rome, Paul III began rebuilding the Capitoline Hill as well as continuing work on St. Peter's. His commissions include some of the finest art and architecture of the late Italian Renaissance. His first major commission brought Michelangelo, after a quarter of a century, back to the Sistine Chapel.

MICHELANGELO'S LATE WORK In his early sixties, Michelangelo complained bitterly of feeling old, but he nonetheless undertook the important and demanding task of painting the **LAST JUDGMENT** on the 48-foot-high end wall above the Sistine Chapel altar between 1536 and 1541 (FIG. 21-38).

21–38 • Michelangelo LAST JUDGMENT, SISTINE CHAPEL
1536–1541. Fresco, 48′ × 44′ (14.6 × 13.4 m).

Dark, rectangular patches intentionally left by recent restorers (visible, for example, in the upper left and right corners) contrast with the vibrant colors of the chapel's frescos. These dark areas show just how dirty the walls had become over the centuries before their recent cleaning.

Read the document related to Michelangelo's poetry on myartslab.com

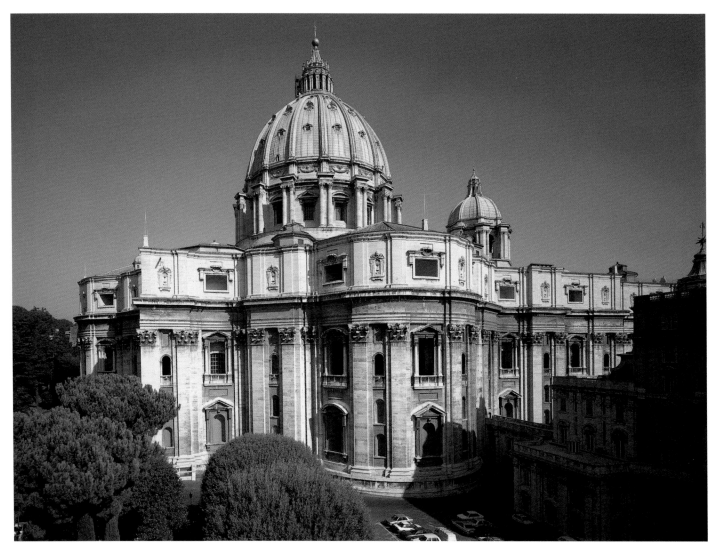

21-39 • Michelangelo ST. PETER'S BASILICA, VATICAN
c. 1546–1564; dome completed 1590 by Giacomo della Porta; lantern 1590–1593. View from the west.

Abandoning the clearly organized medieval conception of the Last Judgment, in which the saved are neatly separated from the damned, Michelangelo painted a writhing swarm of resurrected humanity. At left (on Christ's right side), the dead are dragged from their graves and pushed up into a vortex of figures around Christ, who wields his arm like a sword of justice. The shrinking Virgin under Christ's raised right arm represents a change from Gothic tradition, where she had sat enthroned beside, and equal in size to, her son. To the right of Christ's feet is St. Bartholomew, who in legend was martyred by being skinned alive. He holds his flayed skin, and Michelangelo seems to have painted his own distorted features on the skin's face. Despite the efforts of several saints to save them at the last minute, the damned are plunged toward hell on the right, leaving the elect and still-unjudged in a dazed, almost uncomprehending state. On the lowest level of the mural, right above the altar, is the gaping, fiery entrance to hell, toward which Charon, the ferryman of the dead to the underworld, propels his craft. The painting was long interpreted as a grim and constant reminder to celebrants of the Mass—the pope and his

cardinals—that ultimately they too would face stern judgment at the end of time. Conservative clergy criticized the painting for its frank nudity, and after Michelangelo's death they ordered bits of drapery to be added by artist Daniele da Volterra to conceal the offending areas, earning Daniele the unfortunate nickname *Il Braghettone* ("breeches painter").

Another of Paul III's ambitions was to complete the new St. Peter's, a project that had been under way for 40 years (see "St. Peter's Basilica," page 653). Michelangelo was well aware of the work done by his predecessors—from Bramante to Raphael to Antonio da Sangallo the Younger. The 71-year-old sculptor, confident of his architectural expertise, demanded the right to deal directly with the pope, rather than through a committee of construction deputies. Michelangelo further shocked the deputies—but not the pope—by undoing parts of Sangallo's design, then simplifying and strengthening Bramante's central plan, long associated with shrines of Christian martyrs. Although seventeenth-century additions and renovations dramatically changed the original plan of the church and the appearance of its interior, Michelangelo's

21-40 • Vignola and Giacomo della Porta
PLAN AND FAÇADE OF THE CHURCH OF IL GESÙ, ROME
c. 1573–1584.

apse

crossing

nave

chapels

ST. PETER'S (**FIG. 21-39**) still can be seen in the contrasting forms of the flat and angled exterior walls and the three surviving hemicycles (semicircular structures). Colossal pilasters, blind windows (frames without openings), and niches surround the sanctuary of the church. The current dome, erected by Giacomo della Porta in 1588–1590, retains Michelangelo's basic design: segmented with regularly spaced ribs, seated on a high drum with pedimented windows between paired columns, and surmounted by a tall lantern.

The aging Michelangelo—often described by his contemporaries as difficult, even arrogant—alternated between periods of depression and frenzied activity. Yet he was devoted to his friends and helpful to young artists. He believed that his art was divinely inspired and became increasingly devoted to religious works—many left unfinished—that subverted Renaissance ideals of human perfectibility and denied the idealism of youth. In the process he pioneered new stylistic directions that would inspire succeeding generations of artists.

VIGNOLA A young artist who worked to meet the need for new Roman churches was Giacomo Barozzi (1507–1573), known as Vignola after his native town. He worked in Rome during the late 1530s, surveying ancient Roman monuments and providing illustrations for an edition of Vitruvius. From 1541 to 1543, he was in France with Francesco Primaticcio at the château of Fontainebleau. After returning to Rome, he secured the patronage of the Farnese family and profited from the Counter-Reformation church-building inititatives.

Catholicism's new emphasis on individual, emotional participation brought a focus on sermons and music, requiring churches with wide naves and unobstructed views of the altar, instead of the complex interiors of medieval and earlier Renaissance churches. Ignatius of Loyola was determined to build **IL GESÙ**, the Jesuit headquarters church in Rome, according to these precepts, although he did not live to see it finished (**FIG. 21-40**). The cornerstone was laid in 1540, but construction of Il Gesù did not begin until 1568, after a period of fund-raising. Cardinal Alessandro Farnese (Paul III's namesake and grandson) donated to the project in 1561 and selected Vignola as architect. After Vignola died in 1573, Giacomo della Porta finished the dome and façade to his own designs.

Il Gesù was admirably suited for congregational worship. Vignola designed a wide, barrel-vaulted nave with shallow connected side chapels; there are no aisles and only truncated transepts contained within the line of the outer walls—enabling all worshipers to gather in the central space. A single huge apse and dome over the crossing directed attention to the altar. The design also allows the building to fit compactly into a city block—a requirement that now often overrode the desire to orient a church along an east–west axis. The symmetrical façade, in Vignola's original design as well as della Porta's variation on it, emphasized the central portal with Classical pilasters, engaged columns and pediments, and volutes scrolling out laterally to hide the buttresses of the central vault and to link the tall central section with the lower sides.

As finally built by Giacomo della Porta, the façade design would have significant influence well into the next century. The early Renaissance grid of Classical pilasters and entablatures is abandoned for a two-story design that coordinates paired columns or pilasters, aligned vertically to tie together the two stories of the central block which corresponds with the nave elevation. The main entrance, with its central portal aligned with a tall upper-story window, became the focus of the composition. Centrally aligned pediments break into the level above, leading the eye upward to the cartouches with coats of arms—here of both Cardinal Farnese, the patron, and the Jesuits (whose arms display the initials IHS, the monogram of Christ).

LATER SIXTEENTH-CENTURY ART IN VENICE AND THE VENETO

By the second half of the sixteenth century, Venice ruled supreme as "queen of the Adriatic." Her power was not, however, unchallenged, and the Turks were a constant threat. In 1571, allied with Spain and the pope, the Christian fleet with Venetian ships defeated the Turkish fleet at the Battle of Lepanto, establishing Christian preeminence for future generations. Victorious and wealthy, Venetians built palaces and villas to contain their lavish lifestyle, filling them with lush oil paintings.

OIL PAINTING

Rather than the cool, formal, technical perfection sought by Mannerist painters, Venetian artists expanded upon the manner initiated by Giorgione and Titian, concerning themselves above all with color, light, and expressively loose brushwork.

VERONESE Paolo Caliari (1528–1588) took his nickname "Veronese" from his hometown, Verona, but he worked mainly in Venice. His paintings are nearly synonymous today with the popular image of Venice as a splendid city of pleasure and pageantry sustained by a nominally republican government and great mercantile wealth. Veronese's elaborate architectural settings and costumes, still lifes, anecdotal vignettes, and other everyday details—often unconnected with the main subject—proved immensely appealing to Venetian patrons.

One of Veronese's most famous works is a *Last Supper* that he renamed *Feast in the House of Levi* (see "Veronese is Called before the Inquisition," opposite), painted in 1573 for the Dominican monastery of SS. Giovanni e Paolo. At first glance, the subject of the painting seems to be primarily its architectural setting and only secondarily Christ seated at the table. Symmetrically disposed balustraded stairways lead to an enormous loggia framed by colossal arches, beyond which sits an imaginary city of white marble. Within this grand setting, lifelike figures in lavish costumes strike theatrical poses, surrounded by the sort of anecdotal details loved by the Venetians—like parrots and monkeys—but detested by the Church's inquisitors, who saw them as profane distractions in a representation of the Last Supper.

TINTORETTO Jacopo Robusti (1518–1594), called Tintoretto ("Little Dyer," because his father was a dyer), carried Venetian painting in another direction. Tintoretto's goal, declared on a sign in his studio, was to combine Titian's coloring with the drawing of Michelangelo. His large painting of **THE LAST SUPPER** (**FIG. 21-42**) for the choir of Palladio's church of San Giorgio Maggiore (see **FIG. 21-44**) is quite different from Leonardo da Vinci's painting of the same subject almost a century earlier (see **FIG. 21-3**). Instead of Leonardo's frontal view of a closed and logical space with massive figures reacting in individual ways to Jesus' statement, Tintoretto views the scene from a corner, with the vanishing point on a high horizon line at far right. The table, coffered ceiling, and inlaid floor all seem to plunge dramatically into the distance. The figures, although still large bodies modeled by flowing draperies, turn and move in a continuous serpentine line that unites apostles, servants, and angels. Tintoretto used two internal light sources: one real, the other supernatural. Over the near end of the table, light streams from the oil lamp flaring exuberantly, with angels swirling out from the flame and smoke. A second light emanates from Jesus himself and is repeated in the glow of the apostles' haloes. The intensely spiritual, otherworldly mood is enhanced by deep colors flashed with dazzling highlights on elongated figures, consistent with Mannerist tendencies. The still lifes on the tables and homey details like the cat that peers in the foreground basket connect with viewers' own experiences. And the narrative emphasis has shifted from Leonardo's more worldly study of personal betrayal to Tintoretto's reference to the institution of the Eucharist. Jesus offers bread and wine to a disciple in the manner of a priest administering the sacrament at the altar next to the painting.

The speed with which Tintoretto drew and painted was the subject of comment in his own time, and the brilliance and immediacy so admired in his work today—his slashing brushwork was much appreciated by twentieth-century gestural painters—were occasionally derided as evidence of carelessness in his own time. Rapid production may have been a byproduct of his working methods. Tintoretto had a large workshop of assistants and he usually provided only the original conception, the beginning

According to the New Testament, Jesus revealed his impending death to his disciples during a seder, a meal celebrating the Jewish festival of Passover. This occasion, known to Christians as the Last Supper, and situated in the Gospels on the evening before the Crucifixion, was a popular theme in sixteenth-century European art. But in 1573, when the painter Veronese delivered an enormous canvas of this subject to fulfill a commission (FIG. 21–41), the patrons were shocked. Some were offended by the grandiose pageantry of the scene. Others protested the impiety of surrounding Jesus with a man picking his teeth, scruffy dogs, and foreign soldiers. As a result of the furor, Veronese was called before the Inquisition to explain his painting. There he justified himself first by asserting that the picture actually depicted not the Last Supper, but rather the feast in the house of Simon, a small dinner held shortly before Jesus' final entry into Jerusalem. He also noted that artists customarily invent details in their pictures and that he had received a commission to paint the piece "as I saw fit." His argument fell on unsympathetic ears, and he was ordered to change the painting. Later he sidestepped the issue by changing its title to that of another banquet, one given by the tax collector Levi, whom Jesus had called to follow him (Luke 5:27–32). Perhaps with this change of subject, Veronese took a modest revenge on the Inquisitors: When Jesus himself was criticized for associating with such unsavory people at this meal, he replied, "I have not come to call the righteous to repentance but sinners" (Luke 5:32).

21–41 • Veronese FEAST IN THE HOUSE OF LEVI
From the refectory of the monastery of SS. Giovanni e Paolo, Venice. 1573. Oil on canvas, 18'3" × 42' (5.56 × 12.8 m). Galleria dell'Accademia, Venice.

Read the document related to Paolo Veronese on myartslab.com

drawings, and the final brilliant touches on the finished paintings. Tintoretto's workshop included members of his family—of his eight children, four became artists. His oldest daughter, Marietta Robusti, worked with him as a portrait painter, and two or perhaps three of his sons also joined the shop. So skillfully did Marietta capture her father's style and technique that today art historians cannot identify her work in the shop.

ARCHITECTURE: PALLADIO

Just as Veronese and Tintoretto expanded upon the rich Venetian tradition of oil painting initiated by Giorgione and Titian, Andrea Palladio dominated architecture during the second half of the century by expanding upon the principles of Alberti and ancient Roman architecture. His buildings—whether villas, palaces, or churches—were characterized by harmonious symmetry and controlled ornamentation. Born Andrea di Pietro della Gondola (1508–1580), probably in Padua, Palladio began his career as a stonecutter. After moving to Vicenza, he was hired by the nobleman, humanist scholar, and amateur architect Giangiorgio Trissino, who gave him the nickname "Palladio" for the Greek goddess of wisdom, Pallas Athena, and the fourth-century Roman writer Palladius. Palladio learned

21-42 • Tintoretto THE LAST SUPPER
Church of San Giorgio Maggiore, Venice. 1592–1594. Oil on canvas, 12' × 18'8" (3.7 × 5.7 m).

Tintoretto, who had a large workshop, often developed a composition by creating a small-scale model like a miniature stage set, which he populated with wax figures. He then adjusted the positions of the figures and the lighting until he was satisfied with the entire scene. Using a grid of horizontal and vertical threads placed in front of this model, he could easily sketch the composition onto squared paper for his assistants to copy onto a large canvas. His assistants also primed the canvas, blocking in the areas of dark and light, before the artist himself, free to concentrate on the most difficult passages, finished the painting. This efficient working method allowed Tintoretto to produce a large number of paintings in all sizes.

Latin at Trissino's small academy and accompanied his benefactor on three trips to Rome, where he made drawings of Roman monuments.

Over the years, Palladio became involved in several publishing ventures, including a guide to Roman antiquities and an illustrated edition of Vitruvius. He also published his own books on architecture—including ideal plans for country estates, using proportions derived from ancient Roman buildings—that for centuries would be valuable resources for architectural design. Despite their theoretical bent, his writings were often more practical than earlier treatises. Perhaps his early experience as a stonemason provided him with the knowledge and self-confidence to approach technical problems and discuss them as clearly as he did theories of ideal proportion and uses of the Classical orders. By the eighteenth

century, Palladio's *Four Books of Architecture* had been included in the libraries of most educated people. Thomas Jefferson had one of the first copies in America.

SAN GIORGIO MAGGIORE By 1559, when he settled in Venice, Palladio was one of the foremost architects in Italy. In 1565, he undertook a major architectural commission: the monastery **CHURCH OF SAN GIORGIO MAGGIORE** (**FIG. 21-43**). His variation on the traditional Renaissance façade for a basilica—a wide lower level fronting the nave and side aisles, surmounted by a narrower front for the nave clerestory—creates the illusion of two temple fronts of different heights and widths, one set inside the other. At the center, colossal columns on high pedestals support an entablature and pediment; these columns correspond

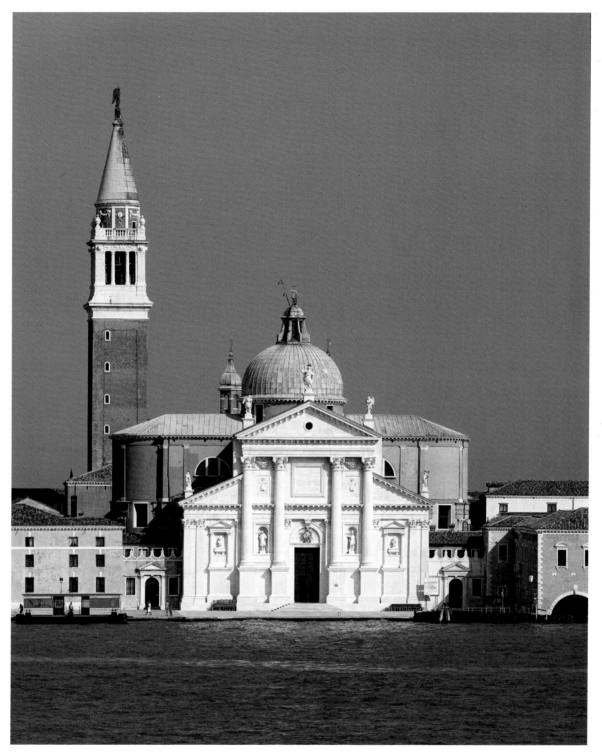

21-43 • Palladio CHURCH OF SAN GIORGIO MAGGIORE, VENICE
Plan 1565; construction 1565–1580; façade 1597–1610; campanile 1791. Finished by Vincenzo Scamozzi following Palladio's design.

to the width of the nave within. Behind the taller temple front, a second front consists of pilasters supporting another entablature and pediment; this wider front spans the entire width of the church, including the triple aisle. Although the façade was not built until after the architect's death, his original design was followed.

The interior of **SAN GIORGIO** (**FIG. 21-44**) is a fine example of Palladio's harmoniously balanced geometry, expressed here in strong verticals and powerfully opened arches. The tall engaged columns and shorter pilasters of the nave arcade piers echo the two levels of orders on the façade, thus helping to unify the building's exterior and interior.

21-44 • NAVE, CHURCH OF SAN GIORGIO MAGGIORE, VENICE
Begun 1566. Tintoretto's *Last Supper* (not visible) hangs to the left of the altar.

THE VILLA ROTONDA Palladio's versatility was already apparent in numerous villas built early in his career. In the 1560s, he started his most famous and influential villa just outside Vicenza (**FIGS. 21–45, 21–46**). Although villas were working farms, Palladio designed this one in part as a retreat, literally a party house. To maximize vistas of the countryside, he placed a porch elevated at the top of a wide staircase on each face of the building. The main living quarters are on this second level, and the lower level is reserved for the kitchen, storage, and other utility rooms. Upon its completion in 1569, the building was dubbed the **VILLA ROTONDA** because it had been inspired by another round building, the Roman Pantheon. The plan shows the geometric clarity of Palladio's conception: a circle inscribed in a small square inside a larger square, with symmetrical rectangular compartments and identical rectangular projections from each of its faces. The use of a central dome on a domestic building was a daring innovation that effectively secularized the dome and initiated what was to become a long tradition of domed country houses, particularly in England and the United States.

21-45 • Palladio PLAN OF VILLA ROTONDA, VICENZA
Italy. Begun 1560s.

21–46 • Palladio EXTERIOR VIEW OF VILLA ROTONDA
Italy. Begun 1560s.

After its purchase in 1591 by the Capra family, the Villa Rotonda became known as the Villa Capra.

Read the document related to Andrea Palladio on myartslab.com

THINK ABOUT IT

21.1 Some art historians have claimed that whereas Rome and Florence were oriented toward drawing, Venice was oriented toward color. Evaluate this claim, discussing specific works from each tradition in forming your answer.

21.2 Analyze either the Palazzo del Tè (FIG. 21–20) or the Villa Rotonda (FIG. 21–46). Explain how the design of the building differs from the design of grand churches during this same period, even though architects clearly used Classical motifs in both sacred and secular contexts.

21.3 Discuss Julius II's efforts to aggrandize the city of Rome and create a new golden age of papal art. Focus your answer on at least two specific works—one in painting and the other architectural—that he commissioned.

21.4 Select either Pontormo's *Deposition* (FIG. 21–30) or Parmigianino's *Madonna of the Long Neck* (FIG. 21–31), and explain why the painting characterizes Mannerist style. How does your chosen work depart from the Classical norms of the High Renaissance? How would you characterize their relationship to Michelangelo's *Last Judgment* (FIG. 21–38)?

CROSSCURRENTS

Ch. 20
Closer Look,
page 628

FIG. 21–33

These two paintings, each commissioned by a powerful political figure, combine Classical and allegorical themes in unusual ways. Each addresses a select audience. Compare the nature of the message each painting presents and evaluate how the style of presentation relates to the traditions and objectives of Florentine art during the period when it was painted.

Study and review on myartslab.com

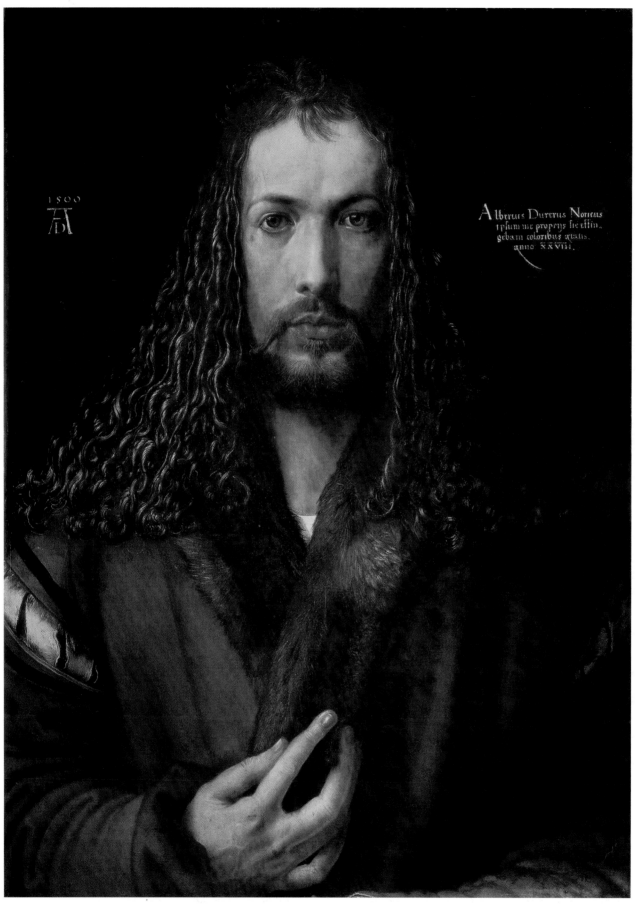

22–1 • Albrecht Dürer SELF-PORTRAIT

1500. Signed "Albrecht Dürer of Nuremberg...age 28." Oil on wood panel, 26¼" × 19¼" (66.3 × 49 cm). Alte Pinakothek, Munich.

📖•⌐ **Read** the document related to Albrecht Dürer on myartslab.com

Sixteenth-Century Art in Northern Europe and the Iberian Peninsula

This striking image (**FIG. 22-1**), dated 1500, seems to depict a blessing Christ, meant to rivet our attention and focus our devotion. But an inscription to the right of the iconic visage identifies this as a **SELF-PORTRAIT** of Albrecht Dürer, painted when he was 28 years old. We are already familiar with the practice of artists painting their own image. Self-portraits appear with some frequency during the Middle Ages (see FIGS. 16–34, 17–23); they truly blossom during the Renaissance (see FIGS. 19–12, 21–34). But this image is still peculiar, marked by an artistic hubris that may embarrass us. The picture becomes less puzzling, however, seen in context.

Dürer strikes an odd pose for a self-portrait—frontal and hieratic, intentionally recalling iconic images of Christ as *Salvator Mundi* (Savior of the World) that were very popular in northern Europe. Dürer even alters the natural color of his own hair to align the image more closely with contemporary notions of Christ's physical appearance. But there is no reason to see this as blasphemous. Since a principal component of contemporary Christian devotion was the attempt to imitate Christ in the believer's own life, Dürer could be visualizing a popular spiritual practice. He could also be literalizing the biblical statement that humans are created in the image of God. But he is also claiming that artists are learned and creative geniuses—perhaps God-like—not laboring crafts-

makers. He wrote, "The more we know, the more we resemble the likeness of Christ who truly knows all things" (Snyder, p. 314).

Dürer had traveled to Italy in 1494–1495, where he encountered a new conception of artists as noble intellectuals, participants in humanistic discourse, purveyors of ideas as well as pictures. In 1498, back in Nuremberg, he published a woodcut series on the Apocalypse (see FIG. 22–7) that brought him a kind of international notice that was new to the German art world. He certainly had reason to feel pride. This stable, triangular composition—so consistent with High Renaissance norms of harmony and balance—could reflect Dürer's Italian adventure. But at its core, this picture fits into a long-standing northern European interest in the meticulous description of surface texture—the soft sheen of human flesh, the reflective wetness of eyes, the matte softness of cloth, and the tactile quality of hair, emphasized here by the way Dürer's hand fingers the fur collar of his outfit, encouraging viewers also to feel it as they see it. Ultimately what is showcased here are Dürer's awesome artistic gifts of hand as much as his intellectual gifts of mind, two aspects perhaps emblemized by the brightly illuminated body parts that align on a vertical axis to dominate this arresting self-portrait.

LEARN ABOUT IT

22.1 Recognize characteristic aspects of earlier Northern Renaissance style that continue into the work of sixteenth-century artists and evaluate the impact of new ideas coming from Italy.

22.2 Assess the relationship between the religious conflicts in northern Europe and the growing interest in new secular subjects in works of art as well as the focus on new themes in sacred art.

22.3 Investigate the broadening of regional interaction in the art of European courts as artists traveled across Europe to work for wealthy patrons and study with acclaimed masters.

22.4 Explore the continuing interest among northern European artists and patrons in the virtuosity of works in media such as wood and gold.

((••—[**Listen** to the chapter audio on myartslab.com

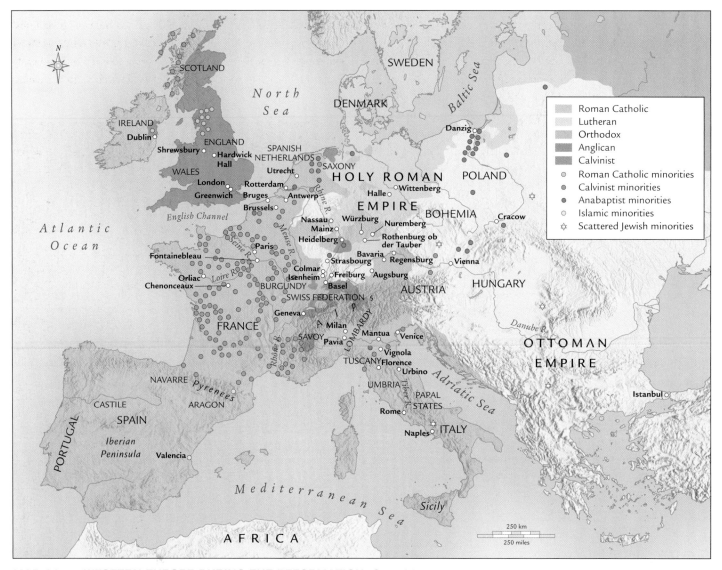

MAP 22-1 • WESTERN EUROPE DURING THE REFORMATION, C. 1560

Sixteenth-century Europe remained largely Roman Catholic, except in Switzerland and the far north, where the impact of the Protestant Reformation was strongest.

THE REFORMATION AND THE ARTS

In spite of the dissident movements and heresies that had challenged the Roman Catholic Church through the centuries, its authority and that of the pope always prevailed—until the sixteenth century (**MAP 22-1**). Then, against a backdrop of broad dissatisfaction with financial abuses and decadent lifestyles among the clergy, religious reformers from within the Church itself challenged first its practices and then its beliefs.

Two of the most important reformers in the early sixteenth century were themselves Catholic priests and trained theologians: Desiderius Erasmus (1466?–1536) of Rotterdam in Holland, who worked to reform the Roman Catholic Church from within, and Martin Luther (1483–1546) in Germany, who eventually broke with it. Indeed, many locate the beginning of the Reformation in 1517, when Luther issued his "95 Theses" calling for Church

reform. Among Luther's concerns were the practice of selling indulgences (guarantees of relief from the punishment required after death for forgiven sins) and the excessive veneration of saints and their relics, which he considered superstitious. Luther and others emphasized individual faith and regarded the Bible as the ultimate religious authority. As they challenged the pope's supremacy, it became clear that the Protestants had to break away from Rome. The Roman Catholic Church condemned Luther in 1521.

Increased literacy and the widespread use of the printing press aided the reformers and allowed scholars throughout Europe to enter the religious debate. In Germany, the wide circulation of Luther's writings—especially his German translation of the Bible and his works maintaining that salvation comes through faith alone—eventually led to the establishment of the Protestant (Lutheran) Church there. In Switzerland, John Calvin (1509–1564) led an even more austere Protestant revolt; and in England, King Henry VIII (r. 1509–1547) broke with Rome in 1534, for reasons of his own. By the end of the sixteenth century, Protestantism in some form prevailed throughout northern Europe.

Leading the Catholic cause was Holy Roman Emperor Charles V. Europe was racked by religious war from 1546 to 1555 as Charles battled Protestant forces in Germany, until a meeting of the provincial legislature of Augsburg in 1555 determined that the emperor must accommodate the Protestant Reformation in his lands. By the terms of the peace, local rulers could select the religion of their subjects—Catholic or Protestant. Tired of the strain of government and prematurely aged, Charles abdicated in 1556 and retired to a monastery in Spain, where he died in 1558. His son Philip II inherited Habsburg Spain and the Spanish colonies, while his brother Ferdinand led the Austrian branch of the dynasty.

The years of political and religious strife had a grave impact on artists and art. Some artists found their careers at an end because of their reformist religious sympathies. Then, as Protestantism gained ascendancy, it was Catholic artists who had to leave their homes to seek patronage abroad. There was also widespread destruction of religious art. In some places, Protestant zealots smashed sculpture and stained-glass windows and destroyed or whitewashed religious paintings to rid churches of what they considered idols—though Luther himself never directly supported iconoclasm (the smashing of religious images). With the sudden loss of patronage for religious art in the newly Protestant lands, many artists turned to portraiture and other secular subjects, including moralizing depictions of human folly and weaknesses, still lifes (paintings of inanimate objects), and landscapes. The popularity of these themes stimulated the burgeoning of a free art market, centered in Antwerp.

GERMANY

In German-speaking regions, the arts flourished until religious upheavals and iconoclastic purges took their toll at mid century. German cities had strong business and trade interests, and their merchants and bankers accumulated self-made, rather than inherited, wealth. They ordered portraits of themselves and fine furnishings for their large, comfortable houses. Entrepreneurial artists, like Albrecht Dürer, became major commercial successes.

SCULPTURE

Although, like the Italians, German Renaissance sculptors worked in stone and bronze, they produced their most original work in wood, especially fine-grained limewood. Most of these wooden images were gilded and painted, continuing an interest in heightening naturalism, until Tilman Riemenschneider began to favor natural wood finishes.

TILMAN RIEMENSCHNEIDER Tilman Riemenschneider (c. 1460–1531) became a master in 1485 and soon had the largest workshop in Würzburg, including specialists in both wood and stone sculpture. Riemenschneider attracted patrons from other cities, and in 1501 he signed a contract with the church of St.

James in Rothenburg, where a relic said to be a drop of Jesus' blood was preserved. The **ALTARPIECE OF THE HOLY BLOOD** (**FIG. 22-2**) is a spectacular limewood construction standing nearly 30 feet high. Erhart Harschner, a specialist in architectural shrines,

22-2 • Tilman Riemenschneider ALTARPIECE OF THE HOLY BLOOD (WINGS OPEN)
Sankt Jakobskirche (church of St. James), Rothenburg ob der Tauber, Germany. Center, *Last Supper*. c. 1499–1505. Limewood, glass, height of tallest figure 39″ (99.1 cm), height of altar 29′6″ (9 m).

In Nuremberg, a city known for its master metalworkers, Hans Krug (d. 1519) and his sons Hans the Younger and Ludwig were among the finest. They created marvelous display pieces for the wealthy, such as this silver-gilt **APPLE CUP** (**FIG. 22-3**). Made about 1510, a gleaming apple, in which the stem forms the handle of the lid, balances on a leafy branch that serves as its base.

The Krug family was responsible for the highly refined casting and finishing of the final product, but several artists worked together to produce such pieces—one drawing designs, another making the models, and others creating the final piece in metal. A drawing by Dürer may have been the basis for the apple cup. Though we know of no piece of goldwork by the artist himself, Dürer was a major catalyst in the growth of Nuremberg as a key center of German goldsmithing. He accomplished this by producing designs for metalwork throughout his career. Designers played an essential role in the metalwork process. With design in hand, the modelmaker created a wooden form for the goldsmith to follow. The result of this artistic collaboration was a technical *tour de force*, an intellectual conceit, and an exquisite object.

22-3 • Workshop of Hans Krug (?) APPLE CUP
c. 1510–1515. Gilt silver, height 8½″ (21.5 cm). Germanisches Nationalmuseum, Nuremberg.

had begun work on the elaborate Gothic frame in 1499, and was paid 50 florins for his work. Riemenschneider was commissioned to provide the figures and scenes to be placed within this frame. He was paid 60 florins for the sculpture, giving us a sense of the relative value patrons placed on their contributions.

The main panel of the altarpiece portrays the moment at the Last Supper when Christ revealed that one of his followers would betray him. Unlike Leonardo da Vinci, who chose the same moment (see FIG. 21-3), Riemenschneider puts Judas at center stage and Jesus off-center at the left. The disciples sit around the table. As the event is described in the Gospel of John (13:21–30), Jesus extends a morsel of food to Judas, signifying that he will be the traitor who sets in motion the events leading to the Crucifixion. One apostle points down, a strange gesture until we realize that he is pointing to the crucifix in the predella, to the relic of Christ's blood, and to the altar table, the symbolic representation of the table of the Last Supper and the tomb of Christ.

Rather than creating individual portraits of the apostles, Riemenschneider repeated an established set of facial types. His figures have large heads, prominent features, sharp cheekbones, sagging jowls, baggy eyes, and elaborate hair with thick wavy locks and deeply drilled curls. The muscles, tendons, and raised veins of hands and feet are also especially lifelike. His assistants and apprentices copied these faces and figures, either from drawings or from three-dimensional models made by the master. In the altarpiece, deeply hollowed folds create active patterns in the voluminous draperies whose strong highlights and dark shadows harmonize the figural composition with the intricate carving of the framework. The Last Supper is set in a "real" room containing actual benches for the figures. Windows in the back wall are glazed with bull's-eye glass so that natural light shines in from two directions to illuminate the scene, producing changing effects depending on the time of day and the weather. Although earlier sculpture had been painted and gilded, Riemenschneider introduced the use of a natural wood finish toned with varnish. This meant that details of both figures and environment had to be carved into the wood itself, not added later with paint. Since this required more skillful carvers and more time for them to carve, this new look was a matter of aesthetics, not cost-saving.

In addition to producing an enormous number of religious images for churches, Riemenschneider was politically active in Würzburg, serving as mayor in 1520. His career ended during the Peasants' War (1524–1526), an early manifestation of the Protestant movement. His support for the peasants led to a fine and imprisonment in 1525, and although he survived, Riemenschneider produced no more sculpture and died in 1531.

22-4 • Nikolaus Hagenauer (central panels and predella) and Matthias Grünewald (wings) **ISENHEIM ALTARPIECE (OPEN)**

From the Community of St. Anthony, Isenheim, Alsace, France. Center panels and predella: *St. Anthony Enthroned between SS. Augustine and Jerome, Christ and the Apostles*, c. 1500. Painted and gilt limewood, center panel 9′9½″ × 10′9″ (2.97 × 3.28 m), predella 2′5½″ × 11′2″ (0.75 × 3.4 m). Wings: *SS. Anthony and Paul the Hermit* (left); *The Temptation of St. Anthony* (right). 1510–1515. Oil on wood panel, 8′2½″ × 3′½″ (2.49 × 0.93 m). Musée d'Unterlinden, Colmar, France.

NIKOLAUS HAGENAUER Prayer was the principal source of solace and relief to the ill before the advent of modern medicine. About 1505, the Strasbourg sculptor Nikolaus Hagenauer (active 1493–1530s) carved an altarpiece for the abbey of St. Anthony in Isenheim near Colmar (**FIG. 22-4**) where a hospital specialized in the care of patients with skin diseases, including the plague, leprosy, and St. Anthony's Fire (caused by eating rye and other grains infected with the ergot fungus). The shrine includes images of SS. Anthony, Jerome, and Augustine. Three tiny men—their size befitting their subordinate status—kneel at the feet of the saints: the donor, Jean d'Orliac, and two men offering a rooster and a piglet.

In the predella below, Jesus and the apostles bless the altar, Host, and assembled patients in the hospital. The flesh of the sculpted figures was painted in lifelike colors, but most of the altarpiece was gilded to enhance its resemblance to a metalwork reliquary. A decade later, Matthias Grünewald painted wooden shutters to cover the shrine (see FIGS. 22-5, 22-6).

PAINTING

The work of two very different German artists has come down to us from the first decades of the sixteenth century. Matthias Grünewald continued currents of medieval mysticism and emotional spirituality to create extraordinarily moving paintings. Albrecht Dürer, on the other hand, used intense observation of the world to render lifelike representations of nature, mathematical perspective to create convincing illusions of space, and a reasoned canon of proportions to standardize depictions of the human figure.

MATTHIAS GRÜNEWALD As a court artist to the archbishop of Mainz, Matthias Grünewald (Matthias Gothart Neithart, c. 1470/1475–1528) was a man of many talents, who worked as an architect and hydraulic engineer as well as a painter. He is best known today for paintings on the shutters or wings attached to Nikolaus Hagenauer's carved Isenheim Altarpiece (see FIG. 22-4). The completed altarpiece is impressive in size and complexity.

22–5 • Matthias Grünewald ISENHEIM ALTARPIECE (CLOSED)

From the Community of St. Anthony, Isenheim, Alsace, France. Center panels: *Crucifixion*; predella: *Lamentation*; side panels: *SS. Sebastian* (left) and *Anthony Abbot* (right). c. 1510–1515. Date 1515 on ointment jar. Oil on wood panel, center panels 9′9½″ × 10′9″ (2.97 × 3.28 m) overall, each wing 8′2½″ × 3′1½″ (2.49 × 0.93 m), predella 2′5½″ × 11′2″ (0.75 × 3.4 m). Musée d'Unterlinden, Colmar, France.

22–6 • Matthias Grünewald ISENHEIM ALTARPIECE (FIRST OPENING)

Left to right: *Annunciation, Virgin and Child with Angels, Resurrection*. c. 1510–1515. Oil on wood panel, center panel 9′9½″ × 10′9″ (2.97 × 3.28 m), each wing 8′2½″ × 3′1½″ (2.49 × 0.93 m). Musée d'Unterlinden, Colmar, France.

Grünewald painted one set of fixed wings and two sets of movable ones, plus one set of panels to cover the predella. The altarpiece could be exhibited in different configurations depending upon the church calendar. The wings and carved wooden shrine complemented one another, the inner sculpture seeming to bring the surrounding paintings to life, and the painted wings protecting the precious carvings.

On weekdays, when the altarpiece was closed, viewers saw a grisly image of the Crucifixion in a darkened landscape, a *Lamentation* below it on the predella, and life-size figures of SS. Sebastian and Anthony Abbot—both associated with the plague—standing on *trompe l'oeil* pedestals on the fixed wings (**FIG. 22–5**). The intensity of feeling here has suggested that Grünewald may have been inspired by the visions of St. Bridget of Sweden, a fourteenth-century mystic whose works—including morbidly detailed descriptions of the Crucifixion—were published in Germany beginning in 1492. Grünewald has scrupulously described the horrific character of the tortured body of Jesus, covered with gashes from his beating and pierced by the thorns used to form a crown for his head. His ashen body, clotted blood, open mouth, and blue lips signal his death. In fact, he appears already to be decaying, an effect enhanced by the palette of putrescent green, yellow, and purplish-red—all described by St. Bridget. She wrote, "The color of death spread through his flesh…." An immaculately garbed Virgin Mary has collapsed in the arms of a ghostlike John the Evangelist, and Mary Magdalen has fallen in anguish to her knees; her clasped hands with outstretched fingers seem to echo Jesus' fingers, cramped in rigor mortis. At the right, John the Baptist points to Jesus and repeats his prophecy, "He shall increase." The Baptist and the lamb, holding a cross and bleeding from its breast into a golden chalice, allude to baptism, the Eucharist, and to Christ as the sacrificial Lamb of God. In the predella below, Jesus' bereaved mother and friends prepare his racked body for burial—an activity that must have been a common sight in the abbey's hospital.

In contrast to these grim scenes, the first opening displays events of great joy—the Annunciation, the Nativity, and the Resurrection—appropriate for Sundays and feast days (**FIG. 22–6**). Praying in front of these pictures, the patients must have hoped for miraculous recovery and taken comfort in these visions of divine rapture and orgiastic color. Unlike the awful darkness of the Crucifixion, the inner scenes are brilliantly illuminated, in part by phosphorescent auras and haloes; stars glitter in the night sky of the Resurrection. The technical virtuosity of Grünewald's painting alone is enough to inspire euphoria.

The central panels show the heavenly and earthly realms joined in one space. In a variation on the northern European visionary tradition, the new mother adores her miraculous Christ Child while envisioning her own future as queen of heaven amid angels and cherubims. Grünewald portrayed three distinct types of angels in the foreground—young, mature, and a feathered hybrid with a birdlike crest on its human head. The range of ethnic types in the heavenly realm may have emphasized the global dominion of the Church, whose missionary efforts were expanding as a result of European exploration. St. Bridget describes the jubilation of the angels as "the glowing flame of love."

The second opening of the altarpiece (see **FIG. 22–4**) reveals Hagenauer's sculpture and was reserved for the special festivals of St. Anthony. The wings in this second opening show to the left the meeting of St. Anthony with the hermit St. Paul, and to the right St. Anthony attacked by horrible demons, perhaps inspired by the horrors of the diseased patients, but also modeled in part on Schongauer's well-known print of the same subject (see **FIG. 19–28**). The meeting of the two hermits in the desert glorifies the monastic life, and in the wilderness Grünewald depicts medicinal plants used in the hospital's therapy. Grünewald painted the face of St. Paul with his own self-portrait, while St. Anthony is a portrait of the donor and administrator of the hospital, the Italian Guido Guersi, whose coat of arms Grünewald painted on the rock next to him.

As with Riemenschneider, Grünewald's involvement with the Peasants' War may have damaged his artistic career. He left Mainz and spent his last years in Halle, whose ruler was the chief protector of Martin Luther and a long-time patron of Grünewald's contemporary Albrecht Dürer.

ALBRECHT DÜRER Studious, analytical, observant, and meticulous—and as self-confident as Michelangelo—Albrecht Dürer (1471–1528) was the foremost artist of the German Renaissance. He made his home in Nuremberg, where he became a prominent citizen. Nuremberg was a center of culture as well as of business, with an active group of humanists and internationally renowned artists. It was also a leading publishing center. Dürer's father was a goldsmith and must have expected his son to follow in his trade (see "German Metalwork: A Collaborative Venture," page 682). Dürer did complete an apprenticeship in gold working, as well as in stained-glass design, painting, and the making of woodcuts—which he learned from Michael Wolgemut, illustrator of the *Nuremberg Chronicle* (see **FIG. 19–29**). It was as a painter and graphic artist, however, that he built his artistic fame.

In 1490, Dürer began traveling to extend his education. He went to Basel, Switzerland, hoping to meet Martin Schongauer, but arrived after the master's death. By 1494, Dürer had moved from Basel to Strasbourg. His first trip to Italy (1494–1495) introduced him to Italian Renaissance ideas and attitudes and, as we considered at the beginning of this chapter, to the concept of the artist as an independent creative genius. In his self-portrait of 1500 (see **FIG. 22–1**), Dürer represents himself as an idealized, Christ-like figure in a severely frontal pose, staring self-confidently at the viewer.

On his return to Nuremberg, Dürer began to publish his own prints to bolster his income, and ultimately it was prints, not paintings, that made his fortune. His first major publication, *The Apocalypse*, appeared simultaneously in German and Latin editions in 1497–1498. It consisted of a woodcut title page and 14 full-page

22-7 • Albrecht Dürer **THE FOUR HORSEMEN OF THE APOCALYPSE**
From *The Apocalypse*. 1497–1498. Woodcut, 15½″ × 11⅛″ (39.4 × 28.3 cm). Metropolitan Museum of Art, New York. Gift of Junius S. Morgan, 1919 (19.73.209)

his late fifteenth-century predecessors, he fills the foreground with large, active figures.

Perhaps as early as the summer of 1494, Dürer began to experiment with engravings, cutting the metal plates himself with an artistry rivaling Schongauer's. His growing interest in Italian art and his theoretical investigations are reflected in his 1504 engraving **ADAM AND EVE** (FIG. 22-8), which represents his first documented use of ideal human proportions based on Roman copies of ancient Greek sculpture. He may have seen figures of Apollo and Venus in Italy, and he would have known ancient sculpture from contemporary prints and drawings. But around these idealized human figures he represents plants and animals with typically northern attention to descriptive detail.

Dürer filled the landscape with symbolic content reflecting the medieval theory that after Adam and Eve disobeyed God, they and their descendants became vulnerable to imbalances in the body fluids that controlled human temperament. An excess of black bile from the liver would produce melancholy, despair, and greed; yellow bile caused anger, pride, and impatience; phlegm in the lungs resulted in lethargy and apathy; and an excess of blood made a person unusually optimistic but also compulsively interested in the pleasures of the flesh. These four human temperaments, or

illustrations with the text printed on the back of each. Perhaps best known is **THE FOUR HORSEMEN OF THE APOCALYPSE** (FIG. 22-7), based on figures described in Revelation 6:1–8: a crowned rider, armed with a bow, on a white horse (Conquest); a rider with a sword, on a red horse (War); a rider with a set of scales, on a black horse (Plague and Famine); and a rider on a sickly pale horse (Death). Earlier artists had simply lined up the horsemen in the landscape, but Dürer created a compact, overlapping group of wild riders charging across the world and trampling its cowering inhabitants, men and women, clerical and lay.

Dürer probably did not cut his own woodblocks but employed a skilled carver who followed his drawings faithfully. Dürer's dynamic figures show affinities with Schongauer's *Temptation of St. Anthony* (see FIG. 19-28). He adapted Schongauer's metal-engraving technique to the woodcut medium, using a complex pattern of lines to model the forms. Dürer's early training as a goldsmith is evident in his meticulous attention to detail, and in his decorative cloud and drapery patterns. Following the tradition established by

22-8 • Albrecht Dürer **ADAM AND EVE**
1504. Engraving, 9⅞″ × 7⅝″ (25.1 × 19.4 cm). Philadelphia Museum of Art. Purchased: Lisa Nora Elkins Fund

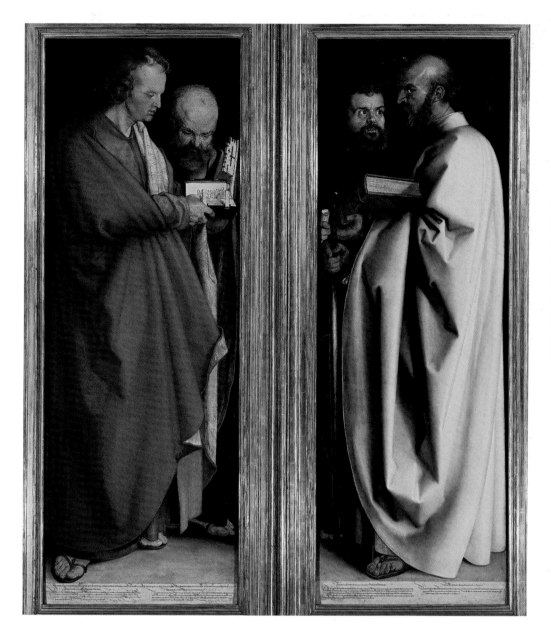

22-9 • Albrecht Dürer
FOUR APOSTLES
1526. Oil on wood panel,
each panel 7'1½" × 2'6" (2.15
× 0.76 m). Alte Pinakothek,
Munich.

Dürer presented these panels to the city of Nuremberg, which had already adopted Lutheranism as its official religion. Dürer wrote, "For a Christian would no more be led to superstition by a picture or effigy than an honest man to commit murder because he carries a weapon by his side. He must indeed be an unthinking man who would worship picture, wood, or stone. A picture therefore brings more good than harm, when it is honourably, artistically, and well made" (Snyder, p. 333).

personalities, are symbolized here by the melancholy elk, the choleric cat, the phlegmatic ox, and the sanguine (or sensual) rabbit. The mouse is a symbol of Satan (see the mousetrap in FIG. 19–11), whose earthly power, already manifest in the Garden of Eden, was capable of bringing human beings to a life of woe through their own bad choices. Adam seems to be releasing the mouse into the world of his paradise as he contemplates eating the forbidden fruit that Eve receives from the snake. Dürer placed his signature prominently on a placard hung on a tree branch in Adam's grasp and on which perches a parrot—possibly symbolizing false wisdom, since it can only repeat mindlessly what it hears.

Dürer's familiarity with Italian art was greatly enhanced by a second, leisurely trip over the Alps in 1505–1506. Thereafter, he seems to have resolved to reform the art of his own country by publishing theoretical writings and manuals that discussed Italian Renaissance problems of perspective, ideal human proportions, and the techniques of painting.

Dürer admired Martin Luther, but they never met. In 1526, the artist openly professed his Lutheranism in a pair of inscribed panels, the **FOUR APOSTLES** (FIG. 22-9). On the left panel, the elderly Peter, who normally has a central position as the first pope, has been displaced with his keys to the background by Luther's favorite evangelist, John, who holds an open Gospel that reads "In the beginning was the Word," reinforcing the Protestant emphasis on the Bible. On the right panel, Mark stands behind Paul, whose epistles were particularly admired by the Protestants. A long inscription on the frame warns the viewer not to be led astray by "false prophets" but to heed the words of the New Testament as recorded by these "four excellent men." Below each figure are excerpts from their letters and from the Gospel of Mark—drawn from Luther's German translation of the New Testament—warning against those who do not understand the true Word of God. These paintings were surely meant to chart the possibility of a Protestant visual art.

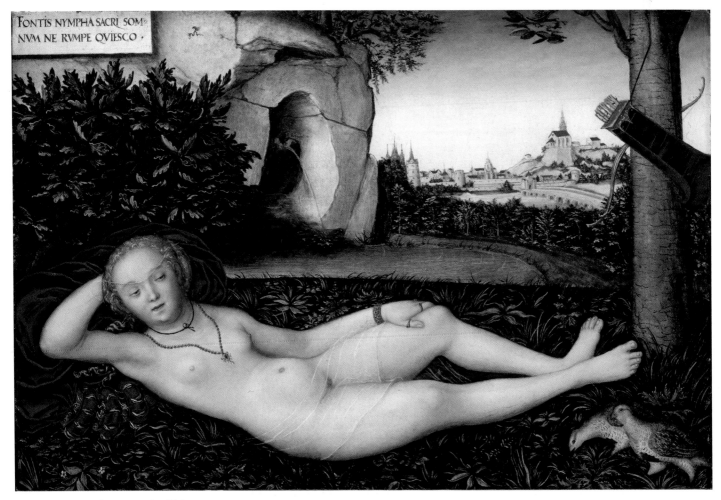

FONTIS NYMPHA SACRI SOM·
NVM NE RVMPE QVIESCO ·

22–10 • Lucas Cranach the Elder **NYMPH OF THE SPRING**
c. 1537. Oil on panel, 19″ × 28½″ (48.5 × 72.9 cm). National Gallery of Art, Washington, DC.

LUCAS CRANACH THE ELDER Martin Luther's favorite painter, Lucas Cranach the Elder (1472–1553), moved his workshop to Wittenberg in 1504, after a number of years in Vienna. In addition to the humanist milieu of its university and library, Wittenberg offered the patronage of the Saxon court. Appointed court painter to Elector Frederick the Wise, Cranach created woodcuts, altarpieces, and many portraits.

Just how far German artists' style and conception of the figure could differ from Italian Renaissance idealism is easily seen in Cranach's **NYMPH OF THE SPRING** (FIG. 22-10), especially when compared with Titian's *"Venus" of Urbino* (see FIG. 21-28). The sleeping nymph was a Renaissance theme, not an ancient one. Cranach was inspired by a fifteenth-century inscription on a fountain beside the Danube, cited in the upper left corner of the painting: "I am the nymph of the sacred font. Do not interrupt my sleep for I am at peace." Cranach records the Danube landscape with characteristic northern attention to detail and turns his nymph into a rather provocative young woman, who glances slyly out at the viewer through half-closed eyes. She has cast aside a fashionable red velvet gown, but still wears her jewelry, which together with her transparent veil enhances rather than conceals

her nudity—especially those coral beads that fall between her breasts, mapping their contours. Unlike other artists working for Protestant patrons, many of whom looked on earthly beauty as a sinful vanity, Cranach seems delighted by earthly things—the lush foliage that provides the nymph's couch, the pair of partridges (symbols of Venus and married love), and Cupid's bow and quiver of arrows hanging on the tree. Could this nymph be a living beauty from the Wittenberg court? She is certainly not an embodiment of an idealized, Classical Venus.

HANS BALDUNG GRIEN Cranach's slightly younger contemporary Hans Baldung (1484/1485–1545)—his nickname tag "Grien" ("green," apparently a favorite color) dates from his apprenticeship days and was used to distinguish him from the numerous other apprentices named Hans—is known for very different visualizations of women. Born into an affluent and well-educated family, Baldung was working in Strasbourg by 1500, before moving to Nuremberg in 1503 and eventually joining Dürer's workshop in 1505–1507. Over the course of his long career, he also worked in Halle and Freiburg, but his principal artistic home was Strasbourg, where he lived out a

22–11 • Hans Baldung Grien DEATH AND THE MATRON

c. 1520–1525. Oil on wood panel, 12⅜″ × 7⅜″ (31.3 × 18.7 cm). Öffentliche Kunstsammlung, Basel.

Although more erotically charged and certainly more dramatic than Dürer's Eve in FIG. 22–8, Baldung's woman is based in certain ways on this famous image, which was engraved while he was assisting in Dürer's workshop. In many respects, the similarities in pose (especially the feet) and form (wide hips with narrowing waist and torso) only point up the differences in expressive content.

prosperous professional life as a painter, printmaker, and stained-glass designer.

During the first half of his career, Baldung created a series of paintings on the theme of **DEATH AND THE MATRON** that juxtapose sensuality with mortality, voluptuousness with decay, attraction with repulsion. The example in **FIG. 22–11** (painted in about 1520–1525 for a private collector in Basel) uses brilliant illumination and expansive posture to draw our attention first to the voluptuous nude, fleshier and considerably more sensual than Cranach's nymph (see FIG. 22–10) or Dürer's Eve (see FIG. 22–8). But this focus is soon overtaken by a sense of surprise that mirrors her own, as she turns her head to discover that the figure stroking

her hair and clutching at her breast is not her lover but Death himself. The putrid decay of his yellowing flesh contrasts sharply with her soft contours, and his bony molting head is the antithesis of her full pink cheeks, flowing tresses, and soft traces of body hair. That the encounter takes place in a cemetery, on top of a tombstone, serves to underline the warning against the transitory pleasures of the flesh, but Baldung also seems to depend on the viewers' own erotic engagement to make the message not only moral but personal.

ALBRECHT ALTDORFER Landscape, with or without figures, became a popular theme in the sixteenth century. In the fifteenth

22-12 • Albrecht Altdorfer
DANUBE LANDSCAPE
c. 1525. Oil on vellum on
wood panel, 12″ × 8½″ (30.5
× 22.2 cm). Alte Pinakothek,
Munich.

century, northern artists had examined and recorded nature with the care and enthusiasm of biologists, but painted landscapes were reserved for the backgrounds of figural compositions, usually sacred subjects. In the 1520s, however, religious art found little favor among Protestants. Landscape painting, on the other hand, had no overt religious content, although it could be seen as a reflection or even glorification of God's works on Earth. The

most accomplished German landscape painter of the period was Albrecht Altdorfer (c. 1480–1538).

Altdorfer probably received his early training in Bavaria from his father, but he became a citizen of Regensburg in 1505 and remained there painting the Danube River Valley for the rest of his life. **DANUBE LANDSCAPE** of about 1525 (**FIG. 22-12**) is an early example of pure landscape painting, without a narrative subject, human figures, or overt religious significance. A small work on vellum laid down on a wood panel, it shows a landscape that seems to be a minutely detailed reproduction of the natural terrain, but the forest seems far more poetic and mysterious than Dürer's or Cranach's carefully observed views of nature. The low mountains, gigantic lacy pines, neatly contoured shrubberies, and fairyland castle with red-roofed towers at the end of a winding path announce a new sensibility. The eerily glowing yellow–white horizon below moving gray and blue clouds in a sky that takes up more than half the composition prefigures the Romanticism of German landscape painting in later centuries.

FRANCE

Renaissance France followed a different path from that taken in Germany. In 1519, Pope Leo X came to an agreement with French King Francis I (r. 1515–1547) that spared the country the turmoil suffered in Germany. Furthermore, whereas Martin Luther had devoted followers in France, French reformer John

Calvin (1509–1564) fled to Switzerland in 1534, where he led a theocratic state in Geneva.

During the second half of the century, however, warring political factions favoring either Catholics or Huguenots (Protestants) competed to exert power over the French crown, with devastating consequences. In 1560, the devoutly Catholic Catherine de' Medici, widow of Henry II (r. 1547–1559), became regent for her young son, Charles IX, and tried, but failed, to balance the warring factions. Her machinations ended in religious polarization and a bloody conflict that began in 1562. When her third son, Henry III (r. 1574–1589), was murdered by a fanatical Dominican friar, a Protestant cousin, Henry, king of Navarre, the first Bourbon king, inherited the throne. Henry converted to Catholicism and ruled as Henry IV. Backed by a country sick of bloodshed, he quickly settled the religious question by proclaiming tolerance of Protestants in the Edict of Nantes in 1598.

A FRENCH RENAISSANCE UNDER FRANCIS I

Immediately after his ascent to the throne, Francis I sought to "modernize" the French court by acquiring the versatile talents of Leonardo da Vinci, who moved to France in 1516. Officially, Leonardo was there to advise the king on royal architectural projects and, the king said, for the pleasure of his conversation. Francis supported an Italian-inspired Renaissance in French art and architecture throughout his long reign.

JEAN CLOUET Not all the artists working at the court of Francis I, however, were Italian. Flemish artist Jean Clouet (c. 1485–c. 1540) found great favor at the royal court, especially as a portrait painter. About the same time that he became principal court painter in 1527, he produced an official portrait of the king (**FIG. 22-13**). Clouet created a flattering image of Francis by modulating the king's distinctive features with soft shading and highlighting the nervous activity of his fingers. At the same time he conceived an image of pure power. Elaborate, puffy sleeves broaden the king's shoulders to fill the entire width of the panel, much as Renaissance parade armor turned scrawny men into giants. The detailed rendering of the delicately worked costume of silk, satin, velvet,

22-13 • Jean Clouet FRANCIS I
1525–1530. Oil and tempera on wood panel, 37¾″ × 29⅛″ (95.9 × 74 cm). Musée du Louvre, Paris.

Women played an important role in the patronage of the arts during the Renaissance. Nowhere is their influence stronger than in the châteaux of the Loire River Valley. At Chenonceau (FIG. 22–14), built beside and literally over the River Cher, a tributary of the Loire, women built, saved, and restored the château. Catherine Briconnet and her husband, Thomas Bohier, originally acquired the property, including a fortified mill, on which they built their country residence. Catherine supervised the construction, which included such modern conveniences as a straight staircase (an Italian and Spanish feature) instead of traditional medieval spiral stairs, and a kitchen inside the château instead of in a distant outbuilding. After Thomas died in 1524 and Catherine in 1526, their son gave Chenonceau to King Francis I.

King Henry II, Francis's son, gave Chenonceau to his mistress Diane de Poitiers in 1547. She managed the estate astutely, increased its revenue, developed the vineyards, added intricately planted gardens in the Italian style, and built a bridge across the Cher. When Henry died in a tournament, his queen, Catherine de' Medici (1519–1589), appropriated the château for herself.

Catherine, like so many in her family a great patron of the arts, added the two-story gallery to the bridge at Chenonceau, as well as outbuildings and additional formal gardens. Her parties were famous:

mock naval battles on the river, fireworks, banquets, dances, and on one occasion two choruses of young women dressed as mermaids in the moat and nymphs in the shrubbery—who were then chased about by young men costumed as satyrs!

When Catherine's third son became king as Henry III in 1574, she gave the château to his wife, Louise of Lorraine, who lived in mourning at Chenonceau after Henry III was assassinated in 1589. She wore only white and covered the walls, windows, and furniture in her room with black velvet and damask. She left Chenonceau to her niece when she died.

In the eighteenth and nineteenth centuries, women continued to determine the fate of Chenonceau. During the French Revolution (1789–1793), the owner, Madame Dupin, was so beloved by the villagers that they protected her and saved her home. Then, in 1864, Madame Pelouze bought Chenonceau and restored it by removing Catherine de' Medici's Italian "improvements."

Chenonceau continued to play a role in the twentieth century. During World War I, it was used as a hospital. During the German occupation in World War II (1940–1942), when the River Cher formed the border with Vichy "Free" France, the gallery bridge at Chenonceau became an escape route.

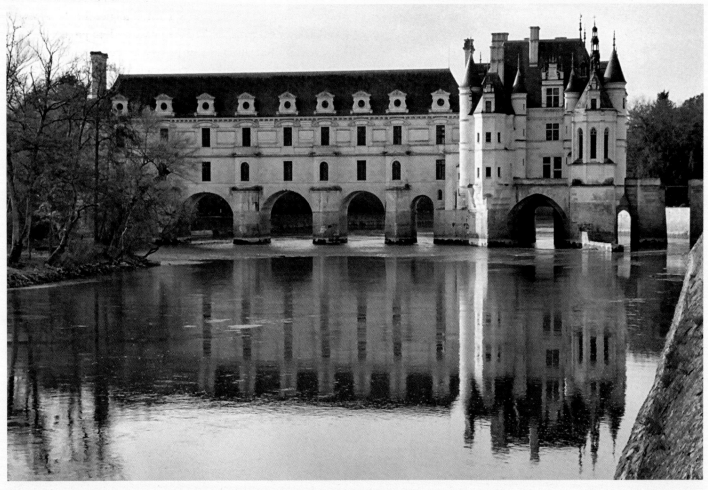

22-14 • CHÂTEAU OF CHENONCEAU
Touraine, France. Original building (at right) 1513–1521; gallery on bridge at left by Philibert de l'Orme, finished c. 1581.

jewels, and gold embroidery could be painted separately from the portrait itself. Royal clothing was often loaned to the artist or modeled by a servant to spare the "sitter" the boredom of posing. In creating such official portraits, the artist sketched the subject, then painted a prototype that, upon approval, became the model for numerous replicas made for diplomatic and family purposes.

THE CHÂTEAU OF CHENONCEAU With the enthusiasm of Francis for things Italian and the widening distribution of Italian books on architecture, the Italian Renaissance style soon infiltrated French architecture. Builders of elegant rural palaces, called **châteaux**, were quick to introduce Italianate decoration to otherwise Gothic buildings, but French architects soon adapted Classical principles of building design as well.

One of the most beautiful châteaux was not built as a royal residence, although it soon became one. In 1512, Thomas Bohier, a royal tax collector, bought the castle of Chenonceau on the River Cher, a tributary of the Loire (see "The Castle of the Ladies," opposite). He demolished the old castle, leaving only a tower. Using the piers of a water mill on the river bank as part of the foundations, he and his wife erected a new Renaissance home. The plan reflects the Classical principles of geometric regularity and symmetry—a rectangular building with rooms arranged on each side of a wide central hall. Only the library and chapel, which are corbelled out over the water, break the line of the walls. In the upper story, the builders used traditional features of medieval castles—battlements, corner turrets, steep roofs, and dormer windows. The owners died soon after the château was finished

in 1521, and their son gave it to Francis I, who turned it into a hunting lodge.

Later, Roman-trained French Renaissance architect Philibert de l'Orme (d. 1570) designed a gallery on a bridge across the river for Catherine de' Medici, completed about 1581 and incorporating contemporary Italianate window treatments, wall molding, and cornices that harmonized almost perfectly with the forms of the original turreted building.

FONTAINEBLEAU Having chosen as his primary residence the medieval hunting lodge at Fontainebleau, Francis I began transforming it into a grand country palace. In 1530, he imported a Florentine artist, the Mannerist painter Rosso Fiorentino (1495–1540), to direct the project. After Rosso died, he was succeeded by his Italian colleague Francesco Primaticcio (1504–1570), who had earlier worked with Giulio Romano in Mantua (see FIG. 21-20), before joining Rosso in 1532, and would spend the rest of his career working on the decoration of Fontainebleau. During that time, he also commissioned and imported a large number of copies and casts of original Roman sculpture, from the newly discovered Laocoön (see FIG. 5-64) to the relief decoration on the Column of Trajan (see FIG. 6-48). These works provided an invaluable visual resource of figures and techniques for the northern European artists employed on the Fontainebleau project.

Among Primaticcio's first projects at Fontainebleau was the redecoration, in the 1540s, of the rooms of the king's official mistress, Anne, duchess of Étampes (FIG. 22-15). The artist combined woodwork, stucco relief, and fresco painting in his complex but

22-15 • Primaticcio STUCCO AND WALL PAINTING, CHAMBER OF THE DUCHESS OF ÉTAMPES, CHÂTEAU OF FONTAINEBLEAU
France. 1540s.

22-16 • Pierre Lescot and Jean Goujon **WEST WING OF THE COUR CARRÉE, PALAIS DU LOUVRE, PARIS**
Begun 1546.

whimsical and graceful interior design. The lithe figures of stucco nymphs, with their elongated bodies and small heads, recall Parmigianino's paintings (see FIG. 21-31). Their spiraling postures and teasing bits of clinging drapery are playfully erotic. Garlands, mythological figures, and Roman architectural ornament almost overwhelm the walls with visual enrichment, yet the whole remains ordered and lighthearted. The first School of Fontainebleau, as this Italian phase of the palace decoration is called, established an Italianate tradition of Mannerism in painting and interior design that spread to other centers in France and into the Netherlands.

THE LOUVRE Before the defeat of Francis I at Pavia by Holy Roman Emperor Charles V, and the king's subsequent imprisonment in Spain in 1525, the French court had been a mobile unit, and the locus of French art resided outside Paris in the Loire Valley. After his release in 1526, Francis made Paris his bureaucratic seat, and the Île-de-France—Paris and its region—took the artistic lead. The move to the capital gave birth to a style of French Classicism when Francis I and Henry II decided to modernize the medieval castle of the Louvre. Work began in 1546, with the replacement of the west wing of the square court, or **COUR CARRÉE (FIG. 22-16)**, by architect Pierre Lescot (c. 1510–1578) working with sculptor Jean Goujon (1510–1568). They designed

a building that incorporated Renaissance ideals of balance and regularity with Classical architectural details and rich sculptural decoration. The irregular rooflines seen in a château such as the one at Chenonceau (see FIG. 22-14, right part of the building) gave way to discreetly rounded arches and horizontal balustrades. Classical pilasters and entablatures replaced Gothic buttresses and stringcourses. A round-arched arcade on the ground floor suggests an Italian loggia. On the other hand, the sumptuousness of the decoration recalls the French Flamboyant style (see Chapter 19), only with Classical pilasters and acanthus replacing Gothic colonnettes and cusps.

SPAIN AND PORTUGAL

The sixteenth century saw the peak of Spanish political power. The country had been united in the fifteenth century by the marriage of Isabella of Castile and Ferdinand of Aragon. Only Navarre (in the Pyrenees) and Portugal remained outside the union of the crowns. (See "Sculpture for the Knights of Christ at Tomar," opposite.) When Isabella and Ferdinand's grandson Charles V abdicated in 1556, his son Philip II (r. 1556–1598) became the king of Spain, the Netherlands, and the Americas, as well as ruler of Milan, Burgundy, and Naples, but Spain was Philip's permanent residence.

ART AND ITS CONTEXTS | Sculpture for the Knights of Christ at Tomar

One of the most beautiful, if also one of the strangest, sixteenth-century sculptures in Portugal seems to float over the cloisters of the convent of Christ in Tomar. Unexpectedly, in the heart of the castle-monastery complex, one comes face to face with the Old Man of the Sea. He supports on his powerful shoulders an extraordinary growth—part roots and trunk of a gnarled tree; part tangled mass of seaweed, algae, ropes, and anchor chains. Barnacle- and coral-encrusted piers lead the eye upward, revealing a large lattice-covered window, the great **WEST WINDOW** of the church of the Knights of Christ (**FIG. 22-17**).

When, in 1314, Pope Clement V disbanded the Templars (a monastic order of knights founded in Jerusalem after the First Crusade), King Dinis of Portugal offered them a renewed existence as the Knights of Christ. As a result, in 1356, they made the former Templar castle and monastery in Tomar their headquarters. When Prince Henry the Navigator (1394–1460) became the grand master of the order, he invested their funds in the exploration of the African coast and the Atlantic Ocean. The Templar insignia, the squared cross, became the emblem used on the sails of Portuguese ships.

King Manuel I of Portugal (r. 1495–1521) commissioned the present church, with its amazing sculpture by Diogo de Arruda, in 1510. So distinctive is the style developed under King Manuel by artists like the Arruda brothers, Diogo (active 1508–1531) and Francisco (active 1510–1547), that Renaissance art in Portugal is called "Manueline." In the window of Tomar, every surface is carved with architectural and natural detail associated with the sea. Twisted ropes form the corners of the window; the coral pillars support great swathes of seaweed. Chains and cables drop through the watery depths to the place where the head of a man—could this Old Man of the Sea be a self-portrait of Diogo de Arruda?—emerges from the roots of a tree. Above the window, more ropes, cables, and seaweed support the emblems of the patron—armillary spheres at the upper outside corners (topped by pinnacles) and at dead center, the coat of arms of Manuel I with its Portuguese castles framing the five wounds of Christ. Topping the composition is the square cross of the Order of Christ—clearly delineated against the wall of the chapel.

The armillary sphere became a symbol of the era. This complex form of a celestial globe, with the sun at the center surrounded by rings marking the paths of the planets, was a teaching device that acknowledged the new scientific theory that the sun, not the Earth, is the center of the solar system. (Copernicus only published his theories in 1531 and 1543.) King Manuel's use of the armillary sphere as his emblem signals his determination to make Portugal the leader in the exploration of the sea. Indeed, in Manuel's reign the Portuguese reached India and Brazil.

22-17 • Diogo de Arruda WEST WINDOW, CHURCH IN THE CONVENT OF CHRIST, TOMAR
Portugal. c. 1510. Commissioned by King Manuel I of Portugal.

For more than half a century, he supported artists in Spain, Italy, and the Netherlands. His navy, the famous Spanish Armada, halted the advance of Islam in the Mediterranean and secured control of most of the Americas. Despite enormous effort, however, Philip could not suppress the revolt of the northern provinces of the Netherlands, nor could he prevail in his war against the English, who destroyed his navy in 1588. He was able to gain control of the entire Iberian peninsula, however, by claiming Portugal in 1580, and it remained part of Spain until 1640.

ARCHITECTURE

Philip built **THE ESCORIAL** (**FIG. 22-18**), the great monastery-palace complex outside Madrid, partly to comply with his father's direction to construct a "pantheon" in which all Spanish kings might be buried and partly to house his court and government. In 1559, Philip summoned from Italy Juan Bautista de Toledo (d. 1567), who had been Michelangelo's supervisor of work at St. Peter's from 1546 to 1548. Juan Bautista's design for the monastery-palace reflected his indoctrination in Bramante's Classical principles in

Rome, but the king himself dictated the severity and size of the structure. The Escorial's grandeur comes from its overwhelming size, fine proportions, and excellent masonry. The complex includes not only the royal residence but also the Royal Monastery of San Lorenzo, a school, a library, and a church, its crypt serving as the royal burial chamber. The plan was said to resemble a gridiron, the instrument of martyrdom of its patron saint, Lawrence, who was roasted alive.

In 1572, Juan Bautista's assistant, Juan de Herrera, was appointed architect, and he immediately changed the design, adding second stories on all wings and breaking the horizontality of the main façade with a central frontispiece that resembled the superimposed temple fronts that were fashionable on Italian churches at this time (see FIGS. 21-40, 21-43). Before beginning the church in the center of the complex, Philip solicited the advice of Italian architects—including Vignola and Palladio. The final design combined ideas that Philip approved and Herrera carried out, and it embodies Italian Classicism in its geometric clarity, symmetry, and superimposed temple-front façade. In its austerity, it embodies the deep religiosity of Philip II.

PAINTING

The most famous painter working in Spain during the last quarter of the sixteenth century was Domenikos Theotokopoulos (1541–1614), who arrived in Spain in 1577 after working for ten years in Italy. "El Greco" ("The Greek"), as he is called, was trained as an icon painter in the Byzantine manner in his native Crete, then under Venetian rule. In about 1566, he entered Titian's studio in Venice, where he also studied the paintings of Tintoretto and Veronese. From about 1570 to 1577, he worked in Rome, living for a time in the Farnese Palace. Probably encouraged by Spanish church officials whom he met in Rome, El Greco eventually settled in Toledo, seat of the Spanish archbishop. He had hoped for a court appointment, but Philip II—a great patron of the Venetian painter Titian and a collector of Netherlandish artists such as Bosch—disliked the painting he had commissioned from El Greco for the Escorial and never again gave him work.

In Toledo, El Greco joined the circle of humanist scholars. He wrote that the artist's goal should be to copy nature, that Raphael relied too heavily on the ancients, and that the Italians' use of mathematics to achieve ideal proportions hindered their painting of nature. At this same time an intense religious revival was under way in Spain, expressed in the impassioned preaching of Ignatius of Loyola, as well as in the poetry of two great Spanish mystics: St. Teresa of Ávila (1515–1582) and her follower St. John of the Cross (1542–1591). El Greco's style—rooted in Byzantine icon painting and strongly reflecting the rich colors and loose brushwork of Venetian painting—was well equipped to express the intense spirituality of these mystics.

In 1586, the Orgaz family commissioned El Greco to paint a large altarpiece honoring an illustrious fourteenth-century ancestor. Count Orgaz had been a great benefactor of the Church, and at his funeral in 1323, SS. Augustine and Stephen were said to have appeared to lower his body into his tomb as his soul was seen ascending to heaven. El Greco's painting the **BURIAL OF COUNT ORGAZ** (FIG. 22-19) captures these miracles in a Mannerist composition that recalls Pontormo (see FIG. 21-30), packing the pictorial field with figures and eliminating specific reference to the spatial setting. An angel lifts Orgaz's ghostly soul along the central axis of the painting toward the enthroned Christ at the apex of the

22-18 • Juan Bautista de Toledo and Juan de Herrera **THE ESCORIAL** Madrid. 1563–1584. Detail from an anonymous 18th-century painting.

22-19 • El Greco BURIAL OF COUNT ORGAZ
Church of Santo Tomé, Toledo, Spain. 1586. Oil on canvas, 16′ × 11′10″ (4.88 × 3.61 m).

🔍 **View** the Closer Look for *Burial of Count Orgaz* on myartslab.com

canvas. The otherworldly luminescence emanating from Christ in this heavenly vision is quite unlike the natural light below, where El Greco surrounded the burial scene with portraits of the local aristocracy and religious notables. He placed his own 8-year-old son at the lower left next to St. Stephen and signed the painting on the boy's white kerchief. El Greco may also have put his own features on the man just above the saint's head, the only other figure who, like the child, looks straight out at the viewer.

THE NETHERLANDS

In the Netherlands, the sixteenth century was an age of bitter religious and political conflict. Despite the opposition of the Spanish Habsburg rulers, the Protestant Reformation took hold in the northern provinces. Seeds of unrest were sown still deeper over the course of the century by continued religious persecution, economic hardship, and inept governors. Widespread iconoclasm characterized 1566–1567, and a long battle for independence began with a revolt in 1568 that lasted until Spain relinquished all claims to the region 80 years later. As early as 1579, when the seven northern Protestant provinces declared themselves the United Provinces, the discord split the Netherlands, eventually dividing it along religious lines into the United Provinces (the present-day Netherlands) and Catholic Flanders (present-day Belgium).

Despite such turmoil, Antwerp and other cities developed into thriving art centers. The Reformation led artists to seek patrons outside the Church. While courtiers and burghers alike continued to commission portraits, the demand arose for small paintings with interesting secular subjects appropriate for homes. For example, some artists became specialists known for their landscapes or satires. In addition to painting, textiles, ceramics, printmaking, and sculpture in wood and metal flourished in the Netherlands. Flemish tapestries were sought after and highly prized across Europe, as they had been in the fifteenth century, and leading Italian artists made cartoons to be woven into tapestries in Flemish workshops (see "Raphael's Cartoons for Tapestries in the Sistine Chapel," page 648). The **graphic arts** emerged as an important medium, providing many artists with another source of income. Pieter Bruegel the Elder, for instance, began his career drawing amusing and moralizing images to be printed and published by At the Four Winds, an Antwerp publishing house.

Like Vasari in Italy, Carel van Mander (1548–1606) recorded the lives of his Netherlandish contemporaries in engaging biographies that mix fact and gossip. He, too, intended his 1604 book *Het Schilder-boeck* (*The Painter's Book*) to be a survey of the history of art, and he included material from the ancient Roman writers Pliny and Vitruvius as well as from Vasari's revised and expanded *Lives*, published in 1568.

ART FOR ARISTOCRATIC AND NOBLE PATRONS

Artistic taste among the wealthy bourgeoisie and noble classes in the early sixteenth-century Netherlands was characterized by a striking diversity, encompassing the imaginative and difficult visions of Hieronymus Bosch, as well as the more Italianate compositions of Jan Gossaert. In the later years of his life, Bosch's membership in a local but prestigious confraternity called the Brotherhood of Our Lady seems to have opened doors to noble patrons such as Count Hendrick III of Nassau and Duke Philip the Fair. His younger contemporary Gossaert left the city of Antwerp as a young man to spend the majority of his active years as the court painter for the natural son of Duke Philip the Good. His art also attracted members of the Habsburg family, including Charles V, who were seduced by Gossaert's combination of northern European and Italian styles.

HIERONYMUS BOSCH Among the most fascinating Netherlandish painters to modern viewers is Hieronymus Bosch (1450–

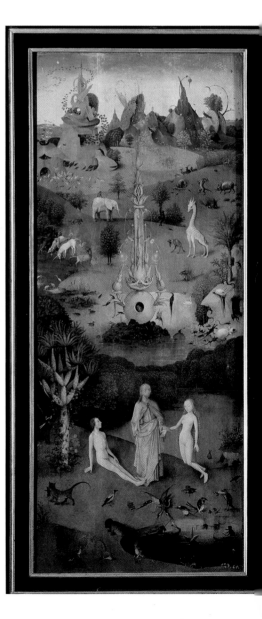

22-20 • Hieronymus Bosch GARDEN OF EARTHLY DELIGHTS (OPEN)
c. 1505–1515. Oil on wood panel, center panel 7′2½″ × 6′4¾″
(2.20 × 1.95 m), each wing 7′2½″ × 3′2″ (2.20 × 0.97 m).
Museo del Prado, Madrid.

Despite—or perhaps because of—its bizarre subject matter, this triptych was woven in 1566 into tapestries, and at least one painted copy was made as well. Bosch's original triptych was sold at the onset of the Netherlands Revolt and sent in 1568 to Spain, where it entered the collection of Philip II.

📖 **Read** the document related to Hieronymus Bosch on myartslab.com

1516), who depicted the sort of imaginative fantasies more often associated with medieval than Renaissance art. A superb colorist and virtuoso technician, Bosch spent his career in the town whose name he adopted, 's-Hertogenbosch. Bosch's religious devotion is certain, and his range of subjects shows that he was well educated. Challenging and unsettling paintings such as his **GARDEN OF EARTHLY DELIGHTS** (**FIG. 22-20**) have led modern scholars to label Bosch both a mystic and a social critic. The subject of the triptych seems to be founded on Christian belief in the natural state of human sinfulness, but it was not painted for a church.

In the left wing, God introduces doll-like figures of Adam and Eve, under the watchful eye of the owl of perverted wisdom. The owl symbolizes both wisdom and folly. Folly had become an important concept to the northern European humanists, who believed in the power of education. They believed that people would choose to follow the right way once they knew it. Here the owl peers out from an opening in the spherical base of a fantastic pink fountain in a lake from which vicious creatures creep out into the world.

In the central panel, the Earth teems with such monsters, but also with vivacious human revelers and luscious huge fruits, symbolic of fertility and sexual abandon. In hell, at the right, sensual pleasures—eating, drinking, music, and dancing—become instruments of torture in a dark world of fire and ice. The emphasis in the right wing on the torments of hell, with no hint of the rewards of heaven, seems to caution that damnation is the natural outcome of a life lived in ignorance and folly, that humans ensure their damnation through their self-centered pursuit of pleasures of the flesh—the sins of gluttony, lust, greed, and sloth—outlined with such fantastic and graphic abandon in the central panel.

One scholar has proposed that the central panel is a parable on human salvation in which the practice of alchemy—the process that sought to turn common metals into gold—parallels Christ's power to convert human dross into spiritual gold. In this theory, the bizarre fountain at the center of the lake in the middle distance can be seen as an alchemical "marrying chamber," complete with the glass vessels for collecting the vapors of distillation. Others see the theme known as "the power of women." In this interpretation, the central pool is the setting for a display of seductive women and sex-obsessed men. Women frolic alluringly in the pool while men dance and ride in a mad circle trying to attract them. In this strange garden, men are slaves to their own lust. An early seventeenth-century critic focused on the fruit, writing that the triptych was known as *The Strawberry Plant* because it represented the "vanity and glory and the passing taste of strawberries or the strawberry plant and its pleasant odor that is hardly remembered once it has passed." Luscious fruits of obvious sexual symbolism—strawberries, cherries, grapes, and pomegranates—appear everywhere in the garden, serving as food, as shelter, and even as a boat. Is human life as fleeting and insubstantial as the taste of a strawberry? Yet another modern reading sees the central tableau imagining the course of life in paradise, assuming that Adam and Even had not consigned humanity to sin by eating the forbidden fruit.

Conforming to a long tradition of triptych altarpieces made for churches, Bosch painted a more sober, *grisaille* picture on the reverse of the side wings. When the triptych is closed, a less enigmatic, but equally fascinating, scene is displayed (**FIG. 22-21**). A transparent, illusionistic rendering of a receding sphere floating within a void encloses the flat circular shelf of Earth on its third day of creation. Fragments of the fantastic fruit that will appear fully formed in the interior pictures float here in the primordial sea, while ominous dark clouds promise the rain that will nurture them into their full seductive ripeness. A tiny crowned figure of God the Creator hovers in a bubble within dark clouds at upper left, displaying a book, perhaps a Bible opened to the words from Psalm 33:9 that are inscribed across the top: "For he spoke, and it came to be; he commanded, and it stood firm."

The *Garden of Earthly Delights* was commissioned by an aristocrat (probably Count Hendrick III of Nassau) for his Brussels town house, and the artist's choice of a triptych format, which suggests an altarpiece, may have been an understated irony. In a private home the painting surely inspired lively discussion, even ribald commentary, much as it does today in the Prado Museum. Perhaps that, rather than a single meaning or interpretation, is the true intention behind this dazzling display of artistic imagination.

JAN GOSSAERT In contrast to the private visions of Bosch, Jan Gossaert (c. 1478–c. 1533) maintained traditional subject matter and embraced the new Classical art of Italy. Gossaert (who later called himself Mabuse after his native city Maubeuge) entered the service of Philip, the illegitimate son of the duke of Burgundy, accompanying him to Italy in 1508, and remaining in his service after Philip became archbishop of Utrecht in 1517.

Gossaert's "Romanizing" style—inspired by Italian Mannerist paintings and decorative details drawn from ancient Roman art—is evident in his painting of **ST. LUKE DRAWING THE VIRGIN MARY** (**FIG. 22-22**), a traditional subject we already know from a painting by Rogier van der Weyden (see FIG. 19-17). In Gossaert's version, the artist's studio is an extraordinary structure of Classical piers and arches, carved with a dense ornament of foliage and medallions. Mary and the Christ Child appear in a blaze of golden light and clouds before the saint, who kneels at a desk, his hand guided by an angel as he records the vision in a drawing. Luke's crumpled red robe replicates fifteenth-century drapery conventions in a seeming reference to Rogier's famous picture. Seated above and behind Luke on a round, columnar structure, Moses holds the Tablets of the Law, referencing his own visions of God on Mount Sinai. Just as Moses had removed his shoes in God's presence, so has Luke in the presence of his vision. Gossaert, like Dürer before him, seems to be staking a claim for the divine inspiration of the artist.

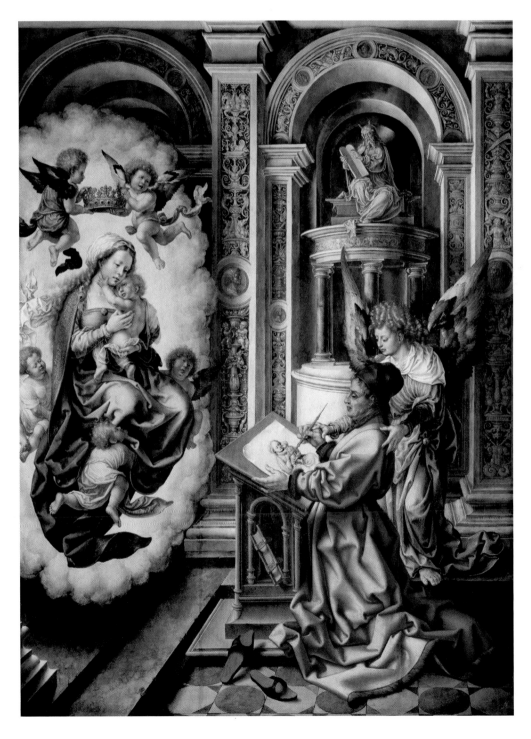

22–22 • Jan Gossaert **ST. LUKE DRAWING THE VIRGIN MARY**
1520. Oil on panel, 43⅜″ × 32¼″ (110.2 × 81.9 cm). Kunsthistorisches Museum, Vienna.

ANTWERP

During the sixteenth century, Antwerp was the commercial and artistic center of the southern Netherlands. Its deep port made it an international center of trade (it was one of the European centers for trade in spices), and it was the financial center of Europe. Painting, printmaking, and book production flourished in this environment, attracting artists and craftsmakers from all over Europe. The demand for luxury goods fostered the birth of the art market, in which art was transformed into a commodity for both local and international consumption. In responding to this market system, many artists became specialists in one area, such as portraiture or landscape, working with art dealers, who emerged as middlemen, further shaping the commodification of art, its production, and its producers.

QUENTIN MASSYS Early accounts of the prosperous Antwerp artist Quentin Massys (1466–1530) claim that he began working in his native Louvain as a blacksmith (his father's profession) but changed to painting to compete with a rival for the affections of a young woman; Carel van Mander claims he was a self-trained

22–23 • Quentin Massys MONEY CHANGER AND HIS WIFE
1514. Oil on panel, 28″ × 26¾″ (71.2 × 68 cm). Kunsthistorisches Museum, Vienna.

artist. We know he entered the Antwerp painters' guild in 1491, and at his death in 1530 he was among its most prosperous and renowned members, supervising a large workshop to meet the market in this burgeoning art center.

One of his most fascinating paintings—**MONEY CHANGER AND HIS WIFE** (**FIG. 22-23**)—recalls, like Gossaert's *St. Luke*, a famous fifteenth-century work, in this case the picture of a goldsmith painted for the Antwerp goldsmiths' guild by Petrus Christus (see "A Closer Look," page 583). Here, however, a couple is in charge of business, and they present us with two different profiles of engagement. The soberly dressed proprietor himself focuses intently on weighing coins in a suspended balance. His brightly outfitted wife—dressed in an archaic fifteenth-century costume that harks back to a golden age of Flemish painting—looks to the side, distracted by her husband's activity from the attention she was giving to the meticulously described Book of Hours spread out on the table in front of her. It would be easy to jump to the conclusion that this is a moral fable, warning of the danger of losing "sight" of religious obligations because of a preoccupation with affairs of business. But the painting is not that simple. An inscription that ran around the original frame quoted Leviticus 19:36—"You shall have honest balances and honest weights"—claiming just business practices as a form of righteous living. Is it possible the moral here juxtaposes not worldliness and spirituality, but attentive and distracted devotional practice? The sidetracked wife seems to have been idly flipping through her prayer book before turning to observe what her husband is doing, whereas a man in a red turban reflected in the convex mirror next to her Book of Hours is caught in rapt attention to the book in front of him, and the nature of his reading is suggested by the church steeple through the window behind him. The sermon here concerns the challenge of godly living in a worldly society, but wealth itself is not necessarily the root of the problem.

CATERINA VAN HEMESSEN Antwerp painter Caterina van Hemessen (1528–1587) developed an illustrious reputation as a portraitist. She had learned to paint from her father, the Flemish Mannerist Jan Sanders van Hemessen, who was dean of the Antwerp painters' guild in 1548, but the quiet realism and skilled rendering of her subjects is distinctively her own. To maintain focus on her foreground subjects, van Hemessen painted

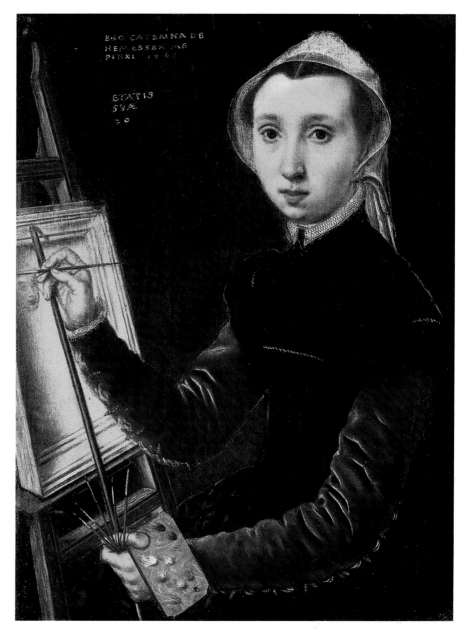

22-24 • Caterina van Hemessen **SELF-PORTRAIT**
1548. Oil on wood panel, 12¼" × 9¼" (31.1 × 23.5 cm). Öffentliche Kunstsammlung, Basel.

them against even, dark-colored backgrounds, on which she identified the sitter by name and age, signing and dating each work. The inscription in her **SELF-PORTRAIT** (**FIG. 22-24**) reads: "I Caterina van Hemessen painted myself in 1548. Her age 20." In delineating her own features, van Hemessen presented a serious young person who looks up to acknowledge us, interrupting her work on a portrait of a woman client. Between the date of this self-portrait and 1552, she painted ten signed and dated portraits of women, which seems to have been a specialty. She became a favored court artist to Mary of Hungary, sister of Emperor Charles V and regent of the Netherlands, for whom she painted not only portraits but also religious works, and whom she followed back to Spain when Mary ceased to be regent in 1556.

Cycles, or series, of paintings unified by a developing theme or allegorical subject—for instance, the Times of the Day, the Four Seasons, or the Five Senses—became popular wall decorations in prosperous Flemish homes during the sixteenth century. In 1565, Pieter Bruegel the Elder was commissioned to paint a series of six large paintings, each over 5 feet wide, surveying the months of the year, two months to a picture. They were made to be hung together in a room—probably the dining room since food figures prominently in these pictures—in the suburban villa of wealthy merchant Nicolaes Jonghelinck, just outside Antwerp.

RETURN OF THE HUNTERS (FIG. 22–25) represents December and January. The bleak landscape is gripped by winter as hunters return home at dusk with meager results: a single rabbit slung over the largest man's shoulder. But the landscape, rather than the figures, seems to be the principal subject here. A row of trees forms a receding set, consistently diminishing in scale, to draw our attention into the space of the painting along the orthogonal descent on the hillside of houses on the left. Like the calendar illustrations of medieval Books of Hours, the landscape is filled with behavior emblematic of the time of year: the singeing of the pig outside the farmhouse at left, the playful movement of ice skaters across frozen fields. We see it all from an omnipotent elevated viewpoint, like one of the birds that perch in the trees or glide across the snow-covered fantasy of an alpine background.

The mood is very different in the painting representing the hazy late summer days of August and September (**FIG. 22–26**). Birds still perch and glide, and a silhouetted tree still dominates the foreground—as if Bruegel wanted to set up obvious relationships between the scenes so that viewers would assess them comparatively—but the setting here is more rural than residential. Architecture keeps its distance or is screened by foliage. Agricultural workers trudge through their labor, harvesting grain, and gathering stalks into tidy sheaves, ready for transport. The figural focus, however, is in the foreground, on a shift of workers on their lunch break—serving themselves from baskets, gnawing on hard pieces of bread, spooning milk from bowls, or gulping from an uplifted jug. One man takes the

22-25 • Pieter Bruegel the Elder RETURN OF THE HUNTERS
1565. Oil on wood panel, 3′10½″ × 5′3¾″ (1.18 × 1.61 m). Kunsthistorisches Museum, Vienna.

22-26 • Pieter Bruegel the Elder **THE HARVESTERS**
1565. Oil on wood panel, 46⅞" × 63¾" (1.17 × 1.6 m). Metropolitan Museum of Art, New York. Rogers Fund, 1919. (19.164)

opportunity of this break for a quick nap. Some have seen in this lounging figure an emblem of sloth, or a wanton display of uncouth behavior, reminiscent of the embarrassing exposure of the peasant couple invited in to warm themselves before the fire in the farmhouse of the February page of Duke Jean de Berry's *Très Riches Heures* (see FIG. 19–5), painted by the Netherlandish Limbourg brothers a century and a half earlier.

Indeed, Bruegel's series of the months invites comparison with this venerable tradition—dating to the early Middle Ages—of showing peasant activity within the calendar cycles of prayer books made for wealthy patrons. Were they amused by peasant behavior? Did they enjoy representations of the productivity of their land and the availability of willing laborers to work it? Or do these vignettes embody their own longings for a

simpler life, idealized for them as a harmony between the natural world and the people who live on it, and off it? But the peasants enjoying the good life in this sunny scene of harvesting are only on a lunch break. Another shift is already hard at work in the fields, and the wealth of the patrons who supported the growth of an art market was dependent on the labor of countless folks like them.

Read the document related to Pieter Bruegel on myartslab.com

A CLOSER LOOK | *The French Ambassadors*

by Hans Holbein the Younger. 1533. Oil on wood panel.
81⅛″ × 82⅝″ (2.07 × 2.1 m). National Gallery, London.

Embossing on the sheath of the dagger tells us that de Dinteville is 28, while an inscription on the edge of the book (Bible?) under de Selve's arm records that he is 24.

This globe has Polisy, the de Dinteville family estate, marked at the center. It was here that this painting was hung when the ambassador returned to France at the end of 1533.

These objects on the top shelf were used to observe natural heavenly phenomena and chart the passage of time. The items displayed on the lower shelf relate more to terrestrial concerns.

Music is a common symbol of harmony in this period, and the broken string on this lute has been understood as an allusion to the discord created by the sweep of Protestant reform across Europe.

This bizarre, but prominently placed skull—as well as the skull badge that appears on de Dinteville's cap—reminded viewers of their own mortality. The foreground skull is distorted by anamorphosis, in which images are stretched horizontally with the use of a trapezoidal grid so that they must be viewed from the side to appear correctly proportioned.

This pavement—known as "Cosmati work" after the thirteenth-century Italian family that specialized in it—is copied from the floor in Westminster Abbey and may proclaim the ambassadors' involvement in a holy enterprise of reconciliation. The artist signed the painting on the left edge of the floor: "Johannes Holbein pingebat, 1533."

This is a Lutheran hymnal published in 1527, open at one of Luther's best-known compositions: "Come, Holy Ghost, our souls inspire." Neither man was a Protestant, but some of de Selve's contemporaries saw him as sympathetic to the cause of the reformers.

🔍 **View** the Closer Look for *The French Ambassadors* on myartslab.com

PIETER BRUEGEL THE ELDER So popular did the works of Hieronymus Bosch remain that, nearly half a century after his death, Pieter Bruegel (c. 1525–1569) began his career by imitating them. Like Bosch, he often painted large narrative works crowded with figures, and he chose moralizing or satirical subject matter. He traveled throughout Italy, but, unlike many Renaissance artists, he did not record the ruins of ancient Rome or the wonders of the Italian cities. Instead, he seems to have been fascinated by the landscape, particularly the formidable jagged rocks and sweeping panoramic views of Alpine valleys, which he recorded in detailed drawings. Back home in his studio, he made an impressive leap of the imagination as he painted the flat and rolling lands of Flanders as broad panoramas, even adding imaginary mountains on the horizon. He also visited country fairs to sketch the farmers and townspeople who became the focus of his paintings, presenting humans not as unique individuals but as well-observed types, whose universality makes them familiar even today.

Bruegel depicted nature in all seasons and in all moods. *Return of the Hunters* (see "Bruegel's Cycle of the Months," page 704) captures the bleak atmosphere of early nightfall during a damp, cold winter, with a freshness that recalls the much earlier paintings of his compatriots the Limbourgs (see FIG. 19-5). The hunters are foregrounded before a sharp plunge into space; the juxtaposition of near and far without middle ground is a typically sixteenth-century device. But this is clearly not an accidental image; it is a slice of everyday life faithfully reproduced within a carefully calculated composition. The same can be said of Bruegel's portrayal of late summer harvest (see FIG. 22-26), where the light is warmer, the landscape lush and verdant, the human activity rooted in agricultural labor or a momentary respite from it. As a depiction of Netherlandish life, these peasant scenes focusing on landscape represent a relative calm before the storm. Three years after they were painted, the anguished struggle of the northern provinces for independence from Spain began.

ENGLAND

Tudor England, in spite of the disruption caused by the Reformation, was economically and politically stable enough to provide sustained support for the arts, as Henry VIII strived to compete with the wealthy, sophisticated court of Francis I. Music, literature, and architecture flourished, but painting was principally left to foreigners.

As a young man, Henry VIII (r. 1509–1547) was loyal to the Church, defending it against Luther's attacks. He was rewarded by the pope in 1521 by being granted the title "Defender of the Faith." But when the pope refused to annul his marriage to Catherine of Aragon, Henry broke with Rome. By action of Parliament in 1534 he became the "Supreme Head on Earth of the Church and Clergy of England." He mandated an English translation of the Bible in every church, and in 1536 and 1539, he dissolved the monasteries, confiscating their great wealth and rewarding his followers with monastic lands and buildings. Shrines and altars were stripped of their jewels and precious metals to bolster the royal purse, and in 1548, during the reign of Henry's son, Edward VI, religious images were officially prohibited.

During the brief reign of Mary (r. 1553–1558), England officially returned to Catholicism, but the accession of Elizabeth in 1558 confirmed England as a Protestant country. So effective was Elizabeth, who ruled until 1603, that the last decades of the sixteenth century in England are called the Elizabethan Age.

ARTISTS IN THE TUDOR COURT

A remarkable record of the appearance of Tudor notables survives in portraiture. Since the Tudors had long favored Netherlandish and German artists, it is hardly surprising that it was a German-born painter, Hans Holbein the Younger (c. 1497–1543), who shaped the taste of the English court and upper classes.

HANS HOLBEIN Holbein first visited London from 1526 to 1528 and was introduced by the Dutch scholar Erasmus to the humanist circle around the English statesman Thomas More. He returned to England in 1532 and was appointed court painter to Henry VIII about four years later. During the 1530s, he created a spectacular series of portraits of nobles and diplomats associated with the Tudor court. The court's climate of international interaction is captured in a double portrait that Holbein painted in 1533 (see "A Closer Look," opposite)—a German painter's rendering in England of two French diplomats, one of them representing the court of Francis I in the Vatican. *The French Ambassadors* foregrounds Holbein's virtuosity as a painter and constructs a rich characterization of Jean de Dinteville, French ambassador to England, and his friend Georges de Selve, bishop of Lavaur and ambassador to the Holy See. With a loving detail that recalls the work of Jan van Eyck, the artist describes the surface textures and luminosity of the many objects placed in the painting to reflect the intellectual gifts and symbolize the political accomplishments of these two men. References in these objects to the conflicts between European states, and within the Catholic Church itself, imply that these bright and confident young ambassadors will apply their considerable diplomatic skills to finding a resolution.

PORTRAITS OF ELIZABETH Queen Elizabeth I carefully controlled the way artists represented her in official portraits and was known to have imprisoned artists whose unofficial images did not meet with her approval. A stark and hieratic regal image by Flemish artist Marcus Gheeraerts typifies the look she was after (**FIG. 22-27**). Called the Ditchley Portrait because it seems to have been commissioned for Ditchley, the estate of her courtier Sir Henry Lee, to commemorate the Queen's visit in 1592, the full-length figure of Elizabeth—more costume than body—stands supreme on a map of her realm with her feet in Oxfordshire, near Ditchley. The stark whiteness of her elaborate dress and the pale abstraction of her severe face assert the virginal purity that she cultivated as a part of her image. A storm passes out of the picture

22-28 • Nicholas Hilliard **GEORGE CLIFFORD, THIRD EARL OF CUMBERLAND**
c. 1595. Watercolor on vellum on card, oval 2¾″ × 2³⁄₁₆″ (7.1 × 5.8 cm). The Nelson-Atkins Museum of Art, Kansas City, Missouri. Gift of Mr. and Mrs. John W. Starr through the Starr Foundation. F58-60/188

on the right while the sun breaks through on the left. It is as if the queen is in control not only of England but of nature itself.

NICHOLAS HILLIARD In 1570, Nicholas Hilliard (1547–1619) arrived in London from southwest England to pursue a career as a jeweler, goldsmith, and painter of miniatures. Hilliard never received a court appointment, but he created miniature portraits of the queen and court notables, including **GEORGE CLIFFORD** (1558–1605), third earl of Cumberland (**FIG. 22-28**). Cumberland was a regular participant in the annual tilts and festivals celebrating the anniversary of Elizabeth's ascent to the throne. In Hilliard's miniature, Cumberland, a man of about 30, wears a richly engraved and gold-inlaid suit of armor, forged for his first appearance in 1583 (see "Armor for Royal Games," opposite). Hilliard gives him a marked air of courtly jauntiness, with a stylish beard, mustache, and curled hair, but Cumberland is also humanized by his direct gaze and receding

The medieval tradition of holding tilting, or jousting, competitions at English festivals and public celebrations continued during Renaissance times. Perhaps most famous were the Accession Day Tilts, held annually to celebrate the anniversary of Elizabeth I's coming to the throne. The gentlemen of the court, dressed in armor made especially for the occasion, held mock battles in the queen's honor. They rode their horses from opposite directions, trying to strike each other with long lances during six passes, as judges rated their performances.

The elegant armor worn by George Clifford, third Earl of Cumberland, at the Accession Day Tilts has been preserved in the collection of the Metropolitan Museum of Art in New York (**FIG. 22–29**). Tudor roses and back-to-back capital *E*s in honor of the queen decorate the armor's surface. As the queen's champion, beginning in 1590, Clifford also wore her jeweled glove attached to his helmet as he met all comers in the tiltyard of Whitehall Palace in London.

Made by Jacob Halder in the royal armories at Greenwich, the 60-pound suit of armor is recorded in the sixteenth-century Almain Armourers' Album along with its "exchange pieces." These allowed the owner to vary his appearance by changing mitts, side pieces, or leg protectors, and also provided backup pieces if one were damaged.

22-29 • Jacob Halder ARMOR OF GEORGE CLIFFORD, THIRD EARL OF CUMBERLAND

Made in the royal workshop at Greenwich, England. c. 1580–1585. Steel and gold, height 5′9½″ (1.77 m). Metropolitan Museum of Art, New York. Munsey Fund, 1932 (32.130.6) hairline. Cumberland's motto—"I bear lightning and water"—is inscribed on a stormy sky, with a lightning bolt in the form of a caduceus, one of his emblems. After all, he was that remarkable Elizabethan type—a naval commander and a gentleman pirate.

ARCHITECTURE

To increase support for the Tudor dynasty, Henry and his successors granted titles to rich landowners. To display their wealth and status, many of these newly created aristocrats embarked on extensive building projects, constructing lavish country residences, which sometimes surpassed the French châteaux in size and grandeur. Rooted in the Perpendicular Gothic style (see FIG. 18-22), Elizabethan architecture's severe walls and broad expanses of glass were modernized by replacing medieval ornament with Classical motifs copied from architectural handbooks and pattern books. The first architectural manual in English, published in 1563, was written by John Shute, one of the few builders who had spent time in Italy. Most influential were the treatises on architectural design by the Italian architect Sebastiano Serlio.

HARDWICK HALL One of the grandest of all the Elizabethan houses was Hardwick Hall, the home of Elizabeth, countess of Shrewsbury, known as "Bess of Hardwick" (FIG. 22-30). When she was in her seventies, the redoubtable countess—who inherited riches from all four of her deceased husbands—employed Robert Smythson (c. 1535–1614), England's first Renaissance architect, to build Hardwick Hall (1591–1597).

The medieval great hall was transformed into a two-story entrance hall, with rooms arranged symmetrically around it—a nod to Classical balance. A sequence of rooms leads to a grand stair up to the long gallery and **HIGH GREAT CHAMBER** on the second floor that featured an ornately carved fireplace (FIG. 22-31). It was here the countess received guests, entertained, and sometimes dined. Illuminated by enormous windows, the room seems designed to showcase a precious set of six Brussels tapestries featuring the story of Ulysses. They serve as yet another reminder of the international character of the lavish decoration of residences created for wealthy Renaissance patrons throughout Europe during the sixteenth century.

22-30 • Robert Smythson HARDWICK HALL
Derbyshire, England. 1591–1597.

22–31 • Robert Smythson HIGH GREAT CHAMBER, HARDWICK HALL
Derbyshire, England. 1591–1597. Brussels tapestries 1550s; painted plaster sculpture by Abraham Smith.

THINK ABOUT IT

22.1 Explore the impact of Italian art and ideas on the work and persona of German artist Albrecht Dürer. Choose one of his works from the chapter, and discuss its Italianate features and the ways in which it departs from and draws on earlier northern European traditions.

22.2 Discuss the impact of the Protestant Reformation on the visual arts in northern Europe, focusing your discussion on types of subject matter that patrons sought.

22.3 Choose one European court that employed artists working in a "foreign" tradition from another part of Europe and assess how this internationalism fostered the breaking down of regional and national boundaries in European art. Be sure to ground your discussion in the work of specific artists.

22.4 Choose a work of art discussed in this chapter that displays extraordinary technical skill in more than one medium. How was its virtuosity achieved, and how is it highlighted as an important factor in the work's significance?

CROSSCURRENTS

FIG. 19–17   FIG. 22–22

Gossaert's painting of St. Luke drawing the Virgin Mary suggests that he knew Rogier van der Weyden's famous earlier painting of the same subject. Compare these two works, separated in date by almost a century, discussing Gossaert's references to Rogier's painting but also characterizing the way each of these two artists embodied the style that characterizes their particular moment in the history of art. What did these paintings mean for their original audience?

✓—Study and review on myartslab.com

23–1 • Gianlorenzo Bernini ST. TERESA OF ÁVILA IN ECSTASY
Cornaro Chapel, church of Santa Maria della Vittoria, Rome. 1645–1652. Marble, height of the group 11′6″ (3.5 m).

Seventeenth-Century Art in Europe

In the church of Santa Maria della Vittoria in Rome, the sixteenth-century Spanish mystic **ST. TERESA OF ÁVILA** (1515–1582, canonized 1622) swoons in ecstasy on a bank of billowing marble clouds (**FIG. 23–1**). A puckish angel tugs open her robe, aiming a gilded arrow at her breast. Gilded bronze rays of supernatural light descend, even as actual light illuminates the figures from a hidden window above. This dramatic scene, created by Gianlorenzo Bernini (1598–1680) between 1645 and 1652, represents a famous vision described with startling physical clarity by Teresa, in which an angel pierced her body repeatedly with an arrow, transporting her to a state of ecstatic oneness with God, charged with erotic associations.

The sculpture is an exquisite example of the emotional, theatrical style perfected by Bernini in response to the religious and political climate in Rome during the period of spiritual renewal known as the Counter-Reformation. Many had seen the Protestant Reformation of the previous century as an outgrowth of Renaissance Humanism with its emphasis on rationality and independent thinking. In response, the Catholic Church took a reactionary, authoritarian position, supported by the new Society of Jesus founded by Ignatius of Loyola (d. 1556, canonized 1622). In the "spiritual exercises" (1522–1523) initiated by St. Ignatius, Christians were enjoined to use all their senses to transport themselves emotionally as they imagined the events on which they were meditating. They were to feel the burning fires of hell or the bliss of heaven, the lashing of the whips and the flesh-piercing crown of thorns. Art became an instrument of propaganda and also a means of leading the spectator to a reinvigorated Christian practice and belief.

Of course, the arts had long been used to convince or inspire, but nowhere more effectively than by the Catholic Church in the seventeenth century. To serve the educational and evangelical mission of the revitalized and conservative Church, paintings and sculpture had to depict events and people accurately and clearly, following guidelines established by religious leaders. Throughout Catholic Europe, painters such as Rubens and Caravaggio created brilliant religious art under official Church sponsorship. And although today some viewers find this sculpture of St. Teresa uncomfortably charged with sexuality, the Church approved of the depictions of such sensational and supernatural mystical visions. They helped worshipers achieve the emotional state of religious ecstasy that was a goal of the Counter-Reformation.

LEARN ABOUT IT

23.1 Explore how the work of Bernini and Caravaggio established a new dramatic intensity, technical virtuosity, and unvarnished naturalism that blossomed into a style we call Baroque that spread across Europe during the seventeenth century.

23.2 Examine the development of portraiture, still life, landscape, and genre scenes as major subjects for painting, especially within the prosperous art market of the Netherlands.

23.3 Analyze the way that seventeenth-century artists created works that embodied the power and prestige of the monarchy as well as works that furthered the Counter-Reformation agenda of the Roman Catholic Church.

23.4 Assess the resurgence of Classicism, especially in the work of seventeenth-century French artists and architects.

((•—[**Listen** to the chapter audio on myartslab.com

"BAROQUE"

The intellectual and political forces set in motion by the Renaissance and Reformation of the fifteenth and sixteenth centuries intensified during the seventeenth century. Religious wars continued, although gradually the Protestant forces gained control in the north, where Spain recognized the independence of the Dutch Republic in 1648. Catholicism maintained its primacy in southern Europe, the Holy Roman Empire, and France through the efforts of an energized papacy, aided by the new Society of Jesus, also known as the Jesuit Order (MAP 23-1). At the same time, scientific advances compelled people to question their worldview. Of great importance was the growing understanding that the Earth was not the center of the universe, but a planet revolving around the sun. As rulers' economic strength began to slip away, artists found patrons in the Church and the secular state, as well as in the newly confident and prosperous urban middle class. What evolved was a style that art historians have called "Baroque." The label may be related to the Italian word *barocco*, a jeweler's term for an irregularly shaped pearl—something beautiful, fascinating, and strange.

Baroque art deliberately evokes intense emotional responses from viewers. Dramatically lit, theatrical compositions often combine several media within a single work as artists highlight their technical virtuosity. But the seventeenth century also saw its own version of Classicism, a more moving and dramatic variant of Renaissance ideals and principles featuring idealization based on observation of the material world; balanced (though often asymmetrical) compositions; diagonal movement in space; rich, harmonious colors; and the inclusion of visual references to ancient Greece and Rome. Many seventeenth-century artists sought lifelike depiction of their world in portraiture, **genre paintings** (scenes from everyday life), still life (paintings of inanimate objects such as food, fruit, or flowers), and religious scenes enacted by ordinary people in ordinary settings. Intense emotional involvement, lifelike renderings, and Classical references may exist in the same work, and are all part of the stylistic complexion of the seventeenth century.

The role of viewers also changed. Italian Renaissance painters and patrons had been fascinated with the visual possibilities of perspective and treasured idealism of form and subject which kept viewers at a distance, reflecting intellectually on what they were seeing. Seventeenth-century masters, on the other hand, sought to engage viewers as participants in the work of art, and often reached out to incorporate or activate the world beyond the frame into the nature and meaning of the work itself. In Catholic countries, representations of horrifying scenes of martyrdom or the passionate spiritual life of mystics in religious ecstasy sought to inspire viewers to a reinvigorated faith by making them feel what was going on, not simply by causing them to think about it. In Protestant countries, images of communal parades and city views sought to inspire pride in civic accomplishments. Viewers participated in works of art like audiences in a theater—vicariously but completely—as the work of art drew them visually and emotionally into its orbit. The

seventeenth-century French critic Roger de Piles (1635–1709) described this exchange when he wrote: "True painting … calls to us; and has so powerful an effect, that we cannot help coming near it, as if it had something to tell us" (Puttfarken, p. 55).

ITALY

Seventeenth-century Italy remained a divided land in spite of a common history, language, and geography. The Kingdom of Naples and Sicily was Spanish; the Papal States crossed the center; Venice maintained its independence as a republic; and the north remained divided among small principalities. Churchmen and their families remained powerful patrons of the arts, especially as they sought to use art in revitalizing the Roman Catholic Church. The Council of Trent (concluded 1563) had set guidelines for Church art that went against the arcane, worldly, and often lascivious trends exploited by Mannerism. The clergy's call for clarity, simplicity, chaste subject matter, and the ability to rouse a very Catholic piety in the face of Protestant revolt found a response in the fresh approaches to subject matter and style offered by a new generation of artists.

ARCHITECTURE AND SCULPTURE IN ROME

A major goal of the Counter-Reformation was the proper embellishment of churches and their settings. Pope Sixtus V (pontificate 1585–1590) had begun the renewal in Rome by cutting long, straight avenues through the city to link the major pilgrimage churches with one another and with the main gates of Rome. Sixtus also ordered open spaces—piazzas—to be cleared in front of major churches, marking each site with an Egyptian obelisk. In a practical vein, he also reopened one of the ancient aqueducts to stabilize the city's water supply. Unchallengeable power and vast financial resources were required to carry out such an extensive plan of urban renewal and to refashion Rome—parts of which had been the victim of rapacity and neglect since the Middle Ages—once more into the center of spiritual and worldly power.

The Counter-Reformation popes had great wealth, although they eventually nearly bankrupted the Church with their building programs. Sixtus began to renovate the Vatican and its library; he completed the dome of St. Peter's and built splendid palaces. The Renaissance ideal of the central-plan church continued to be used for the shrines of saints, but Counter-Reformation thinking called for churches with long, wide naves to accommodate large congregations assembled to hear inspiring sermons as well as to participate in the Mass. In the sixteenth century, the decoration of new churches had been relatively austere, but seventeenth- and eighteenth-century Catholic taste favored opulent and spectacular visual effects to heighten the emotional involvement of worshipers.

ST. PETER'S BASILICA IN THE VATICAN Half a century after Michelangelo had returned St. Peter's Basilica to Bramante's original vision of a central-plan building, Pope Paul V Borghese

MAP 23-1 • SEVENTEENTH-CENTURY EUROPE

Protestantism still dominated northern Europe, while in the south Roman Catholicism remained strong after the Counter-Reformation. The Habsburg empire was now divided into two parts, under separate rulers.

(pontificate 1605–21) commissioned Carlo Maderno (1556–1629) to provide the church with a longitudinal nave and a new façade (**FIG. 23-2**). Construction began in 1607, and everything but the façade bell towers was completed by 1615 (see "St. Peter's Basilica," page 653). Rooted in the design of of Il Gesù's façade (see FIG. 21-40), Maderno's façade for St. Peter's steps forward in three progressively projecting planes: from the corners to the doorways flanking the central entrance area, then the entrance area, then the central doorway itself. Similarly, the colossal orders connecting the first and second stories are flat pilasters at the corners but fully round columns where they flank the doorways. These columns support a continuous entablature that also steps out—following the columns—as it moves toward the central door.

When Maderno died in 1629, Gianlorenzo Bernini (1598–1680), his collaborator of five years, succeeded him as Vatican architect. Bernini was taught by his father, and part of his training involved sketching the Vatican collection of ancient sculpture, such as *Laocoön and His Sons* (see FIG. 5-64), as well as the many examples of Renaissance painting in the papal palace. Throughout his life, Bernini admired antique art and, like other artists of this period, considered himself a Classicist. Today, we not only appreciate his strong debt to the Renaissance tradition but also acknowledge the way he broke through that tradition to develop a new, Baroque style.

When Urban VIII was elected pope in 1623, he unhesitatingly gave the young Bernini the daunting task of designing an enormous bronze baldachin, or canopy, over the high altar of St. Peter's. The church was so large that a dramatic focus on the altar was essential. The resulting **BALDACCHINO** (**FIG. 23-3**), completed in 1633, stands almost 100 feet high and exemplifies the

23-2 • Carlo Maderno and Gianlorenzo Bernini ST. PETER'S BASILICA AND PIAZZA, VATICAN, ROME
Maderno, façade, 1607–1626; Bernini, piazza design, c. 1656–1657.

Perhaps only a Baroque artist of Bernini's talents could have unified the many artistic periods and styles that come together in St. Peter's Basilica (starting with Bramante's original design for the building in the sixteenth century). The basilica in no way suggests a piecing together of parts made by different builders at different times but rather presents itself as a triumphal unity of all the parts in one coherent whole.

Baroque objective to create multimedia works, combining architecture and sculpture—and sometimes painting as well—that defy simple categorization. The gigantic corner columns symbolize the union of Christianity and its Jewish tradition—the vine of the Eucharist climbing the twisted columns associated with the Temple of Solomon. They support an entablature with a crowning element topped with an orb (a sphere representing the universe) and a cross (symbolizing the reign of Christ). Figures of angels and *putti* decorate the entablature, which is hung with tasseled panels in imitation of a cloth canopy. This imposing work not only marks the site of the tomb of St. Peter, but also serves as a tribute to Urban VIII and his family, the Barberini, whose emblems—honeybees and suns on the tasseled panels, and laurel leaves on the climbing vines—are prominently displayed.

Between 1627 and 1641, Bernini and several other sculptors, again in multimedia extravaganzas, rebuilt Bramante's crossing piers as giant reliquaries. Statues of SS. Helena, Veronica, Andrew, and Longinus stand in niches below alcoves containing their relics, to the left and right of the *baldacchino*. Visible through the *baldacchino*'s columns in the apse of the church is another reliquary: the gilded-stone, bronze, and stucco shrine made by Bernini between 1657 and 1666 for the ancient wooden throne thought to have belonged to St. Peter as the first bishop of Rome. The Chair of Peter symbolized the direct descent of Christian authority from Peter to the current pope, a belief rejected by Protestants and therefore deliberately emphasized in Counter-Reformation Catholicism. Above the shrine, a brilliant stained-glass window portrays the Holy Spirit as a dove surrounded by an oval of golden rays. Adoring gilded angels and gilt-bronze rays fan out around the window and seem to extend the penetration of the natural light—and the Holy Spirit—into the apse of the church. The gilding also reflects the light back to the window, creating a dazzling, ethereal effect that the seventeenth century, with its interest in mystics and visions, would equate with the activation of divinity.

At approximately the same time that he was at work on the Chair of Peter, Bernini designed and supervised the building of a

23-3 • Gianlorenzo Bernini BALDACCHINO
St. Peter's Basilica, Vatican, Rome. 1624–1633. Gilt bronze, height approx. 100′ (30.48 m). Chair of Peter shrine, 1657–1666; gilt bronze, marble, stucco, and glass. Pier decorations, 1627–1641; gilt bronze and marble.

colonnade to form a huge double piazza in front of the entrance to St. Peter's (see FIG. 23-2). The open space that he had to work with was irregular, and an Egyptian obelisk and a fountain previously installed by Sixtus V had to be incorporated into the overall plan. Bernini's remarkable design frames the oval piazza with two enormous curved porticos, or covered walkways, supported by Tuscan columns. These curved porticos are connected to two straight porticos, which lead up a slight incline to the two ends of the church façade. Bernini characterized his design as the "motherly arms of the Church" reaching out to the world. He had intended to build a third section of the colonnade closing the side of the piazza facing the church so that only after pilgrims had crossed the Tiber River bridge and made their way through narrow streets, would they encounter the enormous open space before the imposing church. This element of surprise would have made the basilica and its setting an even more awe-inspiring vision. The approach today—along the grand avenue of the Via della Conciliazione running from the Tiber to the Basilica—was conceived by Mussolini in 1936 as part of his masterplan to transform Rome into a grand fascist capital.

BERNINI AS SCULPTOR Even after Bernini's appointment as Vatican architect in 1629, he was still able to accept outside commissions by virtue of his large workshop. In fact, he first became famous as a sculptor, and he continued to create sculpture throughout his career, for both the papacy and private clients. A man of many talents, he was also a painter and even a playwright—an interest that dovetailed with his genius for theatrical and dramatic presentation.

Bernini's **DAVID** (FIG. 23-4), made for a nephew of Pope Paul V in 1623, introduced a new type of three-dimensional composition that intrudes forcefully into the viewer's space. The young hero bends at the waist and twists far to one side, ready to launch the lethal rock at Goliath. Unlike Donatello's sassy boy (see FIG. 20-14) and Verrocchio's poised and proud adolescent (see FIG. 20-34)—both already victorious—or Michelangelo's pensive young man contemplating the task ahead (see FIG. 21-10), Bernini's more mature David, with his lean, sinewy body, tightly clenched mouth, and straining muscles, is all tension, action, and determination. By creating a twisting figure caught in movement, Bernini

23-4 • Gianlorenzo Bernini DAVID
1623. Marble, height 5′7″ (1.7 m). Galleria Borghese, Rome.

23-5 • Gianlorenzo Bernini CORNARO CHAPEL, CHURCH OF SANTA MARIA DELLA VITTORIA, ROME
1642–1652.

Read the document related to Gianlorenzo Bernini on myartslab.com

Watch an architectural simulation about the Cornaro Chapel on myartslab.com

In the center of the chapel and framed by columns in the huge oval niche above the altar, Bernini's marble group *St. Teresa of Ávila in Ecstasy* (see FIG. 23–1) represents a vision described by the Spanish mystic in which an angel pierced her body repeatedly with an arrow, transporting her to a state of indescribable pain, religious ecstasy, and a sense of oneness with God. St. Teresa and the angel, who seem to float upward on clouds, are cut from a heavy mass of solid marble supported on a seemingly drifting pedestal that was fastened by hidden metal bars to the chapel wall. Bernini's skill at capturing the movements and emotions of these figures is matched by his virtuosity in simulating different textures and colors in the pure white medium of marble; the angel's gauzy, clinging draperies seem silken in contrast with Teresa's heavy woolen monastic robe. Bernini effectively used the configuration of the garment's folds to convey the saint's swooning, sensuous body beneath, even though only Teresa's face, hands, and bare feet are actually visible.

Kneeling against what appear to be balconies on both sides of the chapel are marble portrait sculptures of Federigo, his deceased father (a Venetian doge), and six cardinals of the Cornaro family. The figures are informally posed and naturalistically portrayed. Two read from their prayer books, others exclaim at the miracle taking place in the light-infused realm above the altar, and one leans out from his seat, apparently to look at someone entering the chapel—perhaps the viewer, whose space these figures share. Bernini's intent was not to produce a spectacle for its own sake,

incorporates the surrounding space within his composition, implying the presence of an unseen adversary somewhere behind the viewer. Thus, the viewer becomes part of the action, rather than its displaced and dispassionate observer.

From 1642 until 1652, Bernini worked on the decoration of the funerary chapel of Venetian cardinal Federigo Cornaro (**FIG. 23-5**) in the Roman church of Santa Maria della Vittoria, designed by Carlo Maderno earlier in the century. The Cornaro family chapel was dedicated to the Spanish saint Teresa of Ávila, canonized only 20 years earlier. Bernini designed it as a rich and theatrical setting for the portrayal of a central event in Teresa's life. He covered the walls with multicolored marble panels and crowned them with a projecting cornice supported by marble pilasters.

but to capture a critical, dramatic moment at its emotional and sensual height, and by doing so guide viewers to identify totally with the event—and perhaps be transformed in the process.

BORROMINI'S CHURCH OF SAN CARLO The intersection of two of the wide, straight avenues created by Pope Sixtus V inspired city planners to add a special emphasis, with fountains marking each of the four corners of the crossing. In 1634, Trinitarian monks decided to build a new church at the site and awarded the commission for San Carlo alle Quattro Fontane (St. Charles at the Four Fountains) to Francesco Borromini (1599–1667). Borromini, a nephew of architect Carlo Maderno, had arrived in Rome in 1619 from northern Italy to enter his uncle's

workshop. Later, he worked under Bernini's supervision on the decoration of St. Peter's, and some details of the *Baldacchino*, as well as its structural engineering, are now attributed to him, but San Carlo was his first independent commission. Unfinished at Borromini's death, the church was nevertheless completed according to his design.

SAN CARLO ALLE QUATTRO FONTANE stands on a narrow piece of land, with one corner cut off to accommodate one of the fountains that give the church its name (**FIG. 23-6**). To fit the irregular site, Borromini created an elongated central-plan interior space with undulating walls. Robust pairs of columns support a massive entablature, over which an oval dome, supported on pendentives, seems to float (**FIG. 23-7**). The coffers (inset panels in geometric shapes) filling the interior of the oval-shaped dome form an eccentric honeycomb of crosses, elongated hexagons, and octagons. These coffers decrease sharply in size as they approach the apex, or highest point, where the dove of the Holy Spirit hovers in a climax that brings together the geometry used in the chapel: oval, octagon, circle, and—very important—a triangle, symbol of the Trinity as well as of the church's patrons. The dome appears to be shimmering and inflating—almost floating up and away—thanks to light sources placed in the lower coffers and the lantern.

It is difficult today to appreciate how audacious Borromini's design for this small church was. He abandoned the modular, additive system of planning taken for granted by every architect since Brunelleschi. He worked instead from an overriding geometrical scheme, as a Gothic architect might, subdividing modular units to

23-6 • Francesco Borromini FAÇADE (A) AND PLAN (B) OF THE CHURCH OF SAN CARLO ALLE QUATTRO FONTANE
Rome. 1638–1667.

23-7 • Francesco Borromini VIEW INTO THE DOME OF THE CHURCH OF SAN CARLO ALLE QUATTRO FONTANE
Rome. 1638–1667.

obtain more complex, rational shapes. For example, the elongated, octagonal plan of San Carlo is composed of two triangles set base to base along the short axis of the plan (see FIG. 23-6B). This diamond shape is then subdivided into secondary triangular units made by calculating the distances between what will become the concave centers of the four major and five minor niches. Yet Borromini's conception of the whole is not medieval. The chapel is dominated horizontally by a Classical entablature that breaks any surge upward toward the dome. Borromini's treatment of the architectural elements as if they were malleable was also unprecedented. His contemporaries understood immediately what an extraordinary innovation the church represented; the Trinitarian monks who had commissioned it received requests for plans from visitors from all over Europe. Although Borromini's innovative work had little impact on the architecture of Classically minded Rome, it was widely imitated in northern Italy and beyond the Alps.

Borromini's design for San Carlo's façade (see FIG. 23-6A), executed more than two decades later, was as innovative as his planning of the interior. He turned the building's front into an undulating, sculpture-filled screen punctuated with large columns and deep concave and convex niches that create dramatic effects of light and shadow. Borromini also gave his façade a strong vertical thrust in the center by placing over the tall doorway a statue-filled niche, then a windowed niche covered with a canopy, then a giant, forward-leaning cartouche held up by angels carved in such high relief that they appear to hover in front of the wall. The entire composition is crowned with a balustrade broken by the sharply pointed frame of the cartouche. As with the design of the building itself, Borromini's façade was enthusiastically imitated in northern Italy and especially in northern and eastern Europe.

PAINTING

Painting in seventeenth-century Italy followed one of two principal paths: the ordered Classicism of the Carracci or the dramatic naturalism of Caravaggio. Although the leading exponents of these paths were northern Italians—the Carracci family was from Bologna, and Caravaggio was born in or near Milan—they were all eventually drawn to Rome, the center of power and patronage. The Carracci family, like Caravaggio, were schooled in northern Italian Renaissance traditions, with its emphasis on *chiaroscuro*, as well as in Venetian color and *sfumato*. The Carracci quite consciously rejected the artifice of the Mannerist style and fused their northern roots with the central Italian High Renaissance insistence on line (*disegno*), compositional structure, and figural solidity. They looked to Raphael, Michelangelo, and antique Classical sculpture for their ideal figural types and their expressive but decorous compositions. Caravaggio, on the other hand, satisfied the Baroque demand for drama and clarity by developing realism in a powerful new direction. He painted people he saw in the world around him—even the lowlife of Rome—and worked directly from models without elaborate drawings and compositional notes. Unlike the Carracci, he claimed to ignore the influence of the great masters so as to focus steadfastly on a sense of immediacy and invention.

THE CARRACCI The brothers Agostino (1557–1602) and Annibale Carracci (1560–1609) and their cousin Ludovico (1555–1619) shared a studio in Bologna. As their re-evaluation of the High Renaissance masters attracted interest among their peers, they opened their doors to friends and students and then, in 1582, founded an art academy, where students drew from live models and studied art theory, Renaissance painting, and antique Classical sculpture. The Carracci placed a high value on accurate drawing, complex figure compositions, complicated narratives, and technical expertise in both oil and fresco painting. During its short life, the academy had an impact on the development of the arts—and art education—through its insistence on both life drawing (to achieve naturalism) and aesthetic theory (to achieve artistic harmony).

In 1595, Annibale was hired by Cardinal Odoardo Farnese to decorate the principal rooms of his family's immense Roman palace. In the long *galleria* (gallery), to celebrate the wedding of Duke Ranuccio Farnese of Parma to the niece of the pope, the artist was requested to paint scenes of love based on Ovid's *Metamorphoses* (**FIG. 23-8**). Undoubtedly, Annibale and Agostino, who assisted him, felt both inspiration and competition from the important

Farnese collection of antique sculpture exhibited throughout the palace.

The primary image, set in the center of the vault, is *The Triumph of Bacchus and Ariadne*, a joyous procession celebrating the wine god Bacchus's love for Ariadne, whom he rescued after her lover, Theseus, abandoned her on the island of Naxos. Annibale combines the great northern Italian tradition of ceiling

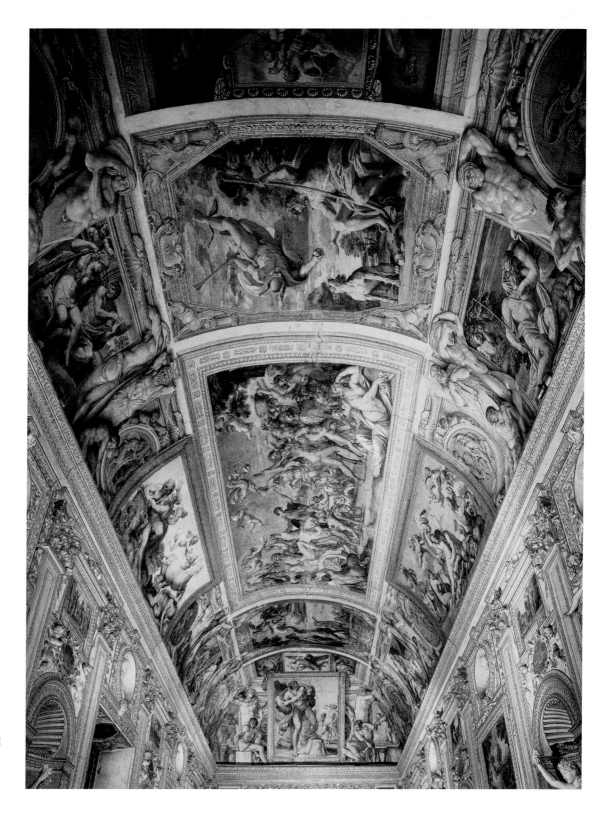

23-8 • Annibale Carracci **CEILING OF GALLERY, PALAZZO FARNESE**
Rome. 1597–1601. Fresco, approx. 68′ × 21′ (20.7 × 6.4 m).

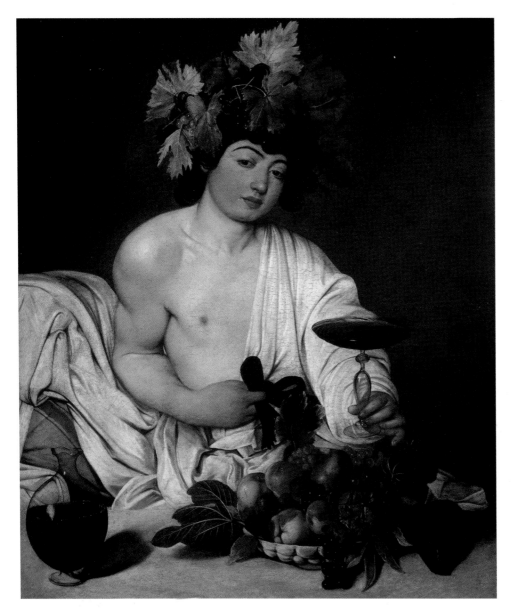

painting—seen in the work of Mantegna and Correggio (see FIGS. 20–32, 21–22)—with his study of central Italian Renaissance painters and the Classical heritage of Rome. Annibale organized his complex theme by using illusionistic devices to create multiple levels of reality. Painted imitations of gold-framed easel paintings called *quadri riportati* ("transported paintings") appear to "rest" on the actual cornice of the vault and overlap "bronze" medallions that are flanked, in turn, by realistically colored *ignudi*, dramatically lit from below. The viewer is invited to compare the warm flesh tones of these youths, and their lifelike poses, with the more idealized "painted" bodies in the framed scenes next to them. Above, paintings of stucco-colored sculptures of herms (plain shafts topped by human torsos) twist and turn as they support the painted framework of the vault, exposing a variety of feelings with their expressions and seemingly communicating with one another. Many of Annibale's ideas are inspired by motifs in Michelangelo's Sistine Chapel ceiling (see FIG. 21–12). The figure types, true to their source, are heroic, muscular, and drawn with precise anatomical accuracy.

But instead of Michelangelo's cool illumination and intellectual detachment, the Carracci ceiling glows with a warm light that recalls the work of the Venetian painters Titian and Veronese, and seems buoyant with optimism and lively engagement.

The ceiling was highly admired, famous from the moment it was finished. The proud Farnese family generously allowed young artists to sketch the figures there, so that Carracci's masterpiece influenced Italian art well into the following century.

CARAVAGGIO Michelangelo Merisi (1571–1610), known as "Caravaggio" after his family's home town in Lombardy, introduced a powerfully frank realism and dramatic, theatrical lighting and gesture to Italian Baroque art. The young painter brought an interest, perhaps a specialization, in still-life painting with him when he arrived in Rome from Milan late in 1592 and found studio work as a specialist painter of fruit and vegetables. When he began to work on his own, he continued to paint still lifes but also began to include half-length figures with them. By this time, his reputation had grown to the extent that an agent offered to market his pictures.

Caravaggio painted for a small, sophisticated circle associated with the household of art patron Cardinal del Monte, where the artist was invited to reside. His subjects from this early period of the 1590s include not only still lifes but also genre scenes featuring fortune-tellers, cardsharps, and glamorous young men dressed as musicians or mythological figures. The **BACCHUS** of 1595–1596 (**FIG. 23-9**) is among the most polished of these early works. Caravaggio seems to have painted exactly what he saw, reproducing the "farmer's tan" of those parts of this partially dressed youth's skin—hand and face—that have been exposed to the sun, as well as the dirt under his fingernails. The figure himself is strikingly androgynous. Made up with painted lips and smoothly arching eyebrows, he seems to offer the viewer the gorgeous goblet of wine held delicately in his left hand, while fingering the black bow that holds his loose clothing together at the waist. Is this a provocative invitation to an erotic encounter or a young actor outfitted for the role of Bacchus, god of wine? Does the juxtaposition of the youth's invitation with a still life of rotting fruit transform this into an image about the transitory nature of sensual pleasure, either admonishing viewers to avoid sins of the flesh or encouraging them to enjoy life's pleasures while they can? The ambiguity seems to make the painting even more provocative.

Most of Caravaggio's commissions after 1600 were religious, and reactions to them were mixed. On occasion, patrons rejected his powerful, sometimes brutal, naturalism as unsuitable to the subject's dignity. Critics differed as well. An early critic, the Spaniard Vincente Carducho, wrote in his *Dialogue on Painting* (Madrid, 1633) that Caravaggio was an "omen of the ruin and demise of painting" because he painted "with nothing but nature before him, which he simply copied in his amazing way" (Enggass and Brown, pp. 173–174). Others recognized him as a great innovator who reintroduced realism into art and developed new, dramatic lighting effects. Seventeenth-century art historian Giovanni Bellori described Caravaggio's painting as

> … reinforced throughout with bold shadows and a great
> deal of black to give relief to the forms. He went so far
> in this manner of working that he never brought his
> figures out into the daylight, but placed them in the dark
> brown atmosphere of a closed room, using a high light
> that descended vertically over the principal parts of the
> bodies while leaving the remainder in shadow in order to
> give force through a strong contrast of light and dark.…
> (Bellori, *Lives of the Painters*, Rome, 1672, in Enggass and
> Brown, p. 79)

Caravaggio's approach has been likened to the preaching of Filippo Neri (1515–1595), the Counter-Reformation priest and mystic who founded a Roman religious group called the Congregation of the Oratory. Neri, called the Apostle of Rome and later canonized, focused his missionary efforts on ordinary people for whom he strove to make Christian history and doctrine understandable and meaningful. Caravaggio, too, interpreted his religious subjects directly and dramatically, combining intensely observed figures, poses, and expressions with strongly contrasting effects of light and color. His knowledge of Lombard painting, where the influence of Leonardo was strong, must have facilitated his development of the technique now known as **tenebrism**, in which forms emerge from a dark background into a strong light that often falls from a single source outside the painting. The effect is that of a theatrical spotlight.

One of Caravaggio's first religious commissions—paintings for the Contarelli Chapel in the French community's church of St. Louis (San Luigi dei Francesi)—included *The Calling of St. Matthew*, painted about 1599–1600 (see "Caravaggio in the Contarelli Chapel," page 724). The subject is conversion, a common Counter-Reformation theme. Jesus calls Levi, the tax collector, to join his apostles (Matthew 9:9; Mark 2:14). Levi—who will become St. Matthew—sits at a table, counting or collecting money, surrounded by elegant young men in plumed hats, velvet doublets, and satin shirts. Nearly hidden behind the back of a beckoning apostle—probably St. Peter—at the right, the gaunt-faced Jesus points dramatically at Levi with a gesture that is repeated in the presumed (other than Jesus, identities are not certain here) tax collector's own surprised response of pointing to himself, as if to say, "Who, me?" An intense raking light enters the painting from upper right, as if it were coming from the chapel's actual window above the altar to spotlight the important features of this darkened scene. Viewers encountering the painting obliquely across the empty space of the chapel interior seem to be witnessing the scene as it is occurring, elevated on a recessed stage opening through the wall before them.

The emotional power of Caravaggio's theatrical approach to sacred narrative is nowhere more evident than in his rendering of **THE CONVERSION OF ST. PAUL** for the Cerasi Chapel in Santa Maria del Popolo (**FIG. 23-12**). This is one of two paintings commissioned for this chapel in 1600; the other portrayed the Crucifixion of St. Peter. The first pair was rejected when Caravaggio delivered them, and they were acquired by a private collector (see also "Caravaggio in the Contarelli Chapel," page 724). This second version of Paul's conversion is direct and simple. Caravaggio focuses on Paul's internal involvement with a pivotal moment, not its external cause. There is no indication of a heavenly apparition, only Paul's response to it. There is no clear physical setting, only mysterious darkness. And Paul's experience is personal. Whereas he has been flung from his horse and threatens to tumble into the viewers' own space—arms outstretched and legs akimbo, bathed in a strong spotlight—the horse and groom behind him seem oblivious to Paul's experience. The horse actually takes up more space in the painting than the saint, and the unsettling position of its lifted foreleg, precariously poised over the sprawled body of Paul, adds further tension to an already charged presentation.

As soon as he had established himself as an up-and-coming artist during the 1590s, Caravaggio turned to a series of important commissions for religious paintings in the chapels of Roman churches. Unlike in the Renaissance, where frescos were applied directly to the walls, Caravaggio produced large oil paintings on canvas in his studio, only later installing them within the chapels to form coordinated ensembles. Several such installations survive, giving us the precious opportunity to experience the paintings as Caravaggio and his patrons intended. One of these intact programs, in the **CONTARELLI CHAPEL** of San Luigi dei Francesi (**FIG. 23–10**), was Caravaggio's earliest religious commission in Rome, perhaps obtained through the efforts of Cardinal del Monte, who had supported the artist through the 1590s.

This church served the French community in Rome, and the building itself was constructed between 1518 and 1589, its completion made possible by the patronage of Catherine de' Medici, queen of France. The chapel Caravaggio decorated was founded in 1565 by Mathieu Cointrel—Matteo Contarelli—a French noble at the papal court who would serve as a financial administrator under Gregory XIII (pontificate 1572–1585). Although earlier artists had been called on to provide paintings for the chapel, it was only after Contarelli's death in 1585 that the executors of his will brought the decoration to completion, hiring Giuseppe Cesare in 1591

to paint the ceiling frescos, and Caravaggio in 1599 to provide paintings of scenes from the life of the patron's patron saint: **THE CALLING OF ST. MATTHEW** on the left wall (**FIG. 23–11**) and *The Martyrdom of St. Matthew* on the right (not visible in FIG. 23–10), both installed in July 1600.

The commissioning document was explicit, requiring the artist to show, in *The Calling of St. Matthew*, the saint rising from his seat to follow Christ in ministry. But Caravaggio was never very good at following the rules. Among the group of smartly dressed Romans who form Matthew's circle of cohorts seated at the left, no one rises to leave. Art historians have

not even been able to agree on which figure is Matthew. Most identify him with a bearded man in the center, interpreting his pointing gesture as a self-referential, questioning response to Jesus' call. But some see Matthew in the figure hunched over the scattered coins at far left, seemingly unmoved by Jesus' presence. In this case, the bearded figure's pointing would question whether this bent-over colleague was the one Jesus sought. The painting is marked by mystery, not by the clarity sought by Counter-Reformation guidelines.

In February 1602, Caravaggio received a second commission for the Contarelli Chapel, this time for a painting over the altar

23–10 • CONTARELLI CHAPEL, SAN LUIGI DEI FRANCESI
Rome. Paintings by Caravaggio 1599–1602.

showing St. Matthew, accompanied by his angelic symbol and writing his Gospel. It was to be completed within three months, but Caravaggio did not receive payment for the picture until September of that year, and the painting he delivered was rejected. The clergy considered Caravaggio's rendering of the saint unacceptably crude and common, his cross-legged pose uncouth and unnecessarily revealing. The fleshiness of the angel, who sidles cozily up to Matthew, was judged inappropriately risqué. In short, the painting was inconsistent with guidelines for saintly decorum set for artists by the Council of Trent. Caravaggio had to paint a second, more decorous altarpiece for the chapel (seen in FIG. 23–10), with a nobler Matthew and a more distant angel. The rejected version was snapped up by Roman collector Vincenzo Giustiniani, who actually paid for the replacement in order to acquire the more sensational original. Unfortunately, this first painting was destroyed in the 1945 bombing of Berlin during World War II.

23-11 • Caravaggio **THE CALLING OF ST. MATTHEW**
Contarelli Chapel, church of San Luigi dei Francesi, Rome. 1599–1600. Oil on canvas, 10′7½″ × 11′2″ (3.24 × 3.4 m).

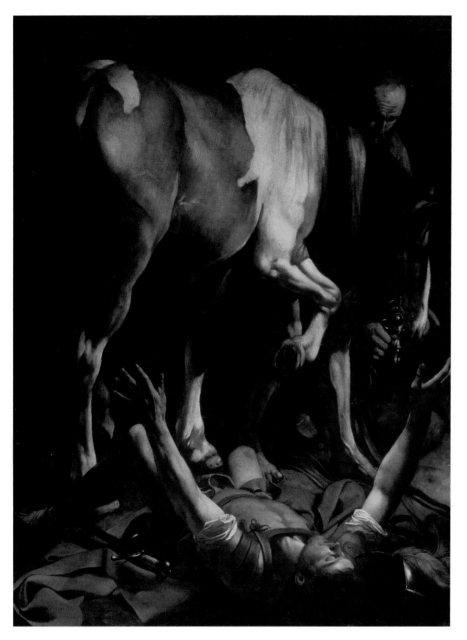

ARTEMISIA GENTILESCHI One of Caravaggio's most brilliant Italian followers was Artemisia Gentileschi (1593–c. 1652/1653), whose international reputation helped spread the Caravaggesque style beyond Rome. Artemisia first studied and worked under her father, Orazio, one of the earliest followers of Caravaggio. In 1616, she moved from Rome to Florence, where she worked for Grand Duke Cosimo II de' Medici and was elected, at the age of 23, to the Florentine Academy of Design.

One of her most famous paintings, and a clear example of her debt to Caravaggio's tenebrism and naturalism, is the painting **JUDITH BEHEADING HOLOFERNES** (**FIG. 23–13**), which she gave to Cosimo II shortly before she left Florence to return to Rome in 1620. The subject is drawn from the biblical book of Judith, which recounts the story of the destructive invasion of Judah by the Assyrian general Holofernes, when the brave and beautiful Jewish widow Judith risked her life to save her people. Using her charm to gain Holofernes' trust, Judith enters his tent with her maidservant while he is drunk and beheads him with his own sword. Gentileschi emphasizes the grisly facts of this heroic act, as the women struggle to subdue the terrified Holofernes while blood spurts wildly from the severing of his jugular. The artist's dramatic spotlighting and a convergence of compositional diagonals rivet our attention on the most sensational aspects of the scene pushed toward us in the foreground. Throughout her life, Gentileschi painted many such images of heroic biblical women, which art historians have interpreted in relation to her own struggle to claim her rightful place in an art world dominated by overpowering men.

Despite the great esteem in which Caravaggio was held by some, especially the younger generation of artists, his violent temper repeatedly got him into trouble. During the last decade of his life, he was frequently arrested, initially for minor offenses such as carrying arms illegally or street brawling. But in May of 1606 he killed a man in a duel fought over a disputed tennis match and had to flee Rome as a fugitive under a death sentence. He supported himself while on the run by painting in Naples, Malta, and Sicily. The Knights of Malta awarded him the cross of their religious and military order in July 1608, but in October he was imprisoned for insulting one of their number, and again he escaped and fled. Caravaggio died on July 18, 1610, just short of his 39th birthday, of a fever contracted during a journey back to Rome where he expected to be pardoned of his capital offense. Caravaggio's unvarnished realism and tenebrism influenced nearly every important European artist of the seventeenth century.

BAROQUE CEILINGS: CORTONA AND GAULLI Theatricality, intricacy, and the opening of space reached an apogee in Baroque ceiling decoration—complex constructions combining architecture, painting, and stucco sculpture. These grand illusionistic projects were carried out on the domes and vaults of churches, civic buildings, palaces, and villas, and went far beyond even Michelangelo's Sistine Chapel ceiling (see FIG. 21–11) or Correggio's dome at Parma (see FIG. 21–22). Baroque ceiling painters sought the drama of an immeasurable heaven that extended into vertiginous zones far beyond the limits of High Renaissance taste. To achieve this, they employed the system of *quadratura* (literally, "squaring" or "gridwork"): an architectural setting painted in meticulous perspective and usually requiring that it be viewed from a specific spot to achieve the desired effect of soaring space. The resulting viewpoint is called *di sotto in sù* ("from below to above"), which we first saw, in a limited fashion, in Mantegna's ceiling in Mantua (see FIG. 20–32).

Because it required such careful calculation, figure painters usually had specialists in *quadratura* paint the architectural frame for them.

Pietro Berrettini (1596–1669), called "Pietro da Cortona" after his hometown, carried the development of the Baroque ceiling away from Classicism into a more strongly unified and illusionistic direction. Trained in Florence and inspired by Veronese's ceiling in the Doge's Palace, which he saw on a trip to Venice in 1637, the artist was commissioned in the early 1630s by the Barberini family of Pope Urban VIII to decorate the ceiling of the audience hall of their Roman palace.

Pietro da Cortona's great fresco **THE GLORIFICATION OF THE PAPACY OF URBAN VIII** became a model for a succession of Baroque illusionistic palace ceilings throughout Europe (**FIG. 23–14**). He structured his mythological scenes around a vault-like skeleton of architecture, painted in *quadratura*, that appears to be attached to the actual cornice of the room. But in contrast

Divine Providence (in gold against an open sky) gestures toward three giant bees surrounded by a huge laurel wreath (both Barberini emblems) carried by Faith, Hope, and Charity. Immortality offers a crown of stars, while other figures present the crossed keys and the triple-tiered crown of the papacy. Around these figures are scenes of Roman gods and goddesses, who demonstrate the pope's wisdom and virtue by triumphing over the vices. So complex was the imagery that a guide gave visitors an explanation, and one member of the household published a pamphlet, still in use today, explaining the painting.

The most spectacular of all illusionistic Baroque ceilings is Giovanni Battista Gaulli's **THE TRIUMPH OF THE NAME OF JESUS AND FALL OF THE DAMNED** (FIG. 23-15), which fills the vault of the Jesuit church Il Gesù (see FIG. 21-40). In the 1560s, Giacomo da Vignola had designed an austere interior for Il Gesù, but when the Jesuits renovated their church a century later, they commissioned a religious allegory to cover the nave's plain ceiling. Gaulli (1639–1709) designed and executed the spectacular illusion between 1672 and 1685, fusing sculpture and painting to eliminate any appearance of architectural division. It is difficult to sort carved three-dimensional figures from the painted imitations, and some paintings are on real panels that extend over the actual architectural frame. Gaulli, who arrived in Rome from Genoa in 1657, had worked in his youth for Bernini, from whom he absorbed a taste for drama and multimedia effects. The elderly Bernini, who worshiped daily at Il Gesù, may well have offered his personal advice to his former assistant, and Gaulli was certainly familiar with other illusionistic paintings in Rome as well, including Pietro da Cortona's Barberini ceiling (see FIG. 23-14).

to Annibale Carracci's neat separations and careful *quadro riportato* framing (see FIG. 23-8), Pietro's figures weave in and out of their setting in active and complex profusion; some rest on the actual cornice, while others float weightlessly against the sky. Instead of Annibale's warm, nearly even light, Pietro's dramatic illumination, with its bursts of brilliance alternating with deep shadows, fuses the ceiling into a dense but unified whole.

The subject is an elaborate allegory of the virtues of the pope. Just below the center of the vault, seated at the top of a pyramid of clouds and figures personifying Time and the Fates,

23-15 • Giovanni Battista Gaulli THE TRIUMPH OF THE NAME OF JESUS AND FALL OF THE DAMNED
Vault of the church of Il Gesù, Rome. 1672–1685. Fresco with stucco figures.

Gaulli's astonishing creation went beyond anything that had preceded it in unifying architecture, sculpture, and painting. Every element is dedicated to creating the illusion that clouds and angels have descended through an opening in the top of the church into the upper reaches of the nave. The extremely foreshortened figures are projected as if seen from below, and the whole composition is focused off-center on the golden aura around the letters IHS, the monogram of Jesus and the insignia of the Jesuits. The subject is, in fact, the Last Judgment, with the elect rising joyfully toward the name of God and the damned plummeting through the ceiling toward the nave floor. The sweeping extension of the work into the nave space, the powerful appeal to the viewer's emotions, and the near-total unity of the multimedia visual effect—all hallmarks of Italian Baroque—were never surpassed.

SPAIN

When the Holy Roman Emperor Charles V abdicated in 1556, he left Spain and its American colonies, as well as the Netherlands, Burgundy, Milan, and the Kingdom of Naples and Sicily to his son Philip II and the Holy Roman Empire (Germany and Austria) to his brother Ferdinand. Ferdinand and the Habsburg emperors who succeeded him ruled their territories from Vienna in Austria, but much of German-speaking Europe remained divided into small units in which local rulers decided on the religion of their territory. Catholicism prevailed in southern and western Germany and in Austria, while the north was Lutheran.

The Spanish Habsburg kings Philip III (r. 1598–1621), Philip IV (r. 1621–1665), and Charles II (r. 1665–1700) reigned over a weakening empire. After repeated local rebellions, Portugal re-established its independence in 1640. The Kingdom of Naples remained in a constant state of unrest. After 80 years of war, the Protestant northern Netherlands—which had formed the United Provinces—gained independence in 1648. Amsterdam grew into one of the wealthiest cities in Europe, and the Dutch Republic became an increasingly serious threat to Spanish trade and colonial possessions. The Catholic southern Netherlands (Flanders) remained under Spanish and then Austrian Habsburg rule.

What had seemed an endless flow of gold and silver from the Americas to Spain diminished, as precious-metal production in Bolivia and Mexico lessened. Agriculture, industry, and trade at home also suffered. As they tried to defend the Roman Catholic Church and their empire on all fronts, the Spanish kings squandered their resources and finally went bankrupt in 1692. Nevertheless, despite the decline of the Habsburgs' Spanish empire, seventeenth-century writers and artists produced some of the greatest Spanish literature and art, and the century is often called the Spanish Golden Age.

PAINTING IN SPAIN'S GOLDEN AGE

The primary influence on Spanish painting in the fifteenth century had been the art of Flanders; in the sixteenth, it had been the art of Florence and Rome. Seventeenth-century Spanish painting, profoundly influenced by Caravaggio's powerfully dramatic art, was characterized by an ecstatic religiosity combined with realistic surface detail that emerges from the deep shadows of tenebrism.

JUAN SÁNCHEZ COTÁN Late in the sixteenth century, Spanish artists developed a significant interest in paintings of artfully arranged objects rendered with intense attention to detail. Juan Sánchez Cotán (1561–1627) was one of the earliest painters of these pure still lifes in Spain. In **STILL LIFE WITH QUINCE, CABBAGE, MELON, AND CUCUMBER** (FIG. 23-16), of about 1602, he contrasts the irregular, curved shapes of the fruits and vegetables with the angular geometry of their setting. His precisely ordered subjects—two of which are suspended from strings—form a long, sagging arc from the upper left to the lower right. The fruits and vegetables appear within a *cantarero* (primitive larder), but it is unclear why they have been arranged in this way. Set in a strong light against impenetrable darkness, this highly artificial arrangement of strikingly lifelike forms suggests not only a fascination with spatial ambiguity, but also a contemplative sensibility and interest in the qualities of objects that look forward to the work of Zurbarán and Velázquez.

JUSEPE DE RIBERA Jusepe (or José) de Ribera (c. 1591–1652) was born in Seville but studied in Rome and settled in Spanish-ruled Naples; in Italy, he was known as "Lo Spagnoletto" ("the Little Spaniard"). He combined the Classical and Caravaggesque styles he had learned in Rome to create a new Neapolitan—and eventually Spanish—style. Ribera became the link extending

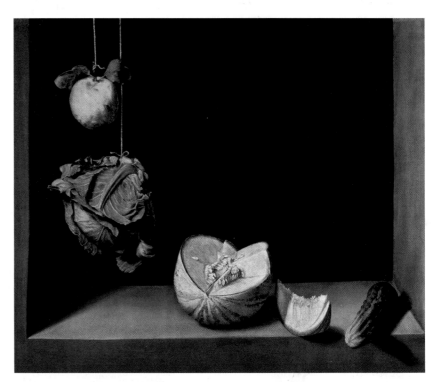

23-16 • Juan Sánchez Cotán STILL LIFE WITH QUINCE, CABBAGE, MELON, AND CUCUMBER
c. 1602. Oil on canvas, 27⅛″ × 33¼″ (68.8 × 84.4 cm). San Diego Museum of Art. Gift of Anne R. and Amy Putnam

compression of the figures into the foreground space heightens our sense of being witness to this scene (see FIG. 23–12).

FRANCISCO DE ZURBARÁN Francisco de Zurbarán (1598–1664) represents another martyrdom, in this case already accomplished, in his 1628 painting of **ST. SERAPION** (FIG. 23–18). Little is known of his early years before 1625, but Zurbarán came under the influence of the Caravaggesque taste prevalent in Seville, the major city in southwestern Spain, while his interest in abstract design has been traced to the heritage of Islamic art in Spain.

Zurbarán primarily worked for the monastic orders. In this painting, he portrays the martyrdom of Serapion, member of the thirteenth-century Mercedarians, a Spanish order founded to rescue the Christian prisoners of the Moors. Following the vows of his order, Serapion sacrificed himself in exchange for Christian captives. The dead man's pallor, his rough hands, and the coarse ropes contrast with the off-white of his creased Mercedarian habit, its folds carefully arranged in a pattern of highlights and varying depths of shadow. The only colors are the red and gold of the insignia. This timelessly immobile composition is like a tragic still life, a study of fabric and flesh become inanimate, silent, and at rest.

23-17 • Jusepe de Ribera MARTYRDOM OF ST. BARTHOLOMEW

1634. Oil on canvas, 41¼″ × 44⅞″ (1.05 × 1.14 m). National Gallery of Art, Washington, DC. Rosenwald Collection (1950.14.744)

from Caravaggio in Italy to the Spanish masters Zurbarán and Velázquez.

During this period, the Church—aiming to draw people back to Catholicism—commissioned portrayals of heroic martyrs who had endured shocking torments as witness to their faith. Ribera's painting of the **MARTYRDOM OF ST. BARTHOLOMEW**, the apostle who was martyred by being skinned alive, captures the horror of the violence to come while emphasizing the saint's spirituality and acceptance (FIG. 23–17). The bound Bartholomew looks heavenward as his executioner tests the sharpness of the knife that he will soon use on his living victim. Ribera has learned the lessons of Caravaggio well, as he highlights the intensely realistic faces with the dramatic light of tenebrism and describes the aging wrinkled flesh in great detail. The

23-18 • Francisco de Zurbarán ST. SERAPION

1628. Oil on canvas, 47½″ × 40¾″ (120.7 × 103.5 cm). Wadsworth Atheneum, Hartford, Connecticut. Ella Gallup Sumner and Mary Catlin Sumner Collection Fund

DIEGO VELÁZQUEZ Diego Rodríguez de Silva y Velázquez (1599–1660), the greatest painter to emerge from the Caravaggesque school of Seville, shared Zurbarán's fascination with objects. He entered Seville's painters' guild in 1617. Like Ribera, he began his career as a tenebrist and naturalist. During his early years, he painted scenes set in taverns, markets, and kitchens, and emphasized still lifes of various foods and kitchen utensils. His early **WATER CARRIER OF SEVILLE** (FIG. 23-19) is a study of surfaces and textures of the splendid ceramic pots that characterized folk art through the centuries. Velázquez was devoted to studying and sketching from life: The man in the painting was a well-known Sevillian waterseller. Like Sánchez Cotán, Velázquez arranged the elements of his paintings with almost mathematical rigor. The objects and figures allow the artist to exhibit his virtuosity in rendering sculptural volumes and describing contrasting textures illuminated by dramatic natural light. Light reflects in different ways off the glazed waterpot at the left and the coarser clay jug in the foreground; it is absorbed by the rough wool and dense velvet of the costumes; it is refracted as it passes through the clear glass held by the man and the waterdrops on the jug's surface.

In 1623, Velázquez moved to Madrid, where he became court painter to the young King Philip IV, a prestigious position that he held until his death in 1660. The opportunity to study paintings in the royal collection, as well as to travel, enabled the development of his distinctive personal style. The Flemish painter Peter Paul Rubens, during a 1628–1629 diplomatic visit to the Spanish court, convinced the king that Velázquez should visit Italy. Velázquez made two trips, the first in 1629–1631 and the second in 1649–1651. He was profoundly influenced by contemporary Italian painting, and on the first trip seems to have taken a special interest in narrative paintings with complex figure compositions.

Velázquez's Italian studies and his growing skill in composition are apparent in both figure and landscape paintings. In **THE SURRENDER AT BREDA** (FIG. 23-20), painted in 1634–1635, Velázquez treats the theme of triumph and conquest in an entirely new way—far removed from traditional gloating military propaganda. Years earlier, in 1625, Ambrosio Spinola, the duke of Alba and the Spanish governor, had defeated the Dutch at Breda. As Velázquez imagined the scene of surrender, the opposing armies stand on a hilltop overlooking a vast valley where the city of Breda burns and soldiers are still deployed. The Dutch commander, Justin of Nassau, hands over the keys of Breda to the victorious Spanish commander. The entire exchange seems extraordinarily gracious, an emblem of a courtly ideal of gentlemanly conduct. The victors stand at attention, holding their densely packed lances upright in a vertical pattern—giving the painting its popular name, "The Lances"—while the defeated Dutch, a motley group, stand out of order, with pikes and banners drooping. In fact, according to reports, no keys were involved and the Dutch were more presentable in appearance than the Spaniards. Velázquez has taken liberties with historical fact to create for his Spanish patron a work of art that rendered the meaning of the surrender, rather than its actual appearance.

Velázquez displays here his compositional virtuosity and his extraordinary gifts as a visual storyteller. A strong diagonal, starting in the sword of the Dutch soldier in the lower left foreground and ending in the checked banner on the

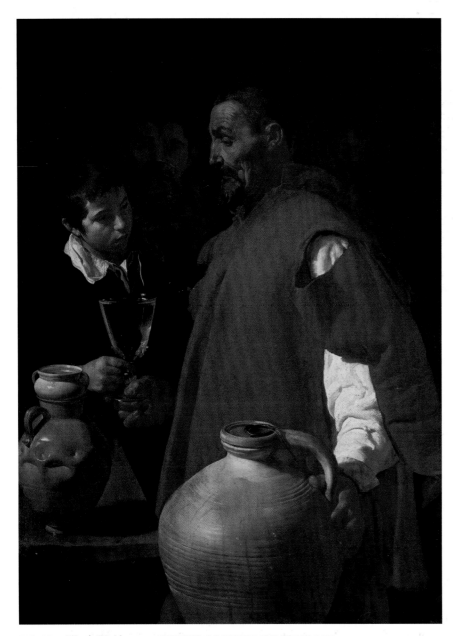

23-19 • Diego Velázquez WATER CARRIER OF SEVILLE
c. 1619. Oil on canvas, 41½″ × 31½″ (105.3 × 80 cm). Victoria & Albert Museum, London.

23–20 • Diego Velázquez THE SURRENDER AT BREDA (THE LANCES)
1634–1635. Oil on canvas, 10'7⅞" × 12'1½" (3.07 × 3.67 m). Museo del Prado, Madrid.

upper right, unites the composition and moves the viewer from the defeated to the victorious soldiers in the direction of the surrender itself. Portraitlike faces, meaningful gestures, and controlled color and texture convince us of the reality of the scene. Across the upper half of the huge canvas, the landscape background is startling. Velázquez painted an entirely imaginary Netherlands in greens and blues worked with flowing, liquid brushstrokes. Luminosity is achieved by laying down a thick layer of lead white and then flowing the layers of color over it. The silvery light forms a background for dramatically silhouetted figures and weapons. Velázquez revealed a breadth and intensity unsurpassed in his century, and became an inspiration to modern artists such as Manet and Picasso.

Perhaps Velázquez's most striking, certainly his most enigmatic work is the enormous multiple portrait, nearly 10½ feet tall and over 9 feet wide, known as **LAS MENINAS (THE MAIDS OF HONOR)** (FIG. **23–21**), painted in 1656, near the end of his life. This painting continues to challenge viewers and stimulate debate

among art historians. Velázquez draws viewers directly into the scene. In one interpretation, the viewer stands in the very space occupied by King Philip and his queen, whose reflections can be seen in the large mirror on the back wall, perhaps a clever reference to Jan van Eyck's *Double Portrait of Giovanni Arnolfini and his Wife* (see FIG. 19–1), which was a part of the Spanish royal collection at this time. Echoing pictorially the claim made in Jan's signature, Velázquez himself is also present, brushes in hand, beside a huge canvas. The central focus, however, is neither the artist nor the royal couple but their brilliantly illuminated 5-year-old daughter, the Infanta (princess) Margarita, who is surrounded by her attendants, most of whom are identifiable portraits.

No consensus exists today on the meaning of this monumental painting. It is a royal portrait; it is also a self-portrait of Velázquez standing at his easel. But fundamentally, *Las Meninas* is a personal statement. Throughout his life, Velázquez had sought respect and acclaim for himself and for the art of painting. Here, dressed as a courtier, the Order of Santiago on his chest (added later) and the

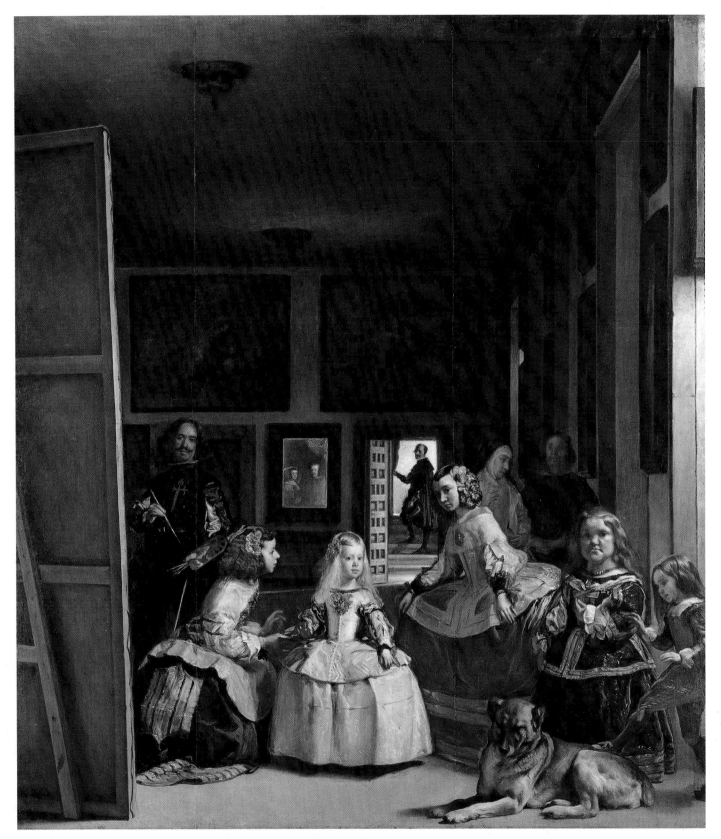

23–21 • Diego Velázquez LAS MENINAS (THE MAIDS OF HONOR)
1656. Oil on canvas, 10′5″ × 9′1½″ (3.18 × 2.76 m). Museo del Prado, Madrid.

The cleaning of *Las Meninas* in 1984 revealed much about Velázquez's methods. He used a minimum of underdrawing, building up his forms with layers of loosely applied paint and finishing off the surfaces with dashing highlights in white, lemon yellow, and pale orange. Rather than using light to model volumes in the time-honored manner, Velázquez tried to depict the optical properties of light reflecting from surfaces. On close inspection his forms dissolve into a maze of individual strokes of paint.

View the Closer Look for *Las Meninas (The Maids of Honor)* on myartslab.com keys of the palace tucked into in his sash, Velázquez proclaims the dignity and importance of painting itself.

BARTOLOMÉ ESTEBAN MURILLO The Madrid of Velázquez was the center of Spanish art. Seville declined after an outbreak of plague in 1649, but it remained a center for trade with the Spanish colonies, where the work of Bartolomé Esteban Murillo (1617–1682) had a profound influence on art and religious iconography. Many patrons wanted images of the Virgin Mary and especially of the Immaculate Conception, the controversial idea that Mary was born free from original sin. Although the Immaculate Conception became Catholic dogma only in 1854, the con-

cept, as well as devotion to Mary, grew during the seventeenth and eighteenth centuries.

Counter-Reformation authorities had provided specific instructions for artists painting the Virgin of the Immaculate Conception: Mary was to be dressed in blue and white, her hands folded in prayer, as she is carried upward by angels, sometimes in large flocks. She may be surrounded by an unearthly light ("clothed in the sun") and may stand on a crescent moon in reference to the woman of the Apocalypse (see FIG. 15–10). Angels often carry palms and symbols of the Virgin, such as a mirror, a fountain, roses, and lilies, and they may vanquish the serpent, Satan. The Church exported to the New World many paintings faithful to these orthodox guidelines by Murillo, Zurbarán, and others. When the indigenous population began to visualize the Christian story (see FIG. 30–46), paintings such as Murillo's **THE IMMACULATE CONCEPTION** (FIG. 23-22) provided prompts for their imaginings.

ARCHITECTURE IN SPAIN

Turning away from the severity displayed in the sixteenth-century El Escorial monastery-palace (see FIG. 22–18), seventeenth-century Spanish architects again embraced the lavish decoration that had characterized their art since the fourteenth century. Profusions of ornament swept back into fashion, first in huge *retablos* (altarpieces), then in portals (main doors often embellished with sculpture), and finally in entire buildings.

THE CATHEDRAL OF SANTIAGO DE COMPOSTELA In the seventeenth century, the role of St. James as patron saint of Spain was challenged by the supporters of St. Teresa of Ávila and then by supporters of St. Michael, St. Joseph, and other popular saints. It became important to the archbishop and other leaders in Santiago de Compostela, where the cathedral of St. James was located, to re-establish their primacy. They reinforced their efforts to revitalize the regular flow of pilgrims to the city, undertaken by Spaniards since the ninth century, and used architecture as part of their campaign.

Renewed interest in pilgrimages to the shrines of saints in the seventeenth century brought an influx of pilgrims, and consequently financial security, to the city and the Church. The cathedral chapter ordered an elaborate façade to be added to the twelfth-century pilgrimage church (FIG. 23-23). A

23-22 • Bartolomé Esteban Murillo **THE IMMACULATE CONCEPTION**
c. 1660–1665. Oil on canvas, 81⅛″ × 56⅝″ (2.06 × 1.44 m). Museo del Prado, Madrid.

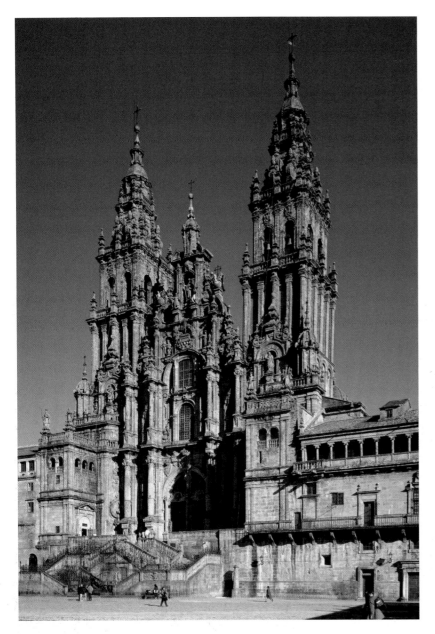

23-23 • WEST FAÇADE, CATHEDRAL OF ST. JAMES, SANTIAGO DE COMPOSTELA, SPAIN
South tower 1667–1680; north tower and central block finished mid 18th century by Fernando de Casas y Nóvoas.

FLANDERS AND THE NETHERLANDS

Led by the nobleman Prince William of Orange, the Netherlands' Protestant northern provinces (present-day Holland) rebelled against Spain in 1568. The seven provinces joined together as the United Provinces in 1579 and began the long struggle for independence, achieved only in the seventeenth century. The king of Spain considered the Dutch heretical rebels, but finally the Dutch prevailed. In 1648, the United Provinces joined emissaries from Spain, the Vatican, the Holy Roman Empire, and France on equal footing in peace negotiations. The resulting Peace of Westphalia recognized the independence of the northern Netherlands.

FLANDERS

After a period of relative autonomy from 1598 to 1621 under Habsburg regents, Flanders, the southern—and predominantly Catholic—part of the Netherlands, returned to direct Spanish rule. Catholic churches were restored and important commissions focused on sacred art. As Antwerp, the capital city and major arts center of the southern Netherlands, gradually recovered from the turmoil of the religious wars, artists of great talent flourished there. Painters like Peter Paul Rubens and Anthony van Dyck established international reputations that brought them important commissions from foreign as well as local patrons.

RUBENS Peter Paul Rubens (1577–1640), whose painting has become synonymous with Flemish Baroque art, was born in Germany, where his father, a Protestant, had fled from his native Antwerp to escape religious persecution. In 1587, after her husband's death, Rubens's mother and her children returned to Antwerp and to Catholicism. Rubens decided in his late teens to become an artist and at age 21 was accepted into the Antwerp painters' guild, a testament to his energy, intelligence, and skill. Shortly thereafter, in 1600, he left for Italy. In Venice, his work came to the attention of the duke of Mantua, who offered him a court post. His activities on behalf of the duke over the next eight years did much to prepare him for the rest of his long and successful career. The duke had him copy famous paintings in collections all over Italy to add to the ducal collection.

Rubens visited every major Italian city, went to Madrid as the duke's emissary, and spent two extended periods in Rome, where he studied the great works of Roman antiquity and the Italian Renaissance. While in Italy, Rubens studied the paintings of two contemporaries, Caravaggio and Annibale Carracci. By 1607

south tower was built in 1667–1680 and then later copied as the north tower.

The last man to serve as architect and director of works at the cathedral, Fernando de Casas y Nóvoas (active 1711–1749), tied the disparate elements together at the west end—towers, portal, stairs—in a grand design focused on a veritable wall of glass, popularly called "The Mirror." His design culminates in a freestanding gable soaring above the roof, visually linking the towers, and framing a statue of St. James. The extreme simplicity of the cloister walls and the archbishop's palace at each side of the portal heightens the dazzling effect of this enormous expanse of glass windows, glittering, jewel-like, in their intricately carved granite frame.

23-24 • Peter Paul Rubens
SELF-PORTRAIT WITH ISABELLA BRANDT
1609–1610. Oil on canvas, 5′9″ × 4′5″ (1.78 × 1.36 m). Alte Pinakothek, Munich.

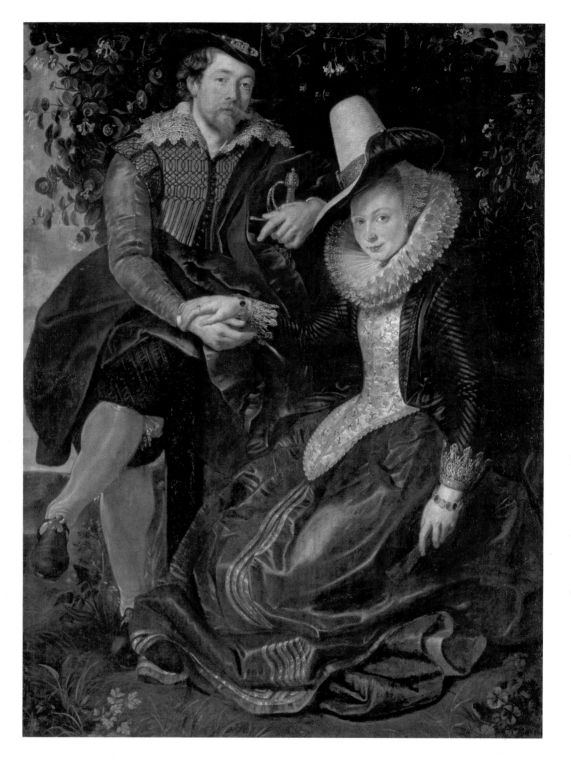

Rubens had persuaded the duke of Mantua to buy the former's *Death of the Virgin* (c. 1601–1602), which had been rejected by Caravaggio's patrons because of its shocking realism.

In 1608, Rubens returned to Antwerp, where in 1609 he accepted a position as court painter to the Habsburg regents of Flanders, Archduke Albert and Princess Isabella Clara Eugenia, the daughter of Philip II. Ten days after that appointment, he married the 18-year-old Isabella Brandt (1596–1626), an alliance that was financially beneficial to the artist, then almost twice the age of his bride. He commemorated the marriage with a spectacular double portrait of himself and his bride seated together in front of a honeysuckle bower that evokes a state of marital bliss (**FIG. 23-24**). The self-confident couple look out to engage viewers directly, and the rich detail of their lavish costumes is described with meticulous precision, foregrounding both the artist's virtuosity and the couple's wealth and sophistication. They join right hands in a traditional gesture of marriage, and the artist slips his foot into the folds of Isabella's flowing red skirt, suggesting a more intimate connection between them. They would have three children before Isabella's untimely death in 1626.

23-25 • Peter Paul Rubens **RUBENS'S HOUSE**
Italianate addition built 1610–1615. Looking toward the garden: house at left, studio at right; house restored and opened as a museum in 1946. From an engraving of 1684. Museum Mayer van den Bergh.

In 1611, Rubens purchased a residence in Antwerp. The original house was large and typically Flemish, but Rubens added a studio in the Italian manner across a courtyard, joining the two buildings by a second-floor gallery over the entrance portal (**FIG. 23-25**). Beyond the courtyard lay the large formal garden, laid out in symmetrical beds. The living room permitted access to a gallery overlooking Rubens's huge studio, a room designed to accommodate large paintings and to house what became virtually a painting factory. The tall, arched windows provided ample light for the single, two-story room, and

23-26 • Peter Paul Rubens **THE RAISING OF THE CROSS**
Made for the Church of St. Walpurga, Antwerp, Belgium. 1610–1611. Oil on panel, center panel 15′1⅞″ × 11′1½″ (4.62 × 3.39 m), each wing 15′1⅞″ × 4′11″ (4.62 × 1.52 m). Now in Cathedral of Our Lady, Antwerp.

23-27 • Peter Paul Rubens HENRY IV RECEIVING THE PORTRAIT OF MARIE DE' MEDICI

1621–1625. Oil on canvas, 12′11⅛″ × 9′8⅛″ (3.94 × 2.95 m). Musée du Louvre, Paris.

📖 **Read** the document related to Peter Paul Rubens on myartslab.com

a large door permitted the assistants to move finished paintings out to their designated owners. Through the gates at one side of the courtyard, one can see the architectural features of the garden.

Rubens's first major commission in Antwerp was a large canvas triptych for the main altar of the church of St. Walpurga, **THE RAISING OF THE CROSS** (**FIG. 23-26**), painted in 1610–1611. He extended the central action and the landscape through all three panels. At the center, Herculean figures strain to haul upright the wooden cross with Jesus already stretched upon it. At the left, the followers of Jesus join in mourning, and at the right, soldiers supervise the execution. The drama and intense emotion of Caravaggio is merged here with the virtuoso technique of Annibale Carracci, but transformed and reinterpreted according to Rubens's own unique ideal of thematic and formal unity. The heroic nude figures, dramatic lighting effects, dynamic diagonal composition, and intense emotions show his debt to Italian art, but the rich

colors and careful description of surface textures reflect his native Flemish tradition.

Rubens's expressive visual language was deemed as appropriate for representing secular rulers as it was for dramatic religious subjects. Moreover, his intelligence, courtly manners, and personal charm made him a valuable and trusted courtier to his royal patrons, who included Philip IV of Spain, Queen Marie de' Medici of France, and Charles I of England. In 1621, Marie de' Medici, who had been regent for her son Louis XIII, asked Rubens to paint the story of her life, to glorify her role in ruling France, and also to commemorate the founding of the new Bourbon royal dynasty. In 24 paintings, Rubens portrayed Marie's life and political career as one continuous triumph overseen by the ancient gods of Greece and Rome.

In the painting depicting the royal engagement (**FIG. 23-27**), Henry IV immediately falls in love with Marie as he gazes at her

A CLOSER LOOK | *Prometheus Bound*

by Peter Paul Rubens and Frans Snyders.
c. 1611–1618. Oil on canvas, 95½″ × 82½″ (2.43 × 2.1 m). Philadelphia Museum of Art.

The struggle between Prometheus and the eagle was interpreted allegorically during the seventeenth century, sometimes as the struggle involved in artistic creativity, or as the heroism involved in enduring suffering of body or soul. Some saw in Prometheus a prototype of the Christ of the Crucifixion, an association furthered here by the placement of the gash on Prometheus' side.

The eagle in this picture was painted by Frans Snyders, a specialist in painting animals and flowers whom Rubens brought in to render the detailed feathers and powerful posture of this bird of prey.

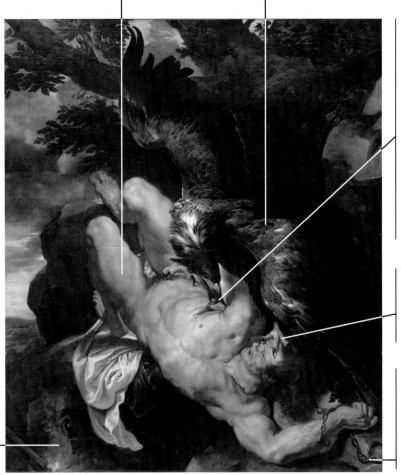

The eagle has pierced Prometheus' side to devour his liver, an action that identifies the subject here. This hero of Greek myth was chained to Mount Caucasus and sentenced to this sensational punishment because, in direct defiance of Zeus' command, he stole fire from Mount Olympus and sneaked it to earth so humankind would no longer be confined to cold and darkness. And since Prometheus' liver regenerated over each night, his fate was to have it plucked out again and again, day after day.

The talons of the eagle are poised to dig into the sensitive areas of the groin and face of the struggling hero to underline for viewers the excruciating nature of his pain.

After the main composition was complete, Rubens added this 17½ inch strip of canvas to the left side of the painting to provide a more expansive space for the dramatic action, allow the inclusion at lower left of the fire that got Prometheus into trouble, and provide the bright light on the horizon that some have interpreted as a touch of optimism to counteract the enduring punishment enacted in the foreground.

These small chains that confine Prometheus to the rock seem hardly adequate to confine the powerfully muscular hero, as Rubens conceives him, leading some to speculate that the artist wanted his incarceration to seem more psychological than physical.

View the Closer Look for *Prometheus Bound* on myartslab.com

portrait, shown to him—at the exact center of the composition—by Cupid and Hymen, the god of marriage. The supreme Roman god Jupiter and his wife Juno look down approvingly from the clouds. A personification of France encourages Henry, outfitted with steel breastplate and silhouetted against a landscape in which the smoke of a battle lingers in the distance, to abandon war for love, as *putti* play below with the rest of his armor. The ripe colors, lavish textures, and dramatic diagonals give sustained visual excitement to these enormous canvases, making them not only important works of art but also political propaganda of the highest order.

To satisfy his clients all over Europe, Rubens employed dozens of assistants, many of whom were, or became, important painters in their own right. Using workshop assistants was standard practice for a major artist, but Rubens was particularly methodical, training or hiring specialists in costumes, still lifes, landscapes, portraiture, and animal painting who together could complete works from his detailed sketches. Some of his most spectacular paintings were collaborations. Frans Snyders (1579–1657), a specialist in painting animals and flowers, was brought in by Rubens to paint the enormous eagle who devours the liver of the mythical hero in **PROMETHEUS BOUND** (see "A Closer Look," above), begun in 1611–12 and perhaps worked on as late as 1618. The dramatic lighting, dynamic composition, and loose, energetic brushwork of this painting—which the artist kept for a while in his own personal collection—was clearly Rubens's own, while the tight and detailed technique of Snyders sets up within the painting a telling representational contrast between the massive predator and its writhing, muscular victim. Among Rubens's other collaborators were his friend and neighbor Jan Brueghel the Elder (1568–1625, son of Pieter Bruegel the Elder, see "Bruegel's Cycle of the Months," page 704) and Anthony van Dyck.

PORTRAITS AND STILL LIFES In addition to collaborating with Rubens, Anthony van Dyck (1599–1641), had an illustrious independent career as a portraitist. Son of an Antwerp silk merchant, he was listed as a pupil of the dean of Antwerp's Guild of St. Luke at age 10. He had his own studio and roster of pupils at age 16 but was not made a member of the guild until 1618, the year after he began his association with Rubens as a specialist in painting heads. The need to blend his work seamlessly with that of Rubens enhanced Van Dyck's technical skill. After a trip to the English court of James I (r. 1603–1625) in 1620, Van Dyck traveled to Italy and worked as a portrait painter for seven years before returning to Antwerp. In 1632, he returned to England as the court painter to Charles I (r. 1625–1649), by whom he was knighted and given a studio, a summer home, and a large salary.

Van Dyck's many portraits of the royal family provide a sympathetic record of their features and demeanor. In **CHARLES I AT THE HUNT** (**FIG. 23-28**), of 1635, Van Dyck was able, by clever manipulation of the setting, to portray the king truthfully and still present him as an imposing figure. Dressed casually for the hunt and standing on a bluff overlooking a distant view (a device used by Rubens to enhance the stature of Henry IV; see FIG. 23-27), Charles, who was in fact very short, appears here taller than his pages and even than his horse, since its head is down and its heavy body is partly off the canvas. The viewer's gaze is diverted from the king's delicate and rather short frame to his pleasant features, framed by his jauntily cocked cavalier's hat and the graceful cascade of his hair. As if in decorous homage, the tree branches bow gracefully toward him, echoing the curving lines of the hat.

Our term, "still life," for paintings of artfully arranged objects on a table, comes from the Dutch *stilleven*, a word coined about 1650. The Antwerp artist Clara Peeters (1594–c. 1657) specialized

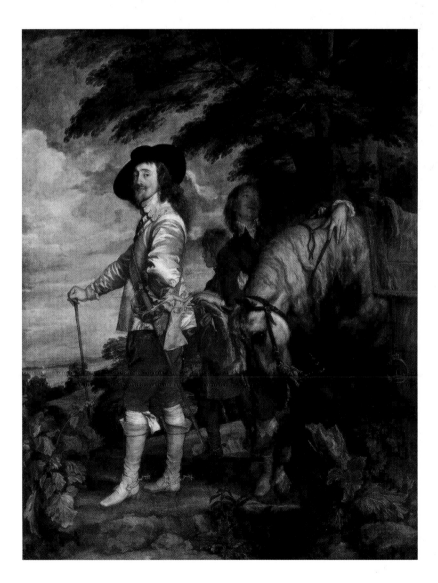

**23-28 • Anthony van Dyck
CHARLES I AT THE HUNT**
1635. Oil on canvas, 8′11″ × 6′11″ (2.75 × 2.14 m). Musée du Louvre, Paris.

23-29 • Clara Peeters STILL LIFE WITH FLOWERS, GOBLET, DRIED FRUIT, AND PRETZELS
1611. Oil on panel, 20½″ × 28¾″ (52 × 73 cm). Museo del Prado, Madrid.

Like many "breakfast pieces," this painting features a pile of pretzels among the elegant tableware. The salty, twisted bread was called *pretzel* (from the Latin *pretiola*, meaning "small reward") because it was invented by German monks to reward children who had learned their prayers. The twisted shapes represented the crossed arms of a child praying.

in still-life tabletop arrangements (see Introduction, "A Closer Look," page xxxiv, FIG. A). She was a precocious young woman whose career seems to have begun before she was 14. Of some 50 paintings now attributed to her (of which more than 30 are signed), many are of the type called "breakfast pieces," showing a table set for a meal of bread and fruit. Peeters was one of the first artists to combine flowers and food in a single painting, as in her **STILL LIFE WITH FLOWERS, GOBLET, DRIED FRUIT, AND PRETZELS** (FIG. 23-29), of 1611. Peeters arranged rich tableware and food against neutral, almost black backgrounds, the better to emphasize the fall of light over the contrasting surface textures. In a display of precious objects that must have appealed to her clients, the luxurious goblet and bowl contrast with simple stoneware and pewter, as do the delicate flowers with the homey pretzels. The pretzels, piled on the pewter tray, are a particularly interesting Baroque element, with their complex multiple curves.

THE DUTCH REPUBLIC

The House of Orange was not notable for its patronage of the arts, but patronage improved significantly under Prince Frederick Henry (r. 1625–1647), and Dutch artists found many other eager patrons among the prosperous middle class in Amsterdam, Leiden, Haarlem, Delft, and Utrecht. The Hague was the capital city and the preferred residence of the House of Orange, but Amsterdam was the true center of power, because of its sea trade and the enterprise of its merchants, who made the city an international commercial center. The Dutch delighted in depictions of themselves and their country—the landscape, cities, and domestic life—not to mention beautiful and interesting objects to be seen in still-life paintings and interior scenes. A well-educated people, the Dutch were also fascinated by history, mythology, the Bible, new scientific discoveries, commercial expansion abroad, and colonial exploration.

23–30 • Hendrick ter Brugghen
ST. SEBASTIAN TENDED BY
ST. IRENE
1625. Oil on canvas, 58¹⁵⁄₁₆″ × 47½″
(149.6 × 120 cm). Allen Memorial
Art Museum, Oberlin College, Ohio.
R.T. Miller Jr. Fund (1953.256)

Visitors to the Netherlands in the seventeenth century noted the popularity of art among merchants and working people. This taste for art stimulated a free market for paintings that functioned like other commodity markets. Artists had to compete to capture the interest of the public by painting on speculation. Specialists in particularly popular types of images were most likely to be financially successful, and what most Dutch patrons wanted were paintings of themselves, their country, their homes, their possessions, and the life around them—characterized by active trade, bustling mercantilism, Protestant religiosity, and jarring class distinctions. The demand for art also gave rise to an active market for the graphic arts, both for original compositions and for copies of paintings, since one copperplate could produce hundreds of impressions, and worn-out plates could be reworked and used again.

THE INFLUENCE OF ITALY Hendrick ter Brugghen (1588–1629) had spent time in Rome, perhaps between 1608 and 1614, where he must have seen Caravaggio's works and became an enthusiastic follower. On his return home, in 1616, Ter Brugghen entered the Utrecht painters' guild, introducing Caravaggio's style into the Netherlands in paintings such as **ST. SEBASTIAN TENDED BY ST. IRENE** (**FIG. 23-30**), and becoming the best known of the Utrecht "Caravaggisti." The sickly gray-green flesh of the nearly dead St. Sebastian, painted in an almost monochromatic palette, contrasts with the brilliant red and gold brocade of what seems to be his crumpled garment. Actually this is the cope of the bishop of Utrecht, which had survived destruction by Protestants and become a symbol of Catholicism in Utrecht. The saint is cast as a heroic figure, his strong, youthful body still bound to the tree. But St. Irene (the patron saint of nurses) delicately removes one of the arrows that pierce him, and her maid reaches to untie his wrists. In a typically Baroque manner, the powerful diagonal created by St. Sebastian's left arm dislodges him from the triangular stability of the group. The immediacy and emotional engagement of the work are enhanced by crowding all the figures into the foreground plane, an effect strengthened by the low horizon line, another aspect of this painting that recalls the work of Caravaggio. The tenebrism and dramatic lighting effects are likewise Caravaggesque, as is the frank realism of the women's faces, with reddened noses and rosy cheeks. Rembrandt, Vermeer, and Rubens all admired Ter Brugghen's painting.

FRANS HALS Frans Hals (c. 1581/1585–1666), the leading painter of Haarlem, developed a style grounded in the Netherlandish love of description and inspired by the Caravaggesque style introduced by artists such as Ter Brugghen. Like Velázquez, he tried to recreate the optical effects of light on the shapes and textures of objects. He painted boldly, with slashing strokes and angular patches of paint. Only when seen at a distance do the colors merge into solid forms over which a flickering light seems to move. In Hals's hands, this seemingly effortless, loose technique suggests the spontaneity of an infectious joy in life. He was known primarily as a portraitist.

Seventeenth-century Dutch portraiture took many forms, ranging from single figures in sparsely furnished settings to allegorical depictions of groups in elaborate costumes surrounded by symbols and attributes. Although the faithful description of facial features and costumes was the most important gauge of a portrait's

success, some painters, like Hals, went beyond likeness to convey a sense of mood or emotion in the sitter. Fundamentally, portraits functioned as social statements of the sitters' status coupled with a clear sense of identity rooted in recognizable faces.

Group portraiture documenting the membership of corporate organizations was a Dutch specialty, and Hals painted some of the greatest examples. These large canvases, filled with many individuals who shared the cost of the commission, challenged painters to present a coherent, interesting composition that nevertheless gave equal attention to each individual portrait. Most artists arranged their sitters in neat rows to depict every face clearly, but in **OFFICERS OF THE HAARLEM MILITIA COMPANY OF ST. ADRIAN** (**FIG. 23-31**) of about 1627, Hals transforms the group portrait into a lively social event. The company, made up of several guard units, was charged with the military protection of Haarlem. Officers came from the upper middle class and held their commissions for three years, whereas the ordinary guards were tradespeople and craftsmakers. Each company was organized like a guild, traditionally under the patronage of a saint, and functioned mainly as a fraternal order, holding archery competitions and taking part in city processions. Hals's composition is based on a strong underlying geometry of diagonal lines—gestures, banners, and sashes—balanced by the stabilizing perpendiculars of table, window, and tall glass. The black suits and hats make the white ruffs and sashes of rose, white, and baby blue even more brilliant.

Although Hals focused his career on portraits of wealthy members of Haarlem's merchant class, he also painted images of eccentric local figures that, although they follow the format of portraiture, functioned as genre paintings by commenting on the

23-31 • Frans Hals
OFFICERS OF THE HAARLEM MILITIA COMPANY OF ST. ADRIAN
c. 1627. Oil on canvas, 6′ × 8′8″ (1.83 × 2.67 m).
Frans Halsmuseum, Haarlem.

23-32 • Frans Hals MALLE BABBE
c. 1630–1633. Oil on canvas, 30⅞″ × 26″ (78.5 × 66.2 cm).
Staatliche Museen, Berlin.

to the same workhouse for the mentally impaired as Hals's own son Pieter, raising the question of whether this lively vignette of pub life was meant as a celebration of local color or as a bracing social commentary.

JUDITH LEYSTER A painting that had long been praised as one of Hals's finest works is actually by Judith Leyster (c. 1609–1660), Hals's contemporary. A cleaning uncovered her distinctive signature, the monogram "JL" with a star, which refers to her surname, meaning "pole star." Leyster's work shows clear echoes of her exposure to the Utrecht painters who had enthusiastically adopted the principal features of Caravaggio's style. Since Leyster signed in 1631 as a witness at the baptism in Haarlem of one of Hals's children, it is assumed they were close; she may also have worked in his shop. She entered Haarlem's Guild of St. Luke in 1633, which allowed her to take pupils into her studio, and her competitive relationship with Frans Hals around that time is made clear by the complaint she lodged against him in 1635 for luring away one of her apprentices.

Leyster is known primarily for informal scenes of daily life, which often carry an underlying moralistic theme. In her lively **SELF-PORTRAIT** of 1635 (**FIG. 23-33**), the artist has interrupted her work to lean back and look at viewers, as if they had just entered the room. Her elegant dress and the fine chair in which

nature of modern life. Among the most striking of these is a painting of the 1630s, portraying a laughing—presumably inebriated—older woman with a large beer tankard in her right hand and a shadowy owl perched on her shoulder, known as **MALLE BABBE** (**FIG. 23-32**). The figure is based on a real individual, a well-known Haarlem barmaid who was eventually confined to a charitable mental institution; the word "Malle" means loony or mad, and the owl was a popular symbol of folly. Hals's painting technique in this character study is looser and more energetic than in most of his formal portraits, where he often restrained his stylistic exuberance to conform to the expectations of his wealthy sitters. Here he felt freer in a painting that may have had personal significance. The historical Malle Babbe was confined

23-33 • Judith Leyster SELF-PORTRAIT
1635. Oil on canvas, 29⅜″ × 25⅝″ (74.6 × 65.1 cm).
National Gallery of Art, Washington, DC.
Gift of Mr. and Mrs. Robert Woods Bliss (1949.6.4)

she sits are symbols of her success as an artist whose popularity was based on the very type of painting in progress on her easel. One critic has suggested that her subject—a man playing a violin—may be a visual pun on the painter with palette and brush. Leyster's understanding of light and texture is truly remarkable. The brushwork she used to depict her own flesh and delicate ruff is more controlled than Hals's loose technique, and forms an interesting contrast to the broad strokes of thick paint she used to create her full, stiff skirt. She further emphasized the difference between her portrait and her painting by executing the image on her easel in lighter tones and softer, looser brushwork. The narrow range of colors sensitively dispersed in the composition and the warm spotlighting are typical of Leyster's mature style.

REMBRANDT VAN RIJN The most important painter working in Amsterdam in the seventeenth century was Rembrandt van Rijn (1606–1669). One of nine children born in Leiden to a miller and his wife, Rembrandt studied under Pieter Lastman (1583–1633), the principal painter in Amsterdam at the time. From Lastman, a history painter who had worked in Rome, Rembrandt absorbed an interest in the naturalism, drama, and tenebrism championed by Caravaggio. By the 1630s, Rembrandt was established in Amsterdam primarily as a portrait painter, although he also painted a wide range of narrative themes and landscapes.

In his first group portrait, **THE ANATOMY LESSON OF DR. NICOLAES TULP** (FIG. 23-34) of 1632, Rembrandt combined his scientific and humanistic interests. Frans Hals had activated the group portrait rather than conceiving it as a simple reproduction of posed figures and faces; Rembrandt transformed it into a charged moment from a life story. Dr. Tulp, head of the surgeons' guild from 1628 to 1653, sits right of center, while a group of fellow physicians gathers around to observe the cadaver and learn from the famed anatomist. Rembrandt built his composition on a sharp diagonal that pierces space from right to left, uniting

23-34 • Rembrandt van Rijn **THE ANATOMY LESSON OF DR. NICOLAES TULP**
1632. Oil on canvas, 5'3¾" × 7'1¼" (1.6 × 2.1 m). Mauritshuis, The Hague.

View the Closer Look for *The Anatomy Lesson of Dr. Nicolaes Tulp* on myartslab.com

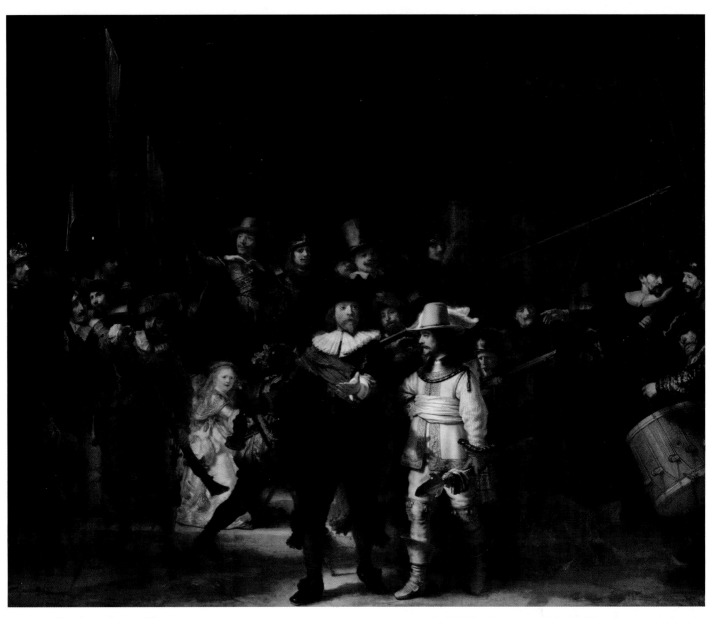

23-35 • Rembrandt van Rijn **THE COMPANY OF CAPTAIN FRANS BANNING COCQ (THE NIGHT WATCH)**
1642. Oil on canvas, 11′11″ × 14′4″ (3.63 × 4.37 m) (cut down from the original size). Rijksmuseum, Amsterdam.

the cadaver on the table, the calculated arrangement of speaker and listeners, and the open book into a dramatic narrative event. Rembrandt makes effective use of Caravaggio's tenebrist technique, as the figures emerge from a dark and undefined ambience, their attentive faces framed by brilliant white ruffs. Radiant light streams down to spotlight the ghostly flesh of the cadaver, drawing our attention to the extended arms of Dr. Tulp, who flexes his own left hand to demonstrate the action of the cadaver's arm muscles that he lifts up with silver forceps. Unseen by the viewers are the illustrations of the huge book, presumably an edition of Andreas Vesalius's study of human anatomy, published in Basel in 1543, which was the first attempt at accurate anatomical illustrations in print. Rembrandt's painting has been seen as an homage to Vesalius and to science, as well as a portrait of the members of the Amsterdam surgeons' guild.

Prolific and popular with his Amsterdam clientele, Rembrandt ran a busy studio, producing works that sold for high prices. The prodigious output of his large workshop and of the many followers who imitated his manner has made it difficult for scholars to define his body of work, and many paintings formerly attributed to Rembrandt have recently been assigned to other artists. Rembrandt's mature work reflected his cosmopolitan city environment, his study of science and nature, and the broadening of his artistic vocabulary by the study of Italian Renaissance art, chiefly from engravings and paintings imported by the busy Amsterdam art market.

In 1642, Rembrandt was one of several artists commissioned by a wealthy civic-guard company to create large group portraits of its members for its new meeting hall. The result, **THE COMPANY OF CAPTAIN FRANS BANNING COCQ** (FIG. **23-35**), carries the idea of a group portrait as a dramatic event even farther. Because

Rembrandt was the first artist to popularize **etching** as a major form of artistic expression. Etching is an intaglio technique, meaning that the design is carved out of the surface of the printing plate. First the metal plate is coated on both sides with an acid-resistant resin that dries hard without being brittle. Then, instead of laboriously cutting the lines of the desired image directly into the plate as in an engraving (see "Woodcuts and Engravings on Metal," page 592) the artist scratches delicately through the resin with a sharp needle to expose the metal. The plate is then immersed in acid, which eats into the metal exposed by the drawn lines. By controlling the time the acid stays on different parts of the plate, the artist can make shallow, fine lines or deep, heavy ones. After the resin coating is removed from the surface of the plate, an impression is taken. If changes need to be made, lines can be "erased" with a sharp metal scraper. Not surprisingly, a complex image with a wide range of tones requires many steps.

Another intaglio technique for registering images with incised lines on a metal plate is called **drypoint**, in which a sharp needle is used to scratch lines directly into the metal. In drypoint, however, the burr (metal pushed up by the drypoint needle) is left in place. Unlike engraving, in which the burr is scraped off, here both the burr and the groove hold the ink. This creates a printed line with a rich black appearance that is impossible to achieve with engraving or etching alone. Unfortunately, drypoint burr is fragile, and no more than a dozen prints can be made before it flattens and loses its character. Rembrandt's earliest prints were entirely etched, but later he added drypoint to develop tonal richness.

Watch a video about the process of intaglio on myartslab.com

a dense layer of grime had darkened and obscured its colors, this painting was once thought to be a nocturnal scene and was therefore called *The Night Watch*. After cleaning and restoration in 1975–1976, it now exhibits a natural golden light that sets afire the palette of rich colors—browns, blues, olive-green, orange, and red—around a central core of lemon yellow in the costume of a lieutenant. To the dramatic group composition, showing a company forming for a parade in an Amsterdam street, Rembrandt added several colorful but seemingly unnecessary figures. While the officers stride purposefully forward, the rest of the men and several mischievous children mill about. The radiant young girl in the left middle ground, carrying a chicken with prominent claws (*klauw* in Dutch), may be a pun on the kind of guns (*klower*) that gave the name (the *Kloveniers*) to the company. Chicken legs with claws also are part of its coat of arms. The complex interactions of the figures and the vivid, individualized likenesses of the militiamen make this one of the greatest group portraits in the Dutch tradition.

In his enthusiasm for printmaking as an important art form with its own aesthetic qualities, Rembrandt was remarkably like Albrecht Dürer (see FIGS. 22-7, 22-8). Beginning in 1627, he focused on etching, which uses acid to inscribe a design on metal

23-36 • Rembrandt van Rijn THREE CROSSES (FIRST STATE)
1653. Drypoint, 15⅛″ × 17¾″ (38.5 × 45 cm). Rijksmuseum, Amsterdam.

23-37 • Rembrandt van Rijn THREE CROSSES (FOURTH STATE)
1653. Drypoint, 15⅛″ × 17¾″ (38.5 × 45 cm). Metropolitan Museum of Art, New York.

plates. About a decade later, he began to experiment with making additions to his compositions in the drypoint technique, in which the artist uses a sharp needle to scratch shallow lines in a plate. Because etching and drypoint allow the artist to work directly on the plate, the style of the finished print can have the relatively free and spontaneous character of a drawing (see "Etching and Drypoint," opposite). In these works Rembrandt alone took charge of the creative process, from the preparation of the plate to its inking and printing, and he constantly experimented with the technique, with methods of inking, and with papers for printing. Rembrandt's prints were sought after, widely collected, and attracted high prices, even in his lifetime.

Rembrandt's deep speculations on the meaning of the life of Christ evolve in a series of prints of the **THREE CROSSES**, that comes down to us in five states, or stages, of the creative and printing process, in this case created exclusively using the drypoint technique. (Only the first and fourth states are reproduced here.) Rembrandt sought to capture the moment described in the Gospels when, during the Crucifixion, darkness covered the Earth and Jesus cried out, "Father, into thy hands I commend my spirit." In the first state (**FIG. 23-36**), the centurion kneels in front of the cross while other terrified people run from the scene. The Virgin Mary and St. John share the light flooding down from heaven. By the fourth state (**FIG. 23-37**), Rembrandt has completely reworked and reinterpreted the theme. As in the first state, the shattered hill of Golgotha dominates the foreground, but now the scene is considerably darker, and some of the people in the first state, including even Mary and Jesus' friends, have almost disappeared. The horseman holding the lance now faces Jesus. The composition has become more compact, the individual elements are simplified, and the emotions are intensified. An oval of light below the base of the cross draws viewers' attention to the figure of Jesus, and the people around him are trapped in mute confrontation. The first state is a detailed rendering of a narrative moment, bustling with detail; the fourth state reduces the event to its mysterious essence. The eternal battles of dark and light, doom and salvation, evil and good—all seem to be waged anew.

As he aged, Rembrandt painted ever more brilliantly, varying textures and paint from the thinnest glazes to thick **impasto** (heavily applied pigments), creating a rich, luminous *chiaroscuro*, ranging from deepest shadow to brilliant highlights in a dazzling display of gold, red, and chestnut-brown. His sensitivity to the human condition is perhaps nowhere more powerfully expressed than in his late self-portraits, which became more searching as he aged. Distilling a lifetime of study and contemplation, he expressed an internalized spirituality new in the history of art. In his **SELF-PORTRAIT** of 1658 (**FIG. 23-38**), the artist assumes a regal pose, at ease, with arms and legs spread, holding a staff as if it were a baton of command. Yet we know that fortune no longer smiled on him; he had declared bankruptcy in 1656, and over the two-year period between that moment and this self-portrait he had sold his private art collection and even his house to cover his debts. It is possible to relate the stress of this situation to the way he represents himself here. A few well-placed brushstrokes suggest the physical tension in the fingers and the weariness of the deep-set eyes. Mercilessly analytical, the portrait depicts the furrowed brow, sagging flesh, and aging face of one who has suffered pitfalls but managed to survive, retaining his dignity.

23-38 • Rembrandt van Rijn SELF-PORTRAIT
1658. Oil on canvas, 52⅝″ × 40⅞″ (133.6 × 103.8 cm). The Frick Collection, New York.

23-39 • Johannes Vermeer VIEW OF DELFT
c. 1662. Oil on canvas, 38½″ × 46¼″ (97.8 × 117.5 cm). Royal Picture Gallery, Mauritshuis, The Hague.

JOHANNES VERMEER One of the most intriguing Dutch artists of this period is Johannes Vermeer (1632–1675), who was also an innkeeper and art dealer. He entered the Delft artists' guild in 1653 and painted only for local patrons. Meticulous in his technique, with a unique and highly structured compositional approach and soft, liquid painting style, Vermeer produced fewer than 40 canvases that can be securely attributed to him. The more these paintings are studied, the more questions arise about the artist's life and his methods. Vermeer's **VIEW OF DELFT** (FIG. **23-39**), for example, is no simple cityscape. Although the artist convinces the viewer of its authenticity, he does not paint a photographic reproduction of the scene; Vermeer moves buildings around to create an ideal composition. He endows the city with a timeless stability by a stress on horizontal lines, the careful placement of buildings, the quiet atmosphere, and the clear, even light that seems to emerge from beneath low-lying clouds. Vermeer may have experimented with the mechanical device known as the **camera obscura** (see Chapter 31, page 968), not as a method of reproducing the image but as another tool in the visual analysis of the composition. The camera obscura would have enhanced optical distortions that led to the "beading" of highlights (seen here on the harbored ships and dark gray architecture), which creates the illusion of brilliant light but does not dissolve the underlying form.

Most of Vermeer's paintings portray enigmatic scenes of women in their homes, alone or with a servant, occupied with some refined activity, such as writing, reading letters, or playing a musical instrument. These are quiet and still interior scenes, gentle in color, asymmetrical but strongly geometric in organization. By creating a contained and consistent architectonic world in which each object adds to the clarity and balance of the composition, Vermeer transports everyday scenes to a level of unearthly perfection. An even, pearly light from a window often gives solidity to the figures and objects in a room. All emotion is subdued, evoking a mood of quiet meditation. Vermeer's brushwork is so controlled that it becomes invisible, except when he paints his characteristic pools of reflected light as tiny, pearl-like droplets of color.

In **WOMAN HOLDING A BALANCE** (FIG. 23-40), studied equilibrium creates a monumental composition and a moment of supreme stillness. The woman contemplates the balance in her right hand, drawing our attention to the act of weighing and judging. Her hand and the scale are central, but directly behind her head, on the wall of the room, is a painting of the Last Judgment, highlighting the figure of Christ the Judge in a gold aureole above her head. The juxtaposition seems to turn Vermeer's genre scene into a metaphor for eternal judgment, a sobering religious reference that may reflect the artist's own position as a Catholic living in a Protestant country. The woman's moment of quiet introspection in front of the gold and pearls displayed on the table before her, shimmering with reflected light from the window, also evokes the *vanitas* theme of the transience of earthly life, allowing the painter to comment on the ephemeral quality of material things.

GENRE SCENES Continuing a long Netherlandish tradition, seventeenth-century genre paintings—generally made for private patrons and depicting scenes of contemporary daily life—were often laden with symbolic references, although their meaning is not always clear to us now. A clean house might indicate a virtuous housewife and mother, while a messy household suggested

laziness and the sin of sloth. Ladies dressing in front of mirrors certainly could be succumbing to vanity, and drinking parties led to overindulgence and lust.

Gerard ter Borch (1617–1681) was one of the most refined of the genre painters. In his painting traditionally known as **THE SUITOR'S VISIT** (**FIG. 23-41**), from about 1658, a well-dressed man bows gracefully to an elegant woman arrayed in white satin, who stands in a sumptuously furnished room in which another woman plays a lute. Another man, in front of a fireplace, turns to observe the newcomer. The painting appears to represent a prosperous gentleman paying a call on a lady of equal social status,

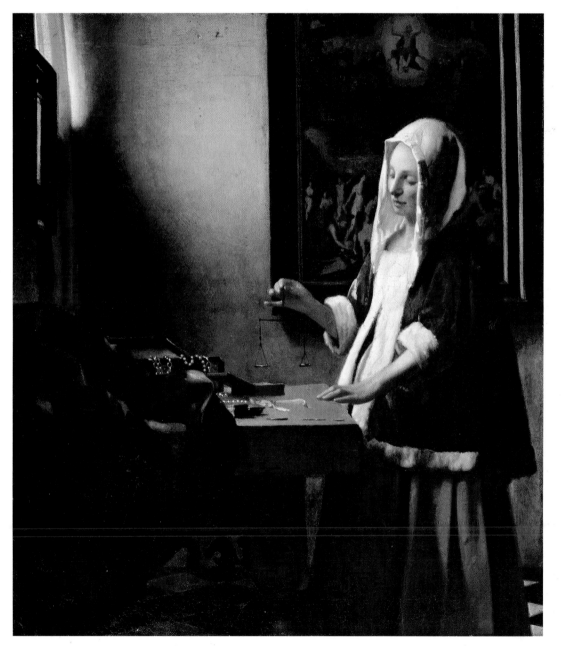

23-40 • Johannes Vermeer WOMAN HOLDING A BALANCE
c. 1664. Oil on canvas, 15⅝″ × 14″ (39.7 × 35.5 cm). National Gallery of Art, Washington, DC.
Widener Collection (1942.9.97)

👁—❙**Watch** a video about Vermeer's *Woman Holding a Balance* on myartslab.com

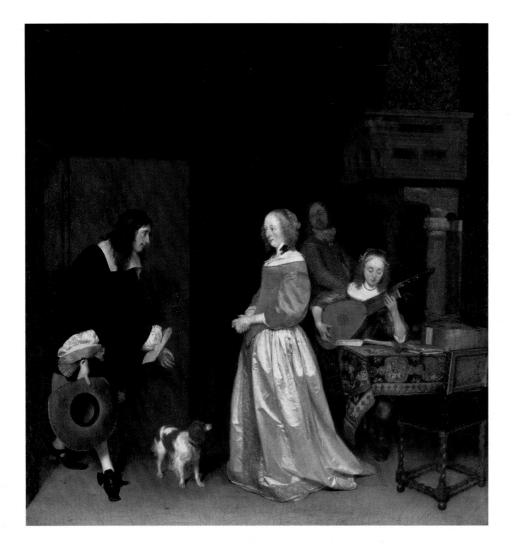

23-41 • Gerard ter Borch THE SUITOR'S VISIT
c. 1658. Oil on canvas, 32½" × 29⅝" (82.6 × 75.3 cm). National Gallery of Art, Washington, DC. Andrew W. Mellon Collection

possibly a courtship scene. The spaniel and the musician seem to be simply part of the scene, but we are already familiar with the dog as a symbol of fidelity, and stringed instruments were said to symbolize, through their tuning, the harmony of souls and thus, possibly, a loving relationship. On the other hand, music making was also associated with sensory pleasure evoked by touch. Ter Borch's exquisite rendering highlights the lace, velvet, and especially the satin of these opulent outfits, potentially symbols of personal excess. If there is a moral lesson, it is presented discreetly and ambiguously.

Another important genre painter is Jan Steen (1626–1679), whose larger brushstrokes contrast with the meticulous treatment of Ter Borch and reveal an artistic affinity with Frans Hals. Steen painted over 800 works but never achieved financial success. Most of his scenes used everyday life to portray moral tales, illustrate proverbs and folk sayings, or make puns to amuse the spectator. Since Steen traveled throughout the Netherlands all his life, and since during the 1670s he was a tavern owner in Leiden, he had many sources of inspiration for the lively human dramas highlighted in his paintings.

Jan Steen's paintings of children are especially remarkable, for he captured not only their childish physiques but also their fleeting moods and expressions with rapid and fluid brushstrokes. A characteristic example is his painting THE FEAST OF ST. NICHOLAS (FIG. 23–42), from the 1660s. Steen's household setting holds none of the intimate order and quiet stillness favored by Vermeer, nor the elegant decorum and guarded interaction portrayed by Ter Borch. This is a scene of noisy commotion within a joyous family get-together, where children react in various ways—disappointment, delight, possessiveness—to the pre-Christmas gifts St. Nicholas has left for them in their shoes. Steen renders the objects scattered in the disordered foreground with meticulous attention to the details of surface texture, but the focus here is the festive atmosphere of a boisterous holiday morning and the folksy figures who delight in the celebration.

Emanuel de Witte (1617–1692) of Rotterdam specialized in architectural interiors, first in Delft in 1640 and then in Amsterdam after settling there permanently in 1652. Although many of his interiors were composites of features from several locations combined in one idealized architectural view, De Witte also painted faithful "portraits" of actual buildings. One of these is his POR-TUGUESE SYNAGOGUE, AMSTERDAM (FIG. 23–43) of 1680. The synagogue shown here, which still stands in Amsterdam, is a rectangular hall divided into one wide central aisle with narrow

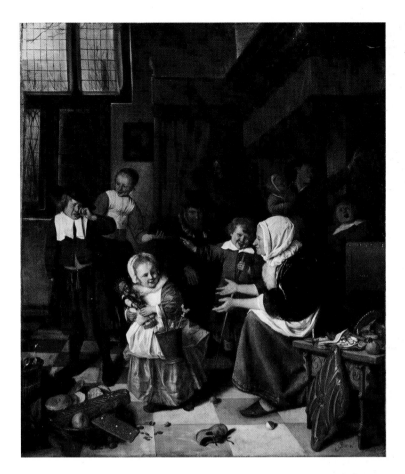

were well-to-do merchants. Fund-raising for a new synagogue began in 1670, and in 1671 Elias Bouman and Daniel Stalpaert began work on the building. With its classical architecture, Brazilian jacaranda-wood furniture, and 26 brass chandeliers, this synagogue was considered one of the most impressive buildings in Amsterdam.

LANDSCAPE The Dutch loved the landscapes and vast skies of their own country, but landscape painters worked in their studios rather than in nature, and they were never afraid to rearrange, add to, or subtract from a scene in order to give their compositions formal organization or a desired mood. Starting in the 1620s, landscape painters generally adhered to a convention in which little color was used beyond browns, grays, and beiges. After 1650, they tended toward more individualistic styles, but nearly all brought a broader range of colors into play. One continuing motif was the emphasis on

side aisles, each covered with a wooden barrel vault resting on lintels supported by columns. De Witte's shift of the viewpoint slightly to one side has created an intriguing spatial composition, and strong contrasts of light and shade add dramatic movement to the simple interior. The elegant couple and the dogs in the foreground provide both a sense of scale for the architecture and some human interest for viewers.

Today, this painting is interesting not only as a work of art, but also as a record of seventeenth-century synagogue architecture, documenting Dutch religious tolerance in an age when European Jews were often persecuted. Expelled from Spain and Portugal from the late fifteenth century on, many Jews had settled in Amsterdam, and their community numbered about 2,300 people, most of whom

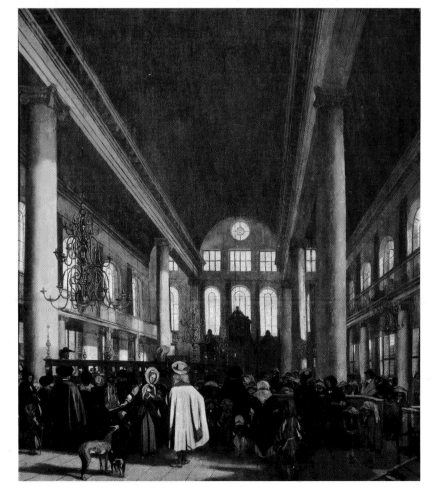

23-43 • Emanuel de Witte PORTUGUESE SYNAGOGUE, AMSTERDAM
1680. Oil on canvas, 43½″ × 39″ (110.5 × 99.1 cm).
Rijksmuseum, Amsterdam.

Architects Daniel Stalpaert and Elias Bouman built the synagogue in 1671–1675.

23-44 • Jacob van Ruisdael VIEW OF HAARLEM FROM THE DUNES AT OVERVEEN
c. 1670. Oil on canvas, 22″ × 24¼″ (55.8 × 62.8 cm). Royal Picture Gallery, Mauritshuis, The Hague.

cloud-filled expanses of sky dominating a relatively narrow horizontal band of earth below.

The Haarlem landscape specialist Jacob van Ruisdael (1628/29–1682), whose popularity drew many pupils to his workshop, was especially adept at both the invention of dramatic compositions and the projection of moods. His **VIEW OF HAARLEM FROM THE DUNES AT OVERVEEN** (**FIG. 23-44**), painted about 1670, celebrates the flatlands outside Haarlem that had been reclaimed from the sea as part of a massive landfill project that the Dutch compared with God's restoration of the Earth after Noah's Flood. Such a religious interpretation may be referenced here in the prominent Gothic church of St. Bavo, looming on the horizon.

There may be other messages as well. While almost three-quarters of this painting is devoted to a rendering of the powerfully cloudy sky, tiny humans can be seen laboring below, caught in the process of spreading white linen across the broad fields to bleach in the sun. This glorification of the industriousness of citizens engaged in one of Haarlem's principal industries must have made the painting particularly appealing to the patriotic local market.

STILL LIFES AND FLOWER PIECES The Dutch were so proud of their still-life painting tradition that they presented a flower painting by Rachel Ruysch to the French queen Marie de' Medici during her state visit to Amsterdam. Like genre paintings,

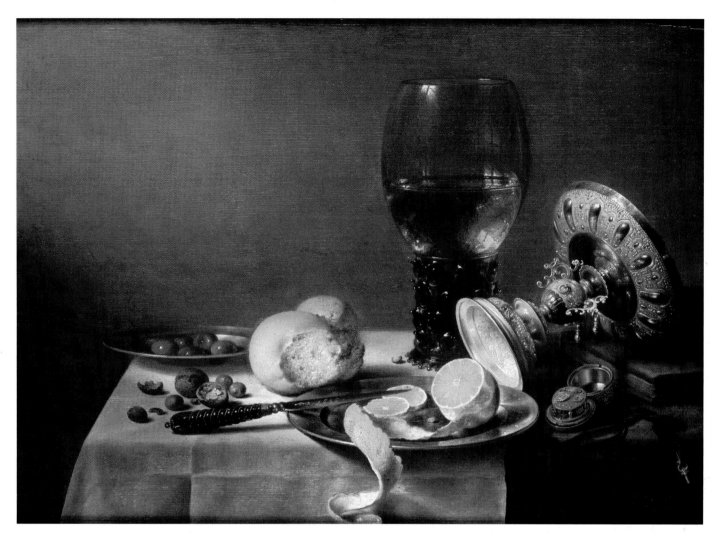

23–45 • Pieter Claesz STILL LIFE WITH TAZZA
1636. Oil on panel, 17⅜″ × 24″ (44 × 61 cm). Royal Cabinet of Paintings Mauritshuis, The Hague.

The heavy round glass is a Roemer, a relatively inexpensive, everyday item, as are the pewter plates. The silver cup (*tazza*) was a typical ornamental piece. Painters owned and shared such valuable props, and this and other showpieces appear in many paintings.

a still-life painting might carry moralizing connotations and commonly had a *vanitas* theme, reminding viewers of the transience of life and material possessions, even art. Yet it can also document and showcase the wealth of its owner.

One of the first Dutch still-life painters was Pieter Claesz (1596/97–1660) of Haarlem, who, like Antwerp artist Clara Peeters (see FIG. 23-29), painted "breakfast pieces," that is, meals of bread, fruits, and nuts. In subtle, nearly monochromatic paintings, such as **STILL LIFE WITH TAZZA** (FIG. 23-45), Claesz seems to give life to inanimate objects. He organizes dishes in diagonal positions to give a strong sense of space—here reinforced by the spiraling strip of lemon peel, foreshortened with the plate into the foreground and reaching toward the viewer's own space—and he renders the maximum contrast of textures within a subtle palette of yellows, browns, greens, and silvery whites. The tilted silver *tazza* contrasts with the half-filled glass, which becomes a towering monumental presence and permits Claesz to display his skill at transparencies

and reflections. Such paintings suggest the prosperity of Claesz's patrons. The food might be simple, but the silver ornamental cup graced the tables of only the wealthy. The meticulously painted timepiece could suggest deeper meanings—it alludes to human technological achievement, but also to the inexorable passage of time and the fleeting nature of human life, thoughts also prompted by the interrupted breakfast, casually placed knife, and toppled tableware.

Still-life paintings in which cut-flower arrangements predominate were referred to simply as "flower pieces." Significant advances were made in botany during the seventeenth century through the application of orderly scientific methods and objective observation (see "Science and the Changing Worldview," page 756). Then, as now, the Dutch were major growers and exporters of flowers, especially the tulips that appear in nearly every flower piece in dozens of exquisite variations. The Dutch tradition of flower painting peaked in the long career of Rachel Ruysch (1664–1750)

From the mid-sixteenth through the seventeenth centuries, new discoveries about the natural world brought a sense of both the grand scale and the microscopic detail of the universe. To publish their theories and research, early scientists learned to draw or depended on artists to draw what they discovered in the world around them. This practice would continue until the invention of photography in the nineteenth century.

Artist and scientist were seldom the same person, but Anna Maria Sibylla Merian (1647–1717) contributed to botany and entomology both as a researcher and as an artist. German by birth and Dutch by training, Merian was once described by a Dutch contemporary as a painter of worms, flies, mosquitoes, spiders, "and other filth." In 1699, the city of Amsterdam subsidized Merian's research on plants and insects in the Dutch colony of Surinam in South America, where she spent two years exploring the jungle and recording insects. On her return to the Dutch Republic, she published the results of her research as **THE METAMORPHOSIS OF THE INSECTS OF SURINAM**, illustrated with 72 large plates engraved after her watercolors (**FIG. 23–46**). For all her meticulous scientific accuracy, Merian carefully arranged her depictions of exotic insects and elegant fruits and flowers into skillful and harmonious compositions.

But interest in scientific exploration was not limited to the Netherlands. The writings of philosophers Francis Bacon (1561–1626) in England and René Descartes (1596–1650) in France helped establish a new scientific method of studying the world by insisting on scrupulous objectivity and logical reasoning. Bacon argued that the facts be established from observation and tested by controlled experiments. Descartes, who was also a mathematician, argued for the deductive method of reasoning, in which conclusions were arrived at logically from basic premises.

In 1543, the Polish scholar Nicolaus Copernicus (1473–1543) published *On the Revolutions of the Heavenly Spheres*, which contradicted the long-held view that the Earth is the center of the universe (the Ptolemaic theory) by arguing instead that it and the other planets revolve around the sun. The Church put Copernicus's work on its *Index of Prohibited Books* in 1616, but Johannes Kepler (1571–1630) continued demonstrating that the planets revolve around the sun in elliptical orbits. Galileo Galilei (1564–1642), an astronomer, mathematician, and physicist, developed the telescope as a tool for observing the heavens and provided further confirmation of Copernican theory but since the Church prohibited its teaching, Galileo was tried for heresy by the Inquisition and forced to recant his views.

The new seventeenth-century science turned to the study of the very small as well as to the vast reaches of space. This included the development of the microscope by the Dutch lens-maker and amateur scientist Anton van Leeuwenhoek (1632–1723). Leeuwenhoek perfected grinding techniques and increased the power of his lenses far beyond what was required for a simple magnifying glass. Ultimately, he was able to study the inner workings of plants and animals and even see micro-organisms.

23-46 • Anna Maria Sibylla Merian PLATE 9 FROM THE METAMORPHOSIS OF THE INSECTS OF SURINAM
1719. Hand-colored engraving, 18⅞″ × 13″ (47.9 × 33 cm). National Museum of Women in the Arts, Washington, DC. Gift of Wallace and Wilhelmina Holladay Collection, funds contributed by Mr. and Mrs. George G. Anderman and an anonymous donor (1976.56)

of Amsterdam. Her flower pieces were highly prized for their sensitive, free-form arrangements and their unusual and beautiful color harmonies. During her 70-year career, she became one of the most sought-after and highest-paid still-life painters in Europe—her paintings brought in twice what Rembrandt's did.

In her **FLOWER STILL LIFE** (**FIG. 23–47**), painted shortly after the end of the century, Ruysch placed the container at the center of the canvas's width, then created an asymmetrical floral arrangement of pale oranges, pinks, and yellows rising from lower left to top right of the picture, offset by the strong diagonal of the tabletop. To further balance the painting, she placed highlighted blossoms and leaves on the dark left half of the canvas and silhouetted them against the light wall area on the right. Ruysch often emphasized the beauty of curving flower stems and enlivened her

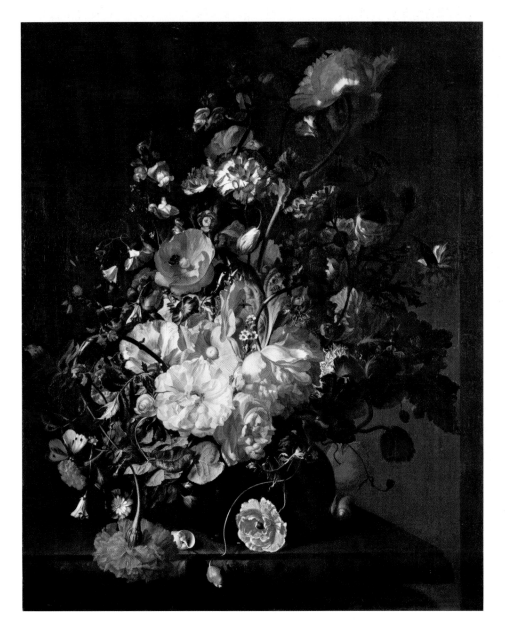

23-47 • Rachel Ruysch FLOWER STILL LIFE
After 1700. Oil on canvas, 30″ × 24″ (76.2 × 61 cm). The Toledo Museum of Art, Ohio. Purchased with funds from the Libbey Endowment. Gift of Edward Drummond Libbey (1956.57)

(regency 1610–1617; see FIG. **23-27**), as regent for her 9-year-old son, Louis XIII (r. 1610–1643). When Louis came of age, the brilliant and unscrupulous Cardinal Richelieu became chief minister and set about increasing the power of the crown at the expense of the French nobility. The death of Louis XIII again left France with a child king, the 5-year-old Louis XIV (r. 1643–1715). His mother, Anne of Austria, became regent, with the assistance of another powerful minister, Cardinal Mazarin. At Mazarin's death in 1661, Louis XIV began his long personal reign, assisted by yet another able minister, Jean-Baptiste Colbert.

An absolute monarch whose reign was the longest in European history, Louis XIV made the French court the envy of every ruler in Europe. He became known as *le Roi Soleil* ("the Sun King") and was sometimes glorified in art through identification with the Classical sun god, Apollo. In a 1701 portrait by court painter Hyacinthe Rigaud (1659–1743), the richly costumed **LOUIS XIV** is framed by a lavish, billowing curtain (**FIG. 23-48**). Proudly showing off his elegant legs, the 63-year-old monarch poses in a blue robe of state, trimmed with gold *fleurs-de-lis* and lined with white ermine. He wears the high-heeled shoes he devised to compensate for his shortness. Despite his pompous pose and magnificent surroundings, the directness of the king's gaze and the frankness of his aging face make him appear surprisingly human.

The arts, like everything else, came under royal control. In 1635, Cardinal Richelieu had founded the French Royal Academy, directing the members to compile a definitive dictionary and grammar of the French language. In 1648, the Royal Academy

compositions with interesting additions, such as casually placed pieces of fruit or insects, in this case a large gray moth (lower left) and two snail shells.

Flower painting was almost never a straightforward depiction of actual fresh flowers. Instead, artists made color sketches of fresh examples of each type of flower and studied scientifically accurate color illustrations in botanical publications. In the studio, using their sketches and notebooks, they would compose bouquets of perfect specimens of a variety of flowers that could never be found blooming at the same time. The short life of flowers was a poignant reminder of the fleeting nature of beauty and of human life.

FRANCE

Early seventeenth-century France was marked by almost continuous foreign and civil wars. The assassination of King Henry IV in 1610 left France in the hands of the queen, Marie de' Medici

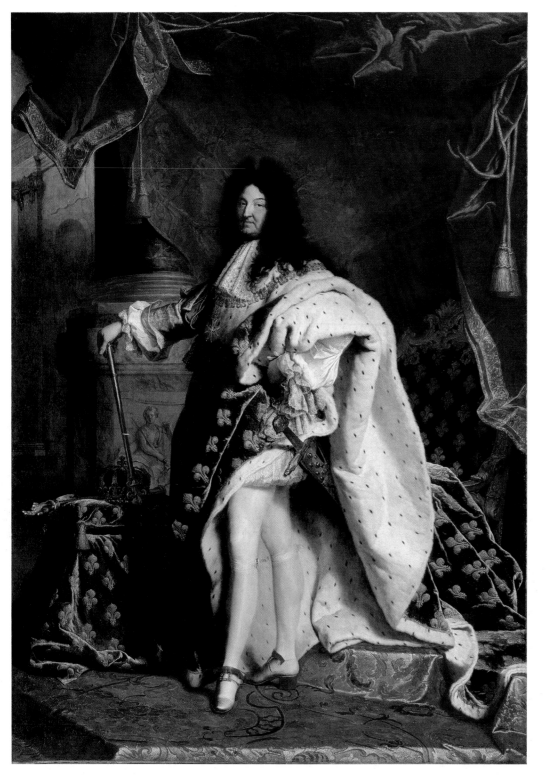

**23-48 • Hyacinthe Rigaud
LOUIS XIV**
1701. Oil on canvas, 9'2" × 7'10¾" (2.19 × 2.4 m). Musée du Louvre, Paris.

Louis XIV had ordered this portrait as a gift for his grandson, the future Philip V of Spain (r. 1700–1746), but when Rigaud finished the painting, Louis liked it too much to give it away and only three years later ordered a copy from Rigaud to give to his grandson. The request for copies of royal portraits was not unusual since the aristocratic families of Europe were linked through marriage. Paintings made appropriate gifts and at the same time memorialized important political alliances by recording them in visual form.

View the Closer Look for *Louis XIV* on myartslab.com

of Painting and Sculpture was founded, which, as reorganized by Colbert in 1663, maintained strict control over the arts (see "Grading the Old Masters," page 763). Although it was not the first European arts academy, none before it had exerted such dictatorial authority—an authority that lasted in France until the late nineteenth century. Membership of the academy assured an artist of royal and civic commissions and financial success, but many talented artists did well outside it.

ARCHITECTURE AND ITS DECORATION AT VERSAILLES

French architecture developed along Classical lines in the second half of the seventeenth century under the influence of François Mansart (1598–1666) and Louis Le Vau (1612–1670). When the Royal Academy of Architecture was founded in 1671, its members developed guidelines for architectural design based on the belief that mathematics was the true basis of beauty. Their chief sources for ideal models were the books of Vitruvius and Palladio.

In 1668, Louis XIV began to enlarge the small château built by Louis XIII at Versailles, not far from Paris. Louis moved to the palace in 1682 and eventually required his court to live in Versailles; 5,000 aristocrats lived in the palace itself, together with 14,000 servants and military staff members. The town had another 30,000 residents, most of whom were royal employees. The designers of the palace and park complex at Versailles were Le Vau, Charles Le Brun (1619–1690), who oversaw the interior decoration, and André Le Nôtre (1613–1700), who planned the gardens (see "Garden Design," page 761). For both political and sentimental reasons, the old château was left standing, and the new building went up around it. This project consisted of two phases: the first additions by Le Vau, begun in 1668; and an enlargement completed after Le Vau's death by his successor, Jules Hardouin-Mansart (1646–1708), from 1670 to 1685.

Hardouin-Mansart was responsible for the addition of the long lateral wings and the renovation of Le Vau's central block on the garden side to match these wings (**FIG. 23-49**). The three-story façade has a lightly rusticated ground floor, a main floor lined with enormous arched windows separated by Ionic columns or pilasters, an attic level whose rectangular windows are also flanked by pilasters, and a flat, terraced roof. The overall design is a sensitive balance of horizontals and verticals relieved by a restrained overlay of regularly spaced projecting blocks with open, colonnaded porches.

In his renovation of Le Vau's center-block façade, Hardouin-Mansart enclosed the previously open gallery on the main level, creating the famed **HALL OF MIRRORS** (**FIG. 23-50**), which is about 240 feet (73 meters) long and 47 feet (13 meters) high. He achieved architectural symmetry and a sense of both splendor and expansiveness by lining the interior wall with Venetian glass mirrors, matching in size and shape the arched windows in the opposing wall. Mirrors were small and extremely expensive in the seventeenth century, and these huge walls of reflective glass were created by fitting 18-inch panels together. They reflect the natural light from the windows and give the impression of an even larger space; at night, the reflections of flickering candles must have turned the mirrored gallery into a shimmering tableau in which the king and courtiers saw themselves as they promenaded.

Inspired by Carracci's Farnese ceiling (see **FIG. 23-8**), Le Brun decorated the vaulted ceiling with paintings on canvas (more stable in the damp northern climate) glorifying the reign and military triumphs of Louis XIV, accompanied by Classical gods. In 1642, Le Brun had studied in Italy, where he came under the influence

23-49 • Louis Le Vau and Jules Hardouin-Mansart GARDEN FAÇADE OF THE PALACE OF VERSAILLES
1678–1685. Foreground: Jean-Baptiste Tuby *Neptune*.

Watch a video about Versailles on myartslab.com

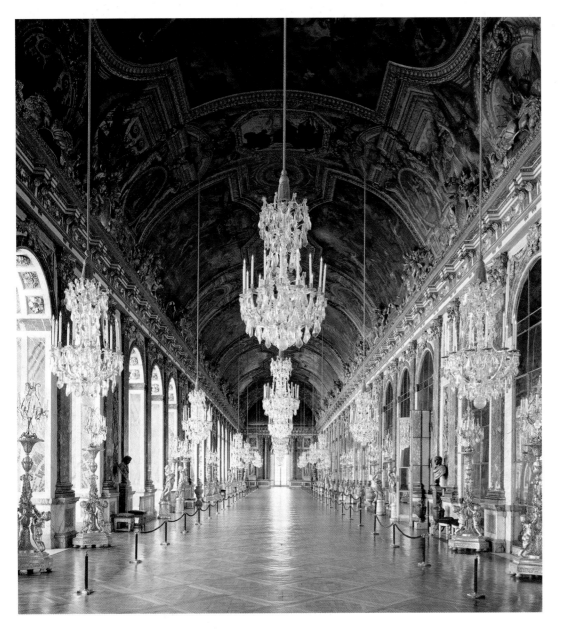

23-50 • Jules Hardouin-Mansart and Charles Le Brun HALL OF MIRRORS, PALACE OF VERSAILLES Begun 1678. Length approx. 240′ (73 m).

In the seventeenth century, mirrors and clear window glass were enormously expensive. To furnish the Hall of Mirrors, hundreds of glass panels of manageable size had to be assembled into the proper shape and attached to one another with glazing bars, which became part of the decorative pattern of the vast room.

of the Classical style of his compatriot Nicolas Poussin. As "first painter to the king" and director of the Royal Academy of Painting and Sculpture, Le Brun controlled art education and patronage from 1661/63 until his death in 1690. He tempered the warmly exuberant Baroque ceilings he had seen in Rome with Poussin's cool Classicism. The underlying theme for his design and decoration of Versailles was the glorification of the king as Apollo the sun god, with whom Louis identified. Louis XIV thought of the duties of kingship, including its pageantry, as a solemn performance, so it is most appropriate that Rigaud's portrait presents him on a raised, stagelike platform, with a theatrical curtain (see FIG. 23-48). Versailles became the splendid stage on which the king played the principal role in the grandiose drama of state.

PAINTING

Sixteenth-century French Mannerism began to give way in the 1620s to Classicism and the impact of Caravaggio, especially his tenebrism and compression of large-scale figures into the foreground. As the century progressed, the control of the Royal Academy and its encouragement of studies of the Classics and the surviving antiquities in Rome, guided French painting toward the Classicism propounded by Le Brun.

CARAVAGGIO'S INFLUENCE: GEORGES DE LA TOUR AND THE LE NAIN BROTHERS One of Caravaggio's most important followers in France, Georges de La Tour (1593–1652) received major royal and ducal commissions and became court painter to Louis XIII in 1639. La Tour may have traveled to Italy in 1614–1616, and in the 1620s he almost certainly visited the Netherlands, where Caravaggio's style was having an impact (see FIG. 23-30). Like Caravaggio, La Tour filled the foreground of his compositions with imposing figures, but in place of Caravaggio's focus on descriptive detail, La Tour's work revels in the dramatic effects of lighting, usually from sources within the paintings

Wealthy and aristocratic French landowners commissioned garden designers to transform their large properties into gardens extending over many acres. The challenge for garden designers was to unify diverse elements—buildings, pools, monuments, plantings, natural land formations—into a coherent whole. At Versailles, André Le Nôtre imposed order upon the vast expanses of palace gardens and park by using broad, straight avenues radiating from a series of round focal points (**FIG. 23–51**). He succeeded so thoroughly that his plan inspired generations of urban designers as well as landscape architects.

In Le Nôtre's hands, the palace terrain became an extraordinary work of art and a visual delight for its inhabitants. Neatly contained expanses of lawn and broad, straight vistas seemed to stretch to the horizon, while the formal gardens became an exercise in precise geometry. The gardens at Versailles are classically harmonious in their symmetrical, geometric design but Baroque in their vast size and extension into the surrounding countryside, where the gardens thickened into woods cut by straight avenues.

The most formal gardens lay nearest the palace, and plantings became progressively less elaborate and larger in scale as their distance from the palace increased. Broad, intersecting paths separated reflecting pools and planting beds, which are called embroidered **parterres** for their colorful patterns of flowers outlined with trimmed hedges. After the formal zone of parterres came lawns, large fountains on terraces, and trees planted in thickets to conceal features such as an open-air ballroom and a colonnade. Statues carved by at least 70 sculptors also adorned the park. A mile-long canal, crossed by a second canal nearly as large, marked the main axis of the garden. Fourteen waterwheels brought the water from the river to supply the canals and the park's 1,400 fountains. Only the fountains near the palace played all day; the others were turned on only when the king approached.

At the north of the secondary canal, a smaller pavilion-palace, the Trianon, was built in 1669. To satisfy the king's love of flowers year-round, the gardens of the Trianon were bedded out with blooming plants from the south, shipped in by the French navy. Even in midwinter, the king and his guests could stroll through a summer garden. The head gardener is said to have had nearly 2 million flowerpots at his disposal. In the eighteenth century, Louis XV added greenhouses and a botanical garden. The facilities of the fruit and vegetable garden that supplied the palace in 1677–1683 today house the National School of Horticulture.

23-51 • Louis Le Vau and André Le Nôtre PLAN OF THE GARDENS OF THE PALACE OF VERSAILLES Versailles, France. c. 1661–1785.

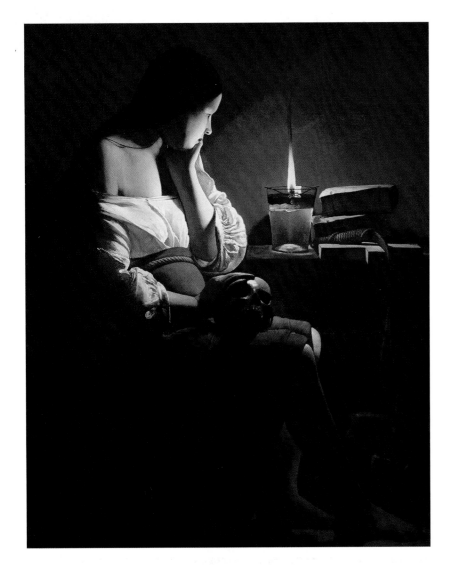

23-52 • Georges de La Tour MARY MAGDALEN WITH THE SMOKING FLAME

c. 1640. Oil on canvas, 46¼″ × 36⅛″ (117 × 91.8 cm). Los Angeles County Museum of Art. Gift of the Ahmanson Foundation (M. 77.73)

themselves. Often, it seems, light is his real subject (see Introduction, "A Closer Look," page xxx FIG. B).

La Tour painted many images of Mary Magdalen. In **MARY MAGDALEN WITH THE SMOKING FLAME** (FIG. 23-52), as in many of his other paintings, the light emanates from an internal source, in this case the flame from an oil lamp. Its warm glow gently brushes over hand and skull—symbol of mortality—to establish the foreground. The compression of the figure into the front of the pictorial space lends a sense of intimacy to the saint's relationship with viewers, although the Magdalen is completely unaware of our presence. Light not only unifies the painting; its controlled character creates its somber mood. Mary Magdalen has put aside her rich clothing and jewels to meditate on the frailty and vanity of human life. Even the flickering light that rivets our attention on her meditative face and gesture is of limited duration.

This same feeling of timelessness, and a comparable interest in effects of light, characterize the

23-53 • Louis or Antoine Le Nain **A PEASANT FAMILY IN AN INTERIOR**

c. 1640. Oil on canvas, 44½″ × 62½″ (1.13 × 1.59 m). Musée du Louvre, Paris.

The members of the French Royal Academy of Painting and Sculpture considered ancient Classical art to be the standard by which contemporary art should be judged. By the 1680s, however, younger artists of the academy began to argue that modern art might equal, or might even surpass, the art of the ancients—a radical thought that sparked controversy.

A debate arose over the relative merits of drawing and color in painting. The conservatives argued that drawing was superior to color because drawing appealed to the mind while color appealed to the senses. They saw Nicolas Poussin as embodying perfectly the Classical principles of subject and design. But the young artists who admired the vivid colors of Titian, Veronese, and Rubens claimed that painting should deceive the eye, and since color achieves this deception more convincingly than drawing, application of color should be valued over drawing. Adherents of the two positions were called poussinistes (in honor of Poussin) and rubénistes (for Rubens).

The portrait painter and critic Roger de Piles (1635–1709) took up the cause of the rubénistes in a series of pamphlets. In The Principles of Painting, de Piles evaluated the most important painters on a scale of 0 to 20 in four categories. He gave no score higher than 72 (18 in each category), since no mortal artist could achieve perfection. Caravaggio received a 0 in expression and a 6 in drawing, while Michelangelo and Leonardo both got a 4 in color and Rembrandt a 6 in drawing.

Most of the painters examined here do not do very well. Raphael and Rubens get 65 points (A on our grading scale), Van Dyck comes close with 55 (C+). Poussin and Titian earn 53 and 51 (solid Cs), while Rembrandt slips by with 50 (C–). Leonardo da Vinci gets 49 (D), and Michelangelo and Dürer with 37 and Caravaggio with 28 are resounding failures in de Piles's view. Tastes change. Someday our own ideas may seem just as misguided as those of the academicians.

---

paintings of the Le Nain brothers, Antoine (c. 1588–1648), Louis (c. 1593–1648), and Mathieu (1607–1677). Although all three were working in Paris by about 1630 and were founding members of the Royal Academy of Painting and Sculpture in 1648, little else is known about their lives and careers. Because they collaborated closely with each other, art historians have only recently begun to sort out their individual styles. They are best known for their painting of genre scenes in which French peasants pause from honest labor for quiet family diversions. **A PEASANT FAMILY IN AN INTERIOR** (FIG. 23-53) of about 1640, probably by Louis Le Nain, is the largest, and one of the most lyrical, of these noble scenes of peasant life. Three generations of this family are gathered around a table. The adults acknowledge our presence—a spotlighted woman at left even seems to offer us some wine—whereas the children remain lost in their dreams or focused on their play. The casualness of costume and deportment is underlined by the foreground clutter of pets and kitchen equipment. It is only after we survey the frieze of figures illuminated around the table that the painting reveals one of its most extraordinary passages—a boy in the left background, warming himself in front of a fireplace and represented only as a dark silhouette from behind, edged by the soft golden firelight. Why the brothers chose to paint these peasant families, and who bought their paintings, are questions still unresolved.

THE CLASSICAL LANDSCAPE: POUSSIN AND CLAUDE LORRAIN French painters Nicolas Poussin (1594–1665) and Claude Gellée (called "Claude Lorrain" or simply "Claude," 1600–1682) pursued their careers in Italy although they usually worked for French patrons. They perfected the French ideal of the "Classical" landscape and profoundly influenced painters for the next two centuries. We refer to Poussin and Claude as Classicists because they organized natural elements and figures into gently illuminated, idealized compositions. Both were influenced by Annibale Carracci and to some extent by Venetian painting, yet each evolved an unmistakably personal style that conveyed an entirely different mood from that of their sources and from each other.

Nicolas Poussin was born in Normandy but settled in Paris, where his initial career as a painter was unremarkable. He arrived in Rome, and the Barberini family became his foremost patrons. Bernini considered Poussin one of the greatest painters in Rome, and others clearly agreed. In 1639, Giovanni Maria Roscioli, secretary to Pope Urban VIII, commissioned from Poussin two large paintings showing the evangelists John and Matthew composing their texts within expansive landscapes dotted with Classical buildings and antique ruins (FIGS. 23-54, 23-55). The paintings were completed by October 1640, just before Poussin left for two years in Paris to work for Louis XIII. Perhaps they were the first installment of a set of four evangelists within landscapes, but only these two had been painted when the patron died in 1644.

These paintings epitomize and are among the earliest examples of a new style of rigorously ordered and highly idealized Classical landscapes with figures—an artistic theme and format created by Poussin that would have a long history in European painting. Although individually composed to create an ordered whole on its own, the paintings were designed as a pair. The large clumps of trees at the outside edges form "bookends" that bring lateral closure to the broad panorama that stretches across both canvases. Their unity is emphasized by the evangelists' postures, turned inward toward each other, and solidified at the lower inside corners where huge blocks of Classical masonry converge from both pictures as coordinated remains of the same ruined monument. A consistent perspective progression in both pictures moves

23-54 • Nicolas Poussin LANDSCAPE WITH ST. MATTHEW AND THE ANGEL
1639–1640. Oil on canvas, 39″ × 53⅛″ (99 × 135 cm). Staatliche Museen, Berlin.

from the picture plane back into the distance through a clearly defined foreground, middle ground, and background, illuminated by an even light with gentle shadows and highlights. In the middle distance, behind St. John, are a ruined temple and an obelisk; the round building in the distant city is Hadrian's Tomb, which Poussin knew from Rome. Precisely placed trees, hills, mountains, water, and even clouds take on a solidity of form that seems almost as structural as this architecture. The subject of Poussin's paintings is not the writing evangelists but the balance and order of nature.

When Claude Lorrain went to Rome in 1613, he first studied with Agostino Tassi, an assistant of Guercino and a specialist in architectural painting. Claude, however, preferred landscape. He sketched outdoors for days at a time, then returned to his studio to compose paintings. Claude was fascinated with light, and his works are often studies of the effect of the rising or setting sun on colors and the atmosphere. A favorite and much-imitated device was to place one or two large objects in the foreground—a tree, building, a figural group, or hill—past which the viewer's eye enters the scene and proceeds, often by diagonal paths, into the distance.

Claude used this compositional device to great effect in paintings such as **A PASTORAL LANDSCAPE** of the late 1640s (**FIG. 23-56**). Instead of balancing symmetrically placed elements in a statement of stable order, Claude leads his viewers actively into the painting in a continuing, zigzagging fashion. A conversing couple frames the composition at the right. Their gestures and the ambling of the cows they are tending lead our attention toward the left on a slightly rising diagonal, where a bridge and the traveler moving across it establish a middle ground. Across the bridge into the distance is a city, setting up a contrast between the warm, soft contours of the pastoral right foreground and the misty angularity of the fortified walls and blocks composing the distant fortress. More distant still are the hazy outlines of hills that seem to take this space into infinity. The picture evokes a city dweller's nostalgia and longing for the simpler and more sensuous life of the country, and it is easy to imagine the foreground shepherd extolling to his companion the superior virtues of their own life in contrast to that in the city, toward which he gestures to underline his point.

**23-55 • Nicolas Poussin
LANDSCAPE WITH ST.
JOHN ON PATMOS**

1640. Oil on canvas, 39½″ ×
53⅝″ (100.3 × 136.4 cm). The Art
Institute of Chicago. A.A. Munger
Collection (1930.500)

Read the document
related to Nicolas Poussin
on myartslab.com

**23-56 • Claude Lorrain
A PASTORAL LANDSCAPE**

c. 1648. Oil on copper, 15½″
× 21″ (39.3 × 53.3 cm). Yale
University Art Gallery, New Haven,
Connecticut. Leonard C. Hanna, Jr.,
B.A. 1913, Fund (1959.47)

23-57 • Inigo Jones BANQUETING HOUSE, WHITEHALL PALACE
London. 1619–1622.

ENGLAND

England and Scotland were joined in 1603 with the ascent to the English throne of James VI of Scotland, who reigned over Great Britain as James I (r. 1603–1625). James increased royal patronage of British artists, especially in literature and architecture. William Shakespeare wrote *Macbeth*, featuring the king's legendary ancestor Banquo, in tribute to the new royal family, and the play was performed at court in December 1606.

Although James's son Charles I was an important collector and patron of painting, religious and political tensions that erupted into civil war cost Charles his throne and his life in 1649. A succession of republican and monarchical rulers who alternately supported Protestantism or Catholicism followed, until the Catholic king James II was deposed in the Glorious Revolution of 1689 by his Protestant son-in-law and daughter, William and Mary. After Mary's death in 1694, William (the Dutch great-grandson of William of Orange, who had led the Netherlands' independence movement) ruled on his own until his death in 1702. He was succeeded by Mary's sister, Anne (r. 1702–1714).

ARCHITECTURE

In sculpture and painting, the English court favored foreign artists. The field of architecture, however, was dominated in the seventeenth century by the Englishmen Inigo Jones, Christopher Wren, and Nicholas Hawksmoor. They replaced the country's long-lived Gothic style with Classicism.

INIGO JONES In the early seventeenth century, Inigo Jones (1573–1652) introduced his version of Renaissance Classicism—based on the style of Italian architect Andrea Palladio—into England. Jones had studied Palladio's work in Venice, and he filled his copy of Palladio's *Four Books of Architecture*—still preserved—with notes. Appointed surveyor-general in 1615, Jones was commissioned to design the Queen's House in Greenwich and the Banqueting House for the royal palace of Whitehall.

The **BANQUETING HOUSE** (**FIG. 23-57**), built in 1619–1622 to replace an earlier hall destroyed by fire, was used for court ceremonies and entertainments such as the popular masques—stylized dramas combining theater, music, and dance in spectacles by a balcony, with antechambers at each end. Ionic columns and pilasters suggest a colonnade but do not impinge on the ideal, double-cube space, which measures 55 feet in width by 110 feet in length by 55 feet in height. In 1630, Charles I commissioned Peter Paul Rubens—who was in England on a peace mission—to decorate the ceiling. Jones had divided the flat ceiling into nine compartments, for which Rubens painted canvases glorifying the reign of James I. Installed in 1635, the central oval shows the triumph of the Stuart dynasty with the king carried to heaven on clouds of glory. The large rectangular panel beyond it depicts the birth of the new nation, flanked by allegorical paintings of heroic strength and virtue overcoming vice. In the long paintings alongside the oval, *putti* holding the fruits of the earth symbolize the peace and prosperity of England and Scotland under Stuart rule. So proud was Charles of the result that, rather than allow the smoke of candles and torches to harm the ceiling decoration, he moved evening entertainments to an adjacent pavilion.

performed by professional actors, courtiers, and even members of the royal family itself. The west front, shown here, consisting of what appears to be two upper stories with superimposed Ionic and Composite orders raised over a plain basement level, exemplifies the understated elegance of Jones's interpretation of Palladian design. Pilasters flank the end bays, and engaged columns subtly emphasize the three bays at the center, a disposition repeated in the balustrade along the roofline. A rhythmic effect results from varying window treatments—triangular and segmental (semicircular) pediments on the first level, cornices with volute (scroll-form) brackets on the second. The sculpted garlands just below the roofline add an unexpected decorative touch.

Although the exterior suggests two stories, the interior of the Banqueting House (**FIG. 23-58**) is actually one large hall divided

CHRISTOPHER WREN After Jones's death, English architecture was dominated by Christopher Wren (1632–1723) who began his professional career in 1659 as a professor of astronomy. For Wren, architecture was a sideline until 1665, when he traveled to France to further his education. While there, he met with French architects and with Bernini, who was in Paris to consult on designs for the Louvre. Wren returned to England with architecture books, engravings, and a greatly increased admiration for French Classical Baroque design. In 1669, he was made surveyor-general, the position once held by Inigo Jones, and in 1673, he was knighted.

After the Great Fire of 1666 destroyed large parts of central London, Wren was continuously involved in rebuilding the city, including more than 50 churches. His major project from 1675

23-59 • Christopher Wren FAÇADE OF ST. PAUL'S CATHEDRAL, LONDON
Designed 1673, built 1675–1710.

Read the document related to Christopher Wren on myartslab.com

to 1710, was the rebuilding of **ST. PAUL'S CATHEDRAL** (**FIGS. 23-59, 23-60**). Attempts to salvage the burned-out Gothic church on the site failed, and a new cathedral was needed. Wren's famous second design for St. Paul's (which survives in the so-called "Great Model" of 1672–1673) was for a centrally planned building with a great dome in the manner of Bramante's original plan for St.

Peter's. This was rejected, but Wren ultimately succeeded both in reconciling Reformation tastes for a basilica and the unity inherent in the use of a dome. St. Paul's has a long nave and equally long sanctuary articulated by small, domed bays. Semicircular, colonnaded porticos open into short transepts that compress themselves against the crossing, where the dome rises 633 feet

23-60 • SCHEMATIC DRAWING OF ST. PAUL'S CATHEDRAL

from ground level. Wren's dome has an interior masonry vault with an oculus and an exterior sheathing of lead-covered wood, but also has a brick cone rising from the inner oculus to support a tall lantern. The ingenuity of the design and engineering remind us that Wren had been a mathematician and professor of astronomy at Oxford. The columns surrounding the drum on the exterior recall Bramante's Tempietto in Rome (see FIG. 21-19), although Wren never went to Italy and knew Italian architecture only from books.

On the façade of St. Paul's (see FIG. 23-59), two levels of paired Corinthian columns support a carved pediment. The deep-set porticos and columned pavilions atop the towers create dramatic areas of light and shadow. Not only the huge size of the cathedral, but also its triumphant verticality, complexity of form, and *chiaroscuro* effects, make it a major monument of English architecture. Wren recognized the importance of the building. On the simple marble slab that forms his tomb in the crypt of the cathedral, he had engraved: "If you want to see his memorial, look around you."

THINK ABOUT IT

23.1 Discuss how Bernini and Caravaggio established the Baroque style in sculpture and painting respectively. Locate the defining traits of the period style in at least one work from the chapter by each of these artists.

23.2 Discuss the development of portraiture, still life, and genre painting in the Dutch Republic during the seventeenth century. What accounts for the increased importance of these subjects at this time?

23.3 Choose two paintings of monarchs in this chapter and explain how the artists who painted them embodied the ruler's prestige and power. Are the strategies of these painters different from those employed by painters of powerful people in the sixteenth century?

23.4 Determine how Poussin's landscapes depart from other stylistic currents at the time. What is meant by the term "Classicism" in relation to Poussin's style? Comment on its importance for the future of French art.

CROSSCURRENTS

Ch. 16
Closer Look,
page 483

FIG. 23–15

These two works visualize the same religious theme—the Last Judgment. But they are placed in different locations within their buildings, engaging different audiences in distinct ways. How do these works represent the cultural goals and stylistic systems of their time and place? Do they have anything other than their subject in common?

✓—Study and review on myartslab.com

Arctic
Ocean

Pacific
Ocean

Arctic
Ocean

Arctic Ocean

RUSSIA

JAPAN

N. KOREA
S. KOREA

TAIWAN

MONGOLIA

CHINA

PHILIPPINES

VIETNAM

BRUNEI

MALAYSIA

INDONESIA

EAST TIMOR

VANUATU

NEW
CALEDONIA

FIJI

NEW
ZEALAND

SOLOMON
ISLANDS

PAPUA
NEW
GUINEA

AUSTRALIA

ANTARCTICA

KAZAKHSTAN

UZBEKISTAN

KYRGYZSTAN

TAJIKISTAN

TURKMENISTAN

AFGHANISTAN

PAKISTAN

NEPAL

BHUTAN

BANGLADESH

MYANMAR

LAOS

THAILAND

CAMBODIA

SRI LANKA

SINGAPORE

INDIA

Indian
Ocean

GEORGIA

ARMENIA

TURKEY

CYPRUS

AZERBAIJAN

IRAN

IRAQ

KUWAIT

SYRIA

LEBANON

ISRAEL

JORDAN

QATAR

U.A.E.

BAHRAIN

SAUDI
ARABIA

OMAN

YEMEN

DJIBOUTI

EGYPT

ERITREA

SUDAN

ETHIOPIA

SOMALIA

UGANDA

KENYA

RWANDA

BURUNDI

TANZANIA

MALAWI

MADAGASCAR

MAURITIUS

MOZAMBIQUE

SWAZILAND

LESOTHO

ZIMBABWE

ZAMBIA

BOTSWANA

NAMIBIA

ANGOLA

DEM. REP.
OF CONGO

CENTRAL
AFRICAN
REP.

CHAD

LIBYA

TUNISIA

ALGERIA

NIGER

MALI

NIGERIA

BENIN

BURKINA
FASO

GUINEA

SIERRA
LEONE

LIBERIA

IVORY COAST

GHANA

TOGO

CAMEROON

EQUATORIAL GUINEA

GABON

CONGO REP.

SOUTH
AFRICA

MAURITANIA

SENEGAL

GAMBIA

GUINEA-
BISSAU

MOROCCO

WESTERN
SAHARA

see inset

ICELAND

GREENLAND
(Denmark)

Atlantic
Ocean

BELIZE

MEXICO

GUATEMALA

HONDURAS

EL SALVADOR

NICARAGUA

COSTA RICA

PANAMA

CUBA

HAITI

JAMAICA

DOMINICAN REPUBLIC

PUERTO RICO

VENEZUELA

COLOMBIA

ECUADOR

GUYANA

SURINAME

FRENCH
GUIANA

PERU

BOLIVIA

BRAZIL

PARAGUAY

URUGUAY

ARGENTINA

CHILE

UNITED
STATES

CANADA

U.S.

Pacific
Ocean

TAHITI

ANTARCTICA

N

2000 km
2000 miles

FINLAND

RUSSIA

ESTONIA

LATVIA

LITHUANIA

RUSSIA

BELARUS

UKRAINE

MOLDOVA

ROMANIA

BULGARIA

TURKEY

Black Sea

GREECE

ALBANIA

MACEDONIA

SERBIA
AND
MONTENEGRO

BOSNIA-
HERZEGOVINA

CROATIA

SLOVENIA

HUNGARY

AUSTRIA

SLOVAK
REP.

CZECH
REP.

POLAND

GERMANY

SWITZ.

ITALY

FRANCE

LUXEMBOURG

BELGIUM

THE
NETHERLANDS

UNITED
KINGDOM

IRELAND

NORWAY

SWEDEN

DENMARK

Baltic
Sea

North
Sea

Atlantic
Ocean

Mediterranean Sea

SPAIN

PORTUGAL

N

400 km
400 miles

Glossary

abacus (p. 108) The flat slab at the top of a **capital**, directly under the **entablature**.

abbey church (p. 239) An abbey is a monastic religious community headed by an abbot or abbess. An abbey church often has an especially large **choir** to provide space for the monks or nuns.

absolute dating (p. 12) A method, especially in archaeology, of assigning a precise historical date at which, or span of years during which, an object was made. Based on known and recorded events in the region, as well as technically extracted physical evidence (such as carbon-14 disintegration). See also **radiometric dating**, **relative dating**.

abstract (p. 7) Of art that does not attempt to describe the appearance of visible forms but rather to transform them into stylized patterns or to alter them in conformity to ideals.

academy (p. 926) An institution established for the training of artists. Academies date from the Renaissance and after; they were particularly powerful, state-run institutions in the seventeenth and eighteenth centuries. In general, academies replaced **guilds** as the venues where students learned the craft of art and were educated in art theory. Academies helped the recognition of artists as trained specialists, rather than craftsmakers, and promoted their social status. An academician is an academy-trained artist.

acanthus (p. 110) A Mediterranean plant whose leaves are reproduced in Classical architectural ornament used on **molding**s, **frieze**s, and **capital**s.

acroterion (*pl.* **acroteria**) (p. 110) An ornament at the corner or peak of a roof.

Action painting (p. 1074) Using broad gestures to drip or pour paint onto a pictorial surface. Associated with mid-twentieth-century American Abstract Expressionists, such as Jackson Pollock.

adobe (p. 399) Sun-baked blocks made of clay mixed with straw. Also: buildings made with this material.

aedicula (p. 609) A decorative architectural frame, usually found around a niche, door, or window. An aedicula is made up of a **pediment** and **entablature** supported by **columns** or **pilasters**.

aerial perspective (p. 626) See under **perspective**.

agora (p. 137) An open space in a Greek town used as a central gathering place or market. Compare **forum**.

aisle (p. 225) Passage or open corridor of a church, hall, or other building that parallels the main space, usually on both sides, and is delineated by a row, or **arcade**, of **columns** or **piers**. Called side aisles when they flank the **nave** of a church.

akropolis (p. 128) The citadel of an ancient Greek city, located at its highest point and housing temples, a treasury, and sometimes a royal palace. The most famous is the Akropolis in Athens.

album (p. 796) A book consisting of a series of paintings or prints (album leaves) mounted into book form.

allegory (p. 627) In a work of art, an image (or images) that symbolizes an idea, concept, or principle, often moral or religious.

alloy (p. 23) A mixture of metals; different metals melted together.

altarpiece (p. xxxiv) A painted or carved panel or ensemble of panels placed at the back of or behind and above an altar. Contains religious imagery (often specific to the place of worship for which it was made) that viewers can look at during liturgical ceremonies (especially the **Eucharist**) or personal devotions.

amalaka (p. 302) In Hindu architecture, the circular or square-shaped element on top of a spire (*shikhara*), often crowned with a **finial**, symbolizing the cosmos.

ambulatory (p. 224) The passage (walkway) around the **apse** in a church, especially a **basilica**, or around the central space in a **central-plan building**.

amphora (*pl.* **amphorae**) (p. 101) An ancient Greek or Roman jar for storing oil or wine, with an egg-shaped body and two curved handles.

animal style or **interlace** (p. 433) Decoration made of interwoven animals or serpents, often found in early medieval Northern European art.

ankh (p. 51) A looped cross signifying life, used by ancient Egyptians.

appropriation (p. xxii) The practice of some Postmodern artists of adopting images in their entirety from other works of art or from visual culture for use in their own art. The act of recontextualizing the appropriated image allows the artist to critique both it and the time and place in which it was created.

apse (p. 192) A large semicircular or polygonal (and usually **vaulted**) recess on an end wall of a building. In a Christian church, it often contains the altar. "Apsidal" is the adjective describing the condition of having such a space.

arabesque (p. 267) European term for a type of linear surface decoration based on foliage and calligraphic forms, thought by Europeans to be typical of Islamic art and usually characterized by flowing lines and swirling shapes.

arcade (p. 170) A series of **arch**es, carried by **column**s or **pier**s and supporting a common wall or **lintel**. In a **blind arcade**, the arches and supports are **engaged** and have a purely decorative function.

arch (p. 95) In architecture, a curved structural element that spans an open space. Built from wedge-shaped stone blocks called **voussoirs** placed together and held at the top by a trapezoidal **keystone**. It forms an effective space-spanning and weight-bearing unit, but requires **buttress**es at each side to contain the outward **thrust** caused by the weight of the structure. *Corbeled arch*: an arch or **vault** formed by **courses** of stones, each of which projects beyond the lower course until the space is enclosed; usually finished with a **capstone**. *Horseshoe arch*: an arch of more than a half-circle; typical of western Islamic architecture. *Round arch*: an arch that displaces most of its weight, or downward thrust along its curving sides, transmitting that weight to adjacent supporting uprights (door or window **jamb**s, **columns**, or **pier**s). *Ogival arch*: a sharply pointed arch created by S-curves. *Relieving arch*: an arch built into a heavy wall just above a **post-and-lintel** structure (such as a gate, door, or window) to help support the wall above by transferring the load to the side walls. *Transverse arch*: an arch that connects the wall **piers** on both sides of an interior space, up and over a stone **vault**.

Archaic smile (p. 114) The curved lips of an ancient Greek statues in the period c. 600–480 BCE, usually interpreted as a way of animating facial features.

architrave (p. 107) The bottom element in an **entablature**, beneath the **frieze** and the **cornice**.

archivolt (p. 478) A band of **molding** framing an **arch**, or a series of stone blocks that form an arch resting directly on flanking **columns** or **piers**.

ashlar (p. 99) A highly finished, precisely cut block of stone. When laid in even **courses**, ashlar masonry creates a uniform face with fine joints. Often used as a facing on the visible exterior of a building, especially as a veneer for the **façade**. Also called **dressed stone**.

assemblage (p. 1026) Artwork created by gathering and manipulating two- and/or three-dimensional found objects.

astragal (p. 110) A thin convex decorative **molding**, often found on a Classical **entablature** and usually decorated with a continuous row of beadlike circles.

atelier (p. 946) The studio or workshop of a master artist or craftsmaker, often including junior associates and apprentices.

atmospheric perspective (p. 183) See under **perspective**.

atrial cross (p. 943) A cross placed in the **atrium** of a church. In Colonial America, used to mark a gathering and teaching place.

atrium (p. 158) An unroofed interior courtyard or room in a Roman house, sometimes having a pool or garden, sometimes surrounded by **columns**. Also: the open courtyard in front of a Christian church; or an entrance area in modern architecture.

automatism (p. 1057) A technique in which artists abandon the usual intellectual control over their brushes or pencils to allow the subconscious to create the artwork without rational interference.

avant-garde (p. 972) Term derived from the French military word meaning "before the group," or "vanguard." Avant-garde denotes those artists or concepts of a strikingly new, experimental, or radical nature for their time.

axis (p. xxvi) In pictures, an implied line around which elements are composed or arranged. In buildings, a dominant line around which parts of the structure are organized and along which human movement or attention is concentrated.

axis mundi (p. 300) A concept of an "axis of the world," which marks sacred sites and denotes a link between the human and celestial realms. For example, in Buddhist art, the axis mundi can be marked by monumental free-standing decorative pillars.

baldachin (p. 472) A canopy (whether suspended from the ceiling, projecting from a wall, or supported by columns) placed over an honorific or sacred space such as a throne or church altar.

bar tracery (p. 510) See under **tracery**.

barbarian (p. 149) A term used by the ancient Greeks and Romans to label all foreigners outside their cultural orbit (e.g., Celts, Goths, Vikings). The word derives from an imitation of what the "barblings" of their language sounded like to those who could not understand it.

barrel vault (p. 187) See under **vault**.

bas-relief (p. 325) Another term for low relief ("bas" is the French word for "low"). See under **relief sculpture**.

basilica (p. 191) A large rectangular building. Often built with a **clerestory**, side **aisles** separated from the center **nave** by **colonnades**, and an **apse** at one or both ends. Originally Roman centers for administration, later adapted to Christian church use.

bay (p. 170) A unit of space defined by architectural elements such as **columns**, **piers**, and walls.

beehive tomb (p. 98) A **corbel-vaulted** tomb, conical in shape like a beehive, and covered by an earthen mound.

Benday dots (p. 1095) In modern printing and typesetting, the individual dots that, together with many others, make up lettering and images. Often machine- or computer-generated, the dots are very small and closely spaced to give the effect of density and richness of tone.

bilum (p. 865) Netted bags made mainly by women throughout the central highlands of New Guinea. The bags can be used for everyday purposes or even to carry the bones of the recently deceased as a sign of mourning.

biomorphic (p. 1058) Denoting the biologically or organically inspired shapes and forms that were routinely included in abstracted Modern art in the early twentieth century.

black-figure (p. 105) A technique of ancient Greek **ceramic** decoration in which black figures are painted on a red clay ground. Compare **red-figure**.

blackware (p. 855) A **ceramic** technique that produces pottery with a primarily black surface with **matte** and glossy patterns on the surface.

blind arcade (p. 780) See under **arcade**.

bodhisattva (p. 311) In Buddhism, a being who has attained enlightenment but chooses to remain in this world in order to help others advance spiritually. Also defined as a potential Buddha.

Book of Hours (p. 549) A prayer book for private use, containing a calendar, services for the canonical hours, and sometimes special prayers.

boss (p. 556) A decorative knoblike element that can be found in many places, e.g. at the intersection of a Gothic **rib vault** or as a buttonlike projection on metalwork.

bracket, bracketing (p. 341) An architectural element that projects from a wall to support a horizontal part of a building, such as beams or the eaves of a roof.

buon fresco (p. 87) See under **fresco**.

burin (p. 592) A metal instrument used in **engraving** to cut lines into the metal plate. The sharp end of the burin is trimmed to give a diamond-shaped cutting point, while the other end is finished with a wooden handle that fits into the engraver's palm.

buttress, buttressing (p. 170) A projecting support built against an external wall, usually to counteract the lateral **thrust** of a **vault** or **arch** within. In Gothic church architecture, a **flying buttress** is an arched bridge above the **aisle** roof that extends from the upper **nave** wall, where the lateral thrust of the main vault is greatest, down to a solid **pier**.

cairn (p. 17) A pile of stones or earth and stones that served both as a prehistoric burial site and as a marker for underground tombs.

calligraphy (p. 275) Handwriting as an art form.

calyx krater (p. 119) See under **krater**.

calotype (p. 969) The first photographic process utilizing negatives and paper positives; invented by William Henry Fox Talbot in the late 1830s.

came (*pl.* **cames**) (p. 501) A lead strip used in the making of leaded or **stained-glass** windows. Cames have an indented groove on the sides into which individual pieces of glass are fitted to make the overall design.

cameo (p. 172) Gemstone, clay, glass, or shell having layers of color, carved in low relief (see under **relief sculpture**) to create an image and ground of different colors.

camera obscura (p. 750) An early cameralike device used in the Renaissance and later for recording images from the real world. It consists of a dark box (or room) with a hole in one side (sometimes fitted with a lens). The camera obscura operates when bright light shines through the hole, casting an upside-down image of an object outside onto the inside wall of the box.

canon of proportions (p. 64) A set of ideal mathematical ratios in art based on measurements, as in the proportional relationships between the basic elements of the human body.

canopic jar (p. 53) In ancient Egyptian culture, a special jar used to store the major organs of a body before embalming.

capital (p. 110) The sculpted block that tops a **column**. According to the **convention**s of the orders, capitals include different decorative elements (see **order**). A *historiated capital* is one displaying a figural composition and/or narrative scenes.

capriccio (*pl.* *capricci*) (p. 915) A painting or print of a fantastic, imaginary landscape, usually with architecture.

capstone (p. 17) The final, topmost stone in a **corbeled arch** or **vault**, which joins the sides and completes the structure.

cartoon (p. 501) A full-scale drawing of a design that will be executed in another **medium**, such as wall painting, **tapestry**, or **stained glass**.

cartouche (p. 187) A frame for a **hieroglyphic** inscription formed by a rope design surrounding an oval space. Used to signify a sacred or honored name. Also: in architecture, a decorative device or plaque, usually with a plain center used for inscriptions or epitaphs.

caryatid (p. 107) A sculpture of a draped female figure acting as a **column** supporting an **entablature**.

cassone (*pl.* *cassoni*) (p. 616) An Italian dowry chest often highly decorated with carvings, paintings, inlaid designs, and gilt embellishments.

catacomb (p. 215) An underground cemetery consisting of tunnels on different levels, having niches for urns and **sarcophagi** and often incorporating rooms (**cubicula**).

cathedral (p. 220) The principal Christian church in a diocese, the bishop's administrative center and housing his throne (*cathedra*).

celadon (p. 358) A high-fired, transparent **glaze** of pale bluish-green hue whose principal coloring agent is an oxide of iron. In China and Korea, such glazes were typically applied over a pale gray **stoneware** body, though Chinese potters sometimes applied them over **porcelain** bodies during the Ming (1368–1644) and Qing (1644–1911) dynasties. Chinese potters invented celadon glazes and initiated the continuous production of celadon-glazed wares as early as the third century CE.

cella (p. 108) The principal interior room at the center of a Greek or Roman temple within which the cult statue was usually housed. Also called the **naos**.

celt (p. 383) A smooth, oblong stone or metal object, shaped like an axe-head.

cenotaph (p. 771) A funerary monument commemorating an individual or group buried elsewhere.

centering (p. 170) A temporary structure that supports a masonry **arch**, **vault**, or **dome** during construction until the mortar is fully dried and the masonry is self-sustaining.

central-plan building (p. 225) Any structure designed with a primary central space surrounded by symmetrical areas on each side, e.g., a **rotunda**.

ceramics (p. 20) A general term covering all types of wares made from fired clay.

chacmool (p. 396) In Maya sculpture, a half-reclining figure probably representing an offering bearer.

chaitya (p. 305) A type of Buddhist temple found in India. Built in the form of a hall or **basilica**, a *chaitya* hall is highly decorated with sculpture and usually is carved from a cave or natural rock location. It houses a sacred shrine or **stupa** for worship.

chamfer (p. 780) The slanted surface produced when an angle is trimmed or beveled, common in building and metalwork.

chasing (p. 432) Ornamentation made on metal by incising or hammering the surface.

château (*pl.* **châteaux**) (p. 693) A French country house or residential castle. A *château fort* is a military castle incorporating defensive works such as towers and battlements.

chattri (p. 780) In Indian architecture, a decorative pavilion with an umbrella-shaped **dome**.

chevron (p. 357) A decorative or heraldic motif of repeated Vs; a zigzag pattern.

chiaroscuro (p. 636) An Italian word designating the contrast of dark and light in a painting, drawing, or print. *Chiaroscuro* creates spatial depth and volumetric forms through gradations in the intensity of light and shadow.

choir (p. 225) The part of a church reserved for the clergy, monks, or nuns, either between the **transept** crossing and the **apse** or extending farther into the **nave**; separated from the rest of the church by screens or walls and fitted with stalls (seats).

cista (*pl.* **cistae**) (p. 157) Cylindrical containers used in antiquity by wealthy women as a case for toiletry articles such as a mirror.

clerestory (p. 57) In a **basilica**, the topmost zone of a wall with windows, extending above the **aisle** roofs. Provides direct light into the **nave**.

cloisonné (p. 257) An **enamel**ing technique in which artists affix wires or strips to a metal surface to delineate designs and create compartments (*cloisons*) that they subsequently fill with enamel.

cloister (p. 448) An enclosed space, open to the sky, especially within a monastery, surrounded by an **arcade**d walkway, often having a fountain and garden. Since the most important monastic buildings (e.g., dormitory, refectory, church) open off the cloister, it represents the center of the monastic world.

codex (*pl.* **codices**) (p. 245) A book, or a group of **manuscript** pages (folios), held together by stitching or other binding along one edge.

coffer (p. 197) A recessed decorative panel used to decorate ceilings or **vault**s. The use of coffers is called coffering.

coiling (p. 848) A technique in basketry. In coiled baskets a spiraling coil, braid, or rope of material is held in place by stitching or interweaving to create a permanent shape.

collage (p. 1025) A composition made of cut and pasted scraps of materials, sometimes with lines or forms added by the artist.

colonnade (p. 69) A row of **columns**, supporting a straight **lintel** (as in a **porch** or **portico**) or a series of **arch**es (an **arcade**).

colophon (p. 438) The data placed at the end of a book listing the book's author, publisher, illuminator, and other information related to its production. In East Asian **handscroll**s, the inscriptions which follow the painting are also called colophons.

column (p. 110) An architectural element used for support and/or decoration. Consists of a rounded or polygonal vertical **shaft** placed on a **base** and topped by a decorative **capital**. In Classical architecture, columns are built in accordance with the rules of one of the architectural **order**s. They can be free-standing or attached to a background wall (**engaged**).

combine (p. 1087) Combination of painting and sculpture using nontraditional art materials.

complementary color (p. 995) The primary and secondary colors across from each other on the color wheel (red and green, blue and orange, yellow and purple). When juxtaposed, the intensity of both colors increases. When mixed together, they negate each other to make a neutral gray-brown.

Composite order (p. 161) See under **order**.

composite pose or **image** (p. 10) Combining different viewpoints within a single representation.

composition (p. xxiii) The overall arrangement, organizing design, or structure of a work of art.

conch (p. 236) A halfdome.

connoisseur (p. 289) A French word meaning "an expert," and signifying the study and evaluation of art based primarily on formal, visual, and stylistic analysis. A connoisseur studies the style and technique of an object to assess its relative quality and identify its maker through visual comparison with other works of secure authorship. See also **Formalism**.

continuous narrative (p. 245) See under **narrative image**.

contrapposto (p. 120) Italian term meaning "set against," used to describe the Classical convention of representing human figures with opposing alternations of tension and relaxation on either side of a central **axis** to imbue figures with a sense of the potential for movement.

convention (p. 31) A traditional way of representing forms.

corbel, corbeling (p. 19) An early roofing and arching technique in which each **course** of stone projects slightly beyond the previous layer (a corbel) until the uppermost corbels meet; see also under **arch**. Also: **bracket**s that project from a wall.

corbeled vault (p. 99) See under **vault**.

Corinthian order (p. 108) See under **order**.

cornice (p. 110) The uppermost section of a Classical **entablature**. More generally, a horizontally projecting element found at the top of a building wall or **pedestal**. A *raking cornice* is formed by the junction of two slanted cornices, most often found in **pediment**s.

course (p. 99) A horizontal layer of stone used in building.

crenellation, crenellated (p. 44) Alternating high and low sections of a wall, giving a notched appearance and creating permanent defensive shields on top of fortified buildings.

crocket (p. 587) A stylized leaf used as decoration along the outer angle of spires, pinnacles, gables, and around **capital**s in Gothic architecture.

cruciform (p. 228) Of anything that is cross-shaped, as in the cruciform plan of a church.

cubiculum (*pl.* **cubicula**) (p. 220) A small private room for burials in a **catacomb**.

cuneiform (p. 28) An early form of writing with wedge-shaped marks impressed into wet clay with a **stylus**, primarily used by ancient Mesopotamians.

curtain wall (p. 1045) A wall in a building that does not support any of the weight of the structure.

cyclopean (p. 93) A method of construction using huge blocks of rough-hewn stone. Any large-scale, monumental building project that impresses by sheer size. Named after the Cyclopes (sing. Cyclops), one-eyed giants of legendary strength in Greek myths.

cylinder seal (p. 35) A small cylindrical stone decorated with **incised** patterns. When rolled across soft clay or wax, the resulting raised pattern or design served in Mesopotamian and Indus Valley cultures as an identifying signature.

dado (*pl.* **dadoes**) (p. 161) The lower part of a wall, differentiated in some way (by a **molding** or different coloring or paneling) from the upper section.

daguerreotype (p. 969) An early photographic process that makes a positive print on a light-sensitized copperplate; invented and marketed in 1839 by Louis-Jacques-Mandé Daguerre.

dendrochronology (p. xxx) The dating of wood based on the patterns of the tree's growth rings.

dentils (p. 110) A row of projecting rectangular blocks forming a **molding** or running beneath a **cornice** in Classical architecture.

desert varnish (p. 406) A naturally occurring coating that turns rock faces into dark surfaces. Artists would draw images by scraping through the dark surface and revealing the color of the underlying rock. Extensively used in southwest North America.

diptych (p. 212) Two panels of equal size (usually decorated with paintings or reliefs) hinged together.

dogu (p. 362) Small human figurines made in Japan during the Jomon period. Shaped from clay, the figures have exaggerated expressions and are in contorted poses. They were probably used in religious rituals.

dolmen (p. 17) A prehistoric structure made up of two or more large upright stones supporting a large, flat, horizontal slab or slabs.

dome (p. 187) A rounded **vault**, usually over a circular space. Consists of curved masonry and can vary in shape from hemispherical to bulbous to ovoidal. May use a supporting vertical wall (**drum**), from which the vault springs, and may be crowned by an open space (**oculus**) and/or an exterior **lantern**. When a dome is built over a square space, an intermediate element is required to make the transition to a circular drum. There are two systems. A dome on **pendentives** incorporates arched, sloping intermediate sections of wall that carry the weight and **thrust** of the dome to heavily **buttress**ed supporting **pier**s. A dome on **squinch**es uses an arch built into the wall (squinch) in the upper corners of the space to carry the weight of the dome across the corners of the square space below. A halfdome or **conch** may cover a semicircular space.

domino construction (p. 1045) System of building construction introduced by the architect Le Corbusier in which reinforced concrete floor slabs are floated on six free-standing posts placed as if at the positions of the six dots on a domino playing piece.

Doric order (p. 108) See **order**.

dressed stone (p. 84) Another term for **ashlar**.

drillwork (p. 188) The technique of using a drill for the creation of certain effects in sculpture.

drum (p. 110) The circular wall that supports a **dome**. Also: a segment of the circular **shaft** of a **column**.

drypoint (p. 748) An **intaglio** printmaking process by which a metal (usually copper) plate is directly inscribed with a pointed instrument (**stylus**). The resulting design of scratched lines is inked, wiped, and printed. Also: the print made by this process.

earthenware (p. 20) A low-fired, opaque **ceramic** ware, employing humble clays that are naturally heat-resistant and remain porous after firing unless **glaze**d. Earthenware occurs in a range of earth-toned colors, from white and tan to gray and black, with tan predominating.

earthwork (p. 1102) Usually very large-scale, outdoor artwork that is produced by altering the natural environment.

echinus (p. 110) A cushionlike circular element found below the **abacus** of a Doric **capital**. Also: a similarly shaped **molding** (usually with egg-and-dart motifs) underneath the **volute**s of an Ionic capital.

electronic spin resonance (p. 12) Method that uses magnetic field and microwave irradiation to date material such as tooth enamel and its surrounding soil.

elevation (p. 108) The arrangement, proportions, and details of any vertical side or face of a building. Also: an architectural drawing showing an exterior or interior wall of a building.

embroidery (p. 397) Stitches applied in a decorative pattern on top of an already-woven fabric ground.

en plein air (p. 987) French term (meaning "in the open air") describing the Impressionist practice of painting outdoors so artists could have direct access to the fleeting effects of light and atmosphere while working.

enamel (p. 255) Powdered, then molten, glass applied to a metal surface, and used by artists to create designs. After firing, the glass forms an opaque or transparent substance that fuses to the metal background. Also: an object created by the enameling technique. See also *cloisonné*.

encaustic (p. 246) A painting **medium** using pigments mixed with hot wax.

engaged (p. 171) Of an architectural feature, usually a **column**, attached to a wall.

engraving (p. 592) An **intaglio** printmaking process of inscribing an image, design, or letters onto a metal or wood surface from which a print is made. An engraving is usually drawn with a sharp implement (**burin**) directly onto the surface of the plate. Also: the print made from this process.

entablature (p. 107) In the Classical **order**s, the horizontal elements above the **column**s and **capital**s. The entablature consists of, from bottom to top, an **architrave**, a **frieze**, and a **cornice**.

entasis (p. 108) A slight swelling of the **shaft** of a Greek **column**. The optical illusion of entasis makes the column appear from afar to be straight.

esquisse (p. 946) French for "sketch." A quickly executed drawing or painting conveying the overall idea for a finished painting.

etching (p. 748) An **intaglio** printmaking process in which a metal plate is coated with acid-resistant resin and then inscribed with a **stylus** in a design, revealing the plate below. The plate is then immersed in acid, and the exposed metal of the design is eaten away by the acid. The resin is removed, leaving the design etched permanently into the metal and the plate ready to be inked, wiped, and printed.

Eucharist (p. 220) The central rite of the Christian Church, from the Greek word for "thanksgiving." Also known as the Mass or Holy Communion, it reenacts Christ's sacrifice on the cross and commemorates the Last Supper. According to traditional Catholic Christian belief, consecrated bread and wine become the body and blood of Christ; in Protestant belief, bread and wine symbolize the body and blood.

exedra (*pl.* **exedrae**) (p. 197) In architecture, a semicircular niche. On a small scale, often used as decoration, whereas larger exedrae can form interior spaces (such as an **apse**).

expressionism (p. 149) Artistic styles in which aspects of works of art are exaggerated to evoke subjective emotions rather than to portray objective reality or elicit a rational response.

façade (p. 52) The face or front wall of a building.

faience (p. 88) Type of **ceramic** covered with colorful, opaque glazes that form a smooth, impermeable surface. First developed in ancient Egypt.

fang ding (p. 334) A square or rectangular bronze vessel with four legs. The *fang ding* was used for ritual offerings in ancient China during the Shang dynasty.

fête galante (p. 910) A subject in painting depicting well-dressed people at leisure in a park or country setting. It is most often associated with eighteenth-century French Rococo painting.

filigree (p. 90) Delicate, lacelike ornamental work.

fillet (p. 110) The flat ridge between the carved-out **flutes** of a **column shaft**.

finial (p. 780) A knoblike architectural decoration usually found at the top point of a spire, pinnacle, canopy, or gable. Also found on furniture. Also the ornamental top of a staff.

flutes (p. 110) In architecture, evenly spaced, rounded parallel vertical grooves incised on **shafts** of **columns** or on columnar elements such as **pilasters**.

flying buttress (p. 503) See under **buttress**.

flying gallop (p. 88) A non-naturalistic pose in which animals are depicted hovering above the ground with legs fully extended backwards and forwards to signify that they are running.

foreshortening (p. xxv) The illusion created on a flat surface by which figures and objects appear to recede or project sharply into space. Accomplished according to the rules of **perspective**.

formal analysis (p. xxiii) An exploration of the visual character that artists bring to their works through the expressive use of elements such as line, form, color, and light, and through its overall structure or composition.

Formalism (p. 1073) An approach to the understanding, appreciation, and valuation of art based almost solely on considerations of form. The Formalist's approach tends to regard an artwork as independent of its time and place of making.

forum (p. 176) A Roman town center; site of temples and administrative buildings and used as a market or gathering area for the citizens.

fresco (p. 81) A painting technique in which water-based pigments are applied to a plaster surface. If the plaster is painted when wet, the color is absorbed by the plaster, becoming a permanent part of the wall (*buon fresco*). *Fresco secco* is created by painting on dried plaster, and the color may eventually flake off. Murals made by both these techniques are called frescos.

frieze (p. 107) The middle element of an **entablature**, between the **architrave** and the **cornice**. Usually decorated with sculpture, painting, or **moldings**. Also: any continuous flat band with **relief sculpture** or painted decoration.

frottage (p. 1057) A design produced by laying a piece of paper over a textured surface and rubbing with charcoal or other soft **medium**.

fusuma (p. 820) Sliding doors covered with paper, used in traditional Japanese construction. *Fusuma* are often highly decorated with paintings and colored backgrounds.

gallery (p. 236) A roofed passageway with one or both of its long sides open to the air. In church architecture, the story found above the side **aisles** of a church or across the width at the end of the **nave** or **transepts**, usually open to and overlooking the area below. Also: a building or hall in which art is displayed or sold.

garbhagriha (p. 302) From the Sanskrit word meaning "womb chamber," a small room or shrine in a Hindu temple containing a holy image.

genre painting (p. 714) A term used to loosely categorize paintings depicting scenes of everyday life, including (among others) domestic interiors, parties, inn scenes, and street scenes.

geoglyph (p. 399) Earthen design on a colossal scale, often created in a landscape as if to be seen from an aerial viewpoint.

gesso (p. 546) A ground made from glue, gypsum, and/or chalk, used as the ground of a wood panel or the priming layer of a canvas. Provides a smooth surface for painting.

gilding (p. 90) The application of paper-thin gold leaf or gold pigment to an object made from another **medium** (for example, a sculpture or painting). Usually used as a decorative finishing detail.

giornata (*pl. giornate*) (p. 539) Adopted from the Italian term meaning "a day's work," a *giornata* is the section of a **fresco** plastered and painted in a single day.

glazing (p. 600) In **ceramics**, an outermost layer of vitreous liquid (**glaze**) that, upon firing, renders the ware waterproof and forms a decorative surface. In painting, a technique used with oil **media** in which a transparent layer of paint (glaze) is laid over another, usually lighter, painted or glazed area. In architecture, the process of filling openings in a building with windows of clear or **stained glass**.

gold leaf (p. 47) Paper-thin sheets of hammered gold that are used in **gilding**. In some cases (such as Byzantine **icons**), also used as a ground for paintings.

gopura (p. 775) The towering gateway to an Indian Hindu temple complex.

Grand Manner (p. 923) An elevated style of painting popular in the eighteenth century in which the artist looked to the ancients and to the Renaissance for inspiration; for portraits as well as history painting, the artist would adopt the poses, compositions, and attitudes of Renaissance and antique models.

Grand Tour (p. 913) Popular during the eighteenth and nineteenth centuries, an extended tour of cultural sites in France and Italy intended to finish the education of a young upper-class person primarily from Britain or North America.

granulation (p. 90) A technique of decoration in which metal granules, or tiny metal balls, are fused onto a metal surface.

graphic arts (p. 698) A term referring to those arts that are drawn or printed and that utilize paper as the primary support.

grattage (p. 1057) A pattern created by scraping off layers of paint from a canvas laid over a textured surface. Compare **frottage**.

grid (p. 65) A system of regularly spaced horizontally and vertically crossed lines that gives regularity to an architectural plan or in the composition of a work of art. Also: in painting, a grid is used to allow designs to be enlarged or transferred easily.

grisaille (p. 540) A style of monochromatic painting in shades of gray. Also: a painting made in this style.

groin vault (p. 187) See under **vault**.

grozing (p. 501) Chipping away at the edges of a piece of glass to achieve the precise shape needed for inclusion in the composition of a **stained-glass** window.

guild (p. 419) An association of artists or craftsmakers. Medieval and Renaissance guilds had great economic power, as they controlled the marketing of their members' products and provided economic protection, political solidarity, and training in the craft to its members. The painters' guild was usually dedicated to St. Luke, their patron saint.

hall church (p. 521) A church with **nave** and **aisles** of the same height, giving the impression of a large, open hall.

halo (p. 215) A circle of light that surrounds and frames the heads of emperors and holy figures to signify their power and/or sanctity. Also known as a nimbus.

handscroll (p. 343) A long, narrow, horizontal painting or text (or combination thereof) common in Chinese and Japanese art and of a size intended for individual use. A handscroll is stored wrapped tightly around a wooden pin and is unrolled for viewing or reading.

hanging scroll (p. 796) In Chinese and Japanese art, a vertical painting or text mounted within sections of silk. At the top is a semicircular rod; at the bottom is a round dowel. Hanging scrolls are kept rolled and tied except for special occasions, when they are hung for display, contemplation, or commemoration.

haniwa (p. 362) Pottery forms, including cylinders, buildings, and human figures, that were placed on top of Japanese tombs or burial mounds during the Kofun period (300–552 CE).

Happening (p. 1087) An art form developed by Allan Kaprow in the 1960s, incorporating performance, theater, and visual images. A Happening was organized without a specific narrative or intent; with audience participation, the event proceeded according to chance and individual improvisation.

hemicycle (p. 512) A semicircular interior space or structure.

henge (p. 17) A circular area enclosed by stones or wood posts set up by Neolithic peoples. It is usually bounded by a ditch and raised embankment.

hierarchic scale (p. 27) The use of differences in size to indicate relative importance. For example, with human figures, the larger the figure, the greater her or his importance.

hieratic (p. 484) Highly stylized, severe, and detached, often in relation to a strict religious tradition.

hieroglyph (p. 52) Picture writing; words and ideas rendered in the form of pictorial symbols.

high relief (p. 307) See under **relief sculpture**.

historiated capital (p. 484) See under **capital**.

historicism (p. 965) The strong consciousness of and attention to the institutions, themes, styles, and forms of the past, made accessible by historical research, textual study, and archaeology.

history paintings (p. 926) Paintings based on historical, mythological, or biblical narratives. Once considered the noblest form of art, history paintings generally convey a high moral or intellectual idea and are often painted in a grand pictorial style.

horizon line (p. 569) A horizontal "line" formed by the implied meeting point of earth and sky. In **linear perspective**, the **vanishing point** or points are located on this "line."

horseshoe arch (p. 272) See under **arch**.

hue (p. 77) Pure color. The saturation or intensity of the hue depends on the purity of the color. Its value depends on its lightness or darkness.

hydria (p. 139) A large ancient Greek or Roman jar with three handles (horizontal ones at both sides and one vertical at the back), used for storing water.

hypostyle hall (p. 66) A large interior room characterized by many closely spaced **columns** that support its roof.

icon (p. 246) An image representing a sacred figure or event in the Byzantine (later the Orthodox) Church. Icons are venerated by the faithful, who believe their prayers are transmitted through them to God.

iconic image (p. 215) A picture that expresses or embodies an intangible concept or idea.

iconoclasm (p. 248) The banning and/or destruction of images, especially **icons** and religious art. Iconoclasm in eighth- and ninth-century Byzantium and sixteenth- and seventeenth-century Protestant territories arose from differing beliefs about the power, meaning, function, and purpose of imagery in religion.

iconography (p. xxvii) Identifying and studying the subject matter and **conventional** symbols in works of art.

iconology (p. xxix) Interpreting works of art as embodiments of cultural situation by placing them within broad social, political, religious, and intellectual contexts.

iconophile (p. 247) From the Greek for "lover of images." In periods of **iconoclasm**, iconophiles advocate the continued use of sacred images.

idealization (p. 134) A process in art through which artists strive to make their forms and figures attain perfection, based on pervading cultural values and/or their own personal ideals.

illumination (p. 431) A painting on paper or parchment used as an illustration and/or decoration in a **manuscript** or **album**. Usually richly colored, often supplemented with gold and other precious materials. The artists are referred to as illuminators. Also: the technique of decorating manuscripts with such paintings.

impasto (p. 749) Thick applications of pigment that give a painting a palpable surface texture.

impluvium (p. 178) A pool under a roof opening that collected rainwater in the **atrium** of a Roman house.

impost block (p. 170) A block of masonry imposed between the top of a **pier** or above the **capital** of a **column** in order to provide extra support at the springing of an **arch**.

incising (p. 118) A technique in which a design or inscription is cut into a hard surface with a sharp instrument. Such a surface is said to be incised.

ink painting (p. 812) A monochromatic style of painting developed in China, using black ink with gray washes.

inlay (p. 30) To set pieces of a material or materials into a surface to form a design. Also: material used in or decoration formed by this technique.

installation, installation art (p. 1051) Contemporary art created for a specific site, especially a gallery or outdoor area, that creates a complete and controlled environment.

intaglio (p. 592) A technique in which the design is carved out of the surface of an object, such as an engraved seal stone. In the **graphic arts**, intaglio includes **engraving**, **etching**, and **drypoint**—all processes in which ink transfers to paper from incised, ink-filled lines cut into a metal plate.

intarsia (p. 618) Technique of **inlay** decoration using variously colored woods.

intuitive perspective (p. 182) See under **perspective**.

Ionic order (p. 107) See under **order**.

iwan (p. 277) In Islamic architecture, a large, vaulted chamber with a monumental arched opening on one side.

jamb (p. 478) In architecture, the vertical element found on both sides of an opening in a wall, and supporting an **arch** or **lintel**.

Japonisme (p. 996) A style in French and American nineteenth-century art that was highly influenced by Japanese art, especially prints.

jasperware (p. 919) A fine-grained, unglazed, white **ceramic** developed in the eighteenth century by Josiah Wedgwood, often with raised designs remaining white above a background surface colored by metallic oxides.

Jataka tales (p. 303) In Buddhism, stories associated with the previous lives of Shakyamuni, the historical Buddha.

joggled voussoirs (p. 268) Interlocking **voussoir**s in an **arch** or **lintel**, often of contrasting materials for colorful effect.

joined-block sculpture (p. 373) Large-scale wooden sculpture constructed by a method developed in Japan. The entire work is made from smaller hollow blocks, each individually carved, and assembled when complete. The joined-block technique allowed production of larger sculpture, as the multiple joints alleviate the problems of drying and cracking found with sculpture carved from a single block.

kantharos (p. 117) A type of ancient Greek goblet with two large handles and a wide mouth.

keep (p. 477) The innermost and strongest structure or central tower of a medieval castle, sometimes used as living quarters, as well as for defense. Also called a donjon.

kente (p. 892) A woven cloth made by the Ashanti peoples of West Africa. *Kente* cloth is woven in long, narrow pieces featuring complex and colorful patterns, which are then sewn together.

key block (p. 828) The master block in the production of a colored **woodblock print**, which requires different blocks for each color. The key block is a flat piece of wood upon which the outlines for the entire design of the print were first drawn on its surface and then all but these outlines were carved away with a knife. These outlines serve as a guide for the accurate **registration** or alignment of the other blocks needed to add colors to specific parts of a print.

keystone (p. 170) The topmost **voussoir** at the center of an **arch**, and the last block to be placed. The pressure of this block holds the arch together. Often of a larger size and/or decorated.

kiln (p. 20) An oven designed to produce enough heat for the baking, or firing, of clay, for the melting of the glass used in **enamel** work, and for the fixing of vitreous paint on **stained glass**.

kiva (p. 405) A subterranean, circular room used as a ceremonial center in some Native American cultures.

kondo (p. 366) The main hall inside a Japanese Buddhist temple where the images of Buddha are housed.

korambo (p. 865) A ceremonial or spirit house in Pacific cultures, reserved for the men of a village and used as a meeting place as well as to hide religious artifacts from the uninitiated.

kore (*pl.* **kourai**) (p. 114) An Archaic Greek statue of a young woman.

koru (p. 872) A design depicting a curling stalk with a bulb at the end that resembles a young tree fern; often found in Maori art.

kouros (*pl.* **kouroi**) (p. 114) An Archaic Greek statue of a young man or boy.

kowhaiwhai (p. 872) Painted curvilinear patterns often found in Maori art.

krater (p. 99) An ancient Greek vessel for mixing wine and water, with many subtypes that each have a distinctive shape. *Calyx krater*: a bell-shaped vessel with handles near the base that resembles a flower calyx. *Volute krater*: a krater with handles shaped like scrolls.

Kufic (p. 275) An ornamental, angular Arabic script.

kylix (p. 120) A shallow ancient Greek cup, used for drinking, with a wide mouth and small handles near the rim.

lacquer (p. 824) A type of hard, glossy surface varnish, originally developed for use on objects in East Asian cultures, made from the sap of the Asian sumac or from shellac, a resinous secretion from the lac insect. Lacquer can be layered and manipulated or combined with pigments and other materials for various decorative effects.

lakshana (p. 306) The 32 marks of the historical Buddha. The *lakshana* include, among others, the Buddha's golden body, his long arms, the wheel impressed on his palms and the soles of his feet, and his elongated earlobes.

lamassu (p. 42) Supernatural guardian-protector of ancient Near Eastern palaces and throne rooms, often represented sculpturally as a combination of the bearded head of a man, powerful body of a lion or bull, wings of an eagle, and the horned headdress of a god, usually possessing five legs.

lancet (p. 505) A tall, narrow window crowned by a sharply pointed arch, typically found in Gothic architecture.

lantern (p. 464) A turretlike structure situated on a roof, vault, or dome, with windows that allow light into the space below.

lekythos (*pl.* **lekythoi**) (p. 141) A slim ancient Greek oil vase with one handle and a narrow mouth.

linear perspective (p. 595) See under **perspective**.

linga shrine (p. 315) A place of worship centered on an object or representation in the form of a phallus (the lingam), which symbolizes the power of the Hindu god Shiva.

lintel (p. 18) A horizontal element of any material carried by two or more vertical supports to form an opening.

literati painting (p. 793) A style of painting that reflects the taste of the educated class of East Asian intellectuals and scholars. Characteristics include an appreciation for the antique, small scale, and an intimate connection between maker and audience.

lithography (p. 953) Process of making a print (lithograph) from a design drawn on a flat stone block with greasy crayon. Ink is applied to the wet stone and adheres only to the greasy areas of the design.

loggia (p. 534) Italian term for a **gallery**. Often used as a corridor between buildings or around a courtyard, a loggia usually features an **arcade** or **colonnade**.

longitudinal-plan building (p. 225) Any structure designed with a rectangular shape and a longitudinal axis. In a cross-shaped building, the main arm of the building would be longer than any arms that cross it. For example, a **basilica**.

lost-wax casting (p. 36) A method of casting metal, such as bronze. A wax mold is covered with clay and plaster, then fired, thus melting the wax and leaving a hollow form. Molten metal is then poured into the hollow space and slowly cooled. When the hardened clay and plaster exterior shell is removed, a solid metal form remains to be smoothed and polished.

low relief (p. 40) See under **relief sculpture**.

lunette (p. 221) A semicircular wall area, framed by an **arch** over a door or window. Can be either plain or decorated.

lusterware (p. 277) Pottery decorated with metallic **glaze**s.

madrasa (p. 277) An Islamic institution of higher learning, where teaching is focused on theology and law.

maenad (p. 104) In ancient Greece, a female devotee of the wine god Dionysos who participated in orgiastic rituals. Often depicted with swirling drapery to indicate wild movement or dance. Also called a Bacchante, after Bacchus, the Roman equivalent of Dionysos.

majolica (p. 573) Pottery painted with a tin **glaze** that, when fired, gives a lustrous and colorful surface.

mandala (p. 302) An image of the cosmos represented by an arrangement of circles or concentric geometric shapes containing diagrams or images. Used for meditation and contemplation by Buddhists.

mandapa (p. 302) In a Hindu temple, an open hall dedicated to ritual worship.

mandorla (p. 479) Light encircling, or emanating from, the entire figure of a sacred person.

manuscript (p. 244) A hand-written book or document.

maqsura (p. 272) An enclosure in a Muslim **mosque**, near the *mihrab*, designated for dignitaries.

martyrium (*pl.* **martyria**) (p. 238) A church, chapel, or shrine built over the grave of a Christian martyr.

mastaba (p. 53) A flat-topped, one-story structure with slanted walls built over an ancient Egyptian underground tomb.

matte (p. 573) Of a smooth surface that is without shine or luster.

mausoleum (p. 175) A monumental building used as a tomb. Named after the tomb of King Mausolos erected at Halikarnassos around 350 BCE.

medallion (p. 222) Any round ornament or decoration. Also: a large medal.

medium (*pl.* **media**) (p. xxiii) The material from which a work of art is made.

megalith (*adj.* **megalithic**) (p. 16) A large stone used in some prehistoric architecture.

megaron (p. 93) The main hall of a Mycenaean palace or grand house.

memento mori (p. 909) From Latin for "remember that you must die." An object, such as a skull or extinguished candle, typically found in a *vanitas* image, symbolizing the transience of life.

menorah (p. 186) A Jewish lampstand with seven or nine branches; the nine-branched menorah is used during the celebration of Hanukkah. Representations of the seven-branched menorah, once used in the Temple of Jerusalem, became a symbol of Judaism.

metope (p. 110) The carved or painted rectangular panel between the **triglyph**s of a Doric **frieze**.

mihrab (p. 265) A recess or niche that distinguishes the wall oriented toward Mecca (*qibla*) in a **mosque**.

millefiori (p. 434) A glassmaking technique in which rods of differently colored glass are fused in a long bundle that is subsequently sliced to produce disks or beads with small-scale, multicolor patterns. The term derives from the Italian for "a thousand flowers."

minaret (p. 274) A tower on or near a **mosque** from which Muslims are called to prayer five times a day.

minbar (p. 265) A high platform or pulpit in a **mosque**.

miniature (p. 245) Anything small. In painting, miniatures may be illustrations within **album**s or **manuscript**s or intimate portraits.

mirador (p. 280) In Spanish and Islamic palace architecture, a very large window or room with windows, and sometimes balconies, providing views to interior courtyards or the exterior landscape.

mithuna (p. 305) The amorous male and female couples in Buddhist sculpture, usually found at the entrance to a sacred building. The *mithuna* symbolizes the harmony and fertility of life.

moai (p. 875) Statues found in Polynesia, carved from tufa, a yellowish brown volcanic stone, and depicting the human form. Nearly 1,000 of these statues have been found on the island of Rapa Nui but their significance has been a matter of speculation.

modeling (p. xxiii) In painting, the process of creating the illusion of three-dimensionality on a two-dimensional surface by use of light and shade. In sculpture, the process of molding a three-dimensional form out of a malleable substance.

module (p. 346) A segment or portion of a repeated design. Also: a basic building block.

molding (p. 319) A shaped or sculpted strip with varying contours and patterns. Used as decoration on architecture, furniture, frames, and other objects.

mortise-and-tenon (p. 18) A method of joining two elements. A projecting pin (tenon) on one element fits snugly into a hole designed for it (mortise) on the other.

mosaic (p. 145) Image formed by arranging small colored stone or glass pieces (**tesserae**) and affixing them to a hard, stable surface.

mosque (p. 265) A building used for communal Islamic worship.

Mozarabic (p. 439) Of an eclectic style practiced in Christian medieval Spain when much of the Iberian peninsula was ruled by Islamic dynasties.

mudra (p. 307) A symbolic hand gesture in Buddhist art that denotes certain behaviors, actions, or feelings.

mullion (p. 510) A slender straight or curving bar that divides a window into subsidiary sections to create **tracery**.

muqarna (p. 280) In Islamic architecture, one of the nichelike components, often stacked in tiers to mark the transition between flat and rounded surfaces and often found on the **vault** of a **dome**.

naos (p. 236) The principal room in a temple or church. In ancient architecture, the **cella**. In a Byzantine church, the **nave** and **sanctuary**.

narrative image (p. 215) A picture that recounts an event drawn from a story, either factual (e.g. biographical) or fictional. In **continuous narrative**, multiple scenes from the same story appear within a single compositional frame.

narthex (p. 220) The vestibule or entrance porch of a church.

nave (p. 191) The central space of a church, two or three stories high and usually flanked by **aisle**s.

necropolis (p. 53) A large cemetery or burial area; literally a "city of the dead."

nemes headdress (p. 51) The royal headdress of ancient Egypt.

niello (p. 90) A metal technique in which a black sulfur **alloy** is rubbed into fine lines engraved into metal (usually gold or silver). When heated, the alloy becomes fused with the surrounding metal and provides contrasting detail.

oculus (*pl.* **oculi**) (p. 187) In architecture, a circular opening. Usually found either as windows or at the apex of a **dome**. When at the top of a dome, an oculus is either open to the sky or covered by a decorative exterior **lantern**.

odalisque (p. 952) Turkish word for "harem slave girl" or "concubine."

oil painting (p. 575) Any painting executed with pigments suspended in a **medium** of oil. Oil paint has particular properties that allow for greater ease of working: among others, a slow drying time (which allows for corrections), and a great range of relative opaqueness of paint layers (which permits a high degree of detail and luminescence).

oinochoe (p. 126) An ancient Greek jug used for wine.

olpe (p. 105) Any ancient Greek vessel without a spout.

one-point perspective (p. 259) See under **perspective**.

orant (p. 220) Of a standing figure represented praying with outstretched and upraised arms.

oratory (p. 228) A small chapel.

order (p. 110) A system of proportions in Classical architecture that includes every aspect of the building's plan, elevation, and decorative system. *Composite*: a combination of the Ionic and the Corinthian orders. The **capital** combines **acanthus** leaves with **volute** scrolls. *Corinthian*: the most ornate of the orders, the Corinthian includes a **base**, a **fluted column shaft** with a capital elaborately decorated with acanthus leaf carvings. Its **entablature** consists of an **architrave** decorated with **moldings**, a **frieze** often containing **relief sculpture**, and a **cornice** with **dentils**. *Doric*: the column shaft of the Doric order can be fluted or smooth-surfaced and has no base. The Doric capital consists of an undecorated **echinus** and **abacus**. The Doric entablature has a plain architrave, a frieze with **metope**s and **triglyph**s, and a simple cornice. *Ionic*: the column of the Ionic order has a base, a fluted shaft, and a capital decorated with volutes. The Ionic entablature consists of an architrave of three panels and moldings, a frieze usually containing sculpted relief ornament, and a cornice with dentils. *Tuscan*: a variation of Doric characterized by a smooth-surfaced column shaft with a base, a plain architrave, and an undecorated frieze. *Colossal* or *giant*: any of the above built on a large scale, rising through two or more stories in height and often raised from the ground on a **pedestal**.

Orientalism (p. 968) A fascination with Middle Eastern cultures that inspired eclectic nineteenth-century European fantasies of exotic life that often formed the subject of paintings.

orthogonal (p. 138) Any line running back into the represented space of a picture perpendicular to the imagined **picture plane**. In **linear perspective**, all orthogonals converge at a single **vanishing point** in the picture and are the basis for a **grid** that maps out the internal space of the image. An orthogonal plan is any plan for a building or city that is based exclusively on right angles, such as the grid plan of many major cities.

pagoda (p. 347) An East Asian **reliquary** tower built with successively smaller, repeated stories. Each story is usually marked by an elaborate projecting roof.

painterly (p. 253) A style of painting which emphasizes the techniques and surface effects of brushwork (also color, light, and shade).

palace complex (p. 41) A group of buildings used for living and governing by a ruler and his or her supporters, usually fortified.

palazzo (p. 602) Italian term for palace, used for any large urban dwelling.

palette (p. 183) A hand-held support used by artists for arranging colors and mixing paint during the process of painting. Also: the choice of a range of colors used by an artist in a particular work, as typical of his or her style. In ancient Egypt, a flat stone used to grind and prepare makeup.

panel painting (p. xxxv) Any painting executed on a wood support, usually planed to provide a smooth surface. A panel can consist of several boards joined together.

parchment (p. 245) A writing surface made from treated skins of animals. Very fine parchment is known as **vellum**.

parterre (p. 761) An ornamental, highly regimented flowerbed; especially as an element of the ornate gardens of a seventeenth-century palace or **château**.

passage grave (p. 17) A prehistoric tomb under a **cairn**, reached by a long, narrow, slab-lined access passageway or passageways.

pastel (p. 914) Dry pigment, chalk, and gum in stick or crayon form. Also: a work of art made with pastels.

pedestal (p. 107) A platform or base supporting a sculpture or other monument. Also: the block found below the base of a Classical **column** (or **colonnade**), serving to raise the entire element off the ground.

pediment (p. 107) A triangular gable found over major architectural elements such as Classical Greek **portico**s, windows, or doors. Formed by an **entablature** and the ends of a sloping roof or a raking **cornice**. A similar architectural element is used decoratively above a door or window, sometimes with a curved upper **molding**. A *broken pediment* is a variation on the traditional pediment, with an open space at the center of the topmost angle and/or the horizontal cornice.

pendant (also **pendent**) (p. 640) One of a pair of artworks meant to be seen in relation to each other as a set.

pendentive (p. 236) The concave triangular section of a **vault** that forms the transition between a square or polygonal space and the circular base of a **dome**.

Performance art (p. 1087) A contemporary artwork based on a live, sometimes theatrical performance by the artist.

peristyle (p. 66) In Greek architecture, a surrounding **colonnade**. A peristyle building is surrounded on the exterior by a colonnade. Also: a peristyle court is an open colonnaded courtyard, often having a pool and garden.

perspective (p. xxi) A system for representing three-dimensional space on a two-dimensional surface. *Atmospheric* or *aerial perspective*: a method of rendering the effect of spatial distance by subtle variations in color and clarity of representation. *Intuitive perspective*: a method of giving the impression of recession by visual instinct, not by the use of an overall system or program. *Oblique perspective*: an intuitive spatial system in which a building or room is placed with one corner in the **picture plane**, and the other parts of the structure recede to an imaginary **vanishing point** on its other side. Oblique perspective is not a comprehensive, mathematical system. *One-point* and multiple-point perspective (also called linear, scientific, or mathematical perspective): a method of creating the illusion of three-dimensional space on a two-dimensional surface by delineating a **horizon line** and multiple **orthogonal** lines. These recede to meet at one or more points on the horizon (vanishing point), giving the appearance of spatial depth. Called scientific or mathematical because its use requires some knowledge of geometry and mathematics, as well as optics. *Reverse perspective*: a Byzantine perspective theory in which the orthogonals or rays of sight do not converge on a vanishing point in the picture, but are thought to originate in the viewer's eye in front of the picture. Thus, in reverse perspective the image is constructed with orthogonals that diverge, giving a slightly tipped aspect to objects.

photomontage (p. 1039) A photographic work created from many smaller photographs arranged (and often overlapping) in a composition, which is then rephotographed.

pictograph (p. 337) A highly stylized depiction serving as a symbol for a person or object. Also: a type of writing utilizing such symbols.

picture plane (p. 575) The theoretical plane corresponding with the actual surface of a painting, separating the spatial world evoked in the painting from the spatial world occupied by the viewer.

picturesque (p. 919) Of the taste for the familiar, the pleasant, and the agreeable, popular in the eighteenth and nineteenth centuries in Europe. Originally used to describe the "picturelike" qualities of some landscape scenes. When contrasted with the **sublime**, the picturesque stood for the interesting but ordinary domestic landscape.

piece-mold casting (p. 334) A casting technique in which the mold consists of several sections that are connected during the pouring of molten metal, usually bronze. After the cast form has hardened, the pieces of the mold are disassembled, leaving the completed object.

pier (p. 270) A masonry support made up of many stones, or rubble and concrete (in contrast to a column **shaft** which is formed from a single stone or a series of **drum**s), often square or rectangular in plan, and capable of carrying very heavy architectural loads.

pietà (p. 230) A devotional subject in Christian religious art. After the Crucifixion the body of Jesus was laid across the lap of his grieving mother, Mary. When other mourners are present, the subject is called the Lamentation.

pietra serena (p. 602) A gray Tuscan sandstone used in Florentine architecture.

pilaster (p. 158) An **engaged** columnlike element that is rectangular in format and used for decoration in architecture.

pilgrimage church (p. 239) A church that attracts visitors wishing to venerate **relic**s as well as attend religious services.

pinnacle (p. 503) In Gothic architecture, a steep pyramid decorating the top of another element such as a **buttress**. Also: the highest point.

plate tracery (p. 505) See under **tracery**.

plein air (p. 989) See under *en plein air*.

plinth (p. 161) The slablike base or **pedestal** of a **column**, statue, wall, building, or piece of furniture.

pluralism (p. 1107) A social structure or goal that allows members of diverse ethnic, racial, or other groups to exist peacefully within the society while continuing to practice the customs of their own divergent cultures. Also: an adjective describing the state of having a variety of valid contemporary styles available at the same time to artists.

podium (p. 138) A raised platform that acts as the foundation for a building, or as a platform for a speaker.

poesia (*pl.* **poesie**) (p. 656) Italian Renaissance paintings based on Classical themes, often with erotic overtones, notably in the mid-sixteenth-century works of the Venetian painter Titian.

polychromy (p. 524) Multicolored decoration applied to any part of a building, sculpture, or piece of furniture. This can be accomplished with paint or by the use of multicolored materials.

polyptych (p. 566) An **altarpiece** constructed from multiple panels, sometimes with hinges to allow for movable wings.

porcelain (p. 20) A type of extremely hard and fine white **ceramic** first made by Chinese potters in the eighth century CE. Made from a mixture of kaolin and petuntse, porcelain is fired at a very high temperature, and the final product has a translucent surface.

porch (p. 108) The covered entrance on the exterior of a building. With a row of **column**s or **colonnade**, also called a **portico**.

portal (p. 40) A grand entrance, door, or gate, usually to an important public building, and often decorated with sculpture.

portico (p. 63) In architecture, a projecting roof or porch supported by **column**s, often marking an entrance. See also **porch**.

post-and-lintel (p. 19) An architectural system of construction with two or more vertical elements (posts) supporting a horizontal element (**lintel**).

potassium-argon dating (p. 12) Archaeological method of **radiometric dating** that measures the decay of a radioactive potassium isotope into a stable isotope of argon, and inert gas.

potsherd (p. 20) A broken piece of **ceramic** ware.

poupou (p. 873) In Pacific cultures, a house panel, often carved with designs.

Prairie Style (p. 1046) Style developed by a group of Midwestern architects who worked together using the aesthetic of the prairie and indigenous prairie plants for landscape design to create mostly domestic homes and small public buildings.

predella (p. 550) The base of an **altarpiece**, often decorated with small scenes that are related in subject to that of the main panel or panels.

primitivism (p. 1022) The borrowing of subjects or forms, usually from non-European or prehistoric sources by Western artists, in an attempt to infuse their work with the expressive qualities they attributed to other cultures, especially colonized cultures.

pronaos (p. 108) The enclosed vestibule of a Greek or Roman temple, found in front of the **cella** and marked by a row of **column**s at the entrance.

proscenium (p. 148) The stage of an ancient Greek or Roman theater. In a modern theater, the area of the stage in front of the curtain. Also: the framing **arch** that separates a stage from the audience.

psalter (p. 256) In Jewish and Christian scripture, a book of the Psalms (songs) attributed to King David.

psykter (p. 126) An ancient Greek vessel with an extended base to allow it to float in a larger **krater**; used to chill wine.

putto (*pl.* **putti**) (p. 224) A plump, naked little boy, often winged. In Classical art, called a cupid; in Christian art, a cherub.

pylon (p. 66) A massive gateway formed by a pair of tapering walls of oblong shape. Erected by ancient Egyptians to mark the entrance to a temple complex.

qibla (p. 274) The **mosque** wall oriented toward Mecca; indicated by the *mihrab*.

quatrefoil (p. 508) A four-lobed decorative pattern common in Gothic art and architecture.

quillwork (p. 847) A Native American technique in which the quills of porcupines and bird feathers are dyed and attached to materials in patterns.

radiometric dating (p. 12) Archaeological method of **absolute dating** by measuring the degree to which radioactive materials have degenerated over time. For dating organic (plant or animal) materials, one radiometric method measures a carbon isotope called radiocarbon, or carbon-14.

raigo (p. 378) A painted image that depicts the Amida Buddha and other Buddhist deities welcoming the soul of a dying believer to paradise.

raku (p. 823) A type of **ceramic** made by hand, coated with a thick, dark glaze, and fired at a low heat. The resulting vessels are irregularly shaped and glazed and are highly prized for use in the Japanese tea ceremony.

readymade (p. 1038) An object from popular or material culture presented without further manipulation as an artwork by the artist.

red-figure (p. 119) A technique of ancient Greek **ceramic** decoration characterized by red clay-colored figures on a black background. The figures are reserved against a painted ground and details are drawn, not engraved; compare **black-figure**.

register (p. 30) A device used in systems of spatial definition. In painting, a register indicates the use of differing groundlines to differentiate layers of space within an image. In **relief sculpture**, the placement of self-contained bands of reliefs in a vertical arrangement.

registration marks (p. 828) In Japanese **woodblock prints**, two marks carved on the blocks to indicate proper alignment of the paper during the printing process. In multicolor printing, which used a separate block for each color, these marks were essential for achieving the proper position or registration of the colors.

relative dating (p. 12) Archaeological process of determining relative chronological relationships among excavated objects. Compare **absolute dating**.

relic (p. 239) Venerated object or body part associated with a holy figure, such as a saint, and usually housed in a **reliquary**.

relief sculpture (p. 5) A three-dimensional image or design whose flat background surface is carved away to a certain depth, setting off the figure. Called *high* or *low (bas-) relief* depending on the extent of projection of the image from the background. Called *sunken relief* when the image is carved below the original surface of the background, which is not cut away.

reliquary (p. 366) A container, often elaborate and made of precious materials, used as a repository for sacred relics.

repoussé (p. 90) A technique of pushing or hammering metal from the back to create a protruding image. Elaborate reliefs are created by pressing or hammering metal sheets against carved wooden forms.

rhyton (p. 88) A vessel in the shape of a figure or an animal, used for drinking or pouring liquids on special occasions.

rib vault (p. 499) See under **vault**.

ridgepole (p. 16) A longitudinal timber at the apex of a roof that supports the upper ends of the rafters.

roof comb (p. 392) In a Maya building, a masonry wall along the apex of a roof that is built above the level of the roof proper. Roof combs support the highly decorated false **façade**s that rise above the height of the building at the front.

rose window (p. 505) A round window, often filled with stained glass set into tracery patterns in the form of wheel spokes, found in the **façade**s of the **nave**s and **transept**s of large Gothic churches.

rosette (p. 105) A round or oval ornament resembling a rose.

rotunda (p. 195) Any building (or part thereof) constructed in a circular (or sometimes polygonal) shape, usually producing a large open space crowned by a **dome**.

round arch (p. 170) See under **arch**.

roundel (p. 158) Any ornamental element with a circular format, often placed as a decoration on the exterior of a building.

rune stone (p. 442) In early medieval northern Europe, a stone used as a commemorative monument and carved or inscribed with runes, a writing system used by early Germanic peoples.

rustication (p. 602) In architecture, the rough, irregular, and unfinished effect deliberately given to the exterior facing of a stone edifice. Rusticated stones are often large and used for decorative emphasis around doors or windows, or across the entire lower floors of a building.

sacra conversazione (p. 630) Italian for "holy conversation." Refers to a type of religious painting developed in fifteenth-century Florence in which a central image of the Virgin and Child is flanked by standing saints of comparable size who stand within the same spatial setting and often acknowledge each other's presence.

salon (p. 907) A large room for entertaining guests or a periodic social or intellectual gathering, often of prominent people, held in such a room. Also: a hall or **gallery** for exhibiting works of art.

sanctuary (p. 102) A sacred or holy enclosure used for worship. In ancient Greece and Rome, consisted of one or more temples and an altar. In Christian architecture, the space around the altar in a church called the chancel or presbytery.

sarcophagus (*pl.* **sarcophagi**) (p. 49) A stone coffin. Often rectangular and decorated with **relief sculpture**.

scarab (p. 51) In ancient Egypt, a stylized dung beetle associated with the sun and the god Amun.

scarification (p. 409) Ornamental decoration applied to the surface of the body by cutting the skin for cultural and/or aesthetic reasons.

school of artists or **painting** (p. 285) An art-historical term describing a group of artists, usually working at the same time and sharing similar styles, influences, and ideals. The artists in a particular school may not necessarily be directly associated with one another, unlike those in a workshop or **atelier**.

scriptorium (*pl.* **scriptoria**) (p. 244) A room in a monastery for writing or copying **manuscript**s.

scroll painting (p. 347) A painting executed on a flexible support with rollers at each end. The rollers permit the horizontal scroll to be unrolled as it is studied or the vertical scroll to be hung for contemplation or decoration.

sculpture in the round (p. 5) Three-dimensional sculpture that is carved free of any background or block. Compare **relief sculpture**.

serdab (p. 53) In ancient Egyptian tombs, the small room in which the *ka* statue was placed.

sfumato (p. 636) Italian term meaning "smoky," soft, and mellow. In painting, the effect of haze in an image. Resembling the color of the atmosphere at dusk, *sfumato* gives a smoky effect.

sgraffito (p. 604) Decoration made by incising or cutting away a surface layer of material to reveal a different color beneath.

shaft (p. 110) The main vertical section of a **column** between the **capital** and the base, usually circular in cross section.

shaft grave (p. 97) A deep pit used for burial.

shikhara (p. 302) In the architecture of northern India, a conical (or pyramidal) spire found atop a Hindu temple and often crowned with an *amalaka*.

shoin (p. 821) A term used to describe the various features found in the most formal room of upper-class Japanese residential architecture.

shoji (p. 821) A standing Japanese screen covered in translucent rice paper and used in interiors.

siapo (p. 876) A type of **tapa** cloth found in Samoa and still used as an important gift for ceremonial occasions.

silkscreen printing (p. 1092) A technique of printing in which paint or ink is pressed through a stencil and specially prepared cloth to reproduce a design in multiple copies.

sinopia (*pl.* **sinopie**) (p. 539) Italian word taken from Sinope, the ancient city in Asia Minor that was famous for its red-brick pigment. In **fresco** paintings, a full-sized, preliminary sketch done in this color on the first rough coat of plaster or *arriccio*.

site-specific (p. 1102) Of a work commissioned and/or designed for a particular location.

slip (p. 118) A mixture of clay and water applied to a **ceramic** object as a final decorative coat. Also: a solution that binds different parts of a vessel together, such as the handle and the main body.

spandrel (p. 170) The area of wall adjoining the exterior curve of an **arch** between its **springing** and the **keystone**, or the area between two arches, as in an **arcade**.

spolia (p. 471) Fragments of older architecture or sculpture reused in a secondary context. Latin for "hide stripped from an animal."

springing (p. 170) The point at which the curve of an **arch** or **vault** meets with and rises from its support.

squinch (p. 238) An **arch** or **lintel** built across the upper corners of a square space, allowing a circular or polygonal **dome** to be securely set above the walls.

stained glass (p. 287) Glass stained with color while molten, using metallic oxides. Stained glass is most often used in windows, for which small pieces of different colors are precisely cut and assembled into a design, held together by lead **came**s. Additional details may be added with vitreous paint.

stave church (p. 443) A Scandinavian wooden structure with four huge timbers (staves) at its core.

stele (*pl.* **stelai**), also **stela** (*pl.* **stelae**) (p. 27) A stone slab placed vertically and decorated with inscriptions or reliefs. Used as a grave marker or commemorative monument.

stereobate (p. 110) In Classical architecture, the foundation upon which a temple stands.

still life (*pl.* **still lifes**) (p. xxix) A type of painting that has as its subject inanimate objects (such as food and dishes) or fruit and flowers taken out of their natural contexts.

stoa (p. 107) In Greek architecture, a long roofed walkway, usually having **column**s on one long side and a wall on the other.

stoneware (p. 20) A high-fired, vitrified, but opaque **ceramic** ware that is fired in the range of 1,100 to 1,200 degrees Celsius. At that temperature, particles of silica in the clay bodies fuse together so that the finished vessels are impervious to liquids, even without glaze. Stoneware pieces are glazed to enhance their aesthetic appeal and to aid in keeping them clean. Stoneware occurs in a range of earth-toned colors, from white and tan to gray and black, with light gray predominating. Chinese potters were the first in the world to produce stoneware, which they were able to make as early as the Shang dynasty.

stringcourse (p. 503) A continuous horizontal band, such as a **molding**, decorating the face of a wall.

stucco (p. 72) A mixture of lime, sand, and other ingredients made into a material that can easily be molded or modeled. When dry, it produces a durable surface used for covering walls or for architectural sculpture and decoration.

stupa (p. 302) In Buddhist architecture, a bell-shaped or pyramidal religious monument, made of piled earth or stone, and containing sacred **relics**.

style (p. xxx) A particular manner, form, or character of representation, construction, or expression that is typical of an individual artist or of a certain place or period.

stylobate (p. 110) In Classical architecture, the stone foundation on which a temple **colonnade** stands.

stylus (p. 28) An instrument with a pointed end (used for writing and printmaking), which makes a delicate line or scratch. Also: a special writing tool for **cuneiform** writing with one pointed end and one triangular.

sublime (p. 955) Of a concept, thing, or state of greatness or vastness with high spiritual, moral, intellectual, or emotional value; or something awe-inspiring. The sublime was a goal to which many nineteenth-century artists aspired in their artworks.

sunken relief (p. 71) See under **relief sculpture**.

symposium (p. 119) An elite gathering of wealthy and powerful men in ancient Greece that focused principally on wine, music, poetry, conversation, games, and love making.

syncretism (p. 220) A process whereby artists assimilate and combine images and ideas from different cultural traditions, beliefs, and practices, giving them new meanings.

taotie (p. 334) A mask with a dragon or animal-like face common as a decorative motif in Chinese art.

tapa (p. 876) A type of cloth used for various purposes in Pacific cultures, made from tree bark stripped and beaten, and often bearing subtle designs from the mallets used to work the bark.

tapestry (p. 292) Multicolored decorative weaving to be hung on a wall or placed on furniture. Pictorial or decorative motifs are woven directly into the supporting fabric, completely concealing it.

tatami (p. 821) Mats of woven straw used in Japanese houses as a floor covering.

temenos (p. 108) An enclosed sacred area reserved for worship in ancient Greece.

tempera (p. 141) A painting **medium** made by blending egg yolks with water, pigments, and occasionally other materials, such as glue.

tenebrism (p. 723) The use of strong *chiaroscuro* and artificially illuminated areas to create a dramatic contrast of light and dark in a painting.

terra cotta (p. 114) A **medium** made from clay fired over a low heat and sometimes left unglazed. Also: the orange-brown color typical of this medium.

tessera (*pl.* **tesserae**) (p. 145) A small piece of stone, glass, or other object that is pieced together with many others to create a **mosaic**.

thatch (p. 16) Plant material such as reeds or straw tied over a framework of poles to make a roof, shelter, or small building.

thermo-luminescence dating (p. 12) A method of **radiometric dating** that measures the irradiation of the crystal structure of material such as flint or pottery and the soil in which it is found, determined by luminescence produced when a sample is heated.

tholos (p. 98) A small, round building. Sometimes built underground, e.g. as a Mycenaean tomb.

thrust (p. 170) The outward pressure caused by the weight of a **vault** and supported by **buttressing**. See also under **arch**.

tondo (*pl.* **tondi**) (p. 126) A painting or **relief sculpture** of circular shape.

torana (p. 302) In Indian architecture, an ornamented gateway arch in a temple, usually leading to the **stupa**.

torc (p. 149) A circular neck ring worn by Celtic warriors.

toron (p. 422) In West African **mosque** architecture, the wooden beams that project from the walls. Torons are used as support for the scaffolding erected annually for the replastering of the building.

tracery (p. 503) Stonework or woodwork forming a pattern in the open space of windows or applied to wall surfaces. In *plate tracery*, a series of openings are cut through the wall. In *bar tracery*, **mullion**s divide the space into segments to form decorative patterns.

transept (p. 225) The arm of a **cruciform** church perpendicular to the **nave**. The point where the nave and transept intersect is called the crossing. Beyond the crossing lies the **sanctuary**, whether **apse**, **choir**, or chevet.

transverse arch (p. 463) See under **arch**.

trefoil (p. 298) An ornamental design made up of three rounded lobes placed adjacent to one another.

triforium (p. 505) The element of the interior elevation of a church found directly below the **clerestory** and consisting of a series of arched openings in front of a passageway within the thickness of the wall.

triglyph (p. 110) Rectangular block between the **metope**s of a Doric **frieze**. Identified by the three carved vertical grooves, which approximate the appearance of the end of wooden beams.

triptych (p. 566) An artwork made up of three panels. The panels may be hinged together in such a way that the side segments (wings) fold over the central area.

trompe l'oeil (p. 618) A manner of representation in which artists faithfully describe the appearance of natural space and forms with the express intention of fooling the eye of the viewer, who may be convinced momentarily that the subject actually exists as three-dimensional reality.

trumeau (p. 478) A **column**, **pier**, or post found at the center of a large **portal** or doorway, supporting the **lintel**.

tugra (p. 288) A calligraphic imperial monogram used in Ottoman courts.

tukutuku (p. 872) Lattice panels created by women from the Maori culture and used in architecture.

Tuscan order (p. 158) See under **order**.

twining (p. 848) A basketry technique in which short rods are sewn together vertically. The panels are then joined together to form a container or other object.

tympanum (p. 478) In medieval and later architecture, the area over a door enclosed by an **arch** and a **lintel**, often decorated with sculpture or mosaic.

ukiyo-e (p. 828) A Japanese term for a type of popular art that was favored from the sixteenth century, particularly in the form of color **woodblock print**s. *Ukiyo-e* prints often depicted the world of the common people in Japan, such as courtesans and actors, as well as landscapes and myths.

undercutting (p. 212) A technique in sculpture by which the material is cut back under the edges so that the remaining form projects strongly forward, casting deep shadows.

underglaze (p. 800) Color or decoration applied to a **ceramic** piece before glazing.

upeti (p. 876) In Pacific cultures, a carved wooden design tablet, used to create patterns in cloth by dragging the fabric across it.

uranium-thorium dating (p. 12) Technique used to date prehistoric cave paintings by measuring the decay of uranium into thorium in the deposits of calcium carbinate that cover the surfaces of cave walls, to determine the minimum age of the paintings under the crust.

urna (p. 306) In Buddhist art, the curl of hair on the forehead that is a characteristic mark of a buddha. The *urna* is a symbol of divine wisdom.

ushnisha (p. 306) In Asian art, a round turban or tiara symbolizing royalty and, when worn by a buddha, enlightenment.

vanishing point (p. 610) In a **perspective** system, the point on the **horizon line** at which **orthogonals** meet. A complex system can have multiple vanishing points.

vanitas (p. xxx) An image, especially popular in Europe during the seventeenth century, in which all the objects symbolize the transience of life. *Vanitas* paintings are usually of **still lifes** or genre subjects.

vault (p. 17) An arched masonry structure that spans an interior space. *Barrel* or *tunnel vault*: an elongated or continuous semicircular vault, shaped like a half-cylinder. *Corbeled vault*: a vault made by projecting **course**s of stone; see also under **corbel**. *Groin* or *cross vault*: a vault created by the intersection of two barrel vaults of equal size which creates four side compartments of identical size and shape. *Quadrant vault*: a half-barrel vault. *Rib vault*: a groin vault with ribs (extra masonry) demarcating the junctions. Ribs may function to reinforce the groins or may be purely decorative.

veduta (*pl.* **vedute**) (p. 915) Italian for "vista" or "view." Paintings, drawings, or prints, often of expansive city scenes or of harbors.

vellum (p. 245) A fine animal skin prepared for writing and painting. See also **parchment**.

verism (p. 168) Style in which artists concern themselves with describing the exterior likeness of an object or person, usually by rendering its visible details in a finely executed, meticulous manner.

vihara (p. 305) From the Sanskrit term meaning "for wanderers." A *vihara* is, in general, a Buddhist monastery in India. It also signifies monks' cells and gathering places in such a monastery.

volute (p. 110) A spiral scroll, as seen on an Ionic **capital**.

votive figure (p. 31) An image created as a devotional offering to a deity.

voussoir (p. 170) Wedge-shaped stone block used to build an **arch**. The topmost voussoir is called a **keystone**. See also **joggled voussoirs**.

warp (p. 292) The vertical threads in a weaver's loom. Warp threads make up a fixed framework that provides the structure for the entire piece of cloth, and are thus often thicker than **weft** threads.

wattle and daub (p. 16) A wall construction method combining upright branches, woven with twigs (wattles) and plastered or filled with clay or mud (daub).

weft (p. 292) The horizontal threads in a woven piece of cloth. Weft threads are woven at right angles to and through the **warp** threads to make up the bulk of the decorative pattern. In carpets, the weft is often completely covered or formed by the rows of trimmed knots that form the carpet's soft surface.

westwork (p. 446) The monumental, west-facing entrance section of a Carolingian, Ottonian, or Romanesque church. The exterior consists of multiple stories between two towers; the interior includes an entrance vestibule, a chapel, and a series of **galleries** overlooking the **nave**.

white-ground (p. 141) A type of ancient Greek pottery in which the background color of the object was painted with a **slip** that turns white in the firing process. Figures and details were added by painting on or incising into this slip. White-ground wares were popular in the Classical period as funerary objects.

woodblock print (p. 591) A print made from one or more carved wooden blocks. In Japan, woodblock prints were made using multiple blocks carved in relief, usually with a block for each color in the finished print. See also **woodcut**.

woodcut (p. 592) A type of print made by carving a design into a wooden block. The ink is applied to the block with a roller. As the ink touches only on the surface areas and lines remaining between the carved-away parts of the block, it is these areas that make the print when paper is pressed against the inked block, leaving the carved-away parts of the design to appear blank. Also: the process by which the woodcut is made.

yaksha, yakshi (p. 301) The male (*yaksha*) and female (*yakshi*) nature spirits that act as agents of the Hindu gods. Their sculpted images are often found on Hindu temples and other sacred places, particularly at the entrances.

yamato-e (p. 374) A native style of Japanese painting developed during the twelfth and thirteenth centuries, distinguished from Japanese painting styles that emulate Chinese traditions.

ziggurat (p. 28) In ancient Mesopotamia, a tall stepped tower of earthen materials, often supporting a shrine.

Bibliography

Susan V. Craig, updated by Carrie L. McDade

This bibliography is composed of books in English that are suggested "further reading" titles. Most are available in good libraries, whether college, university, or public. Recently published works have been emphasized so that the research information would be current. There are three classifications of listings: general surveys and art history reference tools, including journals and Internet directories; surveys of large periods that encompass multiple chapters (ancient art in the Western tradition, European medieval art, European Renaissance through eighteenth-century art, modern art in the West, Asian art, and African and Oceanic art, and art of the Americas); and books for individual Chapters 1 through 33.

General Art History Surveys and Reference Tools

Adams, Laurie Schneider. *Art Across Time*. 4th ed. New York: McGraw-Hill, 2011.

Barnet, Sylvan. *A Short Guide to Writing about Art*. 10th ed. Upper Saddle River, NJ: Pearson/Prentice Hall, 2010.

Bony, Anne. *Design: History, Main Trends, Main Figures*. Edinburgh: Chambers, 2005.

Boström, Antonia. *Encyclopedia of Sculpture*. 3 vols. New York: Fitzroy Dearborn, 2004.

Broude, Norma, and Mary D. Garrard, eds. *Feminism and Art History: Questioning the Litany*. Icon Editions. New York: Harper & Row, 1982.

Chadwick, Whitney. *Women, Art, and Society*. 4th ed. New York: Thames & Hudson, 2007.

Chilvers, Ian, ed. *The Oxford Dictionary of Art*. 4th ed. New York: Oxford Univ. Press, 2009.

Curl, James Stevens. *A Dictionary of Architecture and Landscape Architecture*. 2nd ed. Oxford: Oxford Univ. Press, 2006.

Davies, Penelope J.E., et al. *Janson's History of Art: The Western Tradition*. 8th ed. Upper Saddle River, NJ: Prentice Hall, 2010.

The Dictionary of Art. Ed. Jane Turner. 34 vols. New York: Grove's Dictionaries, 1996.

Frank, Patrick, Duane Preble, and Sarah Preble. *Prebles' Artforms*. 10th ed. Upper Saddle River, NJ: Pearson/Prentice Hall, 2011.

Gaze, Delia, ed. *Dictionary of Women Artists*. 2 vols. London: Fitzroy Dearborn, 1997.

Griffiths, Antony. *Prints and Printmaking: An Introduction to the History and Techniques*. 2nd ed. London: British Museum Press, 1996.

Hadden, Peggy. *The Quotable Artist*. New York: Allworth Press, 2002.

Hall, James. *Dictionary of Subjects and Symbols in Art*. 2nd ed. Boulder, CO: Westview Press, 2008.

Holt, Elizabeth Gilmore, ed. *A Documentary History of Art*. 3 vols. New Haven: Yale Univ. Press, 1986.

Honour, Hugh, and John Fleming. *The Visual Arts: A History*. 7th ed. rev. Upper Saddle River, NJ: Pearson/Prentice Hall, 2010.

Johnson, Paul. *Art: A New History*. New York: HarperCollins, 2003.

Kemp, Martin, ed. *The Oxford History of Western Art*. Oxford: Oxford Univ. Press, 2000.

Kleiner, Fred S. *Gardner's Art through the Ages*. Enhanced 13th ed. Belmont, CA: Thomson/Wadsworth, 2011.

Kostof, Spiro. *A History of Architecture: Settings and Rituals*. 2nd ed. Revised Greg Castillo. New York: Oxford Univ. Press, 1995.

Mackenzie, Lynn. *Non-Western Art: A Brief Guide*. 2nd ed. Upper Saddle River, NJ: Pearson/Prentice Hall, 2001.

Marmor, Max, and Alex Ross, eds. *Guide to the Literature of Art History 2*. Chicago: American Library Association, 2005.

Onians, John, ed. *Atlas of World Art*. New York: Oxford Univ. Press, 2004.

Sayre, Henry M. *Writing about Art*. 6th ed. Upper Saddle River, NJ: Pearson/Prentice Hall, 2009.

Sed-Rajna, Gabrielle. *Jewish Art*. Trans. Sara Friedman and Mira Reich. New York: Abrams, 1997.

Slatkin, Wendy. *Women Artists in History: From Antiquity to the Present*. 4th ed. Upper Saddle River, NJ: Pearson/Prentice Hall, 2001.

Sutton, Ian. *Western Architecture: From Ancient Greece to the Present*. World of Art. New York: Thames & Hudson, 1999.

Trachtenberg, Marvin, and Isabelle Hyman. *Architecture, from Prehistory to Postmodernity*. 2nd ed. Upper Saddle River, NJ: Pearson/Prentice Hall, 2002.

Watkin, David. *A History of Western Architecture*. 4th ed. New York. Watson-Guptill, 2005.

Art History Journals: A Select List of Current Titles

African Arts. Quarterly. Los Angeles: Univ. of California at Los Angeles, James S. Coleman African Studies Center, 1967–.

American Art: The Journal of the Smithsonian American Art Museum. 3/year. Chicago: Univ. of Chicago Press, 1987–.

American Indian Art Magazine. Quarterly. Scottsdale, AZ: American Indian Art Inc., 1975–.

American Journal of Archaeology. Quarterly. Boston: Archaeological Institute of America, 1885–.

Antiquity: A Periodical of Archaeology. Quarterly. Cambridge: Antiquity Publications Ltd., 1927–.

Apollo: The International Magazine of the Arts. Monthly. London: Apollo Magazine Ltd., 1925–.

Architectural History. Annually. Farnham, UK: Society of Architectural Historians of Great Britain, 1958–.

Archives of American Art Journal. Quarterly. Washington, DC: Archives of American Art, Smithsonian Institution, 1960–.

Archives of Asian Art. Annually. New York: Asia Society, 1945–.

Ars Orientalis: The Arts of Asia, Southeast Asia, and Islam. Annually. Ann Arbor: Univ. of Michigan Dept. of Art History, 1954–.

Art Bulletin. Quarterly. New York: College Art Association, 1913–.

Art History: Journal of the Association of Art Historians. 5/year. Oxford: Blackwell Publishing Ltd., 1978–.

Art in America. Monthly. New York: Brant Publications Inc., 1913–.

Art Journal. Quarterly. New York: College Art Association, 1960–.

Art Nexus. Quarterly. Bogota, Colombia: Arte en Colombia Ltda, 1976–.

Art Papers Magazine. Bimonthly. Atlanta: Atlanta Art Papers Inc., 1976–.

Artforum International. 10/year. New York: Artforum International Magazine Inc., 1962–.

Artnews. 11/year. New York: Artnews LLC, 1902–.

Bulletin of the Metropolitan Museum of Art. Quarterly. New York: Metropolitan Museum of Art, 1905–.

Burlington Magazine. Monthly. London: Burlington Magazine Publications Ltd., 1903–.

Dumbarton Oaks Papers. Annually. Locust Valley, NY: J.J. Augustin Inc., 1940–.

Flash Art International. Bimonthly. Trevi, Italy: Giancarlo Politi Editore, 1980–.

Gesta. Semiannually. New York: International Center of Medieval Art, 1963–.

History of Photography. Quarterly. Abingdon, UK: Taylor & Francis Ltd., 1976–.

International Review of African American Art. Quarterly. Hampton, VA: International Review of African American Art, 1976–.

Journal of Design History. Quarterly. Oxford: Oxford Univ. Press, 1988–.

Journal of Egyptian Archaeology. Annually. London: Egypt Exploration Society, 1914–.

Journal of Hellenic Studies. Annually. London: Society for the Promotion of Hellenic Studies, 1880–.

Journal of Roman Archaeology. Annually. Portsmouth, RI: Journal of Roman Archaeology LLC, 1988–.

Journal of the Society of Architectural Historians. Quarterly. Chicago: Society of Architectural Historians, 1940–.

Journal of the Warburg and Courtauld Institutes. Annually. London: Warburg Institute, 1937–.

Leonardo: Art, Science, and Technology. 6/year. Cambridge, MA: MIT Press, 1968–.

Marg. Quarterly. Mumbai, India: Scientific Publishers, 1946–.

Master Drawings. Quarterly. New York: Master Drawings Association, 1963–.

October. Cambridge, MA: MIT Press, 1976–.

Oxford Art Journal. 3/year. Oxford: Oxford Univ. Press, 1978–.

Parkett. 3/year. Zürich, Switzerland: Parkett Verlag AG, 1984–.

Print Quarterly. Quarterly. London: Print Quarterly Publications, 1984–.

Simiolus: Netherlands Quarterly for the History of Art. Quarterly. Apeldoorn, Netherlands: Stichting voor Nederlandse Kunsthistorische Publicaties, 1966–.

Woman's Art Journal. Semiannually. Philadelphia: Old City Publishing Inc., 1980–.

Internet Directories for Art History Information: A Selected List

ARCHITECTURE AND BUILDING,
http://www.library.unlv.edu/arch/rsrce/webresources/
A directory of architecture websites collected by Jeanne Brown at the Univ. of Nevada at Las Vegas. Topical lists include architecture, building and construction, design, history, housing, planning, preservation, and landscape architecture. Most entries include a brief annotation and the last date the link was accessed by the compiler.

ART HISTORY RESOURCES ON THE WEB,
http://witcombe.sbc.edu/ARTHLinks.html
Authored by Professor Christopher L.C.E. Witcombe of Sweet Briar College in Virginia, since 1995, the site includes an impressive number of links for various art-historical eras as well as links to research resources, museums, and galleries. The content is frequently updated.

ART IN FLUX: A DIRECTORY OF RESOURCES FOR RESEARCH IN CONTEMPORARY ART,
http://www.boisestate.edu/art/artinflux/intro.html
Cheryl K. Shurtleff of Boise State Univ. in Idaho has authored this directory, which includes sites selected according to their relevance to the study of national or international contemporary art and artists. The subsections include artists, museums, theory, reference, and links.

ARTCYCLOPEDIA: THE GUIDE TO GREAT ART ON THE INTERNET,
http://www.artcyclopedia.com
With more than 2,100 art sites and 75,000 links, this is one of the most comprehensive Web directories for artists and art topics. The primary search is by artist's name but access is also available by title of artwork, artistic movement, museums and galleries, nationality, period, and medium.

MOTHER OF ALL ART AND ART HISTORY LINKS PAGES,
http://umich.edu/~motherha
Maintained by the Dept. of the History of Art at the Univ. of Michigan, this directory covers art history departments, art museums, fine arts schools and departments, as well as links to research resources. Each entry includes annotations.

VOICE OF THE SHUTTLE,
http://vos.ucsb.edu
Sponsored by Univ. of California, Santa Barbara, this directory includes more than 70 pages of links to humanities and humanities-related resources on the Internet. The structured guide includes specific subsections on architecture, on art (modern and contemporary), and on art history. Links usually include a one-sentence explanation and the resource is frequently updated with new information.

ARTBABBLE,
http://www.artbabble.org/
An online community created by staff at the Indianapolis Museum of Art to showcase art-based video content, including interviews with artists and curators, original documentaries, and art installation videos. Partners and contributors to the project include Art21, Los Angeles County Museum of Art, The Museum of Modern Art, The New York Public Library, San Francisco Museum of Modern Art, and Smithsonian American Art Museum.

YAHOO! ARTS>ART HISTORY,
http://dir.yahoo.com/Arts/Art_History/
Another extensive directory of art links organized into subdivisions with one of the most extensive being "Periods and Movements." Links include the name of the site as well as a few words of explanation.

European Renaissance through Eighteenth-Century Art, General

Black, C.F., et al. *Cultural Atlas of the Renaissance.* New York: Prentice Hall, 1993.

Blunt, Anthony. *Art and Architecture in France, 1500–1700.* 5th ed. Revised Richard Beresford. Pelican History of Art. New Haven: Yale Univ. Press, 1999.

Brown, Jonathan. *Painting in Spain: 1500–1700.* Pelican History of Art. New Haven: Yale Univ. Press, 1998.

Cole, Bruce. *Studies in the History of Italian Art, 1250–1550.* London: Pindar Press, 1996.

Graham-Dixon, Andrew. *Renaissance.* Berkeley: Univ. of California Press, 1999.

Harbison, Craig. *The Mirror of the Artist: Northern Renaissance Art in Its Historical Context.* Perspectives. New York: Abrams, 1995.

Harris, Ann Sutherland. *Seventeenth-Century Art & Architecture.* 2nd ed. Upper Saddle River, NJ: Pearson/Prentice Hall, 2008.

Harrison, Charles, Paul Wood, and Jason Gaiger. *Art in Theory 1648–1815: An Anthology of Changing Ideas.* Oxford: Blackwell, 2000.

Hartt, Frederick, and David G. Wilkins. *History of Italian Renaissance Art: Painting, Sculpture, Architecture.* 7th ed. Upper Saddle River, NJ: Pearson/Prentice Hall, 2011.

Jestaz, Bertrand. *The Art of the Renaissance.* Trans. I. Mark Paris. New York: Abrams, 1994.

Minor, Vernon Hyde. *Baroque & Rococo: Art & Culture.* New York: Abrams, 1999.

Paoletti, John T., and Gary M. Radke. *Art in Renaissance Italy.* 3rd ed. Upper Saddle River, NJ: Pearson/Prentice Hall, 2005.

Smith, Jeffrey Chipps. *The Northern Renaissance.* Art & Ideas. London and New York: Phaidon Press, 2004.

Stechow, Wolfgang. *Northern Renaissance, 1400–1600: Sources and Documents.* Upper Saddle River, NJ: Pearson/Prentice Hall, 1966.

Summerson, John. *Architecture in Britain, 1530–1830.* 9th ed. Pelican History of Art. New Haven: Yale Univ. Press, 1993.

Waterhouse, Ellis K. *Painting in Britain, 1530–1790.* 5th ed. Pelican History of Art. New Haven: Yale Univ. Press, 1994.

Whinney, Margaret Dickens. *Sculpture in Britain: 1530–1830.* 2nd ed. Revised John Physick. Pelican History of Art. London: Penguin, 1988.

Introduction

Acton, Mary. *Learning to Look at Paintings.* 2nd ed. New York: Routledge, 2009.

Arnold, Dana. *Art History: A Very Short Introduction.* Oxford and New York: Oxford Univ. Press, 2004.

Baxandall, Michael. *Patterns of Intention: On the Historical Explanation of Pictures.* New Haven: Yale Univ. Press, 1985.

Clearwater, Bonnie. *The Rothko Book.* London: Tate Publishing, 2006.

Decoteau, Pamela Hibbs. *Clara Peeters, 1594–ca.1640 and the Development of Still-Life Painting in Northern Europe.* Lingen: Luca Verlag, 1992.

Geertz, Clifford. "Art as a Cultural System." *Modern Language Notes* 91 (1976): 1473–1499.

Hochstrasser, Julie Berger. *Still Life and Trade in the Dutch Golden Age.* New Haven: Yale Univ. Press, 2007.

Holstein, Jonathan. *The Pieced Quilt: An American Design Tradition.* New York: Galahad Books, 1973.

Jolly, Penny Howell. "Rogier van der Weyden's Escorial and Philadelphia Crucifixions and Their Relation to Fra Angelico at San Marco." *Oud Holland* 95 (1981): 113–126.

Mainardi, Patricia. "Quilts: The Great American Art." *The Feminist Art Journal* 2/1 (1973): 1, 18–23.

Miller, Angela L., et al. *American Encounters: Art, History, and Cultural Identity.* Upper Saddle River, NJ: Pearson/Prentice Hall, 2008.

Minor, Vernon Hyde. *Art History's History.* Upper Saddle River, NJ: Pearson/Prentice Hall, 2001.

Nelson, Robert S., and Richard Shiff, eds. *Critical Terms for Art History.* 2nd ed. Chicago: Univ. of Chicago Press, 2003.

Panofsky, Erwin. *Studies in Iconology: Humanistic Themes in the Art of the Renaissance.* New York: Oxford Univ. Press, 1939.

———. *Meaning in the Visual Arts.* Phoenix ed. Chicago: Univ. of Chicago Press, 1982.

Preziosi, Donald, ed. *The Art of Art History: A Critical Anthology.* 2nd ed. Oxford and New York: Oxford Univ. Press, 2009.

Rothko, Mark. *Writings on Art.* Ed. Miguel López-Remiro. New Haven: Yale Univ. Press, 2006.

———. *The Artist's Reality: Philosophies of Art.* Ed. Christopher Rothko. New Haven: Yale Univ. Press, 2004.

Schapiro, Meyer. "The Apples of Cézanne: An Essay on the Meaning of Still Life." *Art News Annual* 34 (1968): 34–53. Reprinted in *Modern Art 19th & 20th Centuries: Selected Papers 2,* London: Chatto & Windus, 1978.

Sowers, Robert. *Rethinking the Forms of Visual Expression.* Berkeley: Univ. of California Press, 1990.

Taylor, Joshua. *Learning to Look: A Handbook for the Visual Arts.* 2nd ed. Chicago: Chicago Univ. Press, 1981.

Tucker, Mark. "Rogier van der Weyden's 'Philadelphia Crucifixion.'" *Burlington Magazine* 139 (1997): 676–683.

Wang, Fangyu, et al., eds. *Master of the Lotus Garden: The Life and Art of Bada Shanren (1626–1705).* New Haven: Yale Univ. Press, 1990.

Chapter 18 Fourteenth-Century Art in Europe

Alexander, Jonathan, and Paul Binski, eds. *Age of Chivalry: Art in Plantagenet England, 1200–1400.* London: Royal Academy of Arts, 1987.

Backhouse, Janet. *Illumination from Books of Hours.* London: British Library, 2004.

Boehm, Barbara Drake, and Jiří Fajt, eds. *Prague: The Crown of Bohemia, 1347–1437.* New York: Metropolitan Museum of Art, 2005.

Bony, Jean. *The English Decorated Style: Gothic Architecture Transformed, 1250–1350.* The Wrightsman Lecture, 10. Oxford: Phaidon Press, 1979.

Cennini, Cennino. *The Craftsman's Handbook "Il libro dell'arte."* Trans. D.V. Thompson, Jr. New York: Dover, 1960.

Derbes, Anne, and Mark Sandona, eds. *The Cambridge Companion to Giotto.* Cambridge and New York: Cambridge Univ. Press, 2003.

Fajt, Jiri, ed. *Magister Theodoricus, Court Painter to Emperor Charles IV: The Pictorial Decoration of the Shrines at Karlstejn Castle.* Prague: National Gallery, 1998.

Holt, Elizabeth Gilmore, ed. *A Documentary History of Art.* 2 vols. Princeton, NJ, Princeton Univ. Press, 1982–86.

Ladis, Andrew. ed, *The Arena Chapel and the Genius of Giotto: Padua.* Giotto and the World of Early Italian Art, 2. New York: Garland, 1998.

Meiss, Millard. *Painting in Florence and Siena after the Black Death: The Arts, Religion, and Society in the Mid-Fourteenth Century.* 2nd ed. Princeton, NJ: Princeton Univ. Press, 1978.

Moskowitz, Anita Fiderer. *Italian Gothic Sculpture: c. 1250–c. 1400.* New York: Cambridge Univ. Press, 2001.

Norman, Diana, ed. *Siena, Florence, and Padua: Art, Society, and Religion 1280–1400.* 2 vols. New Haven: Yale Univ. Press, 1995.

Poeschke, Joachim. *Italian Frescoes, the Age of Giotto, 1280–1400.* New York: Abbeville Press, 2005.

Schleif, Corine. "St. Hedwig's Personal Ivory Madonna: Women's Agency and the Powers of Possessing Portable Figures." In *The Four Modes of Seeing: Approaches to Medieval Imagery in Honor of Madeline Harrison Caviness.* Eds. Evelyn Staudinger Lane, Elizabeth Carson Paston, and Ellen M. Shortell. Farnham, Surrey: Ashgate, 2009: 282–403.

Vasari, Giorgio. *The Lives of the Artists.* Trans. Julia Conaway Bondanella and Peter Bondanella. Oxford World's Classics. New York: Oxford Univ. Press, 2008.

Welch, Evelyn S. *Art in Renaissance Italy, 1350–1500.* New ed. Oxford History of Art. Oxford: Oxford Univ. Press, 2000.

White, John. *Art and Architecture in Italy, 1250 to 1400.* 3rd ed. Pelican History of Art. Harmondsworth, UK: Penguin, 1993.

Wieck, Roger S. *Time Sanctified: The Book of Hours in Medieval Art and Life.* 2nd ed. New York: Braziller, 2001.

Chapter 19 Fifteenth-Century Art in Northern Europe

Art from the Court of Burgundy: The Patronage of Philip the Bold and John the Fearless 1364–1419. Dijon: Musée des Beaux-Arts and Cleveland: Cleveland Museum of Art, 2004.

Baxandall, Michael. *The Limewood Sculptors of Renaissance Germany.* New Haven: Yale Univ. Press, 1980.

Blum, Shirley. *Early Netherlandish Triptychs: A Study in Patronage.* California Studies in the History of Art, 13. Berkeley: Univ. of California Press, 1969.

Borchert, Till-Holger. *Age of Van Eyck: The Mediterranean World and Early Netherlandish Painting, 1430–1530.* New York: Thames & Hudson, 2002.

Campbell, Lorne. *The Fifteenth-Century Netherlandish Schools* (National Gallery Catalogues). London: National Gallery, 1998.

Cavallo, Adolph S. *The Unicorn Tapestries at the Metropolitan Museum of Art.* New York: Metropolitan Museum of Art, 1998.

Chastel, Andrè. *French Art: The Renaissance, 1430–1620.* Paris: Flammarion, 1995.

Dhanens, Elisabeth. *Van Eyck: The Ghent Altarpiece.* New York: Viking Press, 1973.

Füssel, Stephan. *Gutenberg and the Impact of Printing.* Trans. Douglas Martin. Burlington, VT: Ashgate, 2005.

Koster, Margaret L. "The *Arnolfini Double Portrait:* A Simple Solution." *Apollo* 157 (September 2003): 3–14.

Lane, Barbara G. *The Altar and the Altarpiece: Sacramental Themes in Early Netherlandish Painting.* New York: Harper & Row, 1984.

Marks, Richard, and Paul Williamson, eds. *Gothic: Art for England 1400–1547.* London: V&A Publications, 2003.

Meiss, Millard. *French Painting in the Time of Jean de Berry: The Limbourgs and their Contemporaries.* 2 vols. New York: Braziller, 1974.

Müller, Theodor. *Sculpture in the Netherlands, Germany, France, and Spain: 1400–1500.* Trans. Elaine and William Robson Scott. Pelican History of Art. Harmondsworth, UK: Penguin, 1966.

Pächt, Otto. *Early Netherlandish Painting: From Rogier van der Weyden to Gerard David.* Ed. Monika Rosenauer. Trans. David Britt. London: Harvey Miller, 1997.

———. *Van Eyck and the Founders of Early Netherlandish Painting.* London: Miller, 1994.

Panofsky, Erwin. *Early Netherlandish Painting, Its Origins and Character.* 2 vols. Cambridge, MA: Harvard Univ. Press, 1966.

Parshall, Peter W., and Rainer Schoch. *Origins of European Printmaking: Fifteenth-Century Woodcuts and their Public.* Washington, DC: National Gallery of Art, 2005.

Plummer, John. *The Last Flowering: French Painting in Manuscripts, 1420–1530, from American Collections.* New York: Pierpont Morgan Library, 1982.

Seidel, Linda. *Jan van Eyck's Arnolfini Portrait: Stories of an Icon.* New York: Cambridge Univ. Press, 1993.

Smith, Jeffrey Chipps. *The Northern Renaissance.* London and New York: Phaidon Press, 2004.

Snyder, James. *Northern Renaissance Art: Painting, Sculpture, the Graphic Arts from 1350 to 1575.* 2nd ed. rev. Larry Silver and Henry Luttikhuizen. Upper Saddle River, NJ: Prentice Hall, 2005.

Vos, Dirk de. *The Flemish Primitives: The Masterpieces.* Princeton, NJ: Princeton Univ. Press, 2002.

Zuffi, Stefano. *European Art of the Fifteenth Century.* Trans. Brian D. Phillips. Art through the Centuries. Los Angeles: J. Paul Getty Museum, 2005.

Chapter 20 Renaissance Art in Fifteenth-Century Italy

Adams, Laurie Schneider. *Italian Renaissance Art.* Boulder, CO: Westview Press, 2001.

Ahl, Diane Cole, ed. *The Cambridge Companion to Masaccio.* New York: Cambridge Univ. Press, 2002.

Ames-Lewis, Francis. *Drawing in Early Renaissance Italy*. 2nd ed. New Haven: Yale Univ. Press, 2000.

———. *The Intellectual Life of the Early Renaissance Artist*. New Haven: Yale Univ. Press, 2000.

Baxandall, Michael. *Painting and Experience in Fifteenth-Century Italy: A Primer in the Social History of Pictorial Style*. 2nd ed. Oxford: Oxford Univ. Press, 1988.

Boskovits, Miklós. *Italian Paintings of the Fifteenth Century*. The Collections of the National Gallery of Art. Washington, DC: National Gallery of Art, 2003.

Botticelli and Filippino: Passion and Grace in Fifteenth-Century Florentine Painting. Milan: Skira, 2004.

Brown, Patricia Fortini. *Art and Life in Renaissance Venice*. Perspectives. New York: Abrams, 1997. Reissue ed. Upper Saddle River, NJ: Pearson/Prentice Hall, 2006.

Brucker, Gene. *Florence: The Golden Age, 1138–1737*. Berkeley: Univ. of California Press, 1998.

Christiansen, Keith, Laurence B. Kanter, and Carl Brandon Strehlke. *Painting in Renaissance Siena, 1420–1500*. New York: Metropolitan Museum of Art, 1988.

Gilbert, Creighton, ed. *Italian Art, 1400–1500: Sources and Documents*. Evanston, IL: Northwestern Univ. Press, 1992.

Heydenreich, Ludwig Heinrich. *Architecture in Italy, 1400–1500*. Revised Paul Davies. Pelican History of Art. New Haven: Yale Univ. Press, 1996.

Hind, Arthur M. *An Introduction to a History of Woodcut*. New York: Dover, 1963.

Hyman, Timothy. *Sienese Painting: The Art of a City-Republic (12/8–14//)*. World of Art. New York: Thames & Hudson, 2003.

King, Ross. *Brunelleschi's Dome: How a Renaissance Genius Reinvented Architecture*. New York: Walker, 2000.

Lavin, Marilyn Aronberg, ed. *Piero della Francesca and his Legacy*. Studies in the History of Art, 48: Symposium Papers, 28. Washington, DC: National Gallery of Art, 1995.

Pächt, Otto. *Venetian Painting in the 15th Century: Jacopo, Gentile and Giovanni Bellini and Andrea Mantegna*. Ed. Margareta Vyoral-Tschapka and Michael Pächt. Trans. Fiona Elliott. London: Harvey Miller, 2003.

Paoletti, John T., and Gary M. Radke. *Art in Renaissance Italy*. 4th ed. Upper Saddle River, NJ: Pearson/Prentice Hall, 2012.

Partridge, Loren W. *The Art of Renaissance Rome, 1400–1600*. 2nd ed. Upper Saddle River, NJ: Pearson/Prentice Hall, 2006.

———. *Art of Renaissance Florence, 1400–1600*. Berkeley: Univ. of California Press, 2009.

de Pisan, Christine. *The Book of the City of Ladies*. Trans. Rosalind Brown-Grant. London: Penguin Books, 1999.

Poeschke, Joachim. *Donatello and His World: Sculpture of the Italian Renaissance*. Trans. Russell Stockman. New York: Abrams, 1993.

Pope-Hennessy, John. *Italian Renaissance Sculpture*. 4th ed. London: Phaidon Press, 1996.

Radke, Gary M., ed. *The Gates of Paradise: Lorenzo Ghiberti's Masterpiece*. New Haven: Yale Univ. Press, 2007.

Randolph, Adrian W.B., *Engaging Symbols: Gender, Politics, and Public Art in Fifteenth-Century Florence*. New Haven: Yale Univ. Press, 2002.

Troncelliti, Latifah. *The Two Parallel Realities of Alberti and Cennini: The Power of Writing and the Visual Arts in the Italian Quattrocento*. Studies in Italian Literature, vol. 14. Lewiston, NY: Mellen Press, 2004.

Turner, Richard. *Renaissance Florence: The Invention of a New Art*. Perspectives. New York: Abrams, 1997. Reissue ed. Upper Saddle River, NJ: Pearson/Prentice Hall, 2006.

Vasari, Giorgio. *The Lives of the Artists*. Trans. Julia Conaway Bondanella and Peter Bondanella. Oxford World's Classics. New York: Oxford Univ. Press, 2008.

Verdon, Timothy, and John Henderson, eds. *Christianity and the Renaissance: Image and Religious Imagination in the Quattrocento*. Syracuse, NY: Syracuse Univ. Press, 1990.

Walker, Paul Robert. *The Feud that Sparked the Renaissance: How Brunelleschi and Ghiberti Changed the Art World*. New York: William Morrow, 2002.

Welch, Evelyn S. *Art and Society in Italy, 1350–1500*. Oxford History of Art. Oxford: Oxford Univ. Press, 1997.

Chapter 21 Sixteenth-Century Art in Italy

Acidini Luchinat, Cristina, et al. *The Medici, Michelangelo, & the Art of Late Renaissance Florence*. New Haven: Yale Univ. Press, 2002.

Bambach, Carmen. *Drawing and Painting in the Italian Renaissance Workshop: Theory and Practice, 1330–1600*. Cambridge: Cambridge Univ. Press, 1999.

Barriault, Anne B., ed. *Reading Vasari*. London: Philip Wilson in assoc. with the Georgia Museum of Art, 2005.

Brambilla Barcilon, Pinin. *Leonardo: The Last Supper*. Chicago: Univ. of Chicago Press, 2001.

Brown, Patricia Fortini. *Art and Life in Renaissance Venice*. Perspectives. New York: Abrams, 1997.

Cellini, Benvenuto. *Autobiography*. Rev. ed. Trans. George Bull. Penguin Classics. New York: Penguin, 1998.

Chelazzi Dini, Giulietta, Alessandro Angelini, and Bernardina Sani. *Sienese Painting: From Duccio to the Birth of the Baroque*. New York: Abrams, 1998.

Cole, Alison. *Virtue and Magnificence: Art of the Italian Renaissance Courts*. Perspectives. New York: Abrams, 1995. Reissue ed. as *Art of the Italian Courts*. Upper Saddle River, NJ: Pearson/Prentice Hall, 2006.

Franklin, David, ed. *Leonardo da Vinci, Michelangelo, and the Renaissance in Florence*. Ottawa: National Gallery of Canada in assoc. with Yale Univ. Press, 2005.

Freedberg, S.J. *Painting in Italy, 1500 to 1600*. 3rd ed. Pelican History of Art. New Haven: Yale Univ. Press, 1993.

Goffen, Rona. *Renaissance Rivals: Michelangelo, Leonardo, Raphael, Titian*. New Haven: Yale Univ. Press, 2002.

———. *Titian's Venus of Urbino*. Masterpieces of Western Painting. Cambridge: Cambridge Univ. Press, 1997.

———. *Titian's Women*. New Haven: Yale Univ. Press, 1997.

Hall, Marcia B. *After Raphael: Painting in Central Italy in the Sixteenth Century*. New York: Cambridge Univ. Press, 1999.

———, ed. *The Cambridge Companion to Raphael*. New York: Cambridge Univ. Press, 2005.

Hollingsworth, Mary. *Patronage in Sixteenth Century Italy*. London: John Murray, 1996.

Hopkins, Andrew. *Italian Architecture: From Michelangelo to Borromini*. World of Art. New York: Thames & Hudson, 2002.

Hughes, Anthony. *Michelangelo*. Art & Ideas. London: Phaidon Press, 1997.

Huse, Norbert, and Wolfgang Wolters. *Art of Renaissance Venice: Architecture, Sculpture, and Painting, 1460–1590*. Trans. Edmund Jephcott. Chicago: Univ. of Chicago Press, 1990.

Joannides, Paul. *Titian to 1518: The Assumption of Genius*. New Haven: Yale Univ. Press, 2001.

Klein, Robert, and Henri Zerner. *Italian Art, 1500–1600: Sources and Documents*. Upper Saddle River, NJ: Pearson/Prentice Hall, 1966.

Kliemann, Julian-Matthias, and Michael Rohlmann. *Italian Frescoes: High Renaissance and Mannerism, 1510–1600*. Trans. Steven Lindberg. New York: Abbeville Press, 2004.

Landau, David, and Peter Parshall. *The Renaissance Print: 1470–1550*. New Haven: Yale Univ. Press, 1994.

Lieberman, Ralph. *Renaissance Architecture in Venice, 1450–1540*. New York: Abbeville Press, 1982.

Lotz, Wolfgang. *Architecture in Italy, 1500–1600*. Revised Deborah Howard. Pelican History of Art. New Haven: Yale Univ. Press, 1995.

Meilman, Patricia, ed. *The Cambridge Companion to Titian*. New York: Cambridge Univ. Press, 2004.

Mitrovic, Branko. *Learning from Palladio*. New York: Norton, 2004.

Murray, Linda. *The High Renaissance and Mannerism: Italy, the North and Spain, 1500–1600*. World of Art. London: Thames & Hudson, 1995.

Partridge, Loren W. *The Art of Renaissance Rome, 1400–1600*. 2nd ed. Upper Saddle River, NJ: Pearson/Prentice Hall, 2006.

———. *Art of Renaissance Florence, 1400–1600*. Berkeley: Univ. of California Press, 2009.

———. *Michelangelo, the Last Judgment: A Glorious Restoration*. New York: Abrams, 1997.

Pilliod, Elizabeth. *Pontormo, Bronzino, Allori: A Genealogy of Florentine Art*. New Haven: Yale Univ. Press, 2001.

Pope-Hennessy, John. *Italian High Renaissance and Baroque Sculpture*. 4th ed. London: Phaidon Press, 1996.

Rosand, David. *Painting in Cinquecento Venice: Titian, Veronese, Tintoretto*. Rev. ed. Cambridge: Cambridge Univ. Press, 1997.

Rowe, Colin, and Leon Satkowski. *Italian Architecture of the 16th Century*. New York: Princeton Architectural Press, 2002.

Rowland, Ingrid D. *The Culture of the High Renaissance: Ancients and Moderns in Sixteenth Century Rome*. Cambridge: Cambridge Univ. Press, 1998.

Shearman, John. *Mannerism*. Harmondsworth, UK: Penguin, 1967. Reissue ed. New York: Penguin, 1990.

Vasari, Giorgio. *The Lives of the Artists*. Trans. Julia Conaway Bondanella and Peter Bondanella. Oxford World's Classics. New York: Oxford Univ. Press, 2008.

Verheyen, Egon. *The Paintings in the Studiolo of Isabella d'Este at Mantua*. Monographs on Archaeology and Fine Arts, 23. New York: New York Univ. Press, 1971.

Williams, Robert. *Art, Theory, and Culture in Sixteenth-Century Italy: From Techne to Metateche*. Cambridge: Cambridge Univ. Press, 1997.

Chapter 22 Sixteenth-Century Art in Northern Europe and the Iberian Peninsula

Bartrum, Giulia. *Albrecht Dürer and his Legacy: The Graphic Work of a Renaissance Artist*. London: British Museum Press, 2002.

_____. *German Renaissance Prints 1490–1550*. London: British Museum Press, 1995.

Brown, Jonathan. *Painting in Spain, 1500–1700*. Pelican History of Art. New Haven: Yale Univ. Press, 1998.

Buck, Stephanie, and Jochen Sander. *Hans Holbein the Younger: Painter at the Court of Henry VIII*. Trans. Rachel Esner and Beverley Jackson. New York: Thames & Hudson, 2004.

Chapuis, Julien. *Tilman Riemenschneider: Master Sculptor of the Late Middle Ages*. Washington, DC: National Gallery of Art, 1999.

Davies, David, and John H. Elliott. *El Greco*. London: National Gallery, 2003.

Dixon, Laurinda. *Bosch*. Art & Ideas. New York: Phaidon Press, 2003.

Foister, Susan. *Holbein and England*. New Haven: Published for Paul Mellon Centre for Studies in British Art by Yale Univ. Press, 2004.

Hayum, Andrée. *The Isenheim Altarpiece: God's Medicine and the Painter's Vision*. Princeton Essays on the Arts, 18. Princeton, NJ: Princeton Univ. Press, 1989.

Hearn, Karen, ed. *Dynasties: Painting in Tudor and Jacobean England, 1530–1630*. New York: Rizzoli, 1996.

Koerner, Joseph Leo. *The Reformation of the Image*. Chicago: Univ. of Chicago Press, 2004.

Kubler, George. *Building the Escorial*. Princeton, NJ: Princeton Univ. Press, 1982.

Nash, Susie. *Northern Renaissance Art*. Oxford History of Art. New York: Oxford Univ. Press, 2008.

Price, David Hotchkiss. *Albrecht Dürer's Renaissance: Humanism, Reformation, and the Art of Faith*. Studies in Medieval and Early Modern Civilization. Ann Arbor: Univ. of Michigan Press, 2003.

Roberts-Jones, Philippe, and Françoise Roberts-Jones. *Pieter Bruegel*. New York: Abrams, 2002.

Smith, Jeffrey Chipps. *Nuremberg, a Renaissance City, 1500–1618*. Austin: Huntington Art Gallery, Univ. of Texas, 1983.

_____. *German Sculpture of the Later Renaissance, c.1520–1580: Art in an Age of Uncertainty*. Princeton, NJ: Princeton Univ. Press, 1994.

_____. *The Northern Renaissance*. London and New York: Phaidon Press, 2004.

Snyder, James. *Northern Renaissance Art: Painting, Sculpture, the Graphic Arts from 1350 to 1575*. 2nd ed. rev. Larry Silver and Henry Luttikhuizen. Upper Saddle River, NJ: Pearson/Prentice Hall, 2005.

Strong, Roy C. *Artists of the Tudor Court: The Portrait Miniature Rediscovered, 1520–1620*. London: V&A Publications, 1983.

Zerner, Henri. *Renaissance Art in France: The Invention of Classicism*. Paris: Flammarion, 2003.

Zorach, Rebecca. *Blood, Milk, Ink, Gold: Abundance and Excess in the French Renaissance*. Chicago: Univ. of Chicago Press, 2005.

Chapter 23 Seventeenth-Century Art in Europe

Adams, Laurie Schneider. *Key Monuments of the Baroque*. Boulder, CO: Westview Press, 2000.

Allen, Christopher. *French Painting in the Golden Age*. World of Art. New York: Thames & Hudson, 2003.

Alpers, Svetlana. *The Art of Describing: Dutch Art in the Seventeenth Century*. Chicago: Chicago Univ. Press, 1983.

_____. *The Making of Rubens*. New Haven: Yale Univ. Press, 1995.

Blankert, Albert. *Rembrandt: A Genius and His Impact*. Melbourne: National Gallery of Victoria, 1997.

Boucher, Bruce. *Italian Baroque Sculpture*. World of Art. New York: Thames & Hudson, 1998.

Brown, Beverly Louise, ed. *The Genius of Rome, 1592–1623*. London: Royal Academy of Arts, 2001.

Brown, Jonathan. *Painting in Spain, 1500–1700*. Pelican History of Art. New Haven: Yale Univ. Press, 1998.

———, and Carmen Garrido. *Velásquez: The Technique of Genius*. New Haven: Yale Univ. Press, 2003.

Careri, Giovanni. *Baroques*. Tran. Alexandra Bonfante-Warren. Princeton: Princeton Univ. Press, 2003.

Chapman, H. Perry. *Rembrandt's Self-Portraits: A Study in 17th-Century Identity*. Princeton: Princeton Univ. Press, 1990.

Chong, Alan, and Wouter Kloek. *Still-Life Paintings from the Netherlands, 1550–1720*. Zwolle: Waanders, 1999.

Enggass, Robert, and Jonathan Brown. *Italian and Spanish Art, 1600–1750: Sources and Documents*. 2nd ed. Evanston, IL: Northwestern Univ. Press, 1992.

Franklin, David, and Sebastian Schütze. *Caravaggio and his Followers in Rome*. New Haven: Yale Univ. Press, 2011.

Frantis, Wayne E., ed. *The Cambridge Companion to Vermeer*. Cambridge: Cambridge Univ. Press, 2001.

———. *Dutch Seventeenth-Century Genre Painting: Its Stylistic and Thematic Evolution*. New Haven: Yale Univ. Press, 2004.

Harbison, Robert. *Reflections on Baroque*. Chicago: Univ. of Chicago Press, 2000.

Keazor, Henry. *Nicolas Poussin, 1594–1665*. Cologne & London: Taschen, 2007.

Kiers, Judikje, and Fieke Tissink. *Golden Age of Dutch Art: Painting, Sculpture, Decorative Art*. London: Thames & Hudson, 2000.

Lagerlöf, Margaretha Rossholm. *Ideal Landscape: Annibale Carracci, Nicolas Poussin, and Claude Lorrain*. New Haven: Yale Univ. Press, 1990.

McPhee, Sarah. *Bernini and the Bell Towers: Architecture and Politics at the Vatican*. New Haven: Yale Univ. Press, 2002.

Millon, Henry A., ed. *The Triumph of the Baroque: Architecture in Europe, 1600–1750*. 2nd ed. rev. New York: Rizzoli, 1999.

Morrissey, Jake. *The Genius in the Design: Bernini, Borromini, and the Rivalry that Transformed Rome*. New York: William Morrow, 2005.

Puttfarken, Thomas. *Roger de Piles' Theory of Art*. New Haven: Yale Univ. Press, 1985.

Rand, Richard. *Claude Lorrain, the Painter as Draftsman: Drawings from the British Museum*. New Haven: Yale Univ. Press; Williamstown, MA: Clark Art Institute, 2006.

Slive, Seymour. *Dutch Painting 1600–1800*. Pelican History of Art. New Haven: Yale Univ. Press, 1995.

Summerson, John. *Inigo Jones*. New Haven: Published for the Paul Mellon Centre for Studies in British Art by Yale Univ. Press, 2000.

Tomlinson, Janis. *From El Greco to Goya: Painting in Spain, 1561–1828*. Perspectives. New York: Abrams, 1997.

Vlieghe, Hans. *Flemish Art and Architecture, 1585–1700*. Pelican History of Art. Reissue ed. 2004. New Haven: Yale Univ. Press, 1998.

Walker, Stefanie, and Frederick Hammond, eds. *Life and the Arts in the Baroque Palaces of Rome: Ambiente Barocco*. New Haven: Yale Univ. Press; for the Bard Graduate Center for Studies in the Decorative Arts, New York, 1999.

Wheelock Jr., Arthur K. *Flemish Paintings of the Seventeenth Century*. Washington, DC: National Gallery of Art, 2005.

Wittkower, Rudolf. *Art and Architecture in Italy, 1600–1750*. 3 vols. 6th ed. Revised Joseph Connors and Jennifer Montague. Pelican History of Art. New Haven: Yale Univ. Press, 1999.

Zega, Andrew, and Bernd H. Dams. *Palaces of the Sun King: Versailles, Trianon, Marly: The Châteaux of Louis XIV*. New York: Rizzoli, 2002.

Credits

Index